T0323250

COALITIONS AND COMPLIANCE

Coalitions and Compliance

The Political Economy of Pharmaceutical
Patents in Latin America

KENNETH C. SHADLEN

OXFORD
UNIVERSITY PRESS

OXFORD

UNIVERSITY PRESS

Great Clarendon Street, Oxford, OX2 6DP,
United Kingdom

Oxford University Press is a department of the University of Oxford.
It furthers the University's objective of excellence in research, scholarship,
and education by publishing worldwide. Oxford is a registered trade mark of
Oxford University Press in the UK and in certain other countries

First Edition published in 2017

Impression: 1

Published in the United States of America by Oxford University Press
198 Madison Avenue, New York, NY 10016, United States of America

British Library Cataloguing in Publication Data
Data available

Library of Congress Control Number: 2017939201

ISBN 978-0-19-959390-3

Printed and bound by
CPI Group (UK) Ltd, Croydon, CR0 4YY

Acknowledgments

Over the course of researching and writing this book I've accumulated more intellectual debts to more people in more countries than I can begin to recount, let alone ever repay. I have had the good fortune of presenting the research at conferences, seminars, and workshops in the UK and Europe, the US and Canada, and throughout Latin America. Doing so allowed me to benefit from the insights of countless people who helped me think about things differently and sharpen my ideas. I am humbled by the extent and array of constructive, feedback that I received in the long process of completing this book. It is an honor and privilege to be part of such a vibrant academic community and to be able to benefit from such rich intellectual networks.

Acknowledgements are where authors recognize colleagues who commented on conference papers or drafts of chapters, and of course I wish to do that. I've also received invaluable feedback from numerous people who took the time to attend seminars and ask thoughtful and challenging questions, or to engage with issues and debates over email. Keeping track of all these formal and informal moments of scholarly communication is nearly impossible, and, regretfully, no doubt some names will be omitted, but in this space I'd like to express my gratitude to many of the individuals who helped along the way: Eduardo Albuquerque, Tahir Amin, Shamnad Basheer, Fabián Biali, Antonio Botelho, Ana Celia Castro, Claudia Chamas, Nitsan Chorev, Ruth Berins Collier, Adam Dean, Ignacio Delgado, Peter Drahos, Ken Dubin, Thomas Eimer, Sebastian Etchemendy, Peter Evans, Jean-Paul Faguet, Felipe Filomeno, Matt Flynn, Elize Fonseca, Kevin Gallagher, John Gerring, Geoff Gershenson, Peter Gourevitch, Alenka Guzmán, Cori Hayden, Sebastian Haunss, Ron Herring, Steffen Hertog, Kathy Hochstetler, Evelyn Huber, Michael Jewess, Jim Mahoney, Scott Mainwaring, Luigi Manzetti, Matt Marostica, Duncan Matthews, Gerry McDermott, Andres Mejia, Kevin Middlebrook, Vicky Murillo, Valbona Muzaka, Joana Naritomi Kimberly Nolan Garcia, Andreas Nölke, Alessandro Octaviani, Pedro Paranaguá, Julia Paranhos, Allison Post, Tim Power, Jerry Reichman, Anderson Ribeiro, Stephanie Rickard, Clemente Ruiz Duran, Marcelo Saguier, Verena Schüren, Bhaven Sampat, Jason Seawright, Leo Stanley, Strom Thacker, Diana Tussie, Alberto Usieto-Blanco, Matthias vom Hau, Robert Wade, Andrew Walter, Peter Yu. Obviously all errors of fact and interpretation are my own.

A special octet deserves particular attention. In May 2015 I hosted a workshop in London to discuss a draft of the book. Marcus Kurtz, Susan Sell, Andrew Schrank, and Ben Ross Schneider travelled internationally; Diego Sanchez-Ancochea came from Oxford; LSE colleagues Cathy Boone, Tasha Fairfield, and Jonathan Hopkin came from various corners of London.

I cannot thank these eight enough for contributing their time and mental energies. Together, we identified weaknesses to address, considered pathways for improvement, and explored avenues to pursue. I am lucky to have such wonderful—and wonderfully insightful—colleagues who would take time out of their lives to work with me in this way. Responding to the feedback received at the workshop and subsequently revising the book were among the most challenging experiences of my career, but also rewarding and well worth the effort.

I received financial support from various sources. Externally to LSE, the British Academy and Nuffield Foundation provided grants that allowed me to undertake the initial research trips. Later, from within LSE, the Santander Travel Research Fund and the Suntory and Toyota International Centres for Economics and Related Disciplines (STICERD) funded additional trips to Argentina, Brazil, and Mexico. I am grateful to all of these organizations and the individuals who helped make all this possible. Likewise, I wish to express my thanks to colleagues at LSE's Research Division.

I could not have completed this book without the excellent support of research assistants who helped with various aspects of the project. These include Nicolás Perrone (Argentina), Fabiola Zibetti (Brazil), Juan Pablo Morales and Rodrigo Martinez Romero (Mexico), and Meriem Bekka, Kim Grauer, Antonio Postigo-Angon, and Elia Trippel at LSE. Nor, more generally, would this book be possible without the help of countless people in Argentina, Brazil, and Mexico who took time out of their busy schedules to meet with me and respond to my many follow-up calls and emails. Some of these people are referred to in the text and cited (anonymously) in the list of interviews, but beyond these specific sources I am extremely grateful to everyone who re-sponded to my requests for interviews or email queries. Similarly, I thank staff at the three countries' patent offices for providing me with data and respond-ing to queries regarding their online databases.

At Oxford University Press, Dominic Byatt and Olivia Wells at Oxford were unfailing in their encouragement and enthusiasm for this book, and they displayed unwavering patience in terms of delivery. Phil Dines was a pleasure to work with on copy-editing the final manuscript, as was Mohana Annamalai in production.

I owe immense thanks to Susan Martin and Louisa Martin Shadlen for their unconditional support over years of my travelling to Latin America and obsessing about this project. *Coalitions and Compliance* has, "basically," been with Louisa for most of her life—and I'll remain thankful to Louisa for her amazing patience for the rest of my life! I also thank my brothers Dave and Mike for their camaraderie and constant support in everything I do. Lastly, I want to express my heartfelt thanks to Jane and Jerry Shadlen, who gave me the greatest gifts I could ever receive: a zest for learning and a green light to pursue my passions. I dedicate this book to my mom and dad.

London
March 2017

Contents

Abbreviations   ix

List of Figures and Tables   xiii

PART I. CONTEXT, THEORY, EXPLANATORY FRAMEWORK

1. Global Change, Political Coalitions, and National Responses   3

2. The Political Economy of Pharmaceutical Patents   28

PART II. INTRODUCING PHARMACEUTICAL PATENTS

3. Power to the Producers: Industrial Legacies, Coalitional Expansion, and Minimalist Compliance in Argentina   63

4. Not If but *How*: NAFTA and Extreme Over-Compliance in Mexico   88

5. Coalitional Clash, Export Mobilization, and Executive Agency: From Reluctant Acquiescence to Enthusiastic Over-Compliance in Brazil   110

PART III. MODIFYING NEW PHARMACEUTICAL PATENT SYSTEMS

6. The Defensive Coalition on the Offensive: National Industry and Argentina's Market-Preserving Patent System   141

7. What's Good for Us is Good for You: The Transnational Pharmaceutical Sector and Mexico's Internationalist Patent System   168

8. Patent Policy in the Shadows of Over-Compliance: Neo-Developmentalism in Brazil   193

PART IV. CONCLUSION

9. Patents and Development in the New Global Economy   227

Fieldwork Appendix   247

References   249

Cited Interviews   289

Index   291

Abbreviations

ABDI	Brazilian Industrial Development Agency
ABE	Association of Brazilian Exporters
ABIA	Brazilian Interdisciplinary AIDS Organization
ABIFINA	Brazilian Pharmo-Chemical Association
ABPI	Brazilian Association for Intellectual Property
ABRABI	Brazilian Association of Biotechnology Firms
AGU	Solicitor General (Brazil)
ALANAC	Association of National Pharmaceutical Firms (Brazil)
AMEGI	Mexican Association of Generic Medicines
AMIF	Mexican Pharmaceutical Industry Association
AMIIF	Mexican Pharmaceutical Research Industry Association
AMPPI	Mexican Intellectual Property Association
ANAFAM	National Association of Drug Manufacturers (Mexico)
ANIERM	National Association of Importers and Exporters (Mexico)
ANMAT	National Agency for Drugs, Food, and Medical Technology (Argentina)
ANPEI	National Association for Research, Development, and Engineering in Innovative Firms (Brazil)
ANVISA	National Agency for Health Surveillance (Brazil)
ARV	Antiretroviral medicine
BIT	Bilateral Investment Treaty
BNDES	National Development Bank (Brazil)
CAEME	Argentinean Chamber of Specialist Medicines
CANIFARMA	National Chamber of the Pharmaceutical Industry (Mexico)
CCE	Business Coordinating Council (Mexico)
CEDIQUIFA	Center for Studies for the Development of the Argentinean Pharmo-Chemical Industry
CEMAI	Mexican Business Council for Foreign Affairs
CERA	Chamber of Argentinean Exporters
CILFA	Chamber of Argentinean Pharmaceutical Industries
CIS	Health Industry Complex (Brazil)
CNBB	Brazilian Confederation of Bishops
CNI	National Confederation of Industry (Brazil)

COECE	Coordinator of Foreign Trade Business Organizations (Mexico)
COFEPRIS	Federal Commission for Protection against Health Risks (Mexico)
CONACYT	National Council for Science and Technology (Mexico)
COOPERALA	Cooperative of Argentinean Specialized Medicines Firms
EU	European Union
FDA	Food and Drug Administration (US)
FIEL	Foundation for Latin American Economic Research (Argentina)
FIESP	Federation of the Industries of the State of São Paulo
FINEP	Brazilian Innovation Agency
FLUC	Forum for the Freedom of Use of Knowledge (Brazil)
GSP	Generalized System of Preferences
GTPI	Intellectual Property Working Group (Brazil)
IMPI	Mexican Institute for Intellectual Property
INPI-AR	National Institute for Industrial Property (Argentina)
INPI-BR	National Institute for Industrial Property (Brazil)
INTERFARMA	Association of the Research-Based Pharmaceutical Industry (Brazil)
IP	Intellectual Property
LFPPI	Law for Development and Promotion of Industrial Property (Mexico)
LIM	Law on Inventions and Trademarks (Mexico)
LPI	Industrial Property Law (Brazil)
LPIMU	Patents and Utility Models Law (Argentina)
MCT	Ministry of Science and Technology (Brazil)
MEI	Business Mobilization for Innovation (Brazil)
MFN	Most-Favored Nation
NAFTA	North American Free Trade Agreement
OECD	Organization for Economic Cooperation and Development
PAN	National Action Party (Mexico)
PCT	Patent Cooperation Treaty
PhRMA	Pharmaceutical Research and Manufacturers of America
PJ	Peronist Party (Argentina)
PMA	Pharmaceutical Manufacturers of America
PRD	Party of the Democratic Revolution (Mexico)
PRI	Institutional Revolutionary Party (Mexico)
PT	Workers Party (Brazil)
PTD	Political Trade Dependence

PVEM	Mexican Green Party
R&D	Research and Development
RMALC	Mexican Action Network on Free Trade
SBPC	Brazilian Society for the Progress of Science
SECOFI	Secretariat of Trade and Industrial Development (Mexico)
SUS	National Health System (Brazil)
TRIPS	Agreement on Trade-Related Aspects of Intellectual Property Rights
UCR	Radical Party (Argentina)
UIA	Argentinean Industrial Union
US	United States
USTR	United States Trade Representative
WHO	World Health Organization
WIPO	World Intellectual Property Organization
WTO	World Trade Organization

List of Figures and Tables

Figures

2.1. Changing Dimensions of Debate in the Politics of Patents   29

2.2. Three Decades of Patenting in the US: All Technologies   34

2.3. Three Decades of Patenting in the US: Pharmaceuticals   34

2.4. Coalitional Dynamics and Forms of Compliance in 1990s   50

2.5. Initial Choices Over Introducing Patents and Subsequent Coalition-Building Possibilities   56

3.1. Structure of Exports to the US: Argentina   83

4.1. Drug Purchases by Mexican Public Sector, 1980–87 (shares)   99

4.2. Structure of Exports to the US: Mexico   102

5.1. FLUC Manifesto   128

5.2. Structure of Exports to the US: Brazil   133

5.3. Political Trade Dependence in Argentina and Brazil   135

6.1. Pharmaceutical and Pharmo-Chemical Applications Filed in Argentina   145

6.2. Granted Pharmaceutical Patents in Argentina, 2000–2012   145

7.1. Pharmaceutical and Pharmo-Chemical Applications Filed in Mexico   171

8.1. Pharmaceutical and Pharmo-Chemical Applications Filed in Brazil   196

8.2. Brazil's Trade Dependence, 1995–2014   213

8.3. Brazil's Political Trade Dependence, 1995–2014   214

Tables

1.1. USTR's Special 301 Reports: Number of Countries Listed   17

2.1. Sources of Pharmaceutical Patents Granted in the US in 1990   35

2.2. Impact of Initial Policy Choices on Patenting of 159 New Drugs Launched from 1996–2004   41

2.3. Pharmaceutical Industries in Argentina, Mexico, and Brazil (mid-1980s to mid-1990s)   47

2.4. Trade Dependence and Political Trade Dependence   49

8.1. ANVISA's Prior Consent (June 2001–July 2010)   203

Part I

Context, Theory, Explanatory Framework

1

Global Change, Political Coalitions, and National Responses

Intellectual property policies affect the processes by which knowledge and information become privately owned, and the terms under which privately owned knowledge and information are used. Because these arrangements influence how citizens and governments access essential knowledge- and information-intensive goods, such as educational materials, medicines, seeds, and software, national policies in this area affect peoples' lives, and countries' trajectories of development in the global economy.

Traditionally, countries around the world enjoyed significant freedom in determining what types of knowledge and information benefited from intellectual property protection, and how much protection rights-owners enjoyed. Intellectual Property (IP) policies were driven by national characteristics, such as levels of income, industrial structure, scientific, and technological capabilities. In general, poorer countries with less technological development tended to adopt more lax IP policies to facilitate the use of knowledge and information, and over the course of acquiring more technological capabilities the amounts of IP protection they made available would increase as a reflection of these changes. Indeed, the close relationship between national conditions and IP policies has long been a staple of case study, comparative historical, and econometric research.[1]

That world is a thing of the past. The late twentieth century was marked by a fundamental transformation in the global politics of IP. In the 1980s and 1990s, as IP became defined as "trade-related," countries wishing to participate in international trade became obligated to undertake significant revisions of

---

[1] See, for example, Chen and Puttitanun (2005), Dutfield and Suthersanen (2005), Hudson and Minea (2013), Kawaura and La Croix (1995), Kim et al. (2012), Kumar (2002), Maskus (2000; 2012), Marron and Steel (2000), May (2000; 2007a; 2013), May and Sell (2006), Odagiri et al. (2010), Ordover (1991), Schiff (1971).

their policies toward patents, copyrights, trademarks, and other forms of IP.[2] The drivers of national IP policy were now international, too.

The cornerstone event in this global sea change was the inclusion of the Agreement on Trade-Related Aspects of Intellectual Property Rights (TRIPS) in the World Trade Organization (WTO), which was founded in 1995.[3] But TRIPS is just part of the story. At the same time as new multilateral rules were being established, the international IP regime was also shaped directly by the actions of larger developed countries that gave the promotion of IP increasingly prominent places in their foreign policy and aid agendas. Similarly, international organizations such as the World Intellectual Property Organization (WIPO) have acted as enthusiastic advocates of increased protection. These shifts replaced a world marked by differentiation, where national IP policies were allowed to correspond to local conditions, with a world of harmonization, where all countries' IP policies are expected to correspond to new international standards.

The global sea change ushered in new IP policies throughout the world, as country after country altered laws and created new state agencies, all toward increasing levels of IP protection. Countries made patent protection available in technological areas where it had previously not been allowed, for example, they strengthened the rights of exclusion that patent owners enjoyed, and they created new administrative agencies and courts to establish and protect these new private property rights. The new approach toward IP is part and parcel of yet another shift, as the focus on privately owned knowledge has been complemented by a focus on "knowledge-based" development. Governments and international organizations have come to embrace, at least rhetorically, the role of IP as a stimulus for innovation, and the importance of innovation as key to increasing firms' competitiveness and national welfare (OECD 2013; Powell and Snellman 2004).

Not surprisingly, as countries reacted to the global sea change, cross-national indices of IP rights have come to reveal across-the-board increases. The mean for ninety-nine developing countries in the most frequently cited index of patent protection, which scores countries from zero to five, increased from 1.6 in 1990 to 2.7 in 2000, reaching 3.1 by 2005 (Park 2008). Similarly, the mean score of "legal transplantation," an index of 121 developing and post-communist countries' similarity with policies of the United States (US), rose by 150 percent from 1995 to 2008 (Morin and Gold 2014).

---

[2] IP is the umbrella term for a range of instruments that confer rights of exclusion to the owners of intangible goods. Patents protect inventions, copyrights, and trademarks protect forms of expression. What they have in common is that they convert knowledge and information into private property.

[3] On TRIPS and, more generally, the establishment of the IP-trade linkage, see, among others, Braithwaite and Drahos (2000), Deere (2008), Drahos (1995), Matthews (2002), Maskus (2012; 2014), May (2000), Muzaka (2011a; 2011b), Orsi and Coriat (2006), Pugatch (2004), Ryan (1998), Sell (2003; 2010a).

Yet even in this context of overarching increases in IP rights, we continue to witness cross-national diversity. Countries reacted differently to the pressures emerging from the global sea change, and then subsequently took different steps in revising these policies and practices. The result of this iterative policymaking process is that countries with new IP systems introduced in response to the new external environment still differ on key characteristics of how they establish and protect privately owned knowledge.

This book analyses this diversity, both cross-national variation in countries' responses to the global sea change and longitudinal patterns of change within countries, in the context of pharmaceutical patents. As of the late 1980s, patents on pharmaceutical products were rarely available in developing countries. Many countries offered patents on pharmaceutical processes, i.e. the manufacturing techniques for making drugs, but few did so for the chemical compounds and medicines themselves. Firms could receive patents for these inventions in most developed countries, but they would not even bother to seek patents on pharmaceutical products in most developing countries because, simply, drugs could not be patented.[4] A key feature—arguably the single most important feature—of the global sea change is to bar countries from retaining the statutory prohibitions that most had until this time: *countries must allow pharmaceutical products to be patented.* By the mid-1990s, virtually all developing countries had committed to introducing pharmaceutical patents, and by the mid-2000s this process was complete in all but the poorest countries.

The shift from pharmaceuticals being largely non-patentable to being nearly universally patentable is striking in terms of the global scope and pace that this occurred—but it is far from the end of the story. Pharmaceutical patents are new, and transitioning from a world where the knowledge associated with medicines was a public good to a world where such knowledge is privately owned and controlled, generated new challenges for state and non-state actors. In response to these challenges, many countries subsequently set out to modify their new patent systems. While the initial policy choices in the 1990s regarded decisions over introducing pharmaceutical patents, policy choices in the 2000s regarded making revisions to the new pharmaceutical patent systems to adjust how they function. The end result of these two episodes of change is that policies continue to vary in important ways. Or, to put it differently, forms and styles of compliance with the new global order of private knowledge in pharmaceuticals differs from country to country.

How to account for variation in national patent systems? This book addresses that question with a two-stage approach. Countries' initial responses to the global sea change varied as a consequence of how industrial legacies interacted with export profiles to affect the possibilities for building coalitions

---

[4] Prior to the late 1970s, pharmaceutical patenting was not available in many developed countries either, as discussed in Chapter 2.

around the issues of when and how pharmaceutical patents should be introduced. How these initial conflicts regarding the introduction of patents were resolved, in turn, conditioned policy choices in the 2000s, around how the new pharmaceutical patent systems function. The two periods of change are linked in that the first set of choices generated distinct challenges to be addressed, and the initial choices also inspired different changes to social structure which, in turn, affected subsequent possibilities for coalition building.

The empirics are drawn from the cases of Argentina, Brazil, and Mexico. None of these countries offered pharmaceutical patents as of the late 1980s, when they were signaled out for their resistance and came under considerable pressure to make pharmaceuticals patentable (Gadbaw and Richards 1988b, 7–8). When they acquiesced to international pressures and agreed to introduce pharmaceutical patents, they did so differently; and when they subsequently revised their new pharmaceutical patent systems they did so differently again. Over the course of these two periods of change, Argentina produced a "market-preserving" patent regime, featuring minimalist, by-the-books adherence to the country's new international obligations, complemented by regulatory changes designed to help local firms adjust to the new status quo and retain a dominant position with respect to international competition. Brazil yielded a "neo-developmentalist" system, with the country adopting global norms in a way that puts IP and innovation at the heart of development policy, but at the same time introducing a range of measures designed to ameliorate the effects of stronger protection. And Mexico produced an "internationalist" patent regime, marked by an expanding embrace of global norms and adoption of "best practices," all with an eye toward attracting foreign investment into the pharmaceutical sector.

The objective of this book is to explain these differences in a way that allows us, more generally, to understand cross-national and longitudinal variation in national policies. While there is an abundance of scholarship on the global politics of IP, explaining for example the integration of IP into international trade rules and conflicts over IP at multilateral and regional levels, as well as a proliferation of case studies of IP policymaking,[5] our understanding of the drivers of national responses to the new external environment remains underdeveloped. This book offers a systematic approach toward studying cross-national and longitudinal variation, one that allows us to understand how the major changes in the global politics of IP migrate to the national level and affect domestic policies and practices over time.

---

[5] See, among others, the contributions to Coriat (2008), Dreyfuss and Rodriguez-Garavito (2014), Haunss and Shadlen (2009), Löfgren and Williams (2013), Mani and Nelson (2013), Shadlen et al. (2011). Important comparative studies (cross-national or within-country longitudinal) also include Deere (2008), Eimer and Lutz (2010), Eren-Vural (2007), Filomeno (2014), Flynn (2011; 2013; 2015), Godoy (2013), Guzmán (2014), Haggart (2014), Matthews (2011), Ramanna (2005), Rodríguez-Franco (2012), Shadlen (2009b; 2012).

Persistent differences in how countries go about establishing the ownership of knowledge, and setting the terms on which privately owned knowledge is used, have important implications for human welfare and economic development. Patents confer exclusive rights over manufacture, distribution, and sales; in a market where a drug is covered by a patent, there will likely be just one supplier of the drug. We expect drugs with single suppliers to be more expensive than drugs with multiple suppliers, so the introduction of pharmaceutical patents can, potentially, create barriers to access of essential drugs. Also, as pharmaceuticals were often a strategic area for industrial promotion and a source of manufacturing employment, new patent systems that endow single firms with control have implications for economic development. Thus, it matters how countries react to the global sea change in IP and position themselves in the new international order.

Before proceeding, it is important to underscore that the relationships between pharmaceutical patents, drug prices, and health outcomes are exceptionally complex. The extent to which patents yield high prices, for example, depends on degrees of competition in given therapeutic segments, the availability of substitutes, the marketing strategies of firms that control patented drugs, and the purchasing practices of public and private healthcare providers. And access to medicines depends on more than the price of drugs: in some countries, poverty and the state of healthcare systems mean that access to medicines and adherence to treatment are problems even when drugs are free. Yet, for all that, when drugs have a single supplier that can set the price, if that price is high, some may suffer from reduced access, and the effects of reduced access can be detrimental for individuals and public health.

And not only are the relationships between patents, prices, and health complex, they are often difficult to observe. Reduced access to key drugs may produce a wide range of setbacks, deprivations, and hardships. Obviously, lack of access to life-saving medicines can be fatal, a scenario that is exemplified in the case of HIV/AIDS, which in the absence of drugs is a death sentence. Not all situations are so stark, but the challenges posed by patents and prices are serious nevertheless. Lack of access to a particular drug might mean that patients rely on inferior treatments and endure more pain and suffering, or perhaps have to live with more discomforting side effects or become more susceptible to other related illnesses. Lack of access to some medicines may compel people to make multiple trips to clinics, for example, perhaps spending more of their family income on transportation, or be unable to continue in their employment. And so on. The effects on health and livelihoods, short of life or death scenarios, are serious too, but these can be hidden and thus difficult for analysts to track and record.[6] And of course the

---

[6] It is often difficult, as Godoy cogently writes, to provide a "body count" (Godoy 2013, 46–7).

allocation of funds to secure access to drugs for one disease or condition, where treatments are more expensive because of patents, may result in diminished access for other patients with other conditions.

The remainder of this chapter consists of three sections. The next section situates the analysis in the context of broader scholarship in comparative and international political economy. In doing so the key building blocks of the coalitional argument are presented. The following section then reviews scholarship on the politics of IP, with an eye toward integrating international and domestic factors. The final section discusses the logic of case selection, the method of data collection and comparative analysis, and the organization of the chapters that follow.

HARMONIZATION, DIFFERENTIATION, AND COALITIONAL POLITICS

The trends witnessed in IP, of big changes sweeping the globe and reflected in currents of national convergence, alongside striking differences between countries, are anything but exceptional. To the contrary, the late twentieth and early twenty-first centuries constituted a period of persistent diversity in the context of overarching convergence in many areas. Democratization swept the world, economic liberalization became the norm, and anti-poverty programs gained a central place on the development agenda, to give just three examples of global trends, but countries continued to exhibit important differences in their democratic political institutions and practices, the extent to which economic actors are subject to market competition, and the characteristics of social protection. Indeed, diversity in the context of convergence is the norm. As countless scholars of comparative and international political economy have shown, broad tendencies toward convergence, be they rooted in international rules, technological change, or the diffusion of new ideas, manifest themselves differently in distinct national contexts.[7]

---

[7] Examples, by no means a comprehensive list, include Brooks (2008) on diversity within the shift toward privatized pension systems, Etchemendy (2011) on diversity in trade and industrial policies in liberalizing countries, Mosley (2003) and Brooks and Kurtz (2012) on diversity of financial regulations in the context of financial globalization and open capital accounts, Murillo (2009) on diversity in national strategies toward privatizing and regulating public utilities, Rudra (2008) on diversity of developing countries' social welfare regimes in the context of globalization and privatization, and Wellhausen (2014) on countries' diverse policies toward foreign investors. Among scholars working on the politics of intellectual property, Haggart's (2014) analysis of digital copyright in Canada, Mexico, and the US is explicitly framed in terms of persistent national diversity as well.

In explaining cross-national and within-country diversity, the focus in this book is placed on the ways that changes to social structure affect political actors' abilities to construct and sustain supportive coalitions. Executives are key players throughout the analysis, as presidents bore the burden of responding to global pressures to adopt new IP systems in the 1990s, and Health Ministries bore the brunt of dealing with the effects of new pharmaceutical patent systems in the 2000s. These events altered Executives' preferences, often in unexpected ways. Yet Executives need room to act. Be they Presidents embracing the global sea change and seeking to introduce new IP regimes in conformity with foreign governments' and foreign investors' wishes or Ministers of Health reacting to the effects of pharmaceutical patents and seeking to revise their countries' new patent systems, Executives need to build coalitions to overcome opposition and secure their desired outcomes, i.e., to see that their policies can be enacted and sustained.

The analytic approach adopted here thus takes seriously Executives' shifting preferences, though placing them in the context of the changing constraints within which Executives act. Political scientists and sociologists that emphasize the constraints on agency often focus on political institutions, such as how constitutions, legislatures, and party systems circumscribe Executive autonomy.[8] I emphasize social structural constraints; how changing constellations of interests create or foreclose opportunities for coalition building and, subsequently, political action.

Attention is placed on two ways that constellations of societal interests are transformed so as to alter the panorama of coalition-building possibilities. First, international politics can reconfigure domestic political processes by differentially empowering and mobilizing rival actors in state and society.[9] The specific focus in this book is on the efforts of the United States Government to make access to the US market conditional upon increasing the level of IP protection. As many researchers have shown, external pressures can encourage exporters to push for policy changes.[10] I build on this research by linking exporters' mobilization to a specific aspect of trade structure: dependence on removable, discretionary trade preferences. Exporters typically have little reason to participate in debates over IP, but threats of diminished market access can change that. In situations where higher shares of exports enter the US market under preferential and removable trading arrangements, exporters, fearing loss of market access, can be mobilized by the advocates of IP protection. I label this process, of otherwise indifferent exporters becoming

[8] Calvo (2014); Carey and Shugart (1998); Corrales (2002); Flores-Macias (2012); Lichbach and Zuckerman (1997); Mainwaring and Shugart (1997); Shugart and Carey (1992).

[9] Brooks and Kurtz (2012); Farrell and Newman (2014); Frieden (1991); Gourevitch (1978; 1986); Katzenstein (1977); Keohane and Milner (1996); Rogowski (1990); Solingen (2009).

[10] Baldwin (1985); Bastos (1994); Bayard and Elliott (1994); Gilligan (1997); Kaempfer et al. (1987).

preoccupied with a new issue and thus wanting their governments to acqui-esce to external demands, "activating agnostics."

That changes in the external environment, such as new international agree-ments or shifting global economic conditions, can alter domestic political pro-cesses, is the cornerstone of much of contemporary political economy. Scholars of "open economy politics" (Frieden 1991; Keohane and Milner 1996; Lake 2009) typically identify the actors with a stake in a particular set of policy choices, observe how these actors' preferences and resources are altered by the relevant international stimuli, and then consider subsequent domestic political processes. Yet external pressures can mobilize *new* actors too (Jacoby 2006). The actors identified *ex ante* as those with a stake in a given policy debate may not constitute the universe of relevant parties. External pressures can also affect domestic politics by creating new constituencies—not just strengthening or weakening already-interested actors, but expanding these actors' range of allies by bringing otherwise uninterested players into policy debates. The mobilization of exporters as advocates of IP protection, i.e. activating agnostics, is an illustration of this phenomenon.

The second way that coalitional possibilities change is that new policies can alter subsequent trajectories of political mobilization (Falleti 2010; Pierson 1993; Thelen 1999; 2003; Weir 2006). Once policies are introduced, however fraught the conflicts over their introduction, actors may subsequently adjust to the new status quo. In such a context, phenomena of increasing and decreas-ing returns affect successive policymaking episodes (Pierson 2000; 2004). Increasing returns allows those engaged in favored activities to accumulate resources, a process that entrenches constituencies for continuity. In contrast, decreasing returns can dilute opposition to new policies once they are imple-mented. New policies may also change the character of the state, by spurring the creation of new agencies, institutions, and organizations, or by giving new prominence and authority to existing bodies. Decisions on major policy issues can shape subsequent trajectories of change and, importantly, the strategies of actors that then work within the parameters established by the new status quo (Farrell and Newman 2014; Immergut 2008; Shaffer 2014).

The asymmetric effects of policy choices on patterns of political mobiliza-tion and subsequent episodes of coalition building invoke notions of path dependence, where policymaking at T_2 is not subject to a "roll of the die" (Weir 2006) but conditioned by choices made at T_1. Initial choices constrain what follows, but, importantly, explanations that take into account the legacies of policy choices need not mechanically demand continuity. Rather, the key is to identify tractable effects of outcomes in one period on outcomes in a subse-quent period.[11] Just as new policies may entrench "winners" and encourage

---

[11] Boas (2007); Capoccia and Kelemen (2007); Chorev (2015); Collier and Collier (1991); Falleti and Mahoney (2015); Mahoney (2000, 2001).

continuity, they may also trigger reactions by actors that seek to modify the new status quo. In both scenarios, policies are producing patterns of political mobilization that, in turn, condition subsequent episodes of policymaking. Nor does an approach that takes seriously the path-dependent effects of policy choices preclude the possibility that politicians may, simply, try to alter policy trajectories. Even once countries have adopted one set of policies, elections can return a new government that seeks change, or more simply political leaders may seek to alter course on account of new ideas or new evidence. Yet actors' range of freedom to alter course is limited: policies adopted in one period, by transforming social structure and the state, cast a shadow over policymaking in subsequent periods.

Together, changes to the international environment and path-dependent policy effects can alter constellations of interests within national political economies. The extent to which external pressures encourage exporters to care about new policy areas affects opportunities for political action on the part of Executives seeking to steer a given course. Likewise, reactions to policies inspire new patterns of mobilization and thus reconfigure constellations of interests, again shifting the social terrain upon which coalitions are constructed. These changes open or foreclose opportunities for political agency. Politicians that seek a particular course of action, in response to external pressures, partisan biases, or new social challenges, need to build coalitions—and their abilities to do so are affected by changes to underlying constellations of interests and social structure.

This approach to changed social structure and thus shifting coalitional possibilities allows us to understand patterns of cross-national and longitudinal variation in IP policies. The global sea change converted Executives into enthusiasts of patent protection in the 1990s. Yet presidents faced opposition to altering their countries' patent systems, and the extent to which they were able to build coalitions to overcome this opposition depended on the ways that the external shocks affected social structure. Then, in the 2000s, when Health Ministers sought to revise their new patent systems, their opportunities for action were constrained by the transformations of social structure induced by the first set of changes. The following section places the coalitional approach in the context of previous research on the drivers of national IP policies.

THE DRIVERS OF COMPLIANCE AND OVER-COMPLIANCE

Coalitional change helps us understand variation in the forms of compliance with international rules and norms. The politics of patents is an iterated process, with key policy choices occurring over two distinct periods. In the 1990s, countries established new patent systems in response to the global sea change; all countries complied with TRIPS, but they did so differently. Then, in the 2000s, many countries sought to reform their new patent systems; again, they did so differently. Just as post-Communist countries of Central and Eastern Europe first introduced private property rights and then subsequently reformed their new private property systems (Bohle and Greskovits 2012; Hancke 2008; Jacoby 2006; Szelényi 2015), or as countries privatized pension systems and utilities and then subsequently introduced regulations to these newly privatized sectors (Brooks 2008; Murillo 2009), countries introduced pharmaceutical patents and then subsequently revised their new patent systems.

How can we account for cross-national and within-country, longitudinal variation in patent policies? As noted, theory and empirics both suggest that IP policies are driven by domestic conditions. As countries acquire more innovative capabilities and their scientific and industrial sectors move closer to the technological frontier, for example, demands for increased IP protection are expected to follow (Acemoglu et al. 2006; Chen and Puttitanun 2005; Kalaycı and Pamukçu 2014). So universal was acceptance of the relationship between national conditions and IP policies that one prominent scholar, in reviewing the literature, characterized the link as "obvious" (Maskus 2000, 102).

As obvious as the relationship may have been, it is also obvious that domestic factors, alone, can no longer adequately account for what has transpired in the current era, when patent regimes of virtually all countries, with varying circumstances, have undergone profound changes. It is hardly conceivable that the relevant national-level variables changed and reached similar thresholds to establish the conditions for increased patent protection in so many countries at the same time. Indeed, historically IP systems have tended to exhibit resistance to abrupt change (David 1993; Lamoreaux et al. 1999; Lerner 2000). The observation of profound transformations in a short period of time poses a puzzle and necessitates taking seriously the international drivers of patent policy change (Shadlen et al. 2005).

But how to think about the international drivers of policy change is not entirely straightforward, either. The obligations imposed by the WTO and TRIPS themselves do not suffice as explanatory factors. All members of the WTO are also parties to TRIPS. Because the Uruguay Round, the multilateral trade negotiations that produced the WTO and the various agreements within the WTO, was completed with a "single undertaking," countries could not pick and choose their agreements, but rather had to become parties to all of the agreements included in the Final Act of 1994.[12] However, while all countries that are members of the WTO needed to comply with TRIPS, they had leeway in determining how to do so, a point driven home emphatically by the

---

[12] There are a few exceptions to this statement, for example, the WTO's Government Procurement Agreement is a "plurilateral" accord that countries can opt in or out of.

abundant legal and policy literature documenting the significant array of TRIPS-acceptable policy options available.[13]

The relevant question is not if countries comply with TRIPS but rather *how* they do so. Some countries may stick strictly to what the international rules require, doing what needs to be done to remain safe from dispute settlement at the WTO, but little more. Some countries may go beyond TRIPS, offering more IP protection than the agreement requires. Forms of compliance—or, more specifically, degrees of "over-compliance"—needs to be the focus of attention.[14] If we conceptualize the outcome as degrees of over-compliance, then to understand variation we need to look beyond the WTO itself. After all, the entire range of variation under study, from minimalist compliance to extreme levels of over-compliance, is compatible with WTO membership. Chapter 2 discusses specific policy choices that were contested in each country. For now, staying at a more general level, the objective is to elucidate the drivers of the different ways that countries comply with the global sea change in IP.

The emergence of regional and bilateral trade agreements with IP provisions that exceed TRIPS is commonly regarded as a driver of over-compliance. The US, European Union (EU), and Japan have all negotiated a large number of trade agreements with developing countries that include IP provisions exceeding those in the WTO.[15] To be sure, countries that enter into bilateral trade agreements of this sort will end up with over-compliant patent systems. Yet attributing IP policy outcomes to bilateral trade agreements may be misleading. Countries might over-comply because they have bilateral trade agreements with major trading partners, but just as well countries might have these agreements because they have over-complied or are prepared to do so. The latter scenario is highly plausible. The US Government, for example, makes it clear that securing levels of IP protection beyond what is required by TRIPS is an objective of negotiating trade agreements with developing countries, and political leaders that enter into negotiations for such agreements do so knowing that they will be expected to alter their IP policies accordingly.

---

[13] Bermudez and Oliveira (2004); Commission on Intellectual Property Rights (2002); Correa (2000b); Hilty and Liu (2014); Kapczynski (2009); Musungu and Oh (2006); Reichman (1996; 2009a; 2009b); Scherer and Watal (2002); Shadlen (2009a); UNCTAD-ICTSD (2005); Watal (1999; 2001).

[14] I borrow the concept of "over-compliance" from Walter (2008; 2014). Gold and Morin (2014), seeking to explain a similar phenomenon, refer to this as different levels of "legal transplantation." Many observers also refer to countries introducing "TRIPS Plus" policies.

[15] The immense literature on IP in bilateral trade agreements includes El-Said (2005; 2007), Fink and Reichenmiller (2005), Krikorian and Szymkowiak (2007), Kuanpoth (2008), Mercurio (2006), Morin (2006; 2009), Roffe and Spennemann (2006), Sell (2007; 2010b), Seuba (2013), von Braun (2012).

Nor can trade agreements comfortably explain countries' subsequent policy choices, those introduced after all relevant steps required by the agreements were taken. Consider the case of Mexico, the one country examined in this book that has a bilateral trade agreement with the US, the North American Free Trade Agreement (NAFTA).[16] Understanding Mexico's patent policy choices in the 1990s necessitates understanding Mexico's pursuit of NAFTA, but the trade agreement's explanatory power for Mexico's subsequent policies is weaker. Because NAFTA's IP provisions are permissive, compared to more recent trade agreements, they left Mexico with ample opportunities to modify the patent system in the 2000s.[17] That Mexico did not do so, and even accentuated the degree of over-compliance, cannot be attributed to obligations that the country incurred as a party to NAFTA. Indeed, the policy changes of the 2000s occurred not because of restrictions imposed by the IP provisions in NAFTA, but rather *despite* the opportunities for policy innovation allowed by NAFTA.

Technical assistance, whereby local officials and policymakers are aided in adopting "best practices" in IP policy by donor governments and international organizations, is also regarded as a driver of over-compliance. The US, EU, and Japan have extensive technical assistance and capacity-building programs, as do international organizations such as the World Intellectual Property Organization.[18] In the mid-1980s, for example, the United States Patent and Trademark Office launched the Global Intellectual Property Academy, to "help countries around the world improve their IP programs and services."[19] Such initiatives, which provide assistance in drafting legislation or training officials, can encourage countries to adopt IP policies and practices that exceed the WTO's requirements.[20] Here again, as with trade agreements, the causal links need to be considered with caution. Countries typically approach foreign governments and international organizations and request technical assistance; the observed outcomes may not be attributable to technical assistance, so much as the conditions that prompted the country to request technical

---

[16] Mexico has trade agreements with the EU and Japan too.

[17] The literature on IP in regional and bilateral trade agreements tends to neglect NAFTA, largely for the reasons discussed in the text. NAFTA was negotiated in the early 1990s, prior to the completion of the TRIPS negotiations and establishment of the WTO, and the IP provisions in NAFTA are more similar to the IP provisions in the WTO than is the case with trade agreements negotiated in the 2000s.

[18] Ghafele and Engel (2012); Matthews and Muñoz-Tellez (2006); May (2004); Morin and Gold (2014); Peterson (2012); Roffe et al. (2007).

[19] See 'History of the Global Intellectual Property Academy', at goo.gl/sFql2h.

[20] In addition to these studies that examine the role of technical assistance in shaping countries' policies, other work focuses on how technical assistance affects implementation. Drahos (2008; 2010), for example, acknowledges cross-national differences in policies, but argues that technical assistance may yield similarities in patent offices' administrative and interpretive practices, a process he refers to as "invisible harmonization."

assistance. Simply put, we are rarely observing countries that were undecided on IP policy and over-complied on account of technical assistance, but, typically, countries that decided to over-comply and requested technical assistance to help them do so.

While neither trade agreements nor technical assistance provide sufficient explanations for countries' initial choices to over-comply, both of these can certainly affect IP policy outcomes, indirectly, over time. As trade agreements cover many policy areas, these can have myriad effects on the economy and society, which in turn can alter coalitional possibilities. Policy options that were available but foregone at one point may no longer be feasible, politically, at a later point, on account of changes to social structure induced by trade agreements. If the broader changes to social structure that trade agreements can bring about are more consequential than the agreements' binding IP provisions per se, trade agreements may be more significant in a political economy sense than strictly legal sense. Technical assistance and capacity-building programs can also affect social structure and the state. Even if the existence of a technical assistance program may reflect (rather than drive) a country's decision to over-comply, it can embolden constituencies within the receiving country. This may happen via the strengthening within the state, in both material and reputational senses, of patent offices, and by increasing national officials' integration into global networks (Drahos 2010). The effects of technical assistance delivered as a consequence of policy choice in one period can alter the state and social structure and thereby constrain policy choice in a subsequent period.

External pressures, in the form of trade sanctions, are another external factor that are commonly cited as drivers of over-compliance.[21] The most visible actor here has been the United States Trade Representative (USTR), which engages in a global monitoring practice, evaluating all countries' IP regimes. Since 1989 the USTR has issued the annual Special 301 Report, essentially a global report card. Each country identified in the Special 301 reports is placed on a "Watch List" or "Priority Watch List," or, more severely, labeled as a "Priority Foreign Country." As countries are placed on the Watch List and then escalated to the Priority Watch List, the threat and likelihood of bilateral trade sanctions increase, and when a country is identified as a Priority Foreign Country, which Drahos (1995, 423) labeled "trade's death row," the USTR is obligated to initiate proceedings to apply trade sanctions.[22] Any assessment system has

---

[21] Deere (2008); Drahos (1995; 2001); Flynn (2015); Morin and Gold (2014); Okedjii (2004); Pechman (1998); Sell (2003; 2010a); Stacy (2004).

[22] Although Priority Foreign Country is meant to trigger the process leading to trade sanctions, countries can be sanctioned without ever being labeled as such. It is worth noting that the 1988 Omnibus Trade Act, which is the law that required the USTR to conduct the Special 301 reviews, did not specify the Watch List or Priority Watch List. Congress instructed the USTR to identify "Priority Foreign Countries," a status that would trigger an immediate

benchmarks against which subjects are being measured, and the benchmark for the USTR's assessments has never been the TRIPS agreement, which of course did not exist yet when the system was introduced in 1989, but rather a vision of "best practices" that go beyond anything required by international agreements. And this continued after the WTO was created and TRIPS came into effect in 1995. According to the "Uruguay Round Agreements Act," failure to provide adequate and effective protection of intellectual property can trigger trade sanctions "notwithstanding the fact that the foreign country may be in compliance with the specific obligations of the TRIPS Agreement."[23] Countries are pressured to over-comply, and threatened with trade sanctions if they do not do so.

Here too the effects of Special 301 need to be considered with caution. To be sure, the USTR keeps a watchful eye on IP practices around the globe and is exceptionally active in pushing countries to adopt over-compliant patent regimes. As Table 1.1 indicates, the number of countries identified has increased greatly since the Special 301 process began, starting at twenty-five countries, consistently twice that number for a period in the 2000s, and even when declining after 2005 always considerably above the 1989 level. Many of the countries targeted by the USTR have indeed over-complied with their TRIPS obligations, but not all countries fall into line; national responses to these bilateral pressures differ greatly. Indeed, notwithstanding the USTR's own touting of Special 301's effectiveness in altering national practices and the considerable attention it attracts, research on the effects of the USTR and Special 301 (and of US trade sanctions more generally) are decidedly ambiguous.[24] Neither small-n comparative case studies nor large-n econometric analyses have been able to demonstrate systematic effects of Special 301 on countries' IP policies.

The challenge is thinking about the conditions under which trade pressures might be effective in altering countries' policies. To elicit a response, threats to punish countries need to be credible, in that the USTR has to be able to take

---

investigation and lead, potentially, to the imposition of retaliatory trade sanctions. In the first year, the USTR exploited ambiguity in the law's phrasing to modify the system and supplement the category of Priority Foreign Country with the Watch List and Priority Watch List. According to the USTR, establishing these incremental levels constituted "an enhancement that we [the USTR] have added to the statute to make it more effective" (Q/A, annexed to the initial Special 301 Report, USTR 1989a). To make the process yet more supple, in 1993 President Bill Clinton's first USTR, Micky Kantor, added "out of cycle reviews" as an additional lever.

[23] I am grateful to Duncan Matthews for bringing this passage of US trade law to my attention.

[24] Studies demonstrating the ambiguous effects of USTR pressures include Bayard and Elliott (1994), Bentolila (2002), Buscaglia and Long (1997), Deere (2008), Elliott and Richardson (1996), Hirst (1998), Knapp (2000), Morin and Gold (2014), Noland (1997), Sell (1995), Shadlen et al. (2005), Zeng (2002).

Table 1.1. USTR's Special 301 Reports: Number of Countries Listed

Year	Number*
1989	25
1990	23
1991	29
1992	34
1993	30
1994	27
1995	32
1996	34
1997	47
1998	49
1999	55
2000	57
2001	51
2002	51
2003	50
2004	52
2005	52
2006	48
2007	43
2008	46
2009	45
2010	41
2011	40
2012	40
2013	41
2014	37
2015	37
2016	34

* Number includes countries included on the Watch List, Priority Watch List, or identified as Priority Foreign Country.

Source: Author's elaboration from USTR's Special 301 Reports

the steps it is threatening to take, and worrisome, in that whatever it is that might be removed as punishment must matter enough to stimulate a reaction. Obviously if two countries engage in little trade than threats to remove market access are unlikely to have much effect. Yet even in the case of countries that engage in extensive trade, the ability to impose restrictions on another country's exports are limited to some degree by the WTO. Because WTO members must grant all other members equivalent market access, known as most-favored nation (MFN) treatment, the US ordinarily cannot raise tariffs on one country's exports of a given good without raising tariffs on all countries' exports of that good, and threats to raise tariffs across the board and thus affecting all exporters, on account of a single country's actions, may lack credibility.

Not all trade takes place on MFN terms, however, and threats to raise tariffs that are not subject to MFN can have more credibility. The WTO allows countries to positively discriminate and grant some countries preferential ("better-than-MFN") market access. The bilateral trade agreements discussed above constitute one example of this, another is through a set of programs known as the Generalized System of Preferences (GSP) that permits preferences outside of reciprocal trade agreements. The United States (along with many other countries) has an array of GSP and GSP-related schemes that offer preferential access on a discretionary basis. Whereas the preferences between partners in bilateral trade agreements are bound by international commitments, preferences granted under the GSP, also above and beyond the MFN concessions of the WTO, are granted at the pleasure of the importing country, and can be removed at the pleasure of the importing country as well. Moreover, and in contrast to MFN-based market access that, if adjusted for one country needs to be adjusted for all countries, the US can *selectively* extend and withdraw preferential market access.

The discretionary and removable attributes of GSP make it an important factor to consider in thinking about the effectiveness of trade sanctions. Pushing countries into altering their IP practices by withdrawing regular, MFN market access can invite retaliation in ways that attempts to do so by withdrawing better-than-MFN preferential market access does not. If the US Government wishes to remove MFN trade benefits from a WTO member, it is constrained in doing so and any measures must be enacted in a non-discriminatory manner; a developing country, even one that is highly dependent on the US market for exports, can challenge the US under the WTO's dispute settlement rules for denying it MFN treatment. Likewise, if the US wishes to remove preferences granted to a partner of a bilateral trade agreement, it is constrained by the terms of the agreement. But importing countries have more discretion with regard to the better-than-MFN trade benefits they make available under GSP schemes.

These characteristics of trade are useful for understanding the conditions under which external pressures may achieve their goals. In their study of legal transplantation in IP, for example, Morin and Gold (2014) find that that USTR pressures were associated with over-compliance in the 1990s but less so in the 2000s, and they attribute this to the inability of the USTR to wield the instrument of removing preferences. The authors refer to a 1999 WTO legal ruling, which called into question importing countries' abilities to unilaterally remove preferences, and suggest that this gave developing countries comfort to ignore the USTR's threats. Trade structure prompts us to think of this differently. It very well might be that countries ignore the USTR because they regard threats to remove preferences as illegal and lacking credibility, but it also may be that countries regard the threats and possibilities of sanctions as genuine, but disregard them anyway because the effects of being punished are minimal. After all, the USTR's pressures were not uniformly effective prior to the 1999 WTO ruling either. As much as an issue of international law, the effectiveness of the USTR's pressures may vary on account of conditions within the targeted countries.

The structure of a country's trading relationship with the US can make the USTR's threats to remove preferential market-access concessions more or less credible, and more or less worrisome. If exporters have minimal dependence on US preferences, either because they export relatively little to the US, or because what they export enters the US under ordinary MFN tariffs or preferences that constitute commitments in bilateral trade agreements, then we would not expect threats—even credible threats—of preferences to be withdrawn to generate much concern. Yet if removable, preferential exports to the US constitute a higher share of overall exports, we might expect the USTR's threats to be more alarming.[25]

The share of a country's exports that enter the US on preferential and removable terms, and thus its sensitivity to the removal of concessionary market access, constitutes its "political trade dependence" (PTD). The adjective "political" is used to emphasize that market access is extended and withdrawn according to political winds in the importing country.[26] The distinctiveness of this measure of trade dependence is critical. A standard measure of bilateral trade dependence is one country's exports to another (e.g. the US) as a share of its total exports. This can be supplemented with a measure of asymmetrical export dependence, which considers country X's exports to the US as a share of total exports, relative to US exports to X as a share of total US exports (Zeng 2002). Neither of these measures captures the level of exporting countries' dependence on market access that is concessionary and subject to withdrawal. All countries that export highly to the US are sensitive to fluctuations in demand derived from changes in the US economy, but they do not experience the same sort of vulnerability as a country with high PTD.

Threats of diminished market access can alter political coalitions and affect IP policy by mobilizing exporters. Most manufacturing firms in basic, labor-intensive industries are generally unconcerned with patents; they neither seek patents for their own inventions nor regard patents as relevant for their access to others' inventions. But when their continued access to the US market depends on revising national practices, these otherwise indifferent and uncommitted firms and their sectoral organizations may be converted into enthusiastic lobbyists for patent protection. Again, this is referred to as

---

[25] Morin and Gold (2014) do not consider countries' trade structure in their analyses, neither of the 1990s when they regard the USTR as important, nor of the 2000s, when the USTR's demands are regarded as less consequential.

[26] The concept of political trade dependence is developed and explored in Manger and Shadlen (2014) and Shadlen (2008).

"activating agnostics" because we would not expect these actors to care one way or the other about patent policy, but they may be made to care on account of their dependence on—and demand for retaining—preferential access to the US market. A country's PTD level should not be regarded as a generator of spontaneous mobilization and predictor of patent policy, but rather a conditional factor that simplifies or complicates coalition building. As presidents and Ministers of Health seek to build coalitions for their desired policy outcomes, they need to cultivate and mobilize bases of support. PTD provides a reading of the social terrain upon which coalitions can be constructed; it is a way that social structure enables or constrains Executive agency.

In addition to mobilizing exporters, another way that external shocks can reconfigure constellations of actors and interests, and thus alter coalitional possibilities, is through the policies themselves. As discussed, even if bilateral trade agreements and technical assistance are not the drivers of initial policy choices, they can alter state and society in such ways as to shape subsequent policymaking episodes. New agencies, institutions, and organizations— sometimes even new ministries—may be created, for example, or new lines of funding put into place. As new challenges emerge, the character of the state confronting these challenges may be fundamentally different from when initial policy decisions were made, and transformed by the earlier choices.

Policy choices can also affect social structure. The introduction of new laws and regulations deters some activities, through outright prohibition or by raising the associated costs. As actors who face decreasing returns adjust to the new status quo, either by adapting to the new regulations or shifting their activities into other areas, they become less available to participate in political coalitions. Some actors that might have participated in political coalitions in one time period, prior to a policy change, may no longer be available in a subsequent period, after the change. Importantly, these patterns of reaction and adjustment do not transpire immediately, so, as shall be discussed further in Chapter 2, a key factor is how long the new policies are in effect and have a chance to settle and alter social structure.

How coalitional possibilities are affected by adjustment to the introduction of pharmaceutical patents is one of the key analytic issues in this book; it is the counterpart to how coalitional possibilities are affected by trade pressures and activation of agnostics.[27] As most pharmaceutical patenting is done by a handful of leading global firms, with industries in developing countries oper- ating far from the technological frontier in this sector, allowing pharmaceut- ical products to be protected by patents is likely to increase transnational

---

[27] The process of actors' patterns of adjustment affecting industrial structure is similar to what evolutionary economists refer to as "selection" and "structured feedback" (Malerba and Orsenigo 2015).

firms' presence in local markets. In the next chapter we will examine the relevant issues in more detail, for now it suffices to note simply that patents allow firms to keep out competitors. Where new products might have had multiple producers in the past, each with shares of the associated revenues, in a system with pharmaceutical patent protection the returns to new products are captured by single patent-owning firms.

How do local firms adjust to this new status quo? Most obviously, trad- itional business models of copying new drugs cease being viable as these become patented locally. Some firms attempt to adjust by trying to become more innovative, investing more in research and development of new drugs. Adjustment along this path can convert these firms into advocates of patent protection. Some firms disappear; barred from continuing with past practices and unable to adopt new viable practices, many industries close.[28] For all their differences, the various forms of adjustment can have similar effects on efforts to revise pharmaceutical patent systems. These firms may have resisted the introduction of pharmaceutical patents in the first place, but, once the country has a patent system, they have adjusted in ways that dampen their opposition. Neither those investing more in R&D nor those that cease to exist constitute useful allies for health officials seeking to build coalitions to ameliorate the effects of pharmaceutical patents. Adjustment can thus cause defensive coali- tions, i.e. the sets of actors that opposed the global sea change in the 1980s and 1990s, to wither.

Yet these two forms of adjustment, trying to be more like "big pharma" or ceasing to exist, do not constitute the universe of responses to the introduction of pharmaceutical patents, and the withering of defensive coalitions is not inevitable. Even in countries with patents, opportunities for production and sales continue to exist in older drugs: because patents expire, pharmaceutical markets include segments featuring firms using knowledge that is no longer privately owned. Some local firms continue to exist, and new firms continue to emerge, selling older drugs where patents are no longer relevant or entering the market with follow-on versions when patents expire. In sum, rather than reacting to the new status quo by becoming originator firms or exiting the sector altogether, many firms adjust to the introduction of pharmaceutical patents by becoming different types of non-originator firms (del Campo 2016; Kale 2010; Shadlen 2007). Local pharmaceutical firms in developing countries may become more like "generic" pharmaceutical firms in developed countries, trying to avoid infringement in their new market segments, while militating against abuse of the patent system. Depending on local firms' abilities to react in this way, defensive coalitions can persist or be reconstituted for subsequent conflicts over how pharmaceutical patent systems function.

---

[28] Some firms may pursue rearguard strategies and continue to make their own versions of patented drugs, but doing so is risky and not the norm.

Differential patterns of adjustment to initial policy choices affect subsequent coalitional possibilities. Policy choices made in the 1990s cast a shadow over policymaking processes in the 2000s. The former does not determine the latter, but, by triggering distinct patterns of adjustment, the first set of choices conditions the second. The two policymaking episodes that are central to this book, introducing pharmaceutical patents and revising new patent systems, are not independent events. Differences in how patent regimes were introduced in the 1990s generate distinct challenges and inspire different patterns of adjustment in domestic pharmaceutical sectors, which in turn affect possibilities for coalition building in the 2000s.

To summarize, the focus here is on two mechanisms by which constellations of actors and interests change in response to external shocks, and as they do so shift the opportunities for coalition building. The first regards trade pressures mobilizing exporters and altering the universe of actors that care about IP policy. The second regards policies, once introduced, inspiring patterns of adjustment and reconfiguring interests around IP policy. Both of these mechanisms shift the social terrain in ways that can enable or constrain policymakers seeking to build coalitions to secure their desired outcomes. Where higher shares of exports enter the US market under preferential and removable trading arrangements, building coalitions for over-compliance in the introduction of pharmaceutical patents becomes easier. And depending on the magnitude and duration of the shock generated by initial policy choices and subsequent transformations of state and society, efforts to modify new patent systems are also constrained.

Finally, and to return to a larger theme of this book, it is important to underscore that both of these mechanisms constitute domestic politics being shifted by *international* changes. While this is easy to see with regard to trade pressures mobilizing exporters, it is also the case when we observe political coalitions reshaped over time by domestic actors' reactions to new policies. The new constellations of interests and patterns of mobilization are the products of an exogenous shock in the first place. If not for the fundamental changes in the global politics of IP, we are unlikely to have witnessed the initial policy changes that transformed the state, inspired adjustment, and subsequently reshuffled social structure. Even if the most important factors accounting for policy variation in subsequent periods are domestic, the entire political economy has been shaped by the initial exogenous shock. This is, essentially, a revised formulation of what Gourevitch (1978) labeled the "second image reversed." In the original, the question asked was how changes in the international environment affect national policies. The answer, which became foundational for decades of research in comparative and international political economy, was that the effects are mediated by national political processes. Here, adopting a longitudinal perspective, we can see how entire political economies can be transformed because of earlier external events. The proximate causes are domestic, but the domestic conditions themselves have international roots.

RESEARCH DESIGN, DATA SOURCES, METHODOLOGY, AND ORGANIZATION

Intellectual property provides a useful terrain to study the national consequences of international change, because without new international rules and the mass of pressures that countries faced in the 1980s and 1990s (i.e. the global sea change) there is little reason to expect developing countries to have revised their IP systems. Other areas of economic policy that also underwent substantial change in this period, such as trade, ownership of state enterprises, and regulations on foreign investment, had typically been contested internally for long periods of time, with some actors seeking the liberalization of imports, privatization of state enterprises, and greater opening to foreign investment. Though countries undeniably were subject to external pressures in these areas too, it is reasonable to expect that, even in the absence of new international rules and overtures from foreign governments, debt crises and deteriorating economic conditions would have yielded significant degrees of policy change. In the case of IP, in contrast, little if any change would have occurred in the absence of external pressures. To illustrate, even as many developing countries were fundamentally revising their development strategies in the 1980s, many continued to fight for international rules endorsing lax IP protection and fiercely resisted overtures to change national practices (Gadbaw and Richards 1988a; Sell 1998). Notwithstanding crises of development strategies and dramatic changes in countries' economic policies, IP is an area where the status quo appeared to be firmly locked in place—until uprooted by an external shock in the late 1980s and early 1990s.

Of course the external shock in this period had implications not just for countries' policies and practices regarding patents, but other forms of IP too, including those regarding copyrights, trademarks, industrial secrets, and so on. Each of these fields animates different sets of interests and mobilizes different sets of actors in society and the state. And even within the realm of patents, patterns of conflict may vary by technology. Focusing on the politics of pharmaceutical patents narrows the scope of research, and in doing so allows us to tighten our analytic lens and present a parsimonious and systematic explanation for the national effects of global shifts in ways that are not possible when assessing the outcome of TRIPS implementation in all its dimensions, as previous scholars have recognized (Deere 2008; Morin and Gold 2014).

A further, substantive, reason to focus on the political economy of pharmaceutical patents is the unrivalled prominence of this particular issue area. In no other sector are patents valued so greatly as mechanisms of appropriation as they are in the drug industry, and pharmaceutical firms spearheaded the global campaign to integrate IP policy into international trade rules. Furthermore, whether or not countries should be obliged to introduce pharmaceutical patents was the singularly most contested and divisive issue during the TRIPS negotiations, and the implications of the subsequent requirement to do so have remained the central point of conflict in the decades since TRIPS entered into effect, attracting an extraordinary amount of attention from analysts, activists, and international organizations. Quite simply, in most countries, political conflicts about complying with TRIPS are, de facto, conflicts over pharmaceutical patenting.

Argentina, Brazil, and Mexico are appropriate cases for comparison, as these were among the countries most heavily targeted by external pressures. As of the late 1980s, none of the three allowed pharmaceutical products to be patented, yet each appeared to offer international drug firms large and potentially lucrative markets, provided that they able to obtain patent protection. In a study of IP protection in Asia and Latin America that the Pharmaceutical Manufacturers of America[29] presented to the US Government in 1987, Argentina, Brazil, and Mexico (along with India) featured as the most "problematic" countries and where industry most wanted the US to act: in these countries the level of protection available was the lowest and the expected gains to transnational firms of obtaining patent protection were greatest, yet these countries were also singled out for being the most reluctant to change their policies (Gadbaw and Richards 1988b; Nogués 1990). The three Latin American countries in particular thus attracted the ire of the transnational pharmaceutical sector and the attention of the US Government, and achieving IP policy changes in these three countries became a key objective of US foreign economic policy (Buscaglia and Long 1997; Elliott and Richardson 1996; Harrison 2004; Hirst 1998). Though each faced considerable external pressures, these three countries demonstrated differences on the key social structure variables that are advanced in this book as the factors affecting diversity in coalitions and compliance: industrial legacies in the local pharmaceutical sectors, and export profiles.

This book utilizes the approach and tools of comparative historical analysis, examining national patterns of change as the outcome of the social forces interacting and unfolding over time (Katznelson 1997; Mahoney and Rueschemeyer 2003; Mahoney and Thelen 2015; Thelen 1999). One of the key insights of the comparative historical approach is that the same factors, even when scored similarly, may affect outcomes differently depending on the

---

[29] In the 1990s this association would insert research into its title and rename itself the Pharmaceutical Research and Manufacturers of America (PhRMA).

pace at which events unfold.[30] Accordingly, the structured comparisons focus on the markedly different ways that similar events occurred in three countries over time, with emphases on timing and the sequential nature of change.

Analytic emphasis is not placed on the behavior of electorates, but rather diverse forms of political action by broad social groups. Coalitions, central to this book, are conceptualized as informal alliances that manifest actors' collective expression of shared interests and objectives in the public sphere. Importantly, coalitions studied this way are identified by the analyst; they are not formal entities, such as agreements between parties in legislatures.[31]

The comparative case studies allow us to adjudicate between rival explanations for political outcomes. Where countries that appear similar in terms of the external pressures they are subject to and the preferences of incumbent Executives yield different responses, for example, we can question the explanatory power of those variables alone. Of course, countries always vary in multiple ways that are out of the researcher's control (i.e., we can neither keep constant nor manipulate all the relevant variables), confounding purely correlational efforts at making causal inference in small-n analyses. Case study research helps us to understand the changing relationship between variables over time, creating a forensic account of what affected what, and how. Within-case analysis and process tracing are used to assess alternative causal pathways of the outcomes of interest: the "causal process observations" obtained through process tracing enable the researcher to determine if the evidence fits one explanation better than another (Collier et al. 2010; Bennett and Checkel 2014a; Fairfield 2013; Fairfield and Charman 2017, forthcoming).

Comparative case studies based on process tracing are also essential for understanding how coalitions are constructed and change. Forms of compliance are not attributable directly to social structure; rather, forms of compliance are tied to the characteristics of political coalitions that social structure both enables and encumbers. This means that we need to build on material and more easily observable indicators, such as the market shares of rival segments of industry, and consider the way actors engage in collective action and cultivate allies, and their strategies to exploit contacts with legislators and Executive officials. We also need to see how Executives, seeking to introduce policy changes, respond to the opportunities and constraints presented by social structure. These sorts of political activities are at the heart of coalition building, and they can only be identified through case studies. Of course, linking changed characteristics of coalitions to policy outcomes is difficult, and the risk of falling into circular reasoning is ever-present. Process tracing allows

---

[30] See, among others, Collier and Collier (1991), Falleti (2005), Falleti and Lynch (2009), Falleti and Mahoney (2015), Grzymala-Busse (2011), Pierson (2003; 2004).

[31] Doner and Schneider (2016, 618) make this distinction as well. See also the contributions to Smith et al. (2014).

us to study the phenomena of coalitions expanding (or shrinking), mobilizing to drive policy change, and, critically, the temporal relationship between these events and the outcomes of interest (Thelen and Mahoney 2015).

The research is based on fieldwork in Argentina, Brazil, and Mexico. In addition to archival sources, press accounts, and statistical data, the research was informed by extensive interviewing. Informants in each country were identified according to functional positions, with the goal of conducting similarly structured interviews with clusters of actors from the same areas and positions in each country. For example, in each country I interviewed representatives from pharmaceutical industries, both subsidiaries of trans-national firms operating locally and national firms, as well as lawyers working with these segments of the pharmaceutical sector. Likewise, in each country I interviewed officials from relevant areas of the Executive, including ministries and secretariats, patent offices and health regulatory agencies, as well as from Congress, including legislators, legislative assistants, and legislative researchers. And in each country I interviewed civil society actors, such as professionals from the medical and health fields, and individuals or organizations focused on the promotion of national science and innovation policies, as well as activists engaged in work around IP, including—but not restricted to—those working specifically on matters related to pharmaceutical patenting and access to medicines. The Fieldwork Appendix presents the location and period of fieldwork in each country, along with information on the informants in each of these functional fields.

Beyond formal, confidential interviews, the research has benefited from a substantial amount of correspondence in other forms. For example with some of the informants I have had ongoing email exchanges over course of multiple years. Though I do not identify informants in the text, where interviews and emails are cited I provide information on the functions and positions of relevant actors (and these cited interviews are listed following the references).

Using interview data presents well-known challenges for causal inference, challenges that have been amply debated (Brady and Collier 2004; Mahoney 2010; Mosley 2013; Rathbun 2008). Most obviously, the pool of subjects interviewed is not random; in fact the pool should not be random when it is essential to communicate with particular individuals about key events. And of course information relayed by informants may be incomplete, self-serving, partial, or inaccurate. One way to address these concerns was to seek "saturation," i.e. to interview multiple people from each functional category to reach the point where additional interviews are not providing new information (Bennett and Checkel 2014b; Bleich and Pekkanen 2013; Lynch 2013). In addition, the information obtained from interviews about the role of actors in events has been cross-checked against information from the public record, newspapers, and archives (often referred to as "triangulation"), and frequently informants were asked to clarify inconsistencies in follow-up interviews or other forms of interaction. Saturation and triangulation thus allow the researcher to be confident that the information obtained from interviews is accurate, and, moreover, as part of a research design based on within-case analysis and process tracing, these steps allows us to use interviews as a method for collecting data to assess rival explanations.

Chapter 2 presents the substance of the policy debates. The chapter provides greater context on IP, patents, and the particular characteristics of pharmaceuticals that have always made this industry a focal point of conflict. In addition to presenting the specific policy issues that were contested as countries introduce pharmaceutical patent systems in the 1990s and then reform these new patent systems in the 2000s, the chapter presents the explanatory framework for understanding cross-national and within-case longitudinal variation in patent policy. That is, while the discussion in this chapter has discussed the relevant variables and mechanisms in more abstract form, Chapter 2 presents this more concretely, with reference to the specific debates over pharmaceutical patents.

The empirical material that follows is divided into two clusters of chapters corresponding to two periods of patent politics. Chapters 3–5 analyze how countries introduced new pharmaceutical patent systems in response to the global sea change of the 1980s and 90s, and Chapters 6–8 analyze how countries went about reforming their new patent systems in the 2000s in response to emerging challenges. In each time period the chapters are presented in the same order, starting with Argentina, followed by Mexico, then Brazil. The chapters are not presented in chronological order, but rather to highlight key aspects of the explanatory framework, namely how changing social structure and export profiles establish the conditions for Executives to build coalitions to secure their desired policy outcomes. Chapter 9 synthesizes the main findings of the book and discusses the implications of the research for the study of comparative and international political economy, and also considers the challenges that developing countries face in adjusting their development strategies to the new world of pharmaceutical patenting.

2

The Political Economy
of Pharmaceutical Patents

This book analyses national responses to the fundamental transformations that the global politics of intellectual property (IP) underwent at the end of the twentieth and start of the twenty-first centuries. The centerpiece of these transformations was the requirement that all countries allow patents on pharmaceutical products. Responses to this global shock varied, both in terms of initial reactions and subsequent policy measures. Thus, one global change yielded diverse national outcomes.

The political economy of pharmaceutical patents proceeds in two stages. With the obligation to introduce pharmaceutical patents imposed, the first set of conflicts revolved around how to do so. Then, once decisions were made about the establishment of pharmaceutical patent systems, the second set of conflicts centered on how the patent systems function. Here the central issue is how countries went about "tailoring" their new patent systems to make them more compatible with national conditions. Of course, prior global debates of the 1980s and 1990s provides the background for the present analysis, for it was the outcome produced in the international politics of IP, most notably that all countries would be expected to grant pharmaceutical patents, that countries were responding to in subsequent episodes of national policy-making. This book focuses on how countries responded to this global shift, the second and third stages in Figure 2.1.

This chapter provides the explanatory framework to account for cross-national and longitudinal variation in national responses to the global sea change. Key contentions of this book are that the politics of patents should be understood as iterative, in that there are successive episodes of conflict that need to be analyzed, and also path dependent, in that the policy choices of one period generate effects that condition influence policymaking in subsequent periods. Accordingly, the explanatory framework links the outcomes of conflicts over tailoring new patent systems to the resolutions of previous conflicts over introducing pharmaceutical patents. Forms of compliance with the new global order are produced by these two sets of conflicts over time.

Global Sea Change   National Responses to the Global Sea Change

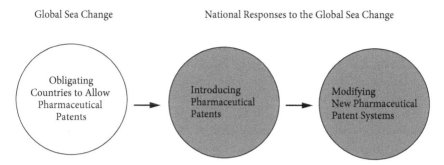

Figure 2.1. Changing Dimensions of Debate in the Politics of Patents

The chapter begins with brief introductions to intellectual property, patents, and pharmaceuticals, to help the reader understand the nature of the conflicts. The second section considers the policy issues that countries addressed in their initial responses to the global sea change, and then in revising their patent systems. The third section hones in on the factors that can account for cross-national variation in the 1990s. The focus is on the ways that social structure, a function of industrial development legacies and export profiles, constrained or enabled Executives seeking to build coalitions for over-compliance. The fourth section then presents an approach for understanding variation in countries' subsequent modifications of their new patent systems in the 2000s. Again, the focus is on changing social structure, here a function of reactions to the initial policy choices, and we see how such changes affect possibilities for the establishment and maintenance of political coalitions for tailoring new patent systems.

INTELLECTUAL PROPERTY, PATENTS, AND PHARMACEUTICAL CONFLICTS

Patents grant exclusive rights over the use of knowledge for limited periods in the territories where they are granted. For as long as a patent in a given country is in effect, the rights to produce and sell goods in that country that include the protected knowledge lie solely with the owner of the patent. By providing actors with means to appropriate the benefits of their investments in research and development, patents can thus create incentives for invention and innovation. Yet because patents convert knowledge, something that is non-rivalrous (everyone can use unlimited amounts without reducing the amount available for anyone else to use), into private property controlled by a single owner, the same instrument that incentivizes inventions and innovations also restricts their diffusion and use. After all, one way that owners recoup their investment expenditures is by selling or licensing their property at high prices for as long as the patent remains in force.

These basic principles of patents allow us to think of the trade-offs involved in policy choice, between dynamic benefits and static costs. Patent protection can create incentives for innovation, but patents can create barriers to the access and use of knowledge. It is difficult to maximize the benefits and minimize the costs simultaneously (Arrow 1962; Maskus 2000; Scotchmer 2004). In the most general of terms, countries may opt for more IP protection to prioritize incentives for innovation, or countries may opt for less protection to avoid the static costs that patents can create.

But what does it mean to refer to a country offering "more" or "less" patent protection? Here it useful to think in terms of two functions that patent systems perform: converting knowledge into property and protecting property. These two functions correspond to two dimensions of property rights, rights of alienation and rights of exclusion (Colombatto 2004; Schlager and Ostrom 1992). With regard to the first function, although a patent endows the owner with a private right of exclusion over knowledge, this does not happen automatically upon possession of knowledge. Patents are granted by the state, and only to inventions that fall within the range of patentable subject matter. Countries' patent laws ordinarily stipulate what sorts of things can be considered inventions,[1] and they may also have provisions declaring that certain inventions are not eligible for patents. Moreover, beyond setting the boundaries of patentable subject matter, where ownership of a given genre of knowledge is permissible, patents are only granted after examiners confirm that the claimed invention satisfies the criteria of novelty, inventiveness, and utility.[2] Countries' patent systems may vary in each of these ways: what constitutes inventions, what inventions are patentable, and how patentability criteria are applied in the course of examination.[3]

With regard to the second function, the protection of property, patents allow the owner, for the duration of the patent term, to control the use of the protected knowledge by providing exclusive rights over manufacturing, import and export, distribution, and sales. But these rights of exclusion can also vary. Once a patent is granted, the rights conferred by the patent include

---

[1] Because of the difficulty of defining "invention," patent laws tend to avoid doing so and instead proceed negatively, stipulating lists of things that are *not* treated as inventions.

[2] In the United States, inventiveness is referred to as "non-obvious." Although legal scholars debate the differences between these two terms (Barton 2003), for the purposes of the political analysis in this book, inventiveness and non-obviousness are synonymous.

[3] Note that the third condition is nested in the first two: if an application is made for a patent on knowledge that is regarded as not constituting an invention or that claims a non-patentable invention, then no assessment of the patentability criteria is made, as the application simply will not undergo substantive examination.

various exceptions to rights-owners' abilities to control the use and distribution of their property.

National patent systems can vary on both of these dimensions, the rights of alienation and rights of exclusion. Depending on how these potential dimensions of variation operate in practice, a country can be said to offer "more" or "less" patent protection. In the simplest sense, where a country allows more types of knowledge to become privately owned and offers more rights of exclusion to the owners of private knowledge we can say that the level of patent protection is greater (or stronger) than in a country that allows fewer types of knowledge to become privately owned and where owners' rights of exclusion are less robust.

The relative weights that countries place on the dynamic benefits versus the static costs of patents have, traditionally, determined whether they offered more or less protection. In general, wealthier countries with more innovative capabilities have opted for more patent protection than developing countries that largely use (rather than produce) knowledge.[4]

Different national approaches to patenting have historically been reflected in international debates. In the broadest of strokes, the international politics of patents has featured efforts by developing countries to affirm their prerogatives to restrict the domain of knowledge which can be privately owned and to reduce rights of exclusion, and efforts by more developed countries to establish norms in favor of expanding the domain of knowledge that can be privately owned and assuring that patent-owners enjoy more extensive rights of exclusion. That is, poorer countries that offered less patent protection have sought international rules confirming their rights to do so, while wealthier countries have sought international rules that would allow knowledge-owners to benefit from patent protection not just locally but globally. International conflicts over patents (and IP more generally) became particularly intense in the 1970s and 1980s, as knowledge- and information-intensive sectors that depend more on IP rights came to play a larger role in economic activity and exert more influence on the foreign economic policy of the US and European states.[5] Quite simply, the level of tolerance of cross-national differentiation subsided, considerably.

Conflicts over patents are particularly acute in the area of pharmaceuticals. Research and development (R&D) costs in drugs are high, because of uncertainties in science (i.e. most research fails to yield marketable products) and the need to undertake clinical trials to receive regulatory approval for new products. Yet drugs, in general, are easy to replicate: it is comparatively simple

---

[4] Chang (2002); Chen and Puttitanun (2005); Maskus (2000); May (2013); May and Sell (2006); Wallerstein et al. (1993).

[5] Harrison (2004); Jaffe and Lerner (2004); Lanoszka (2003); May (2000); Orsi and Coriat (2006); Pugatch (2004); Ryan (1998); Roemer-Mahler (2013); Sell (1998; 2003).

for one firm to produce an identical version of a drug invented or developed by another firm.[6] Together, the high cost of R&D and the relative ease of replication encourage originator firms to utilize patents to ward off competition and thus capture the benefits of their investments in technological innovation and product development.[7] Patents, which erect legal barriers where financial or technological barriers are insufficient to prevent replication, are the most important instrument that originator firms use to secure appropriation of the returns from investments in R&D.[8]

Another characteristic of the pharmaceutical sector that fuels originator firms' interests in obtaining and retaining patent protection are the considerable—and largely unavoidable—delays between invention and launch. Patent applications, to meet standards of novelty, need to be filed early (typically within one year of the invention being made), at a point when the associated drugs that the patent aims to protect ordinarily will still be in the development stage. And the product development stage in pharmaceuticals is long: the path from establishment of a new compound to having a useful product takes considerable time, as do the clinical trials that are necessary to obtain regulatory approval. By the time a drug protected by a patent is placed on the market, a significant chunk of the patent term may have lapsed, making patent owners fiercely concerned with their rights of exclusion in the remaining years.[9] The result of these factors is that there is a window of exclusivity that pharmaceutical firms place a high priority on exploiting. Originator firms will do all they can to ward off competitors during the periods of protection promised by their patents and, if possible, extend periods of protection by acquiring additional patents on new forms and formulations of existing drugs.[10]

Yet pharmaceutical patents bring well-known risks, too. Drugs often have few functional substitutes. Patients with one condition (e.g., hypertension) cannot ordinarily be treated with medicines for other conditions (e.g., chronic pain);

---

[6] The statement regarding the ease of replication is particularly so in the case of the chemical-based pharmaceutical products. Replication of protein-based biological drugs is more complex.

[7] The investments made by pharmaceutical firms may be in-house investments, or they may entail licensing or purchasing patents from smaller firms or public sector researchers. Sampat and Lichtenberg (2011) discuss the relative roles of private and public actors in pharmaceutical research and development.

[8] Dutfield (2003); Grabowski (2002); Levin et al. (1987); Mansfield (1986); Mansfield et al (1981). Pharmaceutical firms also rely on trademarks to promote their brand names and preserve market shares in the absence of patents. The concern with trademarks is not restricted to originator firms, however, as producers of off-patent "branded generics" use trademarks too.

[9] As Budish et al. (2015) show, this can also affect the direction of innovation by encouraging pharmaceutical firms to focus on drugs to treat conditions that require less demanding clinical trials and thus benefit from shorter lag times.

[10] Hemphill and Sampat (2012); Hitchings et al (2012); Howard (2007); Kapczynski et al (2012); Sampat and Shadlen (2017).

nor can pharmaceutical firms that produce hypertension drugs do so using use molecules that reduce pain. Not only is the range of appropriate alternatives in each therapeutic class often limited, but multiple drugs that treat the same condition may have different side effects and be tolerated differently. Thus, for many individuals there is in effect just one useful treatment for their condition. Restricting access to new medicines lacking functional substitutes, via the creation of legal barriers, can thus have profound costs in terms of health and well-being. To appreciate the implications of low functional substitution, contrast drugs with other products: if for example, patents on a new vacuum cleaner make it expensive, the downsides of consumers who cannot afford the new vacuum cleaner using older generations, or brooms, are trivial in comparison with the plight of people who cannot afford a new medication and thus have to use an older generation of treatment, or no drug at all. In light of these factors, many countries have regarded the costs of granting patents on drugs as exceeding the benefits.[11]

Even where countries do grant pharmaceutical patents, health concerns may motivate policymakers and regulators to try to restrict the rights of exclusion that patents confer. They may seek to adjust the patent system to assure that patent-holders' sole rights to sell their products do not lead to prohibitively high prices and impinge on access. And countries with patents may seek to combat originator firms' efforts to extract extra periods of protection, making sure that, once patents expire, competition can ensue quickly.

These conflicting perspectives regarding patent protection, in general, and pharmaceutical patents, in particular, can be further understood by examining data on patenting in the pre-TRIPS era. Figure 2.2 presents data on all patents granted in the US, averaged over five-year periods from 1966–1995. Each bar indicates the relative shares of patents corresponding to inventors from just five countries (France, Germany, Japan, United Kingdom, US) and the rest of the world. Figure 2.3 presents these data at the sectoral level, focusing exclusively on pharmaceutical patents granted in the US. Both figures reveal remarkable levels of growth over time, particularly from the 1980s onward, as well as strikingly high levels of asymmetry in terms of the location of innovation. In pharmaceuticals, these five countries accounted for over 85 percent of patents throughout the time period, and as overall levels of patenting in this sector increased in the 1980s and 1990s, this share did not change. As a further illustration of the asymmetries of capabilities for pharmaceutical patenting, Table 2.1 lists the top twenty pharmaceutical patenting countries in 1990, on the eve of the global requirement to introduce pharmaceutical patents. For each country we see its share of the total, and the cumulative share.

---

[11] Chaudhuri (2005); Dutfield (2003); La Croix and Liu (2008); Mazzoleni and Nelson (1998); Nogués (1990; 1993); Watal (2000); WHO (1997).

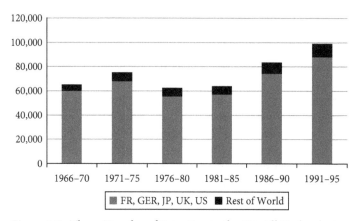

Figure 2.2. Three Decades of Patenting in the US: All Technologies
Source: United States Patent and Trademark Office

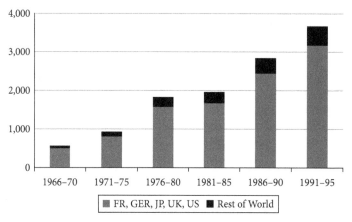

Figure 2.3. Three Decades of Patenting in the US: Pharmaceuticals
Source: United States Patent and Trademark Office

The top ten countries alone surpass 95 percent, and by the time we reach twenty countries we have accounted for more than 99 percent of pharmaceutical patents issued in the US.

In light of the trade-offs between the perceived benefits and costs of pharmaceutical patenting and the intense concentration of capabilities in this area, it is not surprising that so few countries other than the United States allowed pharmaceutical patents prior to the 1980s. Even in Europe, as of 1970 only Britain, France, and West Germany granted pharmaceutical patents; Japan did not begin to do so until 1976. Then from the mid-1970s to the early 1990s, pharmaceutical patenting became the norm throughout the

Table 2.1. Sources of Pharmaceutical Patents Granted in the US in 1990 (by country and share)

Country	Share	(Cumulative Shares)
US	49.0%	
Japan	14.6%	(63.7%)
West Germany	11.1%	(74.8%)
UK	6.8%	(81.6%)
France	5.1%	(86.7%)
Italy	2.9%	(89.5%)
Switzerland	2.8%	(92.3%)
Canada	1.2%	(93.5%)
Belgium	1.0%	(94.4%)
Denmark	0.7%	(95.1%)
Hungary	0.7%	(95.8%)
Sweden	0.6%	(96.5%)
Austria	0.5%	(97.0%)
Israel	0.5%	(97.5%)
Netherlands	0.5%	(98.0%)
Australia	0.4%	(98.3%)
Spain	0.3%	(98.6%)
Ireland	0.2%	(98.8%)
South Korea	0.1%	(99.0%)
Finland	0.1%	(99.1%)

Notes: The total number of pharmaceutical patents granted in 1990 was 3364. The cumulative shares do not always match the corresponding sums on account of rounding.

Source: United States Patent and Trademark Office.

"Global North."[12] At the same time, however, country after country throughout the "Global South" declared pharmaceutical products (and sometimes processes too) non-patentable. As of the early-mid 1980s, roughly fifty or sixty developing (and socialist) countries did not allow patents on pharmaceutical products (Nogués 1990, 4; Qian 2007, 436, footnote 1; UNCTAD 1981, 30, Table 10; WHO 1997, 24).[13]

It was in this context of this gulf, with pharmaceutical patents becoming available in wealthier countries but absent in larger and more industrialized

---

[12] Finland, which allowed pharmaceutical patents in 1995, was the last developed country to do so. La Croix and Liu (2009), Liu and La Croix (2015), and Qian (2007) provide cross-national data. See also, Boldrin and Levine (2008), Cassier (2008), Dutfield (2003), Gaudillière (2008).

[13] Interestingly, there was a moment, in the late 1960s and early 1970s, before many post-colonial countries that had inherited pharmaceutical patent regimes altered their rules and before many wealthier countries began to allow pharmaceutical patents, that more countries in the Global South allowed pharmaceutical patents than did countries in the Global North. Some countries that did not grant patents to pharmaceutical products did, allow pharmaceutical manufacturing processes to be patented, but process patents are easier to circumvent and constitute a weak form of protection.

developing countries, that the transnational pharmaceutical sector mobilized to universalize pharmaceutical patent protection. Though drug firms from the US and Europe did not act alone, these firms and their representatives were among the leading advocates of TRIPS, and more generally of the integration of IP into the trade regime. Making sure that the protection available in developed countries was also available in developing countries was the transnational sector's highest priority.

Through successful lobbying, the transnational pharmaceutical sector made the goal of universalizing patent protection a priority of US and European Governments too. In the 1980s, increasing IP became an important element of the US and European Community's foreign economic policy, a process that culminated in the World Trade Organization's (WTO) TRIPS Agreement. How private firms secured such favorable changes to international legal regimes, the topic of an extensive literature (see references in Chapter 1, fn. 3), is not the focus of attention here. Rather, the global sea change produced by these events, in particular the establishment of the obligation for developing countries to offer pharmaceutical patents, provides the backdrop for the analysis in this book.

TWO PERIODS OF CONFLICT: THE KEY ISSUES

With the centerpiece of the global sea change being the obligation to permit pharmaceutical patenting, the first question all developing countries addressed was when this should happen. While WTO rules allowed developing countries until 2000 to be in compliance with TRIPS, in general, countries that did not grant pharmaceutical patents prior to 1995 could wait until 2005 to do so.[14] Independently of how much of the WTO-authorized transition period countries utilized, TRIPS also obligated countries to receive applications filed as of January 1995, when the Agreement formally entered into effect. These applications would be held, metaphorically, in a "mailbox," to be examined once the country's transition period expired. To illustrate, in the case of a country that introduced pharmaceutical patents starting on the 1st of January 2000, when this date came around the patent office would begin examining applications, and it would do so not only with applications filed as of January 2000 but also with those deposited in the mailbox during the previous five years.

For the transnational pharmaceutical sector and the US Government, the transition periods in TRIPS were too long. These actors had been calling for the introduction of pharmaceutical patents since the mid-1980s, well before

---

[14] Both transition periods are longer in the case of Least Developed Countries.

TRIPS was concluded, and they subsequently wanted countries to begin examining and granting pharmaceutical patents immediately. To be sure, the mailbox provisions mean that applications filed after 1995 could, eventually, be granted, but no property rights would be established until the patents were issued, and that would not happen until after countries' transition periods expired.[15] With the timing of when pharmaceuticals would become patentable of paramount importance, the transnational sector and the US sought over-compliance, demanding that countries begin offering pharmaceutical patents immediately.

Local pharmaceutical industries in developing countries, in contrast, tried to get their governments to use more of the available transition periods. Until pharmaceutical patents became available, no one could exert full control over knowledge, so delaying the onset date would give local actors more time to prepare. Initially, local firms sought to prevent the introduction of pharmaceutical patents altogether, and no doubt for many firms that remained a desirable outcome, but by the early 1990s it was clear that the Uruguay Round negotiations would make pharmaceutical patents obligatory. Lacking the muscle to block the global sea change, local firms mobilized to press their governments to introduce pharmaceutical patents in such a way as to limit the magnitude of the inevitable shock that the new order would bring.

Conflicts regarding the introduction of pharmaceutical patents also regarded the thorny and complicated issue of whether this would be done retroactively. That is, once a date for the onset of pharmaceutical patenting is established, the critical policy choice regards how to treat applications and patents for earlier products that could not benefit from patent protection before the new system was introduced. In the case of pharmaceuticals, this is crucially important because of the lag time between filing patent applications and launching products. To illustrate, imagine a country "Nodrugpatentsland" that introduced a pharmaceutical patent regime in 1996, using one year of the available transition period. Applications filed in the country as of January 1995 would be held in a "mailbox" and examined starting in 1996 after the transition period ended, along with other applications filed after that point. Nodrugpatentsland would not, however, be obligated by TRIPS to acknowledge applications filed abroad prior to 1995. A patent application from 1990, for example, would not have been eligible for a patent in Nodrugpatentsland at the time. Nor would this patent be allowed as of 1996 either, even with the introduction of pharmaceutical patents in Nodrugpatentsland at that point, because patents are not available for knowledge that is already in the public domain; by 1996, when drug patenting commenced, this invention no longer satisfied the criteria of being "new." Since applications on drugs are filed (and

---

[15] This statement is partially qualified by a requirement to provide "exclusive marketing rights" for drugs associated with applications in the mailbox.

patents often obtained) before marketing authority is secured, however, the drug associated to this hypothetical 1990 application would most likely be still in product development—it would be in the pharmaceutical company's "pipeline." Or perhaps the application dates even earlier, to the 1980s, and the patent was already granted in countries with pharmaceutical patent systems. A drug associated with this patent may still be in the pipeline too, awaiting authorization to be placed on the market.

How countries introducing pharmaceutical patents treated drugs in the pipeline constituted a major point of conflict. Do countries acknowledge applications for inventions that were made prior to 1995? Do countries recognize patents already granted elsewhere? During the course of the TRIPS negotiations, the transnational pharmaceutical sector and the US attempted to make so-called pipeline protection obligatory, but developing countries resisted these efforts.[16] Although US negotiators assured that the requirement to offer pipeline protection was included in the IP chapter of NAFTA, it is not part of TRIPS. This means that countries were required to begin accepting applications from 1995 onwards, but TRIPS placed no obligation on countries to recognize earlier applications or patents. Simply put, according to the WTO the world of pharmaceutical patenting starts in 1995.

Conflicts over pipeline patents captured the spotlight in this period because this policy choice would have immediate effects on pharmaceutical firms' revenue streams. To understand the salience and importance of this specific issue, it is worth underscoring the significant degree of heterogeneity in patent applications (Scherer 2001). Firms file applications on virtually all prospective drug candidates, and they do so early in the product development process. But most of these inventions fail in the course of further investigation or clinical trials. Indeed, many applications filed with patent offices are abandoned along the way as firms come to grips with dead ends in product development; most patent applications, and even most granted patents, are associated with drugs that never become marketable products. But this is not so for the specific set of older, pre-1995 applications that firms would still be pursuing after 1995, the ones that could benefit if Nodrugpatentsland allowed pipeline patents, but would never be granted otherwise. These constituted pharmaceutical firms' most important applications and patents. These were the ones associated with products that were still alive, with a shot of surviving the product development and clinical trial phases and, it was hoped, make it to market.

---

[16] The US continued to push for a pipeline requirement throughout the TRIPS negotiations (Matthews 2002, 40–1, 62; WHO 1997, 19). The European Community allied with developing countries. The motives for the EC's opposition to requiring pipeline patents are not well understood, but a plausible source of this position is that some European countries were also just introducing pharmaceutical patent systems in the early 1990s. Japan's position on this issue is unclear.

And the granted patents that were in the balance, patents that had already been issued in countries with pharmaceutical patent systems and would become recognized locally if, but only if, Nodrugpatentsland granted pipeline protection, were even further along and had even greater prospects of being associated with marketable drugs.

For transnational pharmaceutical firms, then, the absence of pipeline protection in TRIPS was an intolerable setback. They feared that the 1995 cut-off date would sharply limit the extent of patent protection they would enjoy for drugs coming on to the market in the 1990s and into the 2000s. The benefits promised by the introduction of pharmaceutical patents would not be enjoyed until well into the future. As the International Federation of Pharmaceutical Manufacturers put it, "The lack of 'pipeline protection' provisions in the TRIPs Agreement is deplored and requires urgent resolution" (IFPMA 1995, 33).[17] Transnational firms and the US Government subsequently attempted to get countries to acknowledge pre-1995 applications and patents, even if not required to do so by TRIPS. They aimed to secure, in the course of implementation, what they were unable to achieve during the Uruguay Round negotiations, pushing for over-compliance in the form of pipeline patents. In contrast, local pharmaceutical firms regarded avoiding pipeline patents, and thus pushing the effects of the new patent system into the future and gaining time to adjust, as equally important.

The distinction between a patent mailbox and pipeline patents is essential for understanding the political importance attached to the latter. Both of these, formally, constitute "retroactivity," in that as of the date that pharmaceuticals become eligible for patents the country will consider older applications that are no longer "new" (Drahos 2010). Yet they differ in crucially important ways. All countries that are members of the WTO and that introduced pharmaceutical patents after 1995 would have a mailbox, with variation in the amount of time countries' mailboxes were operational and receiving applications a function of when pharmaceutical patenting began.[18] But the effects of the mailbox are not felt until after the end of the transition period,

---

[17] See also "TRIPS Transition Period 'Far Too Long': IFPMA," *The Pharma Market Letter*, May 22, 1995. WHO (1997, 28) also emphasizes the particular significance of national policy choices regarding pipeline patents.

[18] Countries that began granting pharmaceutical patents prior to TRIPS could also have created provisions to receive applications in something akin to a mailbox, during the period between when the decision was made to make pharmaceuticals patentable at some date and when that date arrived. My understanding is that this did not happen, that the idea of a mailbox had not yet been hatched. In Mexico, for example, as we shall see in Chapter 4, a 1987 reform to the patent law scheduled pharmaceutical patents to be introduced in 1997, but that reform (which would be overridden in 1991, anyway) did not include mailbox-like provisions. More research into the origins of the mailbox, and the different approaches to introducing pharmaceutical patents adopted by countries in the pre-TRIPS era, would be fruitful.

when pharmaceutical patents start to be examined.[19] The implications of allowing pipeline patents, in contrast, which was not required by TRIPS, are significantly greater. Pipeline protection meant that drugs that were about to be launched would become protected by patents, so it affected the immediacy of the shock produced by the introduction of pharmaceutical patents. As an illustration of significance of pipeline protection, consider that by the end of the 1990s still more than 90 percent of drugs approved for launch in the US relied on pre-1995 patents.[20] In fact, as late as 2006, more than a decade after TRIPS came into effect, the share of new drugs relying on post-1995 patents, and thus likely to benefit from patent protection in the absence of a pipeline, remained less than 25 percent (Sampat and Shadlen 2015a, Figure 2).

The three countries examined in this book varied in important ways on these dimensions. Argentina adopted patents on pharmaceutical products in 2000, without offering pipeline protection to pre-1995 applications and patents. Mexico introduced pharmaceutical patents exceptionally early, in 1991, as well as providing pipeline protection for applications and patents that had been filed prior to 1991 (so much earlier than 1995). In Brazil, pharmaceuticals became eligible for patents in 1997, and here too, like Mexico, pipeline protection was available for earlier applications and patents.

To illustrate the effects of these decisions made in the 1990s, Table 2.2 presents country-level data of patent status of the 159 new drugs that were approved for launch in the US from 1996–2004.[21] In Argentina the delayed introduction of pharmaceutical patents and the absence of a pipeline minimized the extent to which these drugs became patented. Only 23 percent of the drugs in the sample received patents, and even this figure overstates the extent of patenting, as these were issued slowly, beginning in October 2000. As of the end of 2000, only three of these drugs were protected by patents in Argentina, and still only 12 percent by the end of 2001. The effects of earlier choices were much greater in the other two countries. Three-fifths of the drugs in the sample became patent protected in Brazil, with the main reason for this greater share in Brazil being the pipeline. Of the 96 drugs that received patents in Brazil, 80 percent had at least one pipeline patent and 60 percent were protected *exclusively* with pipeline patents; without the decision to

---

[19] In fact the effects may never be felt, because countries with patent mailboxes often included special provisions for these applications (e.g. allowing any firm that had invested in producing a product associated with the application to continue doing so, with payment of a royalty fee, if the patent was eventually granted). Also, although TRIPS required countries with mailboxes to grant exclusive marketing rights to associated drugs, the complex terms under which these were required (WHO 1997, 21) meant that few instances of this would occur.

[20] As drugs tend to be launched early in the United States, US launch dates provide a useful benchmark.

[21] The methodology is explained in the Table. The approach used is similar to that in Sampat and Shadlen (2015b).

Table 2.2. Impact of Initial Policy Choices on Patenting of 159 New Drugs Launched from 1996–2004

	Argentina	Brazil	Mexico
Patents granted	50	140	411
Pipeline patents (% of grants)	—	80 (57%)	46 (11%)
Drugs with at least one patent (% of 159 drugs in sample)	37 (23%)*	96 (60%)	141 (89%)
Drugs with at least one pipeline patent	—	77	39
Drugs with pipeline patents only	—	58	11

* 3 drugs (1.9%) by end of 2000 and 19 drugs (11.9%) by end of 2001

Method and Sources

The analyses producing the data in this table consisted of three steps:

1. A list of all new drugs approved by the US Food and Drug Administration (FDA) between 1996 and 2004 was acquired. For each drug the relevant patents listed in the FDA's "Orange Book" were identified, yielding 626 US patents covering 159 drugs.
2. For each US patent, the corresponding applications filed in Argentina, Brazil, and Mexico were located, supplemented by additional searches undertaken for patent applications filed in these countries covering these 159 drugs. While identifying patents associated with drugs marketed in the US is facilitated by the existence of the FDA's Orange Book, it is more complicated in countries where such databases do not exist. To locate applications in Argentina, Brazil, and Mexico, public and proprietary databases were consulted, using bibliographic information on applications (e.g. titles, priority numbers and dates, names of applicants, names of inventors) to verify matches between the US patents and the corresponding national applications. Applications that were deposited through the pipeline in Brazil and Mexico were recorded as such.
3. National applications were searched individually in the databases of each country's patent office, and the outcomes recorded. The results were then aggregated back to the drug level. Again, pipeline patents were treated separately, as reported in the Table.

Source: Author's construction based on data from US FDA (Orange Book), Derwent World Patents Index, IMS Patent Focus, Lens.org, WIPO (Patenscope), and national patent offices

exceed TRIPS and offer pipeline protection, 58 drugs that were launched from 1996–2004 could have had multiple suppliers in Brazil. In Mexico, which introduced pharmaceutical patents well before either of the other countries, an exceptionally high share (89 percent) of these drugs became patented. Because patents were introduced so early, the pipeline plays a comparatively less important role for this set of drugs, but even here, 28 percent of the drugs that received patents had a pipeline patent, and 8 percent of these were protected in Mexico only because of this choice.

The other main issue that consumed the attention of actors in this period was compulsory licensing. Patents are property rights; they confer owners with sole rights of exclusion. During the time that a patent is in effect, the only actors with the rights to import, produce, or distribute patented products are the owners of the patents and licensees authorized by the owners. Governments can attenuate these rights of exclusion with compulsory licenses, which allow other actors ("third parties") to use privately owned knowledge without the owners' consent.

With regard to pharmaceuticals, the main purpose of provisions on compulsory licenses is to prevent the situation enabled by patents, of single suppliers setting prices, from making drugs prohibitively expensive and undermining access. The way that compulsory licenses achieve this end is that the government requests the patent-holding firm to lower the price, warning that otherwise, regardless of the patent, the government will allow another actor to supply the drug. In other words, the government will "compel" the owner to license the proprietary knowledge claimed in the patent. Though compulsory licensing can occur in any sector where inventions are protected by patents, the issue has particular importance in the case of pharmaceuticals because the ease of replication means that if legal barriers to imitation are relaxed, it is more likely that other producers will be able to enter the market with their own versions of patented drugs.[22] Countries may not need to follow through and issue the compulsory license, but rather use the threat of doing so as a bargaining chip: the patent-holder, fearing loss of control over her property and loss of sales, may respond to the threat by reducing the price. And the threats need not be explicit: if the patent-holder knows that the government approaches the bargaining situation with the ability to issue a compulsory license, there is reason to expect that to affect negotiations.[23]

The ability of a government to use the threat of a compulsory license to obtain price reductions depends on the threat being credible, and whether the threat is credible depends in large part upon the details of the country's patent law. TRIPS leaves countries with significant leeway in this regard. Provided that a minimum set of conditions are satisfied, countries can design their compulsory licensing provisions to give health authorities more or less autonomy to act quickly, for example, to make patent-holders' rights of appeal more or less difficult, or to require royalty payments to be lower or higher.[24] The question, then, is whether the particular provisions of the patent law are drafted

---

[22] In contrast, where replication is more difficult, even if the state issues a compulsory license, competitors to the patent holder face higher barriers to entry. Here it is worth noting that the label "compulsory license" can be misleading, as the patent holder ordinarily does not do anything that constitutes, formally, licensing the right to use the property. Rather, the state allows other actors to use the property, without the owner's permission, pending payment of a royalty. It is precisely the fact that replicating drugs is comparatively easy that compulsory licensing is pertinent. If a potential competitor were to need the owner's help in learning how to manufacture a patented product, because of the difficulty of production or dependence on tacit knowledge that only the patent owner possessed, for example, a legal ruling from the state may not be sufficient to get the patent owner to facilitate competition and ease these technological (non-patent) barriers to entry.

[23] Beall and Kuhn (2012); Cohen and Lybecker (2005); Ford et al. (2007); Kyle and Qian (2014); Meyerhof Salama and Benoliel (2010); Ramani and Urias (2015); Scherer and Watal (2002).

[24] Commission on Intellectual Property Rights (2002); Correa (1999); Gold and Lam (2003); Ho (2011); McManis and Contreras (2014); Reichman (1996; 2009a); Scherer and Watal (2002); Watal (1999; 2001).

such that compulsory licenses are relatively simple issue to issue (and thus the threats more credible) or whether they are more difficult to issue and leave government officials more encumbered (and thus the threats less credible). During the TRIPS negotiations, the transnational pharmaceutical sector and the US Government had sought stricter rules, requesting that compulsory licenses be limited to extraordinary circumstances (Watal 2011, 26–27). Although they ultimately acquiesced to more permissive text, the aspiration for more restrictive provisions continued to inform these actors' demands in the 1990s. As countries introduced new patent systems that would inevitably include some compulsory licensing provisions, the advocates of over-compliance wanted to make sure that these would be designed in such a way as to have minimal effect on how patent-holders exercise their property rights.[25]

Here too, we witness less over-compliance in Argentina than in Brazil or Mexico. Argentina's flexible compulsory licensing rules provided health authorities with a set of practical and useful tools for negotiating with patent holders. In contrast, both Brazil and Mexico adopted more complex provisions that left health officials confronting a series of hurdles that would impede their abilities to act in the public interest were the price of drugs high. Were either Brazilian or Mexican officials to have sought to issue compulsory licenses under the terms of the patent laws adopted in the 1990s, they would have struggled to make their threats credible.

Another dimension of compulsory licensing rules that attracted attention regards countries' rules on "local working" of patents. Most countries will allow compulsory licensing if the owner does not "work" the patent, and the specific question here was whether importation would constitute working or if local manufacturing should be required too.[26] Transnational pharmaceutical firms, which often supply multiple countries from single production sites, were committed to avoiding requirements to manufacture locally. For drugs themselves, firms could satisfy local working requirements by undertaking the final steps of packaging and labelling within countries, but producing pharmo-chemical inputs, such as the active pharmaceutical ingredients (APIs), in each country would be inefficient, and doing so would seriously disrupt these firms' global operations. Local production of pharmo-chemicals would also then

---

[25] In fact, the US issues many compulsory licenses (KEI 2014). Although these fit within the narrow range regarded as acceptable by the US Government, i.e. they are typically issued by courts as remedies for anti-competitive practices, the irony of the same country dissuading use of a policy instrument abroad while using it routinely at home has not gone unnoticed.

[26] In this regard TRIPS is more ambiguous (Correa 2000b; Watal 1999). Although the agreement appears to indicate that importation must be sufficient to meet local working obligations, some legal scholars suggest that when TRIPS is read in conjunction with the Paris Convention that countries may require local production. In the absence of a ruling by the WTO's Appellate Board, the ultimate legal status of such measures remains unclear.

necessitate more involved downstream local production in the formulation of final drugs too. Transnational firms thus sought to assure that importation would be sufficient to satisfy local working requirements, if not directly and explicitly in the text of countries' patent laws, then indirectly by allowing patent-holders to justify decisions to import on economic grounds, such as scale economies. After all, given the small volumes of inputs that are used in preparing medicines, measured in milligrams, such that global supply of most APIs can be satisfied by one or two production facilities, transnational firms can virtually always demonstrate that local production in a given country is economically inefficient.

On this dimension national outcomes appear less consistent with the patterns witnessed so far, in that local manufacturing was not required in Argentina (or Mexico) while in Brazil the patent law included an article that could, under some conditions, require patent-holding firms to produce locally to avoid being subject to compulsory licenses Yet the importance of these differences should not be exaggerated, for, as we shall see in Chapter 5, Brazil's local working requirement was drafted in such a way as to make it easy for patent-holding firms to satisfy. In other words, Brazil does not have, in effect, an operable local working rule either.[27]

To synthesize, developing countries introducing new pharmaceutical patent systems in the 1990s came under intense pressures to do so early, to do so retroactively by offering pipeline patents, and to make compulsory licenses difficult to issue. These policy issues were prominent points of conflict in all countries, and cross-national variation on these dimensions reflects differences in how countries responded to the global sea change.

The 2000s witnessed a second wave of patent politics, as new pharmaceutical patent systems underwent subsequent revisions. While countries varied in the details of how they introduced pharmaceutical patents, the global sea change ushered in a new status quo that was constant across countries: pharmaceutical products were eligible for patents and in most countries, by the 2000s, being granted. The existence of pharmaceutical patents shifts attention from one set of issues to another set, specifically issues regarding how pharmaceutical patent regimes function (the third circle in Figure 2.1). While conflicts in the first period were over the terms under which patent owners would receive private rights of exclusion over the knowledge in pharmaceutical inventions, once patents begin to be issued attention turned to the effective strength and duration of these rights.

---

[27] And in Argentina, a special compulsory licensing provision for applications deposited in the mailbox meant that after 2000, were any of these patents granted, local firms that were already involved in production of the protected drugs could continue to do so with payment of a small royalty to the patent owner.

In contrast with the 1990s, when the focal points of political conflict were common across countries, the specific points of conflict that consumed attention in the 2000s varied from country to country. After all, precisely which dimensions of "how pharmaceutical patent regimes function" are most important depends on local context, including specificities of the patent regime established in the 1990s. Consider, for example, compulsory licensing, an area that has received an enormous amount of attention from academics, activists, and international organizations. As compulsory licenses affect the strength of patent-holders' rights of exclusions, they have more salience in countries where there are more patents, so not surprisingly in light of the data in Table 2.2., among the three countries in this book, revisiting the grounds and procedures for compulsory licenses became a more important topic of debate in Brazil and Mexico than in Argentina.

Other prominent issues that featured in this period include treatment of test data that pharmaceutical firms deposit with local health regulators, enforcement of granted patents against allegations of infringement, approaches toward "secondary" patents on existing drugs that may extend periods of exclusivity, regulations on market entry after patents expire, and measures to control prescription drug pricing. These policy areas are discussed where relevant in Chapters 6–8. For now, the key points are that all of these are issues that affect how countries' new pharmaceutical patent systems function, and here too the relative salience of specific issues in different countries is a function of initial decisions regarding when and how pharmaceutical patents would be introduced.

The context of policy in this second period of patent politics differed too. In contrast to the first period, when state action responded to the imperatives created by the global sea change and it is reasonable to expect that nothing would have happened in the absence of the international shock, policy now had both external and internal motives. Externally, countries remained subject to the demands of the transnational pharmaceutical sector and foreign governments to offer patent owners extensive rights of exclusion; where countries over-complied in the 1990s to make sure that benefits promised were delivered, and where not to get them to over-comply now. Internally, the new status quo introduced by pharmaceutical patents often created challenges for health systems, and as these challenges coincided with a more general concern throughout the development community with social protection (Merrien 2013; Mosley 2001), they often motivated reform efforts. The vector of pressures and challenges orienting policymaking episodes in this period were not uniform across cases, but a function of the respective decisions that countries made in the 1990s. The remainder of this chapter presents the explanatory framework for analyzing these two periods of patent politics.

THE POLITICAL ECONOMY OF INTRODUCING
PHARMACEUTICAL PATENTS

The outcome in the first period is how (including when) countries introduced pharmaceutical patents. As the principal source of resistance to over-compliance in the establishment of new patent systems came from national pharmaceutical firms, understanding countries' responses to the global sea change starts with this sector. Though pharmaceuticals, in general, is an exceptionally internationalized sector with the same set of transnational firms present and dominant in most countries, we witness significant variation in terms of the development of local pharmaceutical industries in the postwar era.[28] Different industrial developmental legacies meant that national pharmaceutical sectors varied in ways that affected their economic and political resources.

Measuring the relative strengths of national and transnational segments of the pharmaceutical industries in different countries in the 1980s and early 1990s is not a straightforward process. Aggregate measures of sectoral employment and output are available (e.g. data from the United Nations Industrial Development Organization), but these figures do not tell us about the relative positions of the domestic vs. foreign segments of industry. One way to assess national firms' position in local markets is by examining their share of sales as share of all domestic pharmaceutical sales, and their standing in rankings of leading firms. For example, in a country with a more developed local pharmaceutical sector, nationally owned firms will have a larger share of sales, and the largest local firms will rank higher among all firms. Both of these measures based on sales data, which are subject to widely recognized limitations,[29] can be complemented with observations of capability development in national pharmaceutical sectors.

Using these indicators, Table 2.3 presents overviews of pharmaceutical sectors of Argentina, Brazil, and Mexico on the eve of the global sea change. The first two rows reveal the greater presence of national firms in the local market in Argentina than elsewhere: Argentinean firms had significantly larger market shares, and the most important firms had significantly more commanding positions in the sector. The third row, placing national firms in the context of the region's largest firms, similarly shows the strength of Argentina: while all fifteen of the region's largest firms were from these three countries, eleven were Argentinean. The fourth row reports the transnational

---

[28] ALADI (1985); Bekerman and Sirlin (2001); Gereffi (1983); Katz (1997a); Lashman Hall (1986); UNCTAD (1981); WHO (1988).

[29] It is rarely possible to obtain comprehensive data on sales that include all outlets (e.g. private pharmacies, hospitals, public sector providers), and all types (e.g. prescription, over-the-counter). IMS Health, for example, the largest provider of such data, collects information on retail pharmacy sales. Governments often will provide information on public sector purchases.

Table 2.3. Pharmaceutical Industries in Argentina, Mexico, and Brazil (mid-1980s to mid-1990s)

	Argentina	Mexico	Brazil
National Firms' Share of Local Retail Market*	45–55%	25–30%	15–20%
Position of Top Four National Firms' in Local Market*	2,3,8,9	18,39,42,50	5,24,35,44
Number of National Firms Among Fifteen Leading Latin American Firms*	11	1	3
National Firms' "Pirate" Sales as Share of TNCs' Expected Local Revenues**	29.6%	15.8%	5.3%
WHO Scoring***	4	3	3

Sources: * ALADI (1985); Katz (1997a)
** Gadbaw and Richards (1988b)
*** WHO (1988)

sector's estimates of the losses they suffered in each market on account of the absence of patent protection. The fifth row refers to an assessment of production capabilities conducted by the World Health Organization (WHO), which scored developing countries' pharmaceutical production capabilities on a 1–4 scale. Again, the Argentinean sector's comparative strengths stand out; in fact Argentina was one of just three countries that received the top score (along with China and India).[30]

With differing capabilities, local pharmaceutical firms were at the heart of each country's "defensive coalition," resisting over-compliance. Yet the abilities of defensive coalitions depend on more than the characteristics of the core actors. Local pharmaceutical sectors could compensate for weak market positions, or buttress their strong positions, by cultivating allies. Business actors' power comes not just from their market position, but also their political strategies for attracting allies and interacting with policymakers (Fairfield 2015; Woll 2008). Some alliance possibilities are functions of developmental legacies too, such as the degree of linkages from laboratories to distribution and retail sectors, and to doctors and hospitals. Greater degrees of downstream linkages, i.e. forward integration, allow pharmaceutical producers to mobilize more actors as political allies.[31]

Coalition partners can come from outside the pharmaceutical and medical communities. Other actors in the industrial sector that also relied on easy

---

[30] The four levels in WHO (1988) were (1) no production capabilities; (2) local production of drugs using imported pharmo-chemicals; (3) production of pharmo-chemicals and final drugs; (4) existence of research capabilities leading, potentially, to the discovery of new chemical entities.

[31] Degrees of upstream linkages to pharmo-chemical producers (i.e. backwards integration) are relevant too, but these are included in the sectoral measures discussed above, as part of the "pharmaceutical" sector.

access to knowledge may ally with local drug producers, for example. While firms from the rest of industry may not have reasons to care much about the details of the introduction of pharmaceutical patents per se, they may have stakes in other elements of new patent laws and be able to be mobilized as allies of pharmaceutical firms in the campaign against over-compliance. Beyond industry, new patent laws had implications for actors concerned about the implications of patents on biodiversity, for example, or the ethics of patenting genetic resources and life forms. The questions of how and when to introduce pharmaceutical patents often intersected with long-standing debates over these other patent-related issues, and the way these different currents came together affected the nature of coalitions attempting to ward off over-compliance.

In the presence of a resilient defensive coalition, the ability of the advocates for over-compliance to broaden their coalition becomes more important. Here too allies might come from other sectors of industry, in this case those firms and sectors that perceive benefits from increased patent protection. Although we have little reason to expect actors throughout the economy to mobilize over the details of pharmaceutical patents, these conflicts were not waged in isolation but rather constituted parts of national debates to new IP systems. Where industrial legacies created actors that desired stronger rights of exclusion for owners of knowledge and information, the advocates of over-compliance had potential alliance partners.[32]

The most important form of coalitional expansion for the advocates of over-compliance was the mobilization of exporters. Threats of trade sanctions can interact with trade structure to convert otherwise indifferent actors in the export sector into enthusiastic supporters of increased patent protection, a process labelled "activating agnostics." Dependence on removable trade preferences makes exporters concerned about the consequences of running afoul of the US, and thus available allies for advocates of over-compliance. This alliance is likely to form in all instances, in that trade sanctions can activate agnostics, but the extent to which exporters constitute a potentially important coalitional participant depends on the extent of their dependence on removable trade preferences. Higher levels of "political trade dependence" enable Executives, transnational pharmaceutical industries, and IP law communities seeking over-compliance to recruit and mobilize important allies to their cause. While these data are analyzed in more details in subsequent chapters, as Table 2.4 shows, political trade dependence was highest in Mexico in the late 1980s and early 1990s, a situation that changes with NAFTA; and in the 1990s, when the introduction of pharmaceutical patenting became contested in the

---

[32] The existence of allies in support of over-compliance is not to be mistaken for the drivers of change. As discussed in Chapter 1, new patent policies in the 1990s were not the outcome of endogenous processes of capability accumulation; none of this would have happened at this time in the absence of the global sea change.

Table 2.4. Trade Dependence and Political Trade Dependence (three year averages)

	Trade Dependence			Political Trade Dependence		
	Argentina	*Brazil*	*Mexico*	*Argentina*	*Brazil*	*Mexico*
1988–1990	13.2%	24.0%	68.8%	3.4%	4.4%	26.8%
1991–1993	10.4%	20.2%	77.7%	2.8%	4.8%	11.9%
1994–1996	9.3%	19.7%	83.8%	2.6%	4.9%	0.0%
1997–1999	9.4%	19.9%	86.6%	1.3%	4.3%	0.0%
2000–2002	11.5%	24.9%	86.7%	1.0%	3.8%	0.0%
2003–2005	10.9%	21.2%	87.4%	1.7%	3.6%	0.0%
2006–2008	8.1%	15.9%	82.4%	1.7%	2.2%	0.0%
2009–2011	5.7%	10.1%	79.8%	0.8%	1.1%	0.0%
2012–2014	5.5%	11.1%	79.0%	0.1%	1.0%	0.0%

Note: **Trade Dependence** is the value of a country's exports to the US divided by the value of the country's global exports. **Political Trade Dependence** is the value of a country's removable, preferential exports to the US divided by the value of the country's global exports.

Sources: Data on preferential exports to US are from the United States International Trade Commission. Data on overall exports to the US and global exports are from UN-COMTRADE

two South American countries, Brazil's dependence on removable preferences was markedly higher than in Argentina.

Variation in these social structure conditions produces distinct scenarios, each with implications for Executive agency (Figure 2.4). Where the local pharmaceutical sector is unable to muster a viable defensive coalition, we should expect to witness over-compliance, because there is simply no one to fight back against the campaign by the US and transnational sector. Industrial structure and the mobilization of exporters can further strengthen the coalition for over-compliance and thus affect the degree and form of this outcome. Similarly, Executive preferences help us understand how over-compliance is achieved. This scenario is what we witness in Mexico, where social structure and Executive preferences combined to produce an early and extreme version of over-compliance.

Where the local pharmaceutical is able to resist the campaign for over-compliance, on account of its own resources or with the help of societal allies, coalitional politics becomes more complex. If transnational firms also benefit from a broad base of support, the expectation is also over-compliance. However, the existence of dual, countervailing forces creates a more symmetrical coalitional clash, which means that the version of over-compliance is likely to be less extreme than in the first instance. This scenario is what we witness in Brazil, where the local pharmaceutical sector was able to overcome its own weakness by participating in a broad alliance that mobilized against the new patent law, but an already powerful transnational sector was supported by a wider set of allies in its campaign for over-compliance. Importantly, Brazil's higher level of dependence on removable and preferential exports also created

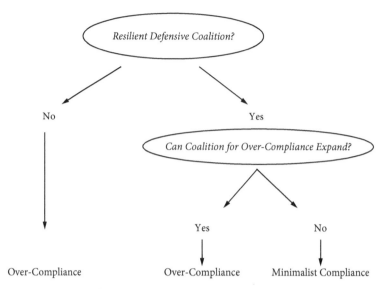

Figure 2.4. Coalitional Dynamics and Forms of Compliance in 1990s

allies that could be mobilized in support of this campaign. Once fully committed to over-compliance, the Brazilian Executive was able to exploit these conditions and secure its desired outcome.

Where the local sector is part of a vibrant defensive coalition and the transnational sector is unable to mobilize allies to its cause, we expect minimalist compliance. Pharmaceutical patents are introduced (to repeat, this is a constant across all cases), but in a way that is furthest from the demands of the transnational sector and foreign governments. We may witness Executives militating for over-compliance, but Executive agency is likely to be frustrated by the prevailing social structure. This scenario is what we witness in the case of Argentina, where the transnational pharmaceutical sector and an Executive enthusiastically committed to over-compliance were unable to overcome the resistance advanced by the local sector's remarkably strong defensive coalition. Despite the relentless efforts of the US Government and the determination of the Argentinean Executive to satisfy these external demands, the campaign for over-compliance was least successful in this country.

The framework thus points to the conditional effects of external pressures and Executive preferences in understanding policy outcomes. For a variety of reasons, Executives may align themselves with foreign governments and transnational pharmaceutical firms and seek over-compliance. It is important to remember that the array of external pressures that developing countries were subject to extended beyond threats of diminished market access. The ability of one country to threaten another country with reduced market access is a function of asymmetric relations (Baldwin 1985; Hirschman 1945), and these asymmetries are manifest in countless other dimensions. Countries may be on the receiving end of diplomatic pressures, for example, have assistance for development projects withdrawn, obtain less support in negotiations with foreign creditors and international financial institutions, face visa restrictions, and so on. For countries undergoing economic liberalization, seeking more foreign investment, and dependent on sound relations with large and wealthier countries, acquiescing to external demands on patents can come to be regarded as a price worth paying. Yet Executives—even committed Executives—may be stymied in the absence of societal bases of support. It is social structure that allows us to understand variation in Executives' abilities to build coalitions to secure their desired outcomes.

THE POLITICAL ECONOMY OF TAILORING PHARMACEUTICAL PATENT SYSTEMS

New pharmaceutical patent systems underwent subsequent revisions in the 2000s, as countries addressed the challenges that emerged from initial policy choices. These efforts are referred to as "tailoring," processes of modifying items that do not fit well to make them more appropriate for local conditions. The feasibility of constructing and retaining coalitions for tailoring is a function of how the new arrangements established in the 1990s altered social structure and created new constellations of actors. To understand the political economy of tailoring, we need to consider both the drivers and context of reform efforts, and how changes to the social terrain altered coalitional possibilities.

The driving force for tailoring new pharmaceutical patent systems ordinarily came from countries' health authorities. Health budgets are most directly affected by the costs imposed by pharmaceutical patents, and Ministries of Health thus found themselves as central actors in patent politics in ways that they had not been previously. Distinguishing between the motives and preferences of Executives, in general, and Health Ministries, in particular, is important, and differences across the two periods of patent politics are evident. In the 1990s, IP policy was bundled with trade policy, and more generally foreign economic policy. This was so at the global level, in that IP became "trade-related" (Maskus 2000; Muzaka 2011b; Sell 2010a), and this connection became reproduced at national levels too. Because of the linkage between IP and trade, in WTO agreements and bilateral pressures, developing countries' patent policies tended to be controlled by actors in the Executive who dealt with countries' strategies of integration in the global economy. Presidents, Ministries of Foreign Affairs, along with top economic officials in Ministries of Economy, Industry, or Trade came to lead on debates over introducing new patent laws. The details varied by country, as countries differ in terms of the titles of their key economic ministries and the division of labor among them, but across countries it was actors in these parts of the Executive—and not from Ministries of Health—that dominated policy-making. Of course health officials in many countries were aware of and sometimes alarmed by the potential effects of introducing pharmaceutical patents, but they tended to be subordinated within Executives, and even when they tried to articulate their concerns, Executives tended to present united fronts in bargaining over new patent laws with their Legislatures. In the second period, in contrast, health officials found themselves with more opportunities to act independently of the rest of the Executive.

A further source of Health Ministries' greater autonomy and visibility in the 2000s is that modifying how patent systems function often regarded the administration and enforcement of laws, or meeting the challenges of imple-menting competing laws. Even where legislative actions were involved, these regarded revisions of particular articles and clauses of the new patent laws, not preparing entirely new laws. Whereas Executives working with Legislatures to design and approve new patent laws tended to stay united in the 1990s, with all officials reading from the same script or remaining quiet, revising specific aspects of these new arrangements in the 2000s provided more space for inter-ministerial divisions to come to fore.

Broader global changes also supported health officials increased involvement in IP policymaking. The World Health Organization and regional bodies, such as the Pan-American Health Organization, became more active in creat-ing countervailing communities to urge national health officials to become involved in dealing with patents. And health officials seeking to revise their patent systems could draw upon a wealth of policy advice. In the aftermath of TRIPS, the study of TRIPS-compatible policy options became an industry of itself, and a large number of international organizations and academics pro-duced what amount to "how-to" manuals for revising patent systems in ways that remain consistent with international obligations.[33]

Yet politicians aiming to tailor their countries' new patent regimes face strong opposition. Foreign governments and transnational drug firms, seek-ing extensive rights of exclusion, tended to react with abhorrence to efforts to modify patent systems, even when such efforts were within the constraints of TRIPS. Just as the US actively pressed countries to over-comply in the 1990s, and regarded deviations from the gold standard as an "unfair" trade practice, the United States Trade Representative (USTR) similarly targeted countries that attempted to tailor their patent regimes in the 2000s. These bilateral

---

[33] Examples include Commission on Intellectual Property Rights (2002), Correa (1999; 2000b; 2007), Ho (2011), Kapczynski (2009), Reichman (1996; 2009b), Scherer and Watal (2002), UNCTAD-ICTSD (2005), Watal (2001). Morin (2014) discusses the role of academics as suppliers of knowledge in this area.

pressures continued, despite international events such as the 2001 "Doha Declaration on TRIPS and Public Health."[34] While the Doha Declaration affirmed countries' rights to implement their TRIPS obligations in health-friendly ways, it did not significantly alter the USTR's behavior.[35] After all, the Doha Declaration clarified that when countries took certain steps they were not in violation of TRIPS, but the US and the transnational sector were never satisfied with countries merely complying with TRIPS.

Again, we expect USTR's pressures to affect patent politics by mobilizing exporters, and the extent to which we are likely to see this depends on countries' trade structures. Commodity booms of the 2000s, increased trade with countries other than the US (e.g. China), and the subsequent diversification of exports, both in terms of products and destination markets, meant that countries tended to be less dependent on exports—particularly preferential exports—to the US (see Table 2.4). As a result, threats of trade sanctions were less likely to activate agnostics and facilitate the widening coalitions for over-compliance.[36] Also, as discussed in Chapter 1, changes to countries' vulnerability rooted in trade structure were complemented by a WTO ruling on the legality of bilateral trade pressures that is claimed to have made the USTR's threats less effective in this period (Morin and Gold 2014).

The principal sources of opposition to tailoring new patent systems are internal, rooted in the accumulated resources of those benefiting from new patent systems. On account of positive feedback and increasing returns, new policies, once introduced, can alter social structure and shape subsequent coalitional possibilities (Pierson 2000). In the case of pharmaceutical patents, the changes introduced by the new status quo can yield material benefits, such as increased market shares and revenues. Transnational firms are no longer dreaming of the day when they may be able to get pharmaceutical patents locally, but now, in this period, increasingly using patents to capture larger shares of markets at higher prices. Likewise, law firms representing the transnational sector have unprecedented levels of business working with international firms on their local patent portfolios (e.g. filing and prosecuting patent applications, maintaining granted patents, monitoring the market to check for potential cases of infringement, and so on).

Beyond the immediate beneficiaries of the new status quo, opposition to— or at least suspicion of—tailoring may come from foreign business actors, not necessarily those engaged in pharmaceutical patenting, but who come to

---

[34] Abbott (2005); Chorev (2012); Reichman and Abbott (2007); Shadlen (2004b); 't Hoen (2002).

[35] Consider the persistently high number of countries identified in the USTR's Special 301 Reports in the years immediately following 2001. See Table 1.1, p. 17.

[36] This is consistent with the finding that commodity revenues and new sources of external finance can enable policy experimentation (Campello 2015; Kaufman 2011; Yang 2006).

regard modifications to the new patent system as potentially damaging the climate for their own operations. They may fear the signaling effect that tailoring may have, i.e. challenging "best practices" in one area may encourage challenging best practices in other areas closer to home. Similarly, once new patent systems are in place, domestic actors in industry and science, even actors that did not seek over-compliance in the 1990s, may come to regard tailoring as a step backwards that reflects the government's lack of commitment to internationalization and that sends worrying signals.

The effects of increasing returns can be manifest in the state too. As patent offices benefit from the revenue streams introduced by receiving more applications and granting more patents, they gain increased prestige and importance in economic policy (Drahos 2010). The introduction of new patent systems and increased attention to "knowledge-based" development often inspires the establishment of new agencies and funding lines for encouraging innovation. These changes to the state, and the accumulation of material and reputational resources, can also establish barriers to tailoring.

Policymakers seeking to tailor their countries' new patent systems thus must confront formidable coalitions nourished by processes of increasing returns and the legacies of initial policy choices. Their abilities to do so are also conditioned by changes unleashed by the global sea change of the 1980s and 1990s. One important effect of the emergence of global pharmaceutical patenting was the triggering of civil society mobilization around the politics of privatized knowledge. Globally and nationally, TRIPS sparked unprecedented degrees of civil society activism around the relationship between patents, drugs, and access to medicines in the late 1990s and early 2000s.[37]

Though not the sole driver, the HIV/AIDS epidemic played a key role in the rise of civil society mobilization, because this was an area where the conflicts between patents and access were most acute. The emergence of new HIV/AIDS treatments created the perfect storm: life-saving drugs that lacked functional substitutes were becoming available at a time that they could be patented globally, because of the global sea change. Thus AIDS drugs became the focal point for what would then become a larger set of conflicts over "access to medicines" and, more generally, "access to knowledge." Not surprisingly, many analyses of patent politics emphasize the important contributions made by non-governmental organizations—particularly AIDS activists—in driving national-level policy changes.[38]

Supplementing scholars' emphasis on civil society, the analysis of coalition building in this book focuses on tailoring-inclined policymakers' abilities to

---

[37] Kapczynski (2008); Kapstein and Busby (2013); Krikorian and Kapczynski (2010); Matthews (2011); Muzaka (2011a); Sell and Prakash (2004); 't Hoen (2002).

[38] Andia (2015); Biehl (2007); d'adesky (2004); Flynn (2015); Klug (2008); Krikorian (2009); Matthews (2011); Smith and Siplon (2006).

obtain the support of local industry. National pharmaceutical sectors were central to the defensive coalitions resisting over-compliance in the 1990s and, depending on what they achieved in the first period these actors had different political resources to deploy in the subsequent period of patent politics. In particular, variation in how pharmaceutical patents were introduced inspired different patterns of adjustment in domestic pharmaceutical sectors, which in turn affected possibilities for coalition building in the 2000s.

Two aspects of the effects of pharmaceutical patenting on local firms need to be underscored, one that is constant across countries and one that varies. By requiring local firms to move into new market segments where they are not infringing property rights, the introduction of pharmaceutical patents reorients local pharmaceutical firms' attention to new sets of issues, and thus transforms them both economically and politically. This happens everywhere: rather than continue to get exercised over the existence of pharmaceutical patents or the terms on which pharmaceutical patents are introduced (e.g. transition periods and whether there should be a pipeline), local firms become concerned about the effective rights of exclusion that patents confer. After all, once a country has a pharmaceutical patent system, it is these issues that affect surviving or new firms' abilities to compete, and the conditions for marketing and distributing their own products.

While the re-orientation of local firms' attention to issues affecting how patent systems function was uniform, the capabilities that they possess to participate in conflicts over these issues were not. Countries' new pharmaceutical patent systems varied in ways that presented local producers with different challenges, and different political resources. How pharmaceutical patents were introduced mattered in terms of the immediacy of the shock that local actors felt, and the amount of time that the new status quo had to settle in. Where this happened earlier, of course, the potential effects were felt earlier too. And where countries introduced pharmaceutical patents retroactively, with a pipeline, patent-protected drugs came on the market immediately.

The timing of the introduction of pharmaceutical patents relative to the 2000s, the era when conflicts over how patent systems function became prominent globally, is important. Timing determines how long the effects introduced by the new status quo had to settle in before coalition-building initiatives around tailoring emerge on the agenda. It does not just matter what happens, but when things happen, both absolutely and relatively; the same measures introduced in one country at one time and another country at another time may have different economic and political effects (Gerschenkron 1962; Levitsky and Way 2015; Pierson 2003; 2004). By the time countries that introduced new patent systems earlier came to address subsequent issues about the functioning of these new arrangements, the effects of the initial policy choices had more years to manifest themselves. These effects complicate tailoring by altering social structure in such a way as to wither away potential participants in supportive coalitions. In contrast, more delayed or more minimally compliant introduction of pharmaceutical patents can leave social conditions that are more amenable to building coalitions for subsequent reforms.

To synthesize, the introduction of pharmaceutical patents increased the presence of foreign pharmaceutical firms, but variation in how and when patents were introduced had different effects, all with implications for coalition building possibilities during subsequent iterations of patent politics. Figure 2.5 provides a basic schematic of how policy choices in the 1990s regarding the introduction of pharmaceutical patents condition opportunities for coalition building for tailoring in the 2000s. Where patents were introduced in such a way as to yield less of a disruption for local pharmaceutical firms, and where the new status quo was incipient at the time that state officials embarked on reforms in the 2000s, the possibilities for coalition building are comparatively enabled by social conditions. In such a case we expect to witness continuity in a minimalist approach to pharmaceutical patenting, yet we also may see policymakers encumbered when they seek policies that are against the wishes of local producers. At the other extreme, where the impacts of the initial policy choices were more substantial and had longer to settle, tailoring is more difficult on account of the evisceration of defensive coalitions. In this scenario we expect to witness continuity in over-compliance, with opportunities for tailoring rarely exploited as health officials are unable to build coalitions to overcome the accumulated resources of those who benefited from the initial policy choices. Where initial policy choices have large immediate impacts but these effects have less time to settle (or when choices with less substantial immediate impacts have more time to settle), officials seeking to build coalitions for tailoring have opportunities to do so, but face constraints created by the enduring effects of earlier choices.

		Time for Impacts of Initial Choices to Settle	
		Less	*More*
Impact of Initial Choices	*Less*	Coalition building comparatively enabled	Coalition building feasible but more constrained by legacies
	More	Coalition building feasible but more constrained by legacies	Coalition building comparatively encumbered

Figure 2.5. Initial Choices Over Introducing Patents and Subsequent Coalition-Building Possibilities

This third scenario leaves greater opportunities for Executive agency to shape outcomes, yet the legacies of initial choices continue to cast a shadow on policy alternatives.

The three countries examined in this book correspond to these scenarios. Argentina's minimalist response to the global sea change of the 1990s meant that, as of the early 2000s, the effects of pharmaceutical patents were comparatively minor, and local producers were able to retain necessary resources to shape subsequent conflicts over the functioning of the new arrangements. While government officials seeking to tailor the patent system could depend on the local sector as a valuable political ally, the legacy of this sector's strength also meant that health officials also found themselves struggling to align industrial development with health priorities. In Mexico, early over-compliance significantly reduced the possibilities for subsequent coalition building. By the time tailoring the patent system emerged as a consideration, the new arrangements had been in place for a considerable amount of time and the country's social structure had been fundamentally altered. When actors had motives to alter the new patent system in the 2000s, their abilities to do so were hemmed in by the social and political conditions created by the policies introduced in the 1990s. In Brazil the effects of policy choices in the 1990s were substantial, but as the initiatives for tailoring emerged so soon after the new patent system was introduced, the effects of over-compliance had less time to settle and health officials seeking to alter course could do so. However, tailoring in Brazil has been significantly encumbered by the changes in state and society engendered by the country's shift toward stronger patent protection in the 1990s.[39]

Before concluding, it is worth underscoring that the second period of patent politics provides useful terrain for examining the impact of Executive preferences on policy outcomes. For a number of reasons, we might expect Executive preferences to be more determinative with regard to revising how new patent systems work than they were with regard to introducing new laws in the first place. As discussed, countries had more policy autonomy on account of the international conjuncture, a condition that could give Executives more scope to act on their own choices (Campello 2015). That debates over patents were particularly focused in this period on health might matter here too, in that governments of the "left" may be more likely to prioritize health policy and be more alarmed by higher drug prices, and they may also be more inclined to challenge global norms.[40] Moreover, the changed arena of action, from

---

[39] There is no case of the scenario in the upper-right quadrant, but we would expect it to demonstrate similar dynamics as witnessed in Brazil.

[40] Here it is notable that discussions of IP are largely omitted from the literature on the return of the "left" in Latin America in the 2000s. Although contributions to Levitsky and Roberts (2011) discuss property rights in the cases of Bolivia and Venezuela, for example, patents and *intellectual* property rights are not addressed.

introducing entirely new laws in the 1990s to implementing and regulating laws in the 2000s, should allow Executive preferences to matter more. As Murillo has shown, in highly technical policy and regulatory areas that rely heavily on expertise, Executives are likely to have more scope to shape policy in their desired directions (Murillo 2009).

Notwithstanding these characteristics of the era and policy area, partisan effects remain rather muted. As growing shares of health expenditures become consumed by the purchase of drugs, Health Ministries, of whatever political stripe, may be spurred into action. As we shall see, efforts to reform patent systems often preceded the election of left presidents or were led by health ministers in conservative governments. And notwithstanding the seemingly technical nature of patent policy in this period, health officials seeking to tailor new patent systems still needed to build and sustain coalitions to secure their desired outcomes, and their opportunities to do so depend on the effects of initial policy choices. Ultimately, even in this period of narrower conflicts and with a more permissive external environment, Executive agency remains conditioned by social structure.

CONCLUSION

The political economy of pharmaceutical patents features two related sets of conflicts. First, in the 1990s, countries needed to decide, in the face of considerable external pressures, how they would introduce patents. Second, in the 2000s, now with the new status quo of patenting in place, conflict turned to how these new arrangements function. The two episodes of conflict are related, in that the way pharmaceutical patents were introduced in the 1990s conditioned the way subsequent conflicts were resolved in the 2000s. Over time, with subsequent iterations, the contours of debate narrow, yet the stakes remain high (Chorev 2015). The remaining variation we observe within this narrowed terrain has important implications for development, for these outcomes continue to affect lives and industries.

This chapter has placed pharmaceutical patenting in broader analyses of intellectual property, reviewed the key issues that formed the central areas of debate, and presented an explanatory framework that allows us to understand cross-national and longitudinal variation in countries' pharmaceutical patent policies. In both periods the central analytic issue regards the abilities of political leaders to forge and sustain coalitions to secure their desired policies. In the 1990s, Executives became enthusiasts of pharmaceutical patents in ways that could not be reliably predicted by the ideologies of the presidents in power or the biases of their political parties, yet Executives' abilities to introduce the types of pharmaceutical patent regimes they desired varied substantially, depending on social structure. Similarly, in the 2000s, when each country's pharmaceutical patent system became subject to revision, health officials seeking to tailor the new arrangements needed to build coalitions, and possibilities to do so were constrained by social structure. The remainder of the book examines the three countries in the two time periods.

Part II

Introducing Pharmaceutical Patents

3

Power to the Producers

Industrial Legacies, Coalitional Expansion, and Minimalist Compliance in Argentina

> Argentina stands today among the few remaining world's most egregious (sic) pirating countries of pharmaceutical patented products. Despite repeated assurances by Argentine officials over the past eight years, Argentina still does not protect pharmaceutical patents while Argentine pirates continue to expand their business presence in other Latin American countries, exporting pirated pharmaceutical inventions and obstructing initiatives to improve the level of protection in the hemisphere... The current Argentine intellectual property regime is, then, protection for intellectual property theft.... At a time when countries such as Brazil and Mexico have enacted patent legislation far superior to TRIPS, Argentina persists in defending the wrong local interests.
>
> (PhRMA 1997)
>
> From the viewpoint of the research-intensive pharmaceutical industry, Argentina has the worst industrial property regime in our Hemisphere.
>
> (PhRMA 2000)

Argentina's Executive sought to over-comply in the 1990s, but was unable to muster the political resources to do so. Assuming power in the midst of an acute economic crisis, President Carlos Menem (1989–1999) embarked on extensive liberalization of the economy. Under the leadership of Menem and Economy Minister Domingo Cavallo, Argentina underwent significant reductions in trade barriers, privatization of state enterprises, and deregulation of foreign investment. Accompanying the President's project for transforming Argentina's development strategy and relationship with the global economy was a proposal for a new patent law, submitted to Congress in 1991. Menem's proposal would replace the existing law, which dated from the mid-nineteenth century, with one that fully satisfied the demands of the US Government and the international pharmaceutical industry. The President aimed to introduce pharmaceutical product patents immediately and retroactively, with a "pipeline" provision to protect applications and patents that had already been filed in other countries. Argentina had opposed the inclusion of intellectual property in the Uruguay Round trade negotiations, but by the early 1990s the country's political leaders embraced over-compliance.

After five years of intense conflict between the Executive and Congress, the new 1996 patent law, the Law on Invention Patents and Utility Models (*Ley de Patentes de Invención y Modelos de Utilidad*, LPIMU), looked little like Menem's original initiative—and was quite some distance from what the US and the global patent community sought. Argentina's patent office would not begin reviewing applications for pharmaceutical patents until late 2000, and retroactive protection would not be available. Drugs with patents applied for prior to 1995 in other countries would never receive protection in Argentina, allowing many new products coming to market in the late 1990s and early 2000s to continue to have multiple suppliers. At the same time, Argentina complemented the LPIMU with a new data protection law that also allowed domestic drug producers to retain a strong position in the local market. In sum, Argentina resisted pressures for over-compliance, introducing pharmaceutical patents in a way that, while meeting the country's new international obligations, differed significantly from the gold standard that foreign governments, the transnational pharmaceutical sector, and, for most of the period, the Executive, demanded.

In explaining this outcome, the analysis in this chapter emphasizes the national pharmaceutical industry's ability to mobilize a campaign to overcome the crusade for over-compliance. The defensive coalition built by Argentina's pharmaceutical firms forced the Executive to accept an outcome that differed sharply from what President Menem and his top cabinet officials pursued. Menem's setback reveals the conditional importance of Executive preferences and power, relative to social structure. Menem's political party was the largest in both bodies of Congress during the period under study, which should have made it possible to obtain approval of a patent law of the President's liking. Independently of the specific composition of Congress, analyses of political institutions classify Argentina as a country with substantial presidential authority (Henisz 2002; Jones 1997; Morgenstern and Nacif 2002). Guillermo O'Donnell (1994) depicted Argentina under Menem as a "delegative democracy," where the President and Congress were both elected but the former had little accountability to the latter. Even constitutionally strong Executives need to bargain with Congress, but we know that in Argentina the Executive negotiated from a position of strength (Corrales 2002; Llanos 2001; Murillo 2009). In fact, if unable to gain legislators' acquiescence Menem had a well-documented track record of legislating through Executive decrees.[1] Yet, these

---

[1] Levitsky and Murillo (2005, 33) note President Menem issued 335 Decrees of Urgency and Necessity from 1989–1994. In contrast his predecessor Raúl Alfonsín issued 10 Decrees from 1983–89.

conditions notwithstanding, Menem was forced to accept an outcome that differed in significant ways from what his government sought. The local pharmaceutical sector's enduring economic and political resources allowed it to construct a broad coalition that mobilized Congress to transform Menem's over-compliant proposal into the minimalist LPIMU.

The case of Argentina in the 1990s also underscores the limits of external pressures, which failed to mobilize exporters sufficiently to enlarge the coalition for over-compliance. The US Government was relentless in its agitation for a new patent law that offered pharmaceutical patent protection immediately and retroactively, including for products about to come on the market, and for much of the period the US had the Executive's support for such a project. Menem's proposed version of the patent law satisfied virtually all of the wishes of the transnational pharmaceutical sector and the US, and throughout the early- and mid-1990s the Executive spared no effort in seeking to deliver over-compliance. Yet even with the Argentinean Executive on its side, the US could not obtain its desired outcome in the face of both the local pharmaceutical sector's intense resistance and the flaccid response of the country's export sector.

Ultimately, the analysis in this chapter shows how industrial legacies can help actors resisting the global sea change build and sustain coalitions for minimalism. Such was the power of Argentina's pharmaceutical firms that they were not just able to beat back the crusade for over-compliance, but successfully alter the Executive's preferences. In response to the new patent and data protection laws, the US upped the ante and applied trade sanctions, yet by this point, rather than try to mobilize support for over-compliance, as it had before, the Executive ignored the external pressures. Social structure not only served as a constraint upon Executive agency, but ultimately transformed Executive preferences: the power of local producers made minimalism state policy in Argentina.

The chapter has four sections. The first section reviews the pathway from Menem's 1991 proposal to the 1996 LPIMU. We see an exceptionally complex—and, for Argentina in this time, atypical—legislative process that featured extensive hearings in Congress, approval of a version of the law that differed greatly from the Executive's, and an ensuing conflict with the Executive that the Legislature's activism triggered. The protracted process resulted in the LPIMU of 1996, an event that was then followed by the rapid introduction of a data protection law that even further distanced Argentina from the demands of the US Government and the transnational pharmaceutical industry. In addition to setting out the outcome of the case, this section illustrates how extensively the US Government and the Argentinean Executive fought for over-compliance. The subsequent three sections explain this outcome in terms of coalitional dynamics. Section two focuses on the interests, resources and capabilities of the key actors at the heart of the two rival coalitions, the transnational and local pharmaceutical sectors. Section three analyzes the broad alliance against over-compliance that the local sector was able to construct, focusing on the relationship between Argentinean pharmaceutical firms and other actors in the industrial sector and health community. Section four, in contrast, analyzes the transnational sector's comparative inability to widen its own coalition in support Menem's proposal. Here we see how Argentina's export structure meant that the principal instrument used to expand coalitions for over-compliance, linking IP to trade and conditioning market access on stronger patent protection so as to mobilize exporters, was ineffective.

EXTERNAL PRESSURES, EXECUTIVE-LEGISLATIVE CONFLICT, AND ARGENTINA'S NEW PATENT LAW

With high per capita income and health spending, and a large middle class with considerable purchasing power, but with a local pharmaceutical sector dominating the market, Argentina was one of the primary countries targeted by the US for IP reform in the 1980s.[2] Pharmaceutical product patents had been unavailable in Argentina since the 1864 Patent Law, and securing the introduction of product patents became a high priority for the transnational pharmaceutical industry and, by extension, the US Government. Complaining that they were largely cut out of the Argentinean market because of the patent system, as well as the country's drug approval and registration practices, international pharmaceutical firms lobbied the United States Trade Representative (USTR) to target Argentina.[3]

External pressures had little traction in the face of entrenched domestic opposition to pharmaceutical patents, and an indifferent Executive that was not prepared to take up the cause. In its submission for the USTR's first-ever Special 301 report in 1989, the transnational pharmaceutical sector complained that "to date the Argentines have limited themselves to stating what they believe they cannot (or will not) do. They have not been forthcoming regarding what they will do."[4] To be sure, throughout the 1980s the local

---

[2] Among the many studies examining the Argentina–US conflict over patents in this period, see Bentolila (2002), Bergallo and Ramón Michel (2014), Boccanera (2005), Buscaglia and Long (1997), Corigliano (2000), Czub (2001), Genovesi (1995), Harrison (2004), Irigoyen (2006), Jauregui (2003), Labaké (2003), Murphy (1997), Richards (1988a), Vicente (1998). See also "Una historia de controversias," *La Nación*, 3 January 1996.

[3] "US Extends Patent Pressure in Latin America," *The Pharma Market Letter*, 8 August 1988; "Argentina to Face U.S. Trade Action," *The Pharma Market Letter*, 22 August 1988.

[4] Letter from Gerald Mossinghoff, President of the Pharmaceutical Manufacturers of America (PMA), to USTR Carla Hills, 16 February 1989 (from USTR archives, copy on file with author).

subsidiaries of transnational firms in Argentina and the country's IP law community had been urging Congress to introduce new legislation, to replace the "obsolete" nineteenth-century patent law, offering patents on pharmaceutical products (Frank 1989, 192–3), yet without the commitment of the Executive branch, such initiatives were futile.[5]

Executive preferences shifted after President Menem took office in July 1989, in the context of a hyperinflationary economic crisis.[6] The conditions of the time created an opportunity to be exploited, and Menem came under immediate pressure to deliver where his predecessor had not. In August, the USTR, which had already launched an investigation of Argentina and included the country on the Watch List in the initial Special 301 Report of 1989, informed the new government that trade sanctions were to follow. Menem, in turn, promised that a new patent law satisfying US demands would be forthcoming within two years (USTR 1989a, 8; 1989b). And, making good on this promise, in October 1991 the Executive presented the Chamber of Deputies with a proposal to introduce pharmaceutical patents immediately, and with pipeline protection for applications and patents that already been filed outside of Argentina.

The course of events in the half-decade between Menem's proposal for a new law in October 1991 and the introduction of the LPIMU in March 1996 is exceptionally confusing, featuring rival bills from Congress and Executive, presidential vetoes and Congressional overrides, decrees, blocking of decrees, and blocking of blocking of decrees.[7] This section reviews the key turning points, not to provide a comprehensive narrative, but to bring out the most salient dimensions of the conflict, namely the high-energy campaign by the Executive and the US to secure the immediate and retroactive introduction of pharmaceutical patents, and the tireless commitment of the Legislature to dilute these efforts.

The initial response to Menem's proposal was dismissive. Although regarded as exemplary by US officials, the transnational pharmaceutical firms, and the international patent community (Rowat 1993, 425),[8] such was the level of internal resistance that the lower house never acted on the bill, allowing it to expire. Deputies insisted that it was not appropriate to begin addressing the

---

[5] For discussions of these unsuccessful initiatives in this period, see Bentolila (2002), FIEL (1990), Grillo (1990), Panadeiros (1991), Richards (1988a), Vázquez (1991).

[6] Such was the extent of crisis that Menem's inauguration was brought forward by half a year, from December.

[7] There was even a "clarifying" bill that was passed with the objective, not entirely achieved, of clarifying the state of affairs. According to one observer, "The end result was a puzzle that only specialized attorneys could understand" (Bentolila 2002, 41).

[8] In Brazil, for example, Menem's proposal was cited as a model to be emulated by legislators and societal actors that sought high levels of patent protection. "Brazil Patents Row in Congress," *The Pharma Market Letter*, November 18, 1991.

issue of pharmaceutical patents until the Uruguay Round negotiations were complete, and the country's new international obligations were explicit (Senado de la Nación 1995, 233, 240). In April 1993, Menem resubmitted the proposal, this time to the Senate where the President's voting bloc appeared more reliable. Addressing a joint session of Congress at the opening of the new legislative session, Menem made an impassioned plea for the patent law to be treated with urgency and passed quickly.

Far from providing Menem with the treatment of his proposal that the President demanded, however, Congress commandeered the process. The Chamber of Deputies and Senate consistently emphasized that they would proceed at their own pace—they would host hearings and undertake internal deliberations, and only then would they present new legislation. In November 1994 the Senate produced its own revised version of a patent law, which was then approved by the Chamber of Deputies and passed in March 1995.

Where Menem said up, Congress said down; where Menem said black, Congress said white. The law passed by the two houses of Congress was essentially the mirror image of what the President had proposed. Menem proposed immediate introduction of pharmaceutical patents supplemented by a pipeline that would have accelerated the impact of the new system, with the effects further amplified by a provision that would have required local firms to begin paying royalties immediately on drugs they were already producing. Under Congress's version, pharmaceuticals would not be patentable until 2003, and without retroactivity. Menem's bill included provisions for compulsory licenses that would give patent holders ample opportunities to delay and block their use, while Congress set out a wide range of grounds to justify the grant of compulsory licenses, including failure to manufacture locally, and procedures that simplified their use.[9]

External reactions to Congress' bill were, not surprisingly, bitter. The US Ambassador to Argentina, James Cheek, exclaimed that what Congress had produced was appropriate "for Third World countries like Surinam or Burundi," but not Argentina. He then went on to charge that "there are sectors interested in keeping Argentina in the category of trading scoundrels" (Corigliano 2000, 69).[10] Argentina had remained on the Special 301 Watch List in the years following Menem's earlier promise of a new patent law, as the USTR kept a watchful eye on the Argentinean Government.[11] By 1993 the US

---

[9] Bergallo and Ramón Michel (2014), Genovesi (1995), Irigoyen (2006), and Murphy (1997) offer detailed comparisons of the two different versions. See also Challú and Levis (1996).

[10] The US was not alone in its reaction. Though using more diplomatic language, the European Union's Ambassador in Buenos Aires also sent a message to the Argentinean Executive expressing concerns over the law passed by Congress.

[11] During this time the transnational pharmaceutical industry continued to campaign for the US to escalate pressures on Argentina, complaining that bilateral consultations were not being fruitful.

had lost patience and elevated Argentina to the Priority Watch List, where the country remained in 1994. Now the USTR referred to Congress's proposed law as "unacceptable" (Harrison 2004, 104) and renewed the threat of trade sanctions.

The Executive, previously frustrated by legislators' delay in passing a new patent law, was now exasperated by what Congress had produced. In testimony to the Senate in June 1994, Cavallo had admonished Congress for not having passed a new patent law nearly three years after Menem's proposal was originally submitted, but accepted, in principle, legislators' prerogative to participate in the process:

> I sincerely believe that it is not good for the citizens of Argentina, it is not good for us, to keep delaying passage of a patent law. If Congress thinks that the Executive's proposal gives too much patent protection, then Congress has the right to decide what level of patent protection it desires. But we maintain that we believe there is no reason to keep delaying passage of a new patent law.
> (Senado de la Nación 1994b, 145–46)

Once passed, however, the Executive was hardly so accommodating: Menem immediately vetoed the provisions where Congress contradicted the Executive, returning a bill that essentially recreated what his team had proposed four years earlier.[12] At the same time the President issued a decree that would introduce the new World Trade Organization's (WTO) agreements into Argentinean law, insisting on a reading of TRIPS whereby Argentina was not eligible to use the transition periods that were afforded to developing countries.[13]

In May 1995 Menem was re-elected to a second term, yet despite his electoral mandate the President remained unable to overcome congressional resistance, as legislators from the two largest blocks, Menem's Peronist party (*Partido Justicialista*, PJ) and the rival Radical party (*Unión Cívica Radical*, UCR), remained united in their opposition.[14] In an emergency session held just three days after the elections, the Senate unanimously overruled the Executive's veto, restoring most of the provisions that Menem had rejected,

---

[12] See Genovesi (1995, 49–91) for details on the specific points that Menem vetoed.

[13] These actions by Menem further aggravated relations with Congress on account of allegedly over-stepping the Executive's constitutional authority (Murphy 1997, 36; Jauregui 2003, 39). Such steps did, however, earn Menem the support of the USTR, which by the time it issued the Special 301 Report in 1995 had lowered Argentina to the Watch List, explicitly citing the veto and decree as the reasons for the revised status. In a section of the report entitled "Progress on Intellectual Property Issues," the USTR noted that "The President of Argentina vetoed troublesome provisions of a recently enacted patent law, and brought into effect by executive decree a new patent law" (USTR 1995, 18).

[14] The 1995 elections gave President Menem a stronger position in Congress, as the PJ gained majorities in both the Chamber of Deputies and the Senate, but the new legislators did not take their seats until the end of the year.

including, importantly, those regarding the timing of when pharmaceutical patents would be introduced and the question of retroactivity. With the restored provisions then approved by the Chamber of Deputies the following week, Congress passed a new version of the patent law to replace that passed two months earlier. Menem refused to accept this either, however, yielding a stalemate. Only the Executive could make a new law official by publishing it in the Official Bulletin, but Congress stubbornly refused to pass a law with the specific, over-compliant provisions that President Menem and his ministers sought.

With the President refusing to authorize the version of the law passed by Congress and Congress demonstrating intransigent opposition to the President's vision, a period of Executive–Legislative negotiations ensued in the form of a mini-summit between the Executive and PJ legislators to break the deadlock. The lines of debate were clear, and unchanged: the Executive, represented most prominently by Economy Minister Cavallo and Foreign Minister Guido di Tella, the most important members of the cabinet, remained adamant that pharmaceutical patents should be available immediately, and Congress continued to insist on longer transition periods without retroactivity. At one point during the June 1995 meetings, Cavallo is reported to have threatened legislators that, were they to continue blocking the Executive's plans, he would advise President Menem to close Congress, as President Fujimori had done in Peru in 1992, and then push the bill through unilaterally—a threat that sparked Deputy Miguel Angel Toma to attempt to punch Cavallo. Toma, who had trained as a boxer in his youth, evidently shouted "I will not put up with someone who defends authoritarianism" as he went after the Economy Minister (Foreign Minister di Tella is reported to have blocked the punch).[15]

Ultimately the two sides compromised, but on terms that were closer to Congress's preferences. The Executive acquiesced to a five-year transition period for the introduction of pharmaceutical product patents, without pipeline patents or requirements of royalty payments that would force firms to discontinue drugs that they were already producing. Congress, in turn, agreed to the inclusion of a "mailbox," as required by TRIPS, whereby the patent office would receive applications as of 1995, to examine after the transition period ended. With regard to compulsory licensing, Congress gave up on its demands for a local manufacturing requirement, but, over the strong objections of the Executive, assured that the final version included a wide range of provisions that simplified the procedures for the Ministry of Health to threaten and issue compulsory licenses to reduce the price of drugs. For example, to

---

[15] "Cavallo, en una pelea que tiene antecedentes," *La Nación*, June 9, 1995. Cavallo, who also threatened to resign if Congress continued to obstruct the Executive, accused legislators of accepting bribes as well.

invoke the public interest grounds for a compulsory license, the Argentinean Government does not need to declare a health emergency, but simply be motivated by serious health concerns and fear that a situation could, potentially, lead to a health emergency (Correa et al. 2011, 24–6; de la Puente et al. 2009, 81).[16]

Before continuing, it is worth underscoring how the inclusion of a mailbox in Argentina illustrates the importance of focusing on degrees of over-compliance, rather than compliance with TRIPS per se. Congress had, initially, adamantly resisted *any* form of retroactivity, but by 1995 TRIPS had gone into effect, and the requirement to offer a mailbox receiving applications from January 1995 onwards was part of the agreement and thus binding for all WTO members. A policy that legislators had regarded as over-compliance when first under consideration, by 1995 constituted mere compliance, and legislators accepted this. But they did so grudgingly, insisting on this being done to minimize its effects as much as possible. While the Executive asked for the mailbox filing option to be available for applications from the early 1990s, Congress set the date in strict accordance with TRIPS. Moreover, the LPIMU stipulated that if an application filed between 1995 and 2000 and kept in the mailbox was, eventually, granted after October 2000, when pharmaceutical patents were to become available, that any firm that was already producing the drug (or had made serious efforts to begin to produce) could continue to do so, subject to a royalty fee.[17]

The agreement reached at the mini-summit did not end the conflict, however, as Menem continued to try to give pharmaceutical patents immediate effect and thereby satisfy the US's principal demand. The President signed and published the compromise law, but in issuing the implementing directive Menem included the provision that would have required local producers to begin making royalty payments immediately on drugs with patents already granted in other countries. Congress refused to buckle, accusing the President of abrogating the agreement they had reached, and unconstitutionally legislating through the use of implementing directives.[18] Despite threats from the USTR that Argentina could have trade preferences removed, the Chamber of Deputies and Senate jointly overrode Menem's directive and reissued the law agreed to in October. Following yet more negotiations, the President at

---

[16] As we shall see later in this book, in the 2000s Brazil altered its patent law in similar ways, to give the Ministry of Health more authority and discretion in issuing (or threatening) compulsory licenses for public interest (Chapter 8), while efforts in Mexico to make much the same sorts of changes were unsuccessful (Chapter 7).

[17] This provision, essentially automatic compulsory licenses for mailbox patents, was also included in India's final amendment to the Patent Act in 2005 (Chaudhuri 2005).

[18] The Executive denied this interpretation, insisting that it was only protecting its constitutional authority to issue implementing orders ("Vetarán parcialmente la última ley de patentes medicinales," *Clarín*, January 3, 1996).

last acquiesced: after all the fighting, Menem accepted that this was the best outcome he was going to get, and the new patent law was published in March 1996.

The LPIMU was a setback for President Menem and the supporters of over-compliance. Consider the international pharmaceutical industry's submission for the 1996 Special 301 review, which concluded that Argentina's new patent law "falls far short of the commitment made by President Menem in 1989 to the United States to enact a patent law in Argentina that would: afford product protection for pharmaceuticals immediately; provide protection to products in the pipeline and a 20-year term, and severely limit the compulsory licensing of patents" (PhRMA 1996). Similarly, an Argentinean observer concluded that the law "ended up completely different from the original project sent by the Executive..." (Irigoyen 2006, 362).

Soon after introducing the new patent law, Argentina also passed a law on data protection that allows the health regulatory agency (*Administración Nacional de Medicamentos, Alimentos y Tecnología Médica*, ANMAT) to rely on information submitted by one firm to grant marketing authorization to follow-on firms. Here too the Executive, acting on behalf of the transnational sector and strongly urged by the US Government, sought legislation that provided a great deal more exclusivity for originator firms; and here too Congress, acting on behalf of the national segment, thwarted such efforts.[19] In the context of the transition period delaying product patents until 2000 and a mailbox, data exclusivity would have offered originator firms a way to gain protection, de facto, for any new drugs introduced in the Argentinean market. They would be able to launch their products in Argentina, and provided that no one could use the data submitted to ANMAT for a period of time, they could have market exclusivity, even without patents. For the local sector, less stringent data protection rules would allow them to get their own versions of new drugs on the market, quickly—both during the transition period and post-2000. Not surprisingly, the data protection law left the transnational sector outraged over what it regarded as "a thinly disguised attempt to invalidate the pharmaceutical patent protection which had just recently been approved" (Vicente 1998, 1107); it "made a bad situation worse" (PhRMA 1998).[20]

The US concurred with this assessment and lost patience. The US had been pushing for a new patent law since the 1990s, only to see the minimalist LPIMU passed in 1996. The USTR reacted by returning Argentina to the Priority Watch List, with another out-of-cycle review scheduled to heighten

---

[19] The data law, the *Ley de Confidencialidad,* "also ended up different from the project submitted by the Executive..." (Irigoyen 2006, 373). "Dos leyes conflictivas," *Clarín,* January 15, 1997.

[20] Bentolila (2002), Bergallo and Ramón Michel (2014), Correa (2000a), Czub (2001), Irigoyen (2006), and Vicente (1998) discuss the data protection law and the reactions it elicited.

the level of scrutiny. The data protection law was the last straw: at this point the USTR stopped threatening and imposed sanctions. Citing both of these new laws, the USTR removed preferential privileges on half of Argentina's exports that went to the US under the Generalized System of Preferences (GSP). Accordingly, more than one hundred products that had been eligible to enter the US market duty-free would now be subject to tariffs.[21]

These actions did not elicit modifications. Menem did not push to reopen the debates over the patent and data laws, nor did the government of Fernando de la Rua (1999–2001) that took office following the 1999 elections and was in power for the rest of the time analyzed in this chapter. Both laws remained in effect. In fact, by this point the Executive's position began to change: rather than conform to external pressures and attempt to impose over-compliance, the Executive shrugged off the significance of trade sanctions and defended the country's new arrangements as satisfactory. Foreign Minister di Tella referred to the US decision to apply sanctions as "an arbitrary and unnecessary" attack on a political and commercial ally and asserted that Argentina "will not modify a law that is entirely satisfactory."[22] The defensive coalition had prevailed; minimalism had become state policy.

In sum, the events of the 1990s in Argentina represent setbacks for the US Government and the transnational pharmaceutical sector. Although a new law allowing for the introduction of pharmaceutical patents was passed, relative to the other countries analyzed in this book the campaign for over-compliance was least successful in Argentina. And by the end of the decade the US no longer had the support of the Argentinean Executive either. The remainder of this chapter examines the social forces that produced this outcome.

POWER AND PREFERENCES IN THE PHARMACEUTICAL INDUSTRY

The principal source of support for Menem's proposal came from transnational pharmaceutical firms, represented by the Argentinean Chamber for Specialized Medicines (*Cámara Argentina de Especialidades Medicinales*, CAEME) and the Center for Studies for the Development of the Argentinean Pharmo-Chemical Industry (*Centro de Estudios para el Desarrollo de la*

---

[21] *Bridges Weekly Trade News Digest*, Vol. 1, Number 3 (February 17, 1997), pp. 1–2; "Trabas de EE.UU. Para Productos Argentinos," *La Nacion*, April 16, 1997. Bentolila (2002, 37, note 132) provides a list of the goods penalized.

[22] "EE UU sancionaría hoy a la Argentina por las patentes," *Clarín*, January 14, 1997. "Trabas de EE.UU. Para Productos Argentinos," *La Nación*, April 16, 1997.

Industria Químico-Farmacéutica Argentina, CEDIQUIFA).[23] For these actors, and their allies in the Argentinean IP law community, all of whom had long called for patent protection for pharmaceutical products, the conjuncture of the early 1990s presented a new opportunity; the prize that had seemed unobtainable was now within their reach. CAEME, CEDIQUIFA, and patent professionals welcomed Menem's proposal with open arms and lobbied actively in support, in the media and in the Congressional hearings.[24] The transnational sector received intellectual support from the Foundation for Latin American Economic Research (*Fundación de Investigaciones Económicas Latinoamericanas*, FIEL), a prominent think tank that published a report on the pharmaceutical industry and medicine prices that recommended drug patents be allowed in Argentina (FIEL 1990). CEDIQUIFA is reported to have commissioned FIEL's report, which both CAEME's and CEDIQUIFA's input into the Senate hearings relied heavily upon.[25]

At the core of the movement opposing Menem's proposal was the national pharmaceutical sector, represented chiefly by the Industrial Chamber of Argentinean Pharmaceutical Firms (*Cámara Industrial de Laboratorios Farmacéuticos Argentinos*, CILFA). CILFA, established in 1964 by Argentinean firms that sought their own trade association separate from the transnational-dominated CAEME, was supported by the Cooperative of Argentinean Specialized Medicines Firms (*Cooperativa de Laboratorios Argentinos de Especialidades Medicinales*, COOPERALA), whose members consisted mostly of smaller firms.[26] These actors initially resisted any modification of the patent law that would introduce pharmaceutical patents, and once it became clear that pharmaceutical patenting was unavoidable they mobilized to shape the way this would happen, participating in Congressional hearings, cultivating relationships with key legislators, and investing considerably in media campaigns to warn of the dire effects that pharmaceutical patenting could have on the Argentinean economy and health system.

To this point the preferences and pattern of conflict are in conformity with expectations: a proposal for over-compliance featuring the immediate introduction of patents with a pipeline elicits the support of the transnational

---

[23] CEDIQUIFA was created in 1972 and functioned as CAEME's research arm.

[24] For illustrations, see CEDIQUIFA (1990) and CAEME's and CEDIQUIFA's testimony in Congress (Senado de la Nación 1993, 321–57; 1994a, 19–49). In addition to testifying himself, CEDIQUIFA's director Félix Rozanski was present at virtually all of the hearings and an active participant.

[25] The other organization that came to the transnational sector's support was the Association of Argentinean Inventors, an association founded in 1990 as the local branch of the International Federation of Inventors' global network (Senado de la Nación 1994a, 213–71). According to one report this association was also linked, institutionally, to CAEME (Labaké 2003).

[26] The Executive Director of CILFA in the early 1990s, and its chief spokesperson and public face, was Pablo Challú, who wrote a series of publications defending the non-patentability of pharmaceutical products (Challú 1991a; 1991b; 1995).

pharmaceutical sector and the opposition of the local pharmaceutical sector. To understand the outcome in Argentina, we need to consider the local pharmaceutical sector's exceptional market strength and coalition-building strategy.

Argentina had the largest and most advanced domestic pharmaceutical sector in Latin America, as we saw in the comparative data presented in Chapter 2 (Table 2.3, p. 47). Among developing countries, only in India and China did capabilities in the pharmaceutical industries match Argentina's (WHO 1988). The degree of local firms' market presence was rare for developing (or even developed) countries, in what is generally a foreign-dominated sector. As of the early 1980s, four Argentinean firms were among the top ten in sales (at places 2, 3, 8, 9), and eleven of the fifteen leading Latin American pharmaceutical firms were Argentinean (ALADI 1985). Local firms' market position improved over the course of the 1980s, as discrimination in favor of Argentinean firms and economic crisis prompted some foreign firms to rely on local firms' distribution channels. By the early 1990s Argentinean firms were dominant: throughout the period when the battle over pharmaceutical patenting was at full pitch, local firms always retained more than 55 percent of the local market, with seven of the ten leading firms Argentinean (Azpiazu 1997, 21; Burachik and Katz 1997, 61–2; Irigoyen 2006, 23).[27]

Local pharmaceutical firms were powerful not just relative to the transnational sector, but as actors on the national industrial scene as well. The sector's contribution to total industrial production led one observer to describe pharmaceuticals as "one of the most dynamic branches of industrial production in Argentina" (Azpiazu 1997, 11). By the time debates over drug patents reached center stage in the early 1990s, pharmaceutical production was the third largest sector in Argentina in terms of output and employment, exceeded only by autos, and petroleum/gas. And these were large enterprises: the average firm size in the pharmaceutical sector, in terms of number of employees, exceeded the industry average by six times, and among the leading firms the average size was significantly greater (Azpiazu 1997, 13; Santoro 2000, 25–9).

The economic strength of the local sector was a legacy, in large part, of precisely the policy and regulatory framework that was under threat in the 1990s. More than any other country in the region, Argentinean firms took advantage of—and their operations depended on—the absence of pharmaceutical patents (UNCTAD 1981). Local firms focused on producing their own versions of drugs that were invented abroad, referred to in Argentina as *copista* products. These drugs were often patented in other markets, but not locally. CILFA estimated that roughly 35 percent of the drugs sold in Argentina by its

---

[27] Two firms (Roemmers, Bagó) were always among the top five, while four others (Sidus, Temis Lostaló, Gador and Phoenix) were consistently in the top ten or fifteen.

members were protected by patents in the US (Senado de la Nación 1993, 294). This figure, though not precise (and slightly higher than other estimates), suggests that Argentinean firms were in direct competition with transnational firms, and that their ability to prevail in this direct competition depended on the existing rules with regard to intellectual property.[28] Not surprisingly, then, Argentinean pharmaceutical producers regarded the introduction of product patents as a major disruption that, if it could not be avoided altogether, needed to be done in such a way as to minimize the immediate effects.

The absence of pharmaceutical patents does not necessarily stimulate the growth of a local sector, but in Argentina the permissive pharmaceutical patent regime was complemented by other measures that also benefitted local firms. In addition to not having to worry about patents, local firms had been protected by high tariffs for final drugs, a drug registration system that allowed local firms to launch their *copista* products quickly, and a regulatory environment that tolerated the close integration between drug producers, distributors, and pharmacies.[29] Broader economic policy and regulatory changes introduced by the Menem Government in the early 1990s were attractive to transnational firms, most importantly, tariff reductions that facilitated importing from foreign production sites, removal of price controls, and drug approval practices that hastened the launch of originator firms' new products, but local firms nevertheless continued to dominate the internal market on account of their close ties to distributors, pharmacies, and the medical community.

For all its prowess in terms of the manufacturing, distribution, and sales of formulated drugs, the local sector's growth was not matched by production of active pharmaceutical ingredients (APIs), for which local firms remained heavily dependent on imports. Some larger firms integrated backwards into pharmo-chemicals to produce the APIs they used, but this tended to be done in small batches, produced largely for themselves, and lacking sufficient scale to become internationally competitive (Irigoyen 2006, 175; Katz 1997b; López 2010). National firms' share of API supply declined from 20 to 25 percent in the 1970s to half of that by the mid-1980s (CEPAL 1987, 84).

These characteristics of the industry help us understand the sector's preferences vis-à-vis the introduction of pharmaceutical patents and its political

---

[28] Bisang (1991) and Panadeiros (1991) both provide lower estimates, but in all cases it is clear that local firms were competing directly with transnationals in the same market segments.

[29] Analyses of dynamics within the Argentinean pharmaceutical industry include Burachik and Katz (1997), Chudnovsky (1979), Correa (1991), CEP (2009), FIEL (1990), Gereffi (1983), Katz (1981), López (2010), Santoro (2000), and White (1983). It is worth noting that the industry's own diagnosis differs somewhat, emphasizing the ways that the policy framework was not as helpful as it could have been (Grillo 1990, 38). See also, "Argentina: Drug Firms Slam Govt Policies," *The Pharma Market Letter*, April 17, 1989.

commitment to the issue. Local pharmaceutical firms competed on the basis of their own brand names and focused on forward integration: they established intermediaries to control distribution, cultivated relationships with pharmacies, physicians, and consumers to maintain a strong retail presence, and intervened in the drug registration process to gain quick authorization.[30] Attention to brand competition and consolidating distribution and sales networks may have been at the expense of integrating backwards into APIs and thus come at a cost economically, but politically—and most importantly for the purposes of this analysis—these efforts placed the local sector in direct and visible competition with transnational firms.

Discussion of the nature of competition within the Argentinean pharmaceutical market in the early 1990s helps us understand why so much seemed at stake. Pipeline protection, making patents available for pre-1995 inventions, would protect drugs that were in clinical trials, but not yet launched. The absence of a pipeline, and strict adherence to a 1995 application date for drug patents to be available in Argentina, would diminish the profitability of these forthcoming products, drugs that originator firms were currently investing resources in developing in preparation of launch. Seen this way, and in the context of the size of the local drug market, one can understand more clearly why the transnational sector and US Government were so focused on obtaining pipeline protection in Argentina—and why CILFA resisted, as these were the sorts of products that Argentinean firms specialized in producing and selling.

And resist it did. CILFA waged an active campaign on multiple fronts. Domestically CILFA participated in the debates in Congress and worked closely with legislators and in the press. Internationally CILFA attempted to coordinate mobilization by pharmaceutical producers throughout Latin America.[31] The association also participated in the USTR's Special 301 process, with submissions that sought to rebut the transnational pharmaceutical sector's characterizations and its requests for Argentina to be listed as a "Priority Foreign Country," and took out advertisements in the *New York Times* and *Washington Post* that criticized US intervention in Argentina's domestic affairs.[32] In fact, with the Executive committed to over-compliance, it was the local pharmaceutical sector that spearheaded Argentina's resistance. Discussing these events two decades later with the director of one of Argentina's

---

[30] CEP (2009) and Sosa (2002, 25–6) and provide data on fusion of the distribution networks. Bekerman and Sirlin (2001, 222) indicate that distribution was heavily concentrated among three firms that were tied to the largest pharmaceutical producers, and linked to retail pharmacies.

[31] CILFA acted as the seat for a regional grouping of associations of national pharmaceutical industries in Latin America.

[32] Ever active, CILFA even participated in congressional debates in Washington, D.C., on healthcare reform in the US.

leading pharmaceutical firms, I suggested that "Argentina resisted in the 1990s," at which point the informant, who was also a former director of CILFA, pounded his fist and exclaimed, "Argentina did not resist, the Menem Government wanted to give everything to the US—*we* resisted" (Interview, December 5, 2014b).

CILFA'S COALITION

The ability of Argentinean pharmaceutical firms to resist and dilute the Executive's initiative is a result of their own capabilities and their coalition-building efforts. Writing in the late 1980s, one observer concluded that opposition to "any general strengthening of the Argentinean patent law comes almost solely from one source—the Argentine national pharmaceutical sector" (Richards 1988a, 113). While that may have accurately characterized the initial reaction to external pressures, by the time pharmaceutical patents were debated in the 1990s local industry had managed to construct a robust coalition to defend its specific interests. From a comparative perspective, Argentina's pharmaceutical sector was remarkably successful in eliciting support for a minimalist response to the global sea change.

The size and organization of the local pharmaceutical industry gave it a prominent position in Argentinean business politics, and CILFA mobilized actors from throughout the industrial community as coalition partners in resisting over-compliance. For example, the General Confederation of Industry and General Economic Confederation, along with the Argentinean Council of Industry attacked Menem's proposal for threatening to destroy the local pharmaceutical sector (Senado de la Nación 1994a, 141–89).[33] That such historically "nationalist" and "industrialist" organizations would come to CILFA's support for a campaign that pitted Argentinean vs foreign industry is not terribly surprising, except for that these associations typically represented small firms, and many of the Argentinean pharmaceutical firms they were defending were anything but small. More revealing are the activities of the Argentinean Industrial Union (*Unión Industrial Argentina,* UIA), nominally the dominant industrial association (Birle 1997; Schneider 2004), and one to which both CILFA and CAEME were affiliates. The association's leadership acknowledged the internal divisions and "conflicting opinions" among its member chambers, but rather than sitting on the sidelines or presenting a compromise position, the UIA ended up echoing CILFA's demands. In what was a comparatively brief intervention, the UIA called for adequate transition

---

[33] Harrison (2004, 104) and Irigoyen (2006, 352) also emphasize these organizations' criticisms of the Executive's proposal.

periods, for example, and rejected the possibility of offering retroactive protection to older inventions.[34]

Participants in these events uniformly note CILFA's commandeering of the UIA, specifically, and the industrial community, more generally, on the issue of pharmaceutical patents, an outcome reflected in the Congressional hearings as well as the broader debate that played itself out in the press. According to a representative from the transnational sector, "CILFA directs the UIA" on issues related to pharmaceutical patents and intellectual property (Interview, November 21, 2007).[35] Recalling these events two decades later, a former President of CILFA was emphatic: the association dedicated itself to influencing the debate on how patents would be introduced as it did with no other issue in the association's history, and a key feature of CILFA's strategy was to get the UIA and other trans-sectoral business organizations in its camp (Interview, December 5, 2014b).[36] In CILFA's fiftieth anniversary memoir, the campaign and strategy vis-à-vis the new patent law was celebrated as a landmark moment in the chamber's history (CILFA 2014, 13). The success of the strategy is clear: of the three countries analyzed in this book, only in Argentina do we witness active mobilization of important business organizations from outside of pharmaceuticals in alliance with local drug producers.

As an indicator of CILFA's dominance and control of the defensive coalition, it is worth noting that other actors from industry did not always parrot CILFA's specific arguments. Many made recommendations that went beyond pharmaceuticals, seeking to convert the obligation to introduce a new patent law into an opportunity to restore a more "knowledge-based" approach to industrial development to spur greater local technological autonomy, yet their concerns were subordinated by CILFA and largely ignored by Congress. Some of the business associations that testified to Congress suggested provisions that would complement the availability of patents with obligations to transfer technology that exceeded anything proposed by CILFA. Likewise, representatives from the Argentinean Association for Technological Development, an association representing mechanical engineers, called for Congress to require patent owners to list their patents and the activities taken to work their patented inventions in a national registry, to facilitate transparency and reduce uncertainty, as well as for complementary revision of the country's competition and anti-trust laws to combat abuse of market power (Senado de la Nación 1994a, 50–62).[37] In short, while CILFA focused on the core issues of

---

[34] Testimony of José Blanco Villegas, President of UIA, November 25, 1993 (Senado de la Nación 1994a, 206–10).

[35] Irigoyen (2006) also emphasizes local laboratories' dominance of the industry-wide association.

[36] A former Executive Director of CILFA in charge of strategy and public relations also emphasized the high priority of prevailing in this conflict (Interview, November 22, 2007a).

[37] This association's spokesman, Julio Maria Grondona, was a former advisor to CILFA. In addition to formal testimony in August 1993, Grondona was a frequent participant in the hearings regularly asking questions from the floor.

when and how pharmaceutical patents would be introduced, the chamber's industrial coalition partners went beyond these issues and also expressed concerns with Argentina's broader technology policies. Yet—and this is a key point for this discussion—the latter actors' own initiatives were unsuccessful. Demands for provisions that were not specifically of interest to the pharmaceutical sector, and that also contradicted the demands of Menem and the US Government, could be safely discarded by Congress. It was the Argentinean pharmaceutical industry that had Congress's ear and controlled the debate.[38]

CILFA was also successful in eliciting the support of actors in the medical and healthcare sector. Some of the industry's characteristics discussed in the previous section facilitated this. In addition to having a large presence in terms of market shares, local firms had extensive ties to drug distributors, pharmacies, and medical professionals. This downstream presence not only helped local firms preserve their market power, but also allowed them to build broader political alliances than might have otherwise been possible. Nearly the entire pharmaceutical production, distribution, and sales chain could be mobilized politically.

During Congress' hearings, one organization after another from the Argentinean health community rejected Menem's proposal; almost in unison, these actors insisted that if new global rules required Argentina to introduce pharmaceutical patents, then the country should do so in a careful, measured, and minimalist way to mitigate the effects. From the Medical Confederation of Argentina, to the Confederation of Argentinean Pharmacists, to the Argentinean Doctors Association, organizations from throughout the health and medical community demanded that Argentina adopt a minimalist approach to introducing pharmaceutical patents: utilize available transition periods, avoid a pipeline, and include extensive and useful compulsory licensing provisions.[39] Even the Argentinean League of Housewives mobilized in support of CILFA, warning of grave threats posed by the introduction of pharmaceutical patents. This last intervention is particularly noteworthy, given that in some therapeutic segments the retail prices of drugs in Argentina tended to be comparatively high, even in the absence of patents (Bisang 1991; Chudnovsky 1979; FIEL 1990; Panadeiros 1991). When the high cost of

---

[38] To provide another example, the School of Pharmacy and Biochemistry at the University of Buenos Aires suggested that Argentinean firms be required to invest a share of sales made during the transition period in research and development (Senado de la Nación 1994a, 124). As CILFA did not support this, the proposal had no traction.

[39] See the transcripts of the Senate hearings, August 12, 1993 (Senado de la Nación 1994a, 75–111) and August 19, 1993 (Senado de la Nación 1994a, 115–37). Some organizations, such as Medical Confederation (p. 85) and the Confederation of Pharmacists (pp. 135–6) proposed that the Ministry of Health participate in patent examination. This suggestion was not adopted, but, as we shall see in Chapter 8, such arrangements were later introduced in Brazil in 2001.

drugs was raised in the hearings, the League of Housewives' representative only lamented what the situation might be like with patents, asking rhetorically "Let me ask a question: do you think that with a patent law Argentineans are going to have the ability to purchase medicines and that the price of drugs will not increase?" (Senado de la Nación 1994a, 129).

The robust defensive coalition created and mobilized by the local pharmaceutical sector fueled Congressional resistance to Menem's push for over-compliance. The national pharmaceutical sector had long-standing ties with the Radical Party, on account of a frequently repeated story that the transnational sector had inspired to remove a UCR President from power in the 1960s, and Radical Deputies and Senators provided the local sector with the most consistent and reliable support.[40] The size and organization of the industry, especially in the city and province of Buenos Aires, made it a natural ally of the industrialist side of the Peronist party too, and many of the sector's outspoken legislative advocates were from the PJ. In fact, support for CILFA's positions on patents largely transcended partisan divisions. During the initial period of debate, contrary to expectations, Congress was united and acted unanimously in support of CILFA; not even the most reliable *menemistas* supported the President's crusade for over-compliance. After the mini-summit in June 1995, partisan divisions emerged, with the UCR still firmly in CILFA's camp and the PJ caucus acting as a bridge to broker a compromise between Congress and the Executive, but even then PJ legislators were quick to react when they sensed that the President was abusing his authority in trying to undermine the compromise bill through the implementation process.

CILFA's ability to broaden the coalition to include the medical community certainly helped its cause in Congress as well. Some of the most active legislators in the Chamber of Deputies and Senate were from the health sector and preoccupied by the effects that pharmaceutical patenting might have on health. In the 1993–95 Legislature, for example, 15.5 percent of UCR deputies and 8.7 percent of PJ deputies came from the medical profession (Corrales 2004, 12), and it was typically these individuals that were most involved in the congressional deliberations. These legislators' opposition to the immediate and retroactive introduction of pharmaceutical patents depended, at least in part, on the case being made that such measures would not just hurt drug producers, but have damaging health consequences.

---

[40] In 1964, over the strong and vocal objections of the transnational sector, Congress passed the *Ley de Medicamentos* which gave the government the ability to impose price controls. After the military took over in 1966 the law was never implemented. For one account, see "Illia y la Ley de Medicamentos," *Crónica*, April 10, 2014 (goo.gl/AF3X9q). At an individual level, the leader of the Radical Party in the 1990s (and President from 1983–89), Raúl Alfonsín is reported to have had close personal relations, dating from childhood years, with the owner of Argentina's leading firm, Roemmers.

EXPORT PROFILE AND CAEME'S UNSUCCESSFUL
POLITICAL MOBILIZATION

The instrument that was expected to help the transnational sector expand its coalition for over-compliance, the engagement and activation of exporters, was not useful in Argentina. By threatening and applying trade sanctions, the USTR aimed to convert otherwise "agnostic" exporters into supporters of over-compliance. Yet these pressures were largely ineffective in generating new allies for CAEME. Consider, for example, the Argentinean Council of Industry, at the time including producers and exporters of light manufactures, which opposed Menem's proposed patent law and explicitly encouraged Congress to ignore the threat of any possible trade sanctions: "There are pressures from the US, pressures that might be transformed into threats and even concrete trade sanctions.... We have the conviction that our legislators will not let themselves be pressured in this way...We must not fear sanctions..." (Senado de la Nación 1994a, 147–8). Likewise, when the USTR announced suspension of GSP treatment in 1997, the reaction of Argentina's leading exporters was largely one of indifference. The Chamber of Argentinean Exporters (*Cámara de Exportadores de la República Argentina*, CERA) emphasized the *minimal* pain that the US sanctions would inflict on the country's export sector.[41] Neither threats of trade sanctions nor, ultimately, trade sanctions, shifted the balance of coalitional forces by converting exporters into advocates for over-compliance. Note that this is the case even though President Menem and the president of the Senate Eduardo Menem (the President's brother) came from a state where exports to the US depended heavily on GSP treatment.[42] To be sure, some individual firms reacted to the sanctions, demanding that Argentina acquiesce to the US demands to retain market access abroad, but these actors were unable to reverse the policies that had been set in course.

Although it is widely acknowledged that US trade sanctions had little effect on Argentinean policy, the reasons why are not adequately understood. External pressures did, initially, transform the Executive's preferences, but they did not have sufficient effects on social structure to alter coalitional dynamics. Overall export dependence on the US market was low throughout this period, always at or about 10 percent. The country's principal exports to the US, beef and cereals, did not enter under GSP and thus were not affected by the removal of trade preferences. Figure 3.1 plots Argentina's trade dependence on the US market, both overall trade and preferential trade from 1985 to 2000. The data reveal political trade dependence, always low, declining in the period when the

---

[41] "Trabas de EE.UU. para productos argentinos," *La Nacion*, April 16, 1997.
[42] A leading leather-producing firm was owned by President Menem's former brother in-law.

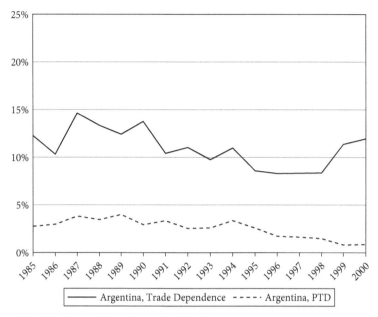

Figure 3.1. Structure of Exports to the US: Argentina

Note: Data on preferential exports to the US are from the United States International Trade Commission; data on overall exports to the US and global exports are from UN-COMTRADE.

debates over pharmaceutical patenting were most intense. That is, Argentina became less sensitive to US threats of GSP removal at the time that the threats were ratcheted up and then finally acted upon. Preferential exports potentially expose countries to external pressures, as these can be removed at the discretion of the importing country. Argentina's low levels of preferential exports relative to total exports help us understand why trade sanctions were so ineffective. External pressures did successfully activate some agnostics, but these actors' peripheral position in the national political economy meant that the effects on coalitional politics were insignificant.

The inability of the US to elicit change in Argentina merits attention. It certainly was not for lack of effort. Argentina was regularly lambasted in the Special 301 reports and trade sanctions were consistently on the horizon.[43] Indeed, the level of public activism on the part of US officials in Buenos Aires throughout this period is remarkable. We have already noted the remarks of

---

[43] The US had also attempted to make Argentina's eligibility for debt restructuring under the Brady Plan conditional on passage of a new patent law, as well as US support for loans from the International Monetary Fund and the Inter-American Development Bank.

Ambassador James Cheek.[44] Throughout the period of most intense debate over the LPIMU, Menem and Cavallo had monthly meetings with officials from the US Embassy in Buenos Aires to discuss the proposed legislation, in addition to visits in the first half of 1995 by USTR Micky Kantor, Vice-President Al Gore, and Commerce Secretary Ron Brown.[45] US officials were explicit that they were using Argentina as an example, to send a signal to other developing countries about the consequences of failure to accord the level of patent protection that the US desired. To be sure, the variety of external pressures applied mobilized Argentinean officials, who expressed concerns about the broader effects that resisting US demands on patents might have on the country's foreign relations and reputation for foreign investors. And, as noted, they mobilized some exporters too. However, external threats, promises, and sanctions appear to have had little effect in terms of widening CAEME's coalition.

One might claim that the US's pressures were effective in that Argentina's response to the global sea change, though "minimalist," was not as minimalist as it could have been. Argentina could have waited until 2005 to introduce pharmaceutical patents, for example, and Argentina could have made the compulsory licensing clauses more vigorous with explicit requirements of local manufacturing. After the LPIMU was passed, Congress considered revising it immediately in both of these ways, but did not do so. There is, thus, a correlation between external pressures being ratcheted up, from the USTR threatening trade sanctions to applying trade sanctions, and the outcome of Argentina not further reducing the country's degree of over-compliance. Yet there are multiple reasons to question the causal inference. Most importantly, it is clear that the US did not achieve the outcome it desired. The US Government was explicit throughout the entire period that its objective was to pressure Argentina to introduce pharmaceutical patents quickly and with a pipeline for pre-1995 applications and patents, not simply to prevent them from being delayed even longer, and that it sought to prevent ANMAT from authorizing drugs on the basis of "proprietary" data. These outcomes were not achieved. The USTR's pressures and sanctions did not deliver what they were designed to deliver: pharmaceutical patents would not become available until late 2000, only inventions from 1995 onwards would ever be eligible for protection, and ANMAT's practices would continue to help local firms place their *copista* drugs on the market easily and quickly. As for the contemplated revisions to the compulsory licensing clauses, no doubt US

---

[44] Ambassador Cheek's interventions in the press were so regular, and so critical of Congress, that the UCR bloc in the Chamber of Deputies petitioned Menem to request the Ambassador be replaced. Cheek's predecessor in Buenos Aires, Terence Todman, was also extremely outspoken.

[45] Even ex-President George H.W. Bush got involved. In an April 1995 visit to Buenos Aires the ex-President discussed the patent law with Menem over lunch and then declared to the press that the stalemate would be resolved ("Se va a solucionar," *Pagina/12*, April 4, 1995).

officials were pleased by these changes not being made, but attributing this to external pressures reverses cause and effect: Argentina's Congress threatened this change as a reaction to the US sanctions.[46]

CONCLUSION

Although Argentina adopted a new patent system as demanded by the WTO in the 1990s, the outcome differs—in fundamentally key ways—from the desires of the transnational pharmaceutical industry and US Government, as well as from the initial desires of the Argentinean Executive. Whereas President Menem's 1991 proposal called for the immediate and retroactive introduction of pharmaceutical patents, patents were not introduced until late 2000, without a pipeline or any sort of protection for drugs that would enter the market in the 1990s. Of the three cases examined in this book, Argentina is the one in which the campaign for over-compliance was least successful.

That Argentina's political leaders would become committed to satisfying the US with regard to patents in the early 1990s is to be expected, given the extent of external pressures as well as the ideological proclivities of the top officials of the Menem Government at this time (Dominguez 1997). But the Executive was unable to push the project through on its desired terms, and instead accepted an outcome that corresponded much more closely to what the opponents of over-compliance sought. Writing about the exceptionally rapid implementation of structural reforms in the early 1990s, Levitsky and Murillo conclude as such: "Had President Menem been held fully account-able to Congress and the judiciary, the reform process would almost certainly have been slower and less far-reaching" (Levitsky and Murillo 2005, 33). In the case of pharmaceutical patents, where Congress showed an exceptional degree of activism and demanded that President Menem and his policy-making team remained accountable, the reform process was, indeed, pro-tracted and less far-reaching.

To be sure, the Executive tried to bypass Congress. Although Cavallo promised the Legislature in June 1994 that pharmaceutical patent protection would not be introduced by decree, at the same time, and foreshadowing events of the following year, he insisted on the Executive's prerogative to use a partial veto to get its way (Senado de la Nación 1994a, 156–8). And in June 1995 Cavallo is alleged to have made the more authoritarian threat discussed above. But ultimately the Executive succumbed to the considerable opposition

---

[46] Another initiative contemplated in Congress at the time, dubbed "Helms-Burton Law in Reverse," would have blocked US firms from participating in public tenderings in Argentina by making firms from countries that impose trade sanctions on Argentina ineligible (Czub 2001).

it faced. One explanation for this outcome may be that the Argentinean Executive never really cared so much about this piece of legislation. Jones, for example, asserts that the patent law was not brought to Congress to seek passage but rather to appease the US Government (Jones 2002, 158). Yet the evidence that the Executive sought to pass the patent law, and a particularly over-compliant version of the patent law, is overwhelming. This was demanded and fought for in Congress by the very top officials in the Executive; the fact that the President sent Cavallo and di Tella to the mini-summit in June 1995 reflects the Menem Government's priorities. Moreover, US officials made it abundantly clear that they would not be satisfied by Argentina simply passing a new patent law: the US demanded a particular type of patent law, and it eventually punished Argentina for the legislation that was passed.

Rather than a function of the Executive's questionable commitment to over-compliance, the analysis in this chapter points to the conditional nature of the Argentinean Executive's power. Consistent with Llanos's and Murillo's analyses of privatization and regulation, even constitutionally strong Executives need to bargain with Congress (Llanos 2001; Murillo 2009). The key issue, then, is what limited Menem's authority in this instance and why the President struggled to obtain the support of legislators on the terms he sought. The explanation here has focused on the strength and resilience of the defensive coalition constructed by the local pharmaceutical sector. Industrial legacies and market structure allowed CILFA, the organization representing these firms, to harness a wide range of allies that, collectively, mobilized Congress to neuter Menem's over-compliant proposal. In the absence of significant export mobilization to produce countervailing societal opposition to CILFA's coalition, the result was Argentina's minimalist approach to pharmaceutical patents.

By the late 1990s minimalism became state policy in Argentina. The Executive stopped trying to impose over-compliance on a resistant society and instead fell into step with the local pharmaceutical sector and the defensive coalition. In fact, the Argentinean Government came to defend the new patent regime against further external attacks, a pattern that would continue into the 2000s. That minimalism became state policy may not be terribly surprising following the 1999 elections, which put President Fernando de la Rua from the CILFA-friendly Radical Party in power, and the subsequent economic crises of the early 2000s, but it is important to underscore that we see this revision in Executive preferences in the latter years of the Menem Government too. As discussed, after the new patent and data laws were passed, President Menem accepted and defended them. One explanation for this may be the departure of Cavallo from the cabinet in July 1996. That is, it may be that, once this leading official was gone, intra-Executive conflicts between Cavallo and his adversaries shifted in favor of the latter, and thus the Menem Government's enthusiasm for globalization and adoption of "best practices" in IP subsided. Yet Cavallo's successor as Minister of Economy, Roqué Fernandez, who had been President of the Central Bank, was also a committed "neoliberal" technocrat, and in other areas of policy Menem's globalizing zest remained.[47]

Another, more mundane, explanation is that, in the latter half of the 1990s, other issues simply consumed the government's attention: a slumping economy, scandals over arms sales, and so on. Having fought about patents for so long, Menem just decided enough was enough and that he would accept the compromise outcome rather than keep fighting. This is entirely plausible, but also consistent with the explanation put forward in this chapter. We only reached this point of Executive exhaustion on account of the enduring strength of the coalition for minimalism in the 1990s. Had Argentina's pharmaceutical firms and their allies not put up so much resistance in the early- and mid-1990s, then Menem would already have prevailed at the time when over-compliance was still a high priority for his government.

Argentina's patent system was, however, revolutionized in this period: as of 2000 Argentina would begin granting patents on pharmaceutical products, something the country had not previously done. Yet the fact that pharmaceutical patents were introduced in the way they were, because of the policy choices of the 1990s, had important consequences going forward. How the minimalist regime implemented in the 1990s shaped subsequent politics of patents in the 2000s will be the subject of Chapter 6.

---

[47] For example, Menem contemplated replacing convertibility, by which the Argentinean peso was fixed at equal value to the US dollar and both could be used interchangeably, with formal adoption of the US dollar as the local currency (i.e. "dollarization").

4

Not If but *How*

NAFTA and Extreme Over-Compliance in Mexico

Mexico must enact an adequate patent law before it can ever initiate a successful free-trade agreement with the U.S. and Canada.

(PMA 1991)

[Mexico's 1991 patent law is] the most modern of its kind in the world"

("Mexican Patent Law Introduced, *The Pharma Market Letter,* July 8, 1991)

Mexico's response to the global sea change was abrupt, early, and extreme. In June 1991, well before the TRIPS Agreement was finalized, Mexico introduced an over-compliant patent law that radically restructured the country's approach to knowledge ownership. The Law for the Development and Protection of Industrial Property (*Ley de Fomento y Protección de la Propiedad Industrial,* LFPPI) introduced patents immediately, offered generous protection for patents on older drugs that were still in the "pipeline," and gave patent-holders strong rights of control over the use of their private knowledge.

This chapter explains the radical and abrupt changes introduced in Mexico. Quite simply, once external pressures converted the Executive to the cause, the presence of a domineering transnational pharmaceutical sector seeking extensive protection and a highly mobilized export sector preoccupied with preferential access to the US market established the conditions for over-compliance.

Yet there are degrees of compliance and over-compliance, and what transpired in Mexico stands out both in terms of outcome and process. The key issue in this first period of patent politics is not if countries introduced pharmaceutical patents, but *how* they did so, and the way this occurred in Mexico would have enduring effects. In contrast to the protracted and highly visible debates witnessed elsewhere, fundamental changes to the patent system went largely unnoticed in Mexico. President Carlos Salinas de Gortari (1988–1994) submitted an initiative for a new patent law in December 1990, and in six months the LFPPI was passed, virtually unaltered. The new law was subject to only the lightest of treatment by the Legislature, and the entire affair received scant attention from the media. Political economy changes that consumed legislatures and publics in other countries transpired seemingly without notice in Mexico. The result of this nearly substance-free process was a new law that would set Mexico down the path of ever-increasing patent protection.

An obvious explanation for early and extreme over-compliance in Mexico might be that the party of the President, the Institutional Revolutionary Party (*Partido Revolucionario Institucional,* PRI), had commanding major-ities in the Legislature, and the Mexican Executive's authority in the early 1990s was exceptionally strong (Weldon 1997). Accordingly, once Executive preferences shifted in favor of over-compliance, as they had by 1990, the outcome was a foregone conclusion: a new patent law offering strong and extensive protection for pharmaceuticals was going to pass in Mexico. It nevertheless remains surprising that the Executive was able to obtain all of what it wanted, so easily. "Presidentialist" arguments, i.e. explanations for outcomes based on the power of the Executive, rest on a presumption of resistance that the Executive was able to overcome. To be sure, were there resistance to Salinas's proposal, the Executive would almost certainly have prevailed, as it did on most proposed legislation in this period (Casar 2002; Saiegh 2011). But analysis of this case reveals only minimal mobilization against the Salinas Government's proposals regarding the introduction of pharmaceutical patents, and thus scarcely any resistance for the Executive to overcome.

The lack of substantial resistance to Salinas's proposal needs to be under-stood, because it shaped the outcome. After all, Presidentialism is not to be equated with absolutism: even strong Executives typically need to bargain with dissenters and legislators from within their own parties (Llanos 2001; Murillo et al. 2011), processes that can shape the terms on which powerful Executives secure their desired policies. Indeed, in debates over other policies in Mexico in this period, such as Salinas's proposed education reforms, revision of the land tenure system, utility privatization, and modification of consumer pro-tection laws, for example, resistance from PRI legislators forced the Executive to bargain and make concessions. We do not observe resistance and bargain-ing around the new patent law, however, and the absence of such processes affected the outcomes in ways that would have long-term effects on Mexican political economy. Thus, to understand extreme and early over-compliance in Mexico—not just why the patent law passed but why this LFPPI with these provisions on drug patents—we need to understand why there was so little resistance and mobilization.

The analysis in this chapter pays special attention to the significance of the North American Free Trade Agreement (NAFTA), in particular to how the NAFTA process shaped patterns of political mobilization and coalition building around patents. This agreement, which Mexico signed with the United States and Canada in 1993, and which entered into effect in January 1994, is the first bilateral or regional trade agreement between developed and developing countries to include rules on intellectual property. The most immediate effect of NAFTA was that it helped convert Mexican officials into patent enthusiasts. Securing the trade agreement was the highest priority for the Salinas Government (Castañeda 1990; Golob 1997; Ortiz Mena 2004), and, as the first quotation in the chapter's epigraph suggests, a new patent law was a condition for achieving this goal (Cameron and Tomlin 2002; Lustig 1992; Gasman 1995).

Not only did the promise of NAFTA shift the Executive's preferences, but it transformed the broader political economy of patents in this period. By bundling patents with a range of other policy issues, NAFTA altered the domestic pharmaceutical sector's focus and inspired a political strategy that was more oriented toward affecting policy on government purchasing than the details of drug patents. In addition, the prospect of a trade agreement sparked the coordinated mobilization of exporters in a way that was unwitnessed in other countries, and the subsequent negotiating process restructured the network of business organization in a way that marginalized the voice of potentially dissenting actors from the domestic pharmaceutical sector. In sum, NAFTA created new Executive preferences and new coalitional possibilities; externally-induced changes to domestic politics shaped the way that Mexico introduced pharmaceutical patents in the early 1990s.

This chapter has four sections. The first section reveals the transformation of Executive preferences, examining Mexico's responses to external pressures beginning in the mid-1980s. We begin with analysis of moderate reforms to the country's patent law in 1987, when Mexico resisted pressures from the transnational pharmaceutical sector and US Government for the immediate introduction of patents, and we then examine the subsequent turnaround that yielded the over-compliant LFPPI of 1991. The second section focuses on the resources and strategies of the core antagonists, the national and transnational pharmaceutical sectors. We see how economic liberalization in the late 1980s and the NAFTA negotiating process affected the national sector both economically and politically, making an already weakened defensive coalition even less resilient. The third section, focusing on the strategies of the transnational sector, emphasizes how trade structure as well as the opportunities presented by NAFTA helped the coalition for over-compliance attract allies from throughout the Mexican business community. The fourth section uses examination of the legislative process by which Mexico adopted pharmaceutical patents in 1991 to illustrate these stark coalitional asymmetries. We observe a defensive coalition stripped of the will to fight and an expansive and energized coalition for over-compliance.

EXTERNAL PRESSURES, NEW OPPORTUNITIES, AND CHANGING EXECUTIVE PREFERENCES

Mexico was one of the first countries targeted by the international pharmaceutical industry and the US Government. Pharmaceutical products and processes had been ineligible for patents since the 1976 Law on Inventions and Trademarks (*Ley de Invenciones y Marcas*, LIM), and the "Ad Hoc Group on Mexican Industrial Property," a loose collection of US investors and legal professionals, had been pressuring Mexico since nearly this time. In 1984 the Pharmaceutical Manufacturers of America (PMA) identified Mexico as a priority country for the United States Trade Representative (USTR) to target, and Mexico was one of the first countries to be threatened with trade sanctions on account of IP practices (Gwynn 1988, 235; Pemberton and Soni 1992, 105; Sherwood et al. 1991, 175).

In 1986, to relieve external pressures, President Miguel de la Madrid (1982–88) proposed a reform to the LIM that was passed by the Legislature and entered into law in January 1987. Not surprisingly, pharmaceutical patents were the key issue (Becerra Ramírez 2009; Gwynn 1988; Rangel-Ortiz 1988). What de la Madrid proposed, and what the LIM sanctioned, was for process patents to be allowed immediately, and for pharmaceutical products to become patentable as of 1997, after a ten year transition period.

The 1986–87 LIM reform is best understood as a grudging response to external pressures, one that reflected the government's approach, at the moment, to patent policy. The US and the transnational pharmaceutical sector wanted much faster movement, but were unable to overcome the the de la Madrid Government's commitment to gradualism. At one point, the Special Commission responsible for steering the bill through the Senate reduced the transition period proposed by President de la Madrid to five years, a move that of course was cheered by transnational pharmaceutical firms in Mexico and met with disdain by local producers (Cámara de Senadores 1987, 607–11; Gwynn 1988, 239; Rangel-Ortiz 1988, 858). Yet the Executive insisted on delaying the introduction of pharmaceutical product patents for ten years, as in the original version it had sent to Congress. This was as much as Mexican officials were prepared to deliver.

The evidence suggests that the Executive intervened to impose its preferences for a longer transition period. The head of the Special Commission in the Senate was Raul Salinas Lozano, the father of future-President Carlos Salinas de Gortari. At the time, Carlos Salinas was the Secretary of Planning and Budget, and had recently emerged from an intra-cabinet battle as the key economic policymaker under President de la Madrid (Centeno 1997). The Special Commission's revision of the Executive's proposal essentially pit father (Legislature) against son (Executive). Had the de la Madrid Government been prepared to bend to pressures and introduce pharmaceutical patents more quickly, this was an opportunity. Yet it held firm. The Executive reiterated its commitment to the more delayed introduction of pharmaceutical patents, and the head of the Special Commission, the father of the most important—and rising—economic policy official in the country, immediately agreed to respect the Executive's preferences, without defending in any way his Commission's own proposed amendment. When the full Senate met to vote on the LIM reform in December 1986, for example, a PRI Senator demanded restoration of the ten-year transition period for pharmaceutical product patents, as in the Executive's original proposal. In response to this intervention, neither Senator Salinas nor any members of the Special Commission attempted to defend the change they had proposed and make the case for a quicker introduction of pharmaceutical patents. Rather, Senator Salinas simply thanked his colleague for his input and agreed to restore the transition period to ten years, and the LIM was then passed as such (Cámara de Senadores 1987, 618–21).

The LIM experience shows that the Mexican Government of the mid-1980s, even as it became committed to a liberalized and export-oriented economic development strategy, still did not regard patent protection for pharmaceutical products as appropriate. Mexico had not, yet, embraced the global sea change in IP, hook, line, and sinker. In contrast to other economic policy areas where Mexico introduced substantial policy shifts in the 1980s, such as the removal of trade barriers and relaxation of regulations on foreign investors (Lustig 1992; Moreno-Brid and Ros 2009; Ten Kate 1992; Whiting 1992), IP policy changes were substantially less dramatic. De la Madrid and Salinas were prepared to introduce some modifications to mollify Mexico's external critics, but they were not yet committed to a patent regime of the type being demanded by external actors; what the US and the transnational pharmaceutical sector were demanding remained a step too far.

It is tempting to claim that the reforms to the LIM only appear as moderate in hindsight. That is, in 1987, with negotiations in the Uruguay Round on a new multilateral IP agreement hardly off the ground, the changes introduced—allowing process patents and scheduling for product patents to be available a decade later—may have been radical for the moment. Yet Mexico's reforms were regarded, at the time, as being minimal. The US Government, the transnational pharmaceutical sector, and the Mexican IP law community immediately criticized the alterations to the LIM for their meekness and expressed frustration at de la Madrid's unwillingness, specifically, to accelerate pharmaceutical patenting. After all, other countries (e.g. South Korea, Turkey) were introducing product patents in this period. The PMA regarded process patents as "inadequate and ineffective and, consequently, a totally unsatisfactory substitute for product protection" (PMA 1989).[1] These actors also expressed

---

[1] See also, "PMA Disappointed with Mexican Patent Law," *The Pharma Market Letter* January 19, 1987; Gwynn (1988, 235).

concern about the LIM's failure to alter Mexico's compulsory licensing clauses, which required patent-holders to demonstrate that they were manufacturing patented products in the country, left government officials with authority to carry out inspections to verify local production, and did not provide opportunities to justify decisions to not produce patented products within the country.[2] Given that Mexico did not yet have pharmaceutical patents the compulsory licensing provisions remained irrelevant to that field, but they were indications of the government's approach to IP policy at the time. The reformed LIM did not even create a patent office; patent applications would continue to be handled by a division within the Secretariat of Trade and Industrial Development (*Secretaría de Comercio y Fomento Industrial*, SECOFI). For its part, the Mexican Executive also regarded the revised LIM as a minimalist response, and defended the changes as appropriate measures for the country's level of development and economic strategy.[3] Government officials and PRI legislators went to great lengths to emphasize that they regarded the patent system as an instrument to promote national technological development; its function was not to cater to the demands of knowledge owners, but rather to aid in the diffusion of knowledge. From the de la Madrid Government's perspective, the reforms reflected an effort to match the country's IP system with its conditions and needs.

Mexico came under immediate pressures to revisit these issues. The US insisted that Mexico eliminate the transition period to make pharmaceutical product patents available without delay, and that the local manufacturing requirement in the compulsory licensing provisions be removed too (Gwynn 1988; Sherwood et al. 1991; USITC 1990). In fact, the external pressures faced by Mexico were greater after the 1987 reform than they had been before. As punishment for failure to satisfy its demands with regard to patents, the US removed preferential treatment from US$200 million of Mexican exports that had been entering the US under the Generalized System of Preferences (GSP), and denied Mexico's application for a waiver that would have allowed another US$500 million of exports to enter under preferential terms (Gwynn 1988, 235; Lustig 1992, 129; Pemberton and Soni 1992, 105). In 1989, the first year that the USTR published the Special 301 report on IP practices, Mexico was placed on the Priority Watch List.

At the same time as the USTR brandished the stick of trade sanctions, the US Government also extended a carrot: the opportunity to stabilize and expand preferential market access by negotiating a bilateral trade agreement.

---

[2] If anything, by clarifying and streamlining the compulsory licensing procedures, the revised LIM reduced patent-holders' effective rights of exclusion (Rangel-Ortiz 1981; 1988).

[3] See, for example, President de la Madrid's letter to Congress accompanying the Executive's original submission, emphasizing the relationship between a reformed LIM and Mexico's National Program for Scientific and Technological Development (Cámara de Senadores 1987, 580–1).

For many goods, Mexico already had preferential market access to the US, through the GSP, but these preferences could be reduced or removed at any time, as the experience of the late 1980s demonstrated. A reciprocal trade agreement offered to make Mexico's preferential market access stable and permanent, and also promised to broaden Mexico's preferential market access to areas not covered by the GSP (Manger and Shadlen 2014; Shadlen 2008).[4]

To obtain stable and broader preferential market access, however, Mexico would have to thoroughly revamp its IP system, far beyond the reforms to the LIM introduced in 1987. When President Salinas approached the United States to negotiate what would, eventually, become NAFTA, the US officials made it clear that negotiations would not begin until Mexico first introduced a new patent system that included product patents in pharmaceuticals. Sure enough, in what Lustig refers to as a "tacit exchange" (Lustig 1992, 129), Mexico promised that new patent legislation would be forthcoming, and the US removed its neighbor from the Priority Watch List that year and opened the door to negotiating the trade agreement.[5]

The promise of NAFTA shifted the Executive's preferences regarding the appropriate patent policy for Mexico. The proposed law that Salinas submitted to Congress in December 1990 marked an abrupt departure from recent Mexican policy. As a columnist wrote in one of Mexico's leading business newspapers, "it is a truly revolutionary proposal that has surprised specialists in the area who never believed that the government would dare to go so far."[6] Patent provisions that only four years earlier were regarded as sacred and critical aspects of the country's development strategy were now discarded as Mexico's new approach to IP reflected the government's broad goal of inter-nationalizing the Mexican economy and desire to out-compete other countries in pursuit of foreign investment. In the "National Program for Industrial Modernization and Foreign Trade" (SECOFI 1990), the Salinas Government had lamented that the lack of pharmaceutical patent protection was deterring investment (p. 167) and indicated its intentions to submit a new patent law to Congress "so that patent protection offered in Mexico would be similar to that available in industrialized countries..." (p. 173). Later that year, in presenting the initiative to Congress, President Salinas exclaimed that "Mexico has the

---

[4] An agreement with the US would also allow exporters from Mexico to access the US market on the same terms as exporters from Canada could, following the Canada-US bilateral trade agreement that came into effect in 1989 (Gruber 2001).

[5] "U.S. Exempts Mexico from Any Retaliation on Proprietary Rights," *Wall Street Journal*, January 25, 1990; "Mexico to Improve Patent Protection," *Financial Times*, January 22, 1990. For a former Mexican policymaker's view of the undesirability of increasing patent protection to the level the US wanted, but the imperative of doing so to retain healthy trading relations, see de María y Campos (1991). Sell (1995, 331) also notes that the promise of NAFTA led Mexican officials to reassess the costs and benefits of altering IP policies. Although the LFPPI was widely regarded as a precondition to NAFTA, Mexican trade officials deny the link (Robert 2000, 237).

[6] Luis Mercado, "Propiedad Industrial," *El Economista*, December 14, 1990.

opportunity to jump ahead of countries. Being in the vanguard in making the changes required to compete effectively at the international level brings advantages to the country in terms of positioning ourselves strategically to profit from international flows of trade, investment and technology" (Cámara de Senadores 1990, 4). Whereas the de la Madrid Government had touted the reformed LIM as comprehensive and far-sighted legislation that appropriately matched the level of patent protection to the country's capabilities and needs, by 1990 the Executive (indeed, the same individuals: Salinas was the chief policymaker, now he was the President) depicted the LIM as "obsolete" and used similar adjectives and rationale as before (comprehensive, far-sighted, etc.) in support of the proposed new law.[7]

As a further illustration of how the opportunities presented by NAFTA shifted the Executive's preferences, consider the issue of pipeline patents. Even when Salinas agreed to introduce pharmaceutical patents in order to secure the trade agreement with the US, the government was not contemplating pipeline protection to drugs already patented outside of the country, and the original initiative drafted by SECOFI did not include such a provision. Yet after the USTR indicated that this omission put the NAFTA negotiations at peril, this too became part of the Executive's vision regarding what sort of patent law was optimal for Mexico, and the pipeline provision was included in the initiative that Salinas submitted to Congress in 1990 for approval the following year (Becerra Ramírez 2009, 79; Paine and Santoro 1992, 13).

Mexico's new patent law exhibits over-compliance on virtually all dimensions, not only pre-dating TRIPS by a number of years but exceeding the standards that would be agreed in the Uruguay Round. Patenting of pharmaceutical products, which had been programmed to start in 1997, was introduced immediately, in 1991. Pharmaceutical patents would also be allowed retroactively, in that the LFPPI included a pipeline provision to offer recognition of patents already granted, and applications already filed, outside of Mexico.[8] The exceptionally permissive conditions for receiving pipeline protection underscore the extreme aspects of Mexico's new pharmaceutical patent system: patents would eligible so long as the associated products had not been put on the market in Mexico itself. This means that Mexico would allow drugs that had already been launched in other countries to become patented—and thus controlled by a single supplier—in Mexico, in contrast to limiting this form of retroactive protection to drugs yet to be marketed

---

[7] For additional illustrations of the Executive's new orientation, see Mexico's Secretary of Trade and Industry, Jaime Serra Puche, exclaiming the virtues of the proposed law in a speech at Glaxo's Mexico subsidiary ("Protegerá México la propiedad industrial para darle alicientes: Serra," *El Economista*, March 6, 1991), and "México podría tener el mejor marco legal para propiedad intelectual," *El Economista*, May 6, 1991).

[8] Note that in the absence of any transition period, there was no need for a "mailbox" to receive applications.

anywhere (i.e. genuinely in the originator firm's product pipeline). The LFPPI also stipulated that pipeline patents would expire in Mexico at the same time as they expire in the first country of application, and that in no case could the period of patent protection exceed twenty years. However, the twenty-year maximum period is counted from the date of filing in Mexico, which for pipeline patents will, by definition, be later than the original international filing date. This means that any extensions of patent terms given in the original filing country would be adopted in Mexico, without risk of bumping into the twenty-year maximum.[9] Mexico's compulsory licensing provisions were transformed too, with the LFPPI explicitly defining "local working" to include importation. As regards compulsory licensing for public use, the new law's provisions established a series of steps and conditions that would need to be met, and thus did not provide health officials with a useful tool to bargain with patent-holders for lower prices (Correa 2000a; Oliveira et al. 2004). Finally, to note, the new law called for the establishment of an autonomous patent office, what would become the Mexican Institute for Industrial Property (*Instituto Mexicano de Propiedad Industrial*, IMPI).[10]

To repeat, the key question in this period is not if countries introduced pharmaceutical patent systems, but how. Mexico's early and extreme response to the global sea change would have enduring effects on pharmaceutical politics. The remainder of this chapter examines how this outcome came about.

LIBERALIZATION, NAFTA, AND PHARMACEUTICAL PATENTS

The main advocates of over-compliance in Mexico, as elsewhere, were transnational pharmaceutical firms and the IP law community, represented locally by the Mexican Pharmaceutical Industry Association (*Asociación Mexicana de la Industria Farmacéutica*, AMIF)[11] and the Mexican Intellectual Property Association (*Asociación Mexicana para la Protección de la Propiedad Intelectual*, AMPPI), respectively. Both associations had reacted

---

[9] NAFTA introduces further ambiguity here, for the provision that requires pipeline protection does not include the wording that limits the period of protection to a maximum of twenty years (Becerra Ramírez 2009, 78).

[10] For more detailed overviews of Mexico's new patent system, see Becerra Ramírez (2009; 2013), Correa (2000a), Jalife Daher (2009), Pemberton and Soni (1992), Rowat (1993), Villareal Gonda (1991). In 1994 the patent law was revised, mostly to comply with NAFTA. These revisions also addressed the governance of IMPI.

[11] In 1994 AMIF would insert the word "research" into its title, thus changing from AMIF to AMIIF (*Asociación Mexicana de Industrias de Investigación Farmacéutica*). This change paralleled that of the PMA, which became PhRMA.

with profound disappointment to the 1987 LIM reform and, once it became clear that a change of direction was in the works, both worked closely with Executive officials and PRI legislators in the design and subsequent passage of the new patent law. AMIF demanded the immediate patentability of pharmaceutical products, eliminating the LIM's transition period, and, of course, a pipeline option to secure exclusivity for recently-launched and soon-to-be-launched drugs that could not yet, at the time, be patented in Mexico. AMIF also requested that the compulsory licensing system rules be made significantly more restrictive, to make the possibility of deployment much less likely. Only in a very restricted set of conditions would Mexico be authorized to issue a compulsory license, for example, and AMIF demanded that importation explicitly constitute "working," to avoid the situation of having to produce patented pharmo-chemicals locally in order to retain exclusivity in the Mexican market (AMIF 1990). AMIF mobilized its members and allies to help draft the initiative that Salinas proposed in 1990 and also to work with officials from the Executive and Congress to secure amendments to the final LFPPI.

Neither the transnational sector's preferences nor its strategy of political mobilization were unique to Mexico. What transnational pharmaceutical firms wanted in Mexico and how AMIF tried to secure what its members wanted in Mexico were nearly identical to what we witness in other countries. Yet in Mexico transnational pharmaceutical firms were exceptionally successful, on account of factors both internal and external to the sector.

The transnational sector was fighting from a position of strength. Over the course of the postwar period, foreign firms had become increasingly dominant in the Mexican pharmaceutical industry: by the 1980s they accounted for forty-six of the leading fifty pharmaceutical firms operating in Mexico (ALADI 1985; Brodovsky 1997), including all of the top ten, and roughly three-quarters of sales in the private retail market (Gruner Kronhein 1991, 183, Table 5.1; USITC 1990, 4–8, note 50).[12] Although the promotion of a national pharmaceutical sector had been a development objective from the 1960s onwards, the transnational sector's economic and political dominance grew nonetheless, and Mexican firms were not in a position to present strong resistance to the advocates of over-compliance in the early 1990s.[13]

In discussing the political economy of Mexico's pharmaceutical industry, distinguishing between upstream pharmo-chemical and downstream

[12] ALADI (1985) reports four Mexican firms in the top fifty and one in the top twenty, with the largest at 18th position; Katz (1997a, 61–2), based on 1987 data, notes that the top two Mexican firms were ranked 15th and 17th.

[13] Analyses of Mexican pharmaceutical policies and development in the sector include Brodovsky (1997), Gasman (1995; 2008), Gereffi (1978; 1983), González Pier (2008), Gruner Kronhein (1991), Hayden (2008), Laveaga (2009), Salomón (1997), Wionczek (1983), Zúñiga and Combe (2002).

pharmaceutical (drug) producers is important, for these two sectors bene-fited from different types of promotional measures, and experienced different fates in the 1980s. Measures to support pharmo-chemical firms, such as import protection, direct subsidies, and tax incentives, had succeeded in creating a local sector with increasing capabilities in the production of active pharmaceutical ingredients (APIs). In 1960 the API sector consisted of about ten firms, mostly in steroids.[14] By the late 1980s, ninety firms, of which more than 70 percent were Mexican-owned, produced over three hundred different types of APIs and supplied roughly 60 percent of the market (Brodovsky 1997, 173).[15] Yet the pharmo-chemical sector was subject to extensive trade liberalization in the late 1980s. Though pharmo-chemical producers were not immediately exposed to international competition following the first moves toward trade liberalization in 1985 (Ten Kate 1992), they soon would be. In 1988 licensing requirements were removed from most types of pharmo-chemical imports and tariffs were reduced (Salomón 1997; Secretaría de Salud 2005, 33–5; USITC 1990). Roughly half of Mexico's pharmo-chemical firms disappeared after liberalization, many of them selling their assets to foreign firms (Brodovsky 1997; CEPAL 1999; Gonsen and Jasso 2000).[16] The dismantling of the pharmo-chemical sector was essentially a pre-emptive strike. According to the director of a national firm and former President of the National Association of Drug Manufacturers (*Asociación Nacional de Fabricantes de Medicamentos*, ANAFAM), the dramatic changes that firms were experiencing, with even the most successful struggling for survival, stripped Mexico's pharmo-chemical sector of the economic and political resources to mount a challenge against the AMIF-inspired project for pharmaceutical patents (Interview, August 21, 2007).

With regard to firms producing final drugs, the key promotional instrument throughout the post-war period had been discriminatory government pur-chasing practices (Brodovsky 1997; Gasman 1995; Gruner Kronhein 1991). Mexico had two principle forms of health coverage for formal sector workers, the Mexican Institute for Social Security and the Institute for Security and Social Services for State Employees, for private and public sector employees, respectively (Dion 2010; Ward 1986). Both offered broad coverage, including drugs, and both secured their pharmaceutical products disproportionately from Mexican firms. By 1987 Mexican firms accounted for 70 percent of

---

[14] The Mexican pharmaceutical industry's historic base in steroid production is related to a key plant for steroid synthesis (barbasco) being native to southern Mexico (Gereffi 1978; Laveaga 2009).

[15] Gruner Kronheim (1991, 184) also notes the growing technological development of the sector. CEPAL's (1987) analysis of pharmo-chemical industries in Latin America indicates that backwards integration progressed furthest in Mexico, and likewise Katz's (1997b, 68) estimate that roughly 40 percent of pharmo-chemical inputs were sourced locally in Mexico is signifi-cantly higher than the 25 percent estimates reported for Argentina and Brazil.

[16] Brodovsky (1997) provides details on Mexican companies that closed or were absorbed by foreign firms.

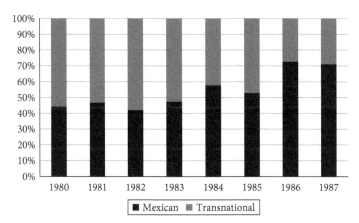

Figure 4.1. Drug Purchases by Mexican Public Sector, 1980–87 (shares)

Note: Transnational includes importation.

Source: CANIFARMA (1988, 19)

public sector purchases (Figure 4.1). Whereas subsidiaries of foreign firms retained overwhelming shares of private markets, both in pharmacies and through private insurance, local firms dominated sales to the state. This segmentation is captured in the comparative data on sales presented in Chapter 2 (Table 2.3, p. 47) as well, where we see the leading position of transnational firms.

Although preferential purchasing practices meant that liberalization was less of a shock for drug producers than for pharmo-chemical firms, the focus on providing medicines to the public sector had multiple consequences. Because state purchasers demanded low prices, Mexican firms selling drugs to public healthcare providers benefited from small margins and thus were not major players in the local economy.[17] And because selling to the state meant that they needed to invest less in distribution, commercialization, and marketing, Mexican firms benefited less from forward linkages. They never cultivated networks of allies in the production-distribution-retail chain that they could rely on politically, as their counterparts did in Argentina. Dependence on public sector purchasing practices also affected the local sector's political strategy, in that the state-centric orientation made government purchasing regulations exceptionally important.

In this regard, the NAFTA negotiations, which put government purchasing on the table too, along with IP, are of paramount significance. By bundling together multiple issues that would affect the pharmaceutical sector, negotiations reoriented the local sector's political strategy. Mexican pharmaceutical

---

[17] This demand for low prices also contributed to the segmentation described in the text, as it dampened many foreign firms' interest in selling to the state sector at this time.

firms had two concerns in this period, retaining the 1997 transition period for the introduction of product patents, and retaining favorable government procurement practices. In ordinary debates over IP, only the first of these would be subject to contestation. In Mexico, however, because of the bundling of the LFPPI and NAFTA, pharmaceutical firms would have to engage with both issues, and they were obsessed with retaining favorable government procurement practices.[18] A long-standing participant in both ANAFAM and the National Chamber of the Pharmaceutical Industry (*Cámara Nacional de la Industria Farmacéutica*, CANIFARMA) with years of experience in the pharmaceutical industry recalled a meeting organized by SECOFI, in which the Salinas Government brought together national firms and essentially promised to preserve its favorable government purchasing practices if the local industry would not make a fuss about the introduction of pharmaceutical patents. According to this informant, in a follow-up exchange to an interview in Mexico City (Interview, March 30, 2010), "the SECOFI official said (more or less), you have two things to your advantage, government procurement rules and the absence of pharmaceutical product patents, and you'll have to give up one."[19] Faced with such options, the local sector's representatives acquiesced to the immediate introduction of product patents. In the informant's words, ANAFAM and CANIFARMA "decided to accept patents in exchange for retaining preferences in public sector purchases." Whether or not this was really a decision that local firms made or one that was made for them is another issue; Mexican firms could not have blocked the introduction of pharmaceutical patents, but mobilizing resistance around patents might have altered when and how this happened. By reorienting local firms' preferences and political strategies, NAFTA made Mexico's defensive coalition weaker, and its resistance less firm, than it otherwise would have been.[20]

Nor did Mexico's pharmaceutical producers benefit from allies in civil society that might have pushed back against over-compliance. Although the 1980s and early 1990s was a period of increasing popular mobilization (Bruhn 1997b; Foweraker 1990), the complex of patents, phamarmaceutical industries, access to drugs, and public health never became one of the concerns.

---

[18] For a statement of the local sector's position, with ANAFAM emphasizing the importance of retaining favorable government purchasing arrangements, see "Deben excluir del TLC las compras de medicamentos del sector público: ANFM," *El Economista*, April 3, 1991. Robert (2000) and Swift (2006) also emphasize the attention that Mexico's pharmaceutical firms placed on this issue.

[19] Email, January 14, 2011.The informant has worked in management in a Mexican pharmaceutical firm since the late 1980s, and throughout this time participated in both ANAFAM and CANIFARMA.

[20] As it turns out, Mexican firms were unable to exclude pharmaceuticals entirely from the government procurement provisions in NAFTA, instead securing an eight-year transition period (Robert 2000; Swift 2006). Not surprisingly, the informant from the local sector quoted in the text went on to lament that local firms "ended up losing on both fronts."

Even as the the NAFTA debate triggered an unprecedented degree of societal mobilization on Mexico's trade and foreign policies, patents were not on the radar screen. Civil society and non-governmental organizations were consumed by other aspects of the trade agreement and changing economic policy environment, as well as other policies being introduced during the Salinas presidency that were not part of NAFTA (e.g. revisions of the *ejido* system). Documents and reports of the coordinating group, Mexican Action Network on Free Trade (*Red Mexicana de Acción Frente al Libre Comercio*, RMALC), made no reference to the LFPPI; similarly, intereviews with RMALC leaders also revealed lack of awareness of, or interest in, the issue.[21]

COMPLETING THE ROUT: NAFTA, BUSINESS POLITICS, AND THE EXPANSIVE COALITION FOR OVER-COMPLIANCE

The NAFTA context also helped the transnational sector further its political advantages. By making negotiation of the trade agreement conditional on changes to Mexico's IP system, not only did the US make Mexican policy-makers intensely pro-IP, but, importantly, this linkage facilitated the entry of new actors into the coalition. As indicated, NAFTA offered to convert discretionary and removable preferences granted unilaterally into stable preferences delivered via a reciprocal agreement. The promise of stable, preferential market access allowed the actors at core of the coalition for the early and retroactive introduction of pharmaceutical patents (state officials, transnational pharmaceutical firms, and IP lawyers) to cultivate allies from throughout the Mexican political economy, particularly non-traditional exporters and firms linked to this growing sector.

Data on Mexico's trade structure help understand these patterns of mobilization. Figure 4.2 presents data on Mexico's exports to the US, from 1985 to 2000. Overall dependence on the US market was exceptionally high, and continued as such through the period. Levels of political trade dependence (PTD) were high too, prior to NAFTA. In the late 1980s Mexico's PTD relative to the US rose astronomically, and even after falling in the early 1990s (on account of increased petroleum exports and also more export diversification in anticipation of NAFTA), at over 10 percent this share remained comparatively high.

---

[21] Nor, for example, are these issues covered in Wise et al.'s (2003) book on social mobilization in Mexico.

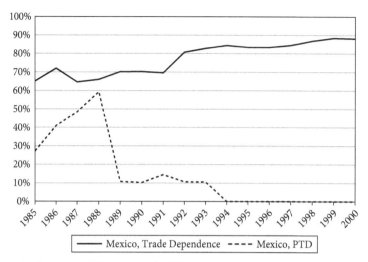

Figure 4.2. Structure of Exports to the US: Mexico

Note: Data on preferential exports to the US are from the United States International Trade Commission; data on overall exports to the US and global exports are from UN-COMTRADE.

Exports under removable preference schemes expose countries to the threats of trade sanctions, as the benefits derived from these sorts of preferences depend on the discretion of the importing country. Mexico's PTD was high during the revisions of the LIM too (in fact, higher), but at that time exporters' ability to continue enjoying preferences was not being conditioned explicitly on the country's IP policies. Once this link was made in the late 1980s, exporters became readily available for participation in the coalition for over-compliance, and the promise to lock preferences in with a bilateral trade agreement accentuated this effect substantially.

As exporters came to regard the treatment of pharmaceutical patents as a linchpin for their continued access to the US market, key organizations such as the National Association of Importers and Exporters (*Asociación Nacional de Importadores y Exportadores de la República Méxicana*, ANIERM) and Mexican Business Council for Foreign Affairs (*Consejo Empresarial Mexicano para Asuntos Internacionales*, CEMAI) became enthusiastic advocates of over-compliance. Again, these organizations and the firms they represent did not have direct interests in IP, but had indirect interests in that they stood to gain from a change to the patent law that satisfied the US's demands, i.e. they were "activated agnostics." Rapid passage of the LFPPI was something that needed to happen to retain—indeed, improve—preferential access to the US market, and they actively pushed for it. Exporters and their representatives in associations linked to the export sector thus visibly and

actively campaigned for over-compliance, emphasizing both the dire consequences Mexico would suffer if a satisfactory patent law were not approved, and
the benefits that would accrue if Mexico were to meet the US's demands.[22] In
sum, with NAFTA conditioned on a new patent law that introduced pharmaceutical patents immediately and retroactively, dependence on removable
preferences made exporters in Mexico available for mobilization in favor of
this outcome.

The NAFTA process also provoked a reorganization of government-
business relations, a process that further assisted the efforts of the transnational pharmaceutical sector and local IP lawyers to broaden the coalition
in support of over-compliance. Negotiations for the trade agreement provided the stimulus for exporters to commandeer the system of business
representation in Mexico. A new body, the Coordinator of Foreign Trade
Business Organizations (*Coordinadora de Organismos Empresariales de
Comercio Exterior*, COECE), formed in 1990, functioned as the principal
representative and interlocutor on trade and "trade-related" policy issues in
this period (Arriola 1994; Puga 1993; Thacker 2000). COECE's prominent
position in business politics broadened, de facto, the coalition for over-
compliance. The peak business organization representing large Mexican
firms, the Business Coordinating Council (*Consejo Coordinador Empresarial*,
CCE), also provided enthusiastic and active support for the new patent law.
As previous analyses of this period have observed, the new structure of
business representation that emerged at the start of the 1990s stifled dissenting voices and gave the Mexican private sector a united front to work with
the government in ushering in key economic policy changes (Fairbrother
2007; Schneider 2004; Shadlen 2004a). With pursuing exporters' objective of
securing the trilateral trade agreement as its highest priority, and with over-
compliance in how Mexico introduced pharmaceutical patents a prerequisite
for the trade agreement, COECE and the CCE served as reliable allies of
the LFPPI's principal advocates. Here again, these leading organizations in
the Mexican business community did not proactively seek a new patent
regime that immediately introduced pharmaceutical patents and did so
with generous pipeline provisions and weak compulsory licensing provisions,
for example, virtually no one in the Mexican business community set out
unprovoked to reverse the policy choices made just a few years earlier
regarding pharmaceutical patents, but key actors came to regard doing so
as an obvious step and a price worth paying to obtain what they really
wanted—NAFTA.

---

[22] For one newspaper account of such an event, a seminar organized by the American
Chamber of Commerce in Mexico City, see "Estados Unidos puede usar el garrotte," *El
Financiero*, June 14, 1991.

MOBILIZATION, COALITIONS, AND PATENT POLITICS

The conditions analyzed in the previous sections—an enthusiastic Executive committed to over-compliance, a weak defensive coalition made yet weaker and stripped of the will to fight about patents by the NAFTA context, and a dominant transnational pharmaceutical sector benefitting from widespread support throughout the business sector—all combined to make for an exceptionally uneventful legislative process. In six months, with hardly any substantive debate, Salinas's proposal was passed in virtually unaltered form. Though the Senate received Salinas's initiative in December, it did not act on the law until May, when it was discussed and voted on in part of a single day's ordinary business. The law received similarly pro-forma treatment in the Chamber of Deputies in June.

Remarkably little attention was paid to a subject that, in other countries, consumed legislatures for years. As one observer puts it, the new patent law was "rushed through an ignorant Congress" (Nadal 1995, 135). Those supporting Salinas's proposal not infrequently repeated the Executive's lines: texts of statements made on the floor of the Senate and Chamber of Deputies show remarkable similarities to the texts of statements made by government officials; in one instance *La Jornada* reports the President of the Senate's Trade Commission reading a SECOFI press release, on how the LFPPI will increase national competitiveness, on the floor of the Senate, as if it were his own speech.[23]

Nor, importantly, did the few legislators voicing any opposition have much to say about the substance of patent policy, rather they focused on the legislative process or expressed broader and more abstract concerns regarding globalization and imperialism. Some deputies, for example, opposed the "ultra-rapid, supersonic" process for getting the law through, and requested that the vote be delayed to have more consultations, which is of course what happened in other countries, but these demands were ignored. In contrast to the LIM reform of 1986–87, where PRI legislators demonstrated divisions on substantive issues, in 1991 opposition—as it were—came almost exclusively from the newly formed Party of the Democratic Revolution (*Partido de la Revolución Democrática*, PRD), a center-left party founded in the late 1980s by a mix of PRI dissidents and smaller leftist parties (Bruhn 1997a). But even the PRD's criticisms remained extremely broad, about the perils of IP harmonization and the need for the state to continue to play a role in technology transfer, not about particular patent policy measures or what any of this might mean for the pharmaceutical sector or health. Legislatures in other countries fiercely debated the details of when pharmaceutical patents should be introduced and whether to make patent protection retroactive, and what the

---

[23] "Aprobó el Senado la Ley" *La Jornada*, 17 May 1991.

grounds should be for compulsory licenses, and other provisions. In Mexico, the LFPPI was passed with hardly any attention whatsoever paid to such issues.

In the rare instances where substantive dimensions did receive attention, the process is also revealing about the state of political mobilization. Local pharmaceutical firms expressed concerns regarding changes to the compulsory licensing provisions, specifically the Salinas proposal's explicit statement that importation would satisfy the local working requirement. As discussed in Chapter 2, new international rules that would come in the mid-1990s with the launch of the World Trade Organization would be ambiguous on this point, and so too was the draft of the TRIPS Agreement that was current as of this time (and NAFTA negotiations had not yet begun[24]), so such an explicit statement as included in Salinas's proposal went far beyond Mexico's international obligations. Representatives of the Mexican pharmaceutical sector expressed concern that this provision would reduce incentives for local production, production that could, in turn, facilitate spillovers to local industry.[25] At one point ANAFAM referred to this as a "fatal blow" and requested in the press that the language be tempered, but the request was ignored by the Senate, which approved Salinas's proposal.[26] Then, in the Chamber of Deputies, the provisions dealing with compulsory licensing and local working were altered in the other direction, to provide patent owners with yet stronger rights of exclusion. The original version, as passed by the Senate, indicated that failure to work a patent within three years of grant could be grounds for a compulsory license, except when SECOFI judged that non-working was justified. According to the President of the commission responsible for the legislation in the Chamber of Deputies, the Commission on Patrimony and Industrial Development, the "Mexican Pharmochemical Association" contacted him the night before and requested that the wording of the article be changed to remove discretion from SECOFI, and instead allow the patent holder to make the case that failure to work the patent locally was economically justified (Cámara de Diputados 1991, 41). This amendment was approved, with no discussion and only a single objection, from a PRD deputy who accused the PRI of denuding SECOFI's ability to act in the public interest (Cámara de Diputados 1991, 54).[27] The fact that, on the day of the Chamber of Deputy's vote, the head of the Commission in charge of the legislation would explain, on the record to the full House, that the previous night he was

---

[24] The wording in NAFTA would be the same as in TRIPS.

[25] "Latente el fortalecimento de los monopolios de empresas farmacéuticas estadounidenses: ANFM," *El Economista*, April 8, 1991; "Inquietud por la próxima Ley de Fomento y Protección de la Propiedad Intelectual," May 14, 1991.

[26] "Se resentirán a largo plazo los efectos de la nueva Ley de Fomento y Protección a la Propiedad Industrial," *El Economista*, May 20, 1991.

[27] This last-minute change is the one substantive provision criticized by the PRD in these hearings.

contacted by a group—one with an intense interest in the outcome—requesting a revision, and that therefore he was making the revision (as if someone had pointed out a typographical error), and that this would proceed unopposed and almost without comment, speaks to the state of the legislative process.[28]

The point of this anecdote is not simply that it reinforces what we already know about the state of Mexican legislative politics in 1991, but rather it serves as an illustration of the asymmetrical mobilization by opponents and supporters of the LFPPI. Congressional "ignorance," and more generally the lack of attention that the introduction of pharmaceutical patents received in Mexico's legislature, reflected social structure and the nature of social coalitions. Intellectual property is an extremely technical area, not one where we would expect legislators to have expertise and competence. Senators and Deputies rely on information they receive from social actors. This was particularly the case with Mexico at this time, when legislators worked with thinly staffed committees and had minimal budgets to hire researchers and consultants. The local pharmaceutical sector failed to mobilize and supply potential legislative allies with means to respond to the lobbying of the transnational sector. Deputies and Senators from the governing PRI came armed with arguments in favor of the LFPPI, fed by the law's supporters in the private sector (industry and law) and the Executive. The PRD, in contrast, opposed the Salinas Government's economic policies in general but had little to say on the details of IP, and even less on the issue of pharmaceutical patents. PRD legislators knew that they did not like the LFPPI, but they do not seem to have known why they did not like the LFPPI, beyond the fact that it was proposed by Salinas and associated with a broader package of policies that they disliked. That the PRD could not block the LFPPI is not surprising, but that they so rarely articulated subtstantive criticisms of relevant aspects of the law is an indication of how thin—and demobilized—were the societal actors that did oppose. The NAFTA context altered the local pharmaceutical sector's priorities and reoriented its political strategy, and the subsequent lack of mobilization on patents left legislative opponents undernourished and thus contributed to the congressional debate being substance-free. Indeed, the only substantive change made to Salinas's proposal *increased* the strength of protection made available to pharmaceutical patent-holders.[29]

---

[28] For what it's worth, the "Mexican Pharmochemical Association" cited by the President of the Commission appears to be a phantom organization. In none of the interviews I conducted was anyone able to tell me what this organization was. Nor does the association appear in the press coverage of this period. The likely conclusion is, simply, that head of the Commission recorded the name incorrectly, that he made an error and was referring to AMIF, the transnational sector's trade body.

[29] This was recognized—indeed applauded—by observers too: "Nueva Ley de propiedad industrial para el TLC," *El Economista*, June 19, 1991.

CONCLUSION

In many countries the introduction of pharmceutical patents was highly polarized, protracted, and conflictual. In Mexico it was not. In December 1990, President Salinas sent a draft of a new patent law to Congress and by July of the next year this was the law of the land. Mexico introduced pharmaceutical patents immediately, with a generously designed pipeline provision to protect inventions that pre-dated the law and were associated with drugs yet to be launched in Mexico, and with strong rights of exclusion for patent owners. This is not just over-compliance, but early and extreme over-compliance. Appreciating this, the US Government touted Mexico's approach to pharmaceutical patents as a model to be emulated, and USTR Carla Hills personally distributed copies of Mexico's LFPPI on an August 1991 trip through Latin America (Marques 1993, 74).

Mexico stands out not just for the outcome, but the process. In contrast to the protracted period of congressional deliberation and Executive–Legislative conflict that marked passage of new patent laws in Argentina (and, as we shall see, Brazil), the passage of the LFPPI in Mexico was quick and simple. The legislative process endured six months in total, but, in effect, just six weeks: the Senate received the initiative in December but did nothing until May, when it was dispensed with quickly, and then approved with similarly little attention to detail by the Chamber of Deputies. Neither body of Congress had public hearings. The Chamber of Deputies' Commission on Patrimony and Industrial Development met three times with SECOFI officials and twice with private sector groups (Cámara de Diputados 1991), but no public records were made of these meetings (or if they were, the records were lost). The Commission evidently received roughly seventy written submissions on all aspects of the law (including trademarks), though these are also unavailable.[30] In comparative perspective, the vacuum in institutional and historical memory is telling, for the same events were recorded in abundance in other countries, and recollections of similarly placed informants remain vivid.

It was not just the Mexican legislature that paid little attention to the issue; the media did not either. With the help of a research assistant in Mexico I conducted a search of media coverage of the LFPPI from December 1990 through the end of 1991. While NAFTA received abundant coverage, attention to the patent law itself was almost non-existent. Neither of two major political magazines (the monthly *Nexos* nor the weekly *Proceso*) reported on the LFPPI, nor did Mexico's most visible business magazine (the biweekly

---

[30] According to the former Deputy who was Secretary on the Commission responsible for the new law, most of the submissions regarding patents came from international pharmaceutical firms and their lawyers (Interview, March 23, 2010).

Expansión). The sparse newspaper coverage included a handful of stories in *El Economista, El Financiero, El Universal, Excelsior,* and *La Jornada.*[31] What coverage the press did provide was remarkably superficial. Sometimes newspapers simply repackaged the government's press releases. Two of the articles in *El Economista,* for example, are little more than reprinted versions of SECOFI documents and press releases.[32] The day after the Senate approved the LFPPI in May 1991, *El Economista*'s front-page headline noted this, but the article that followed was split between reporting this event and reporting that the Senate also voted to allow a PRI Senator to be seconded to the Supreme Court.[33] In other words, the Senate's passage of the LFPPI was covered in a single article which was really a report on the day's activities in Congress. And while the headline referred to "20 modifications" made by the Senate, nowhere in the text of the article does the newspaper provide information on which aspects of the President's proposal had been modified.[34]

To explain both the extreme outcome and the substance-free debates that produced this outcome, this chapter has focused on the interaction between the country's social structure and the political context created by NAFTA. The promise of NAFTA converted Mexico's Executive, which had just a few years earlier warded off pressures for extensive IP reform, into an enthusiastic supporter of over-compliance in the area of pharmaceutical patents. The Salinas Government's obsession with securing NAFTA fed its commitment not just to a new patent law, but to rapid passage of this particular version of a new patent law.

In addition to altering Executive preferences, the NAFTA process shaped coalitions, in decidedly asymmetric ways. On the one hand, the bundling of policies on patents and policies on government purchasing re-oriented both the interests and political strategies of local pharmaceutical firms. As a result, by the time the new patent law was being considered in 1991, Mexico's defensive coalition consisted of a weakened pharmo-chemical sector undergoing dramatic transformation on account of liberalization, and a final drugs sector that was compelled to care more about preservation of favorable government purchasing arrangements than patents. An already-weak defensive coalition was made weaker and sapped of the will to fight. On the other hand, the promise of NAFTA converted exporters into fervent IP enthusiasts and prompted a fundamental restructuring of business politics

---

[31] The newspaper *Reforma* did not yet exist at this time.

[32] "México podría tener el mejor marco legal para propiedad intelectual," *El Economista,* May 6, 1991; "Facilitará competitividad y seguridad a los negocios e inventores mexicanos," *El Economista,* May 17, 1991. The circuit of the latter is particularly impressive: SECOFI wrote it, the press reported it as news, and, as we have seen, a Senator used the report as a speech!

[33] "Con 20 modificaciones el Senado aprobó la Ley de Fomento y Protección de la Propiedad Industrial," *El Economista,* May 17, 1991.

[34] Haggart (2014, 211) similarly notes that Mexico's 1997 copyright law, offering enhanced rights of exclusion to content owners, also passed with minimal debate and little public notice.

that marginalized dissenting voices. Not only did the coalition for over-compliance thus feature a dominant transnational pharmaceutical sector, but it also was able to mobilize the most important actors in Mexico's business community on behalf of the cause.

These coalitional dynamics, in particular the absence of any serious internal resistance to the crusade for over-compliance, were consequential for when and how pharmaceutical patents were introduced in Mexico. Even powerful Executives need to bargain when confronted with opposition. Yet the lack of opposition meant that the Executive had to concede little to secure the outcome it wanted. Taking a step back, one could imagine internal mobilization against aspects of the proposed LFPPI having encouraged Mexico's negotiators to bargain more externally, citing domestic opposition to make some concessions seem to be more of a sacrifice. That is, domestic resistance could have encouraged the Executive to hold back on some changes, using further IP concessions as bargaining chips to obtain other benefits. In the logic of a simple two-level game (Putnam 1988), Mexican negotiators would be using external pressures to push through domestic changes and also using domestic resistance to secure other goals externally. Yet there is little evidence of this either. To the contrary, when the Senate did not act on the bill in the legislative session immediately upon receiving the Executive's proposal, in April 1991, on the eve of the following legislative session, President Salinas called the heads of the two legislative bodies to *Los Pinos* to secure assurance that passing the new patent law would be prioritized in both house's agendas.[35] Some observers speculated at the time that Salinas might use the Legislature's delay as a bargaining chip with the US.[36] This could and might have happened, if there was any opposition to the LFPPI—but there was not. Congress simply had a cluttered agenda and, until receiving signals from the Executive, did not fully appreciate the urgency. Once the stakes were made clear, the Legislature then proceeded to rubber stamp the Executive's proposal.

Mexico's early and extreme over-compliance provides the point of departure for the subsequent analysis of patent politics in Mexico in Chapter 7. By the early 2000s Mexico would have had pharmaceutical patents for a decade, and local firms no longer would benefit from preferential government purchasing either. The way Mexico introduced patents would have profound effects on pharmaceutical markets and industrial structure. The abilities of subsequent reform-minded politicians to build coalitions to address the emerging sets of challenges would be constrained by the policy choices of the early 1990s.

---

[35] "A Debate Parlamentario, la Nueva Ley Sobre Propiedad Industrial," *El Financiero*, April 4, 1991.
[36] "Negociará México el proyecto de Propiedad Industrial en las pláticas de junio con EUA y Canadá," *El Economista*, March 7, 1991.

5

Coalitional Clash, Export Mobilization, and Executive Agency

From Reluctant Acquiescence to Enthusiastic Over-Compliance in Brazil

On May 1, 1991, the Government of President Collor introduced its draft patent law into Congress. Unfortunately the law is seriously flawed and falls short of the commitment made by the Brazilian Government to introduce an adequate patent law in exchange for the elimination of U.S. trade sanctions.

(PMA 1992)

This new industrial property law represents a complete turnabout of the thinking in Brazil, which can be attributed to strong forward-looking leadership by President Cardoso and many in the Brazilian Congress, as well as tireless advocacy for enhanced protections on the part of many others who remain nameless here.

(PhRMA 1997)

Brazil's patent policies underwent complete transformation in the 1990s. Brazil had spearheaded developing countries' efforts to block the inclusion of intellectual property in the Uruguay Round negotiations and, failing on that front, negotiated actively to produce a final agreement that preserved developing countries' policy options. Brazil fought to make sure that, were the TRIPS Agreement to make the introduction of pharmaceutical patenting obligatory, countries would have transition periods to meet this requirement, would not be expected to offer protection retroactively to older inventions, and, more generally, that measures to balance the rights of knowledge users with knowledge owners would remain available.[1] In the

---

[1] The immense literature on Brazil's international leadership in global debates over IP includes Barbosa (2004; 2013), Deere (2008), Matthews (2002), Sell (1998), Watal (2001; 2011), Yu (2009).

course of implementing TRIPS locally, however, Brazil's reaction was over-compliance: the new Industrial Property Law (*Lei de Propriedade Industrial*, LPI), passed in 1996 after five years of extensive debate in Congress, failed to take advantage of the same policy options that the country had fought for in the multilateral arena. Most importantly, the LPI offered protection, via pipeline patents, to earlier inventions that pre-dated TRIPS.

Analyses of Brazil's path from resistance to enthusiastic embrace of the global sea change have tended to focus on the role of external pressures and the ideology of Fernando Henrique Cardoso, who was the key official in the Executive from 1993–95 and then President from 1995–2003.[2] Brazil was indeed subject to considerable external pressures, including trade sanctions in the late 1980s and constant threats of more penalties to be imposed throughout the period in which the new patent law was being debated. And by the mid-1990s the Brazilian Executive, after initially resisting, had adopted the position that over-compliance was in the country's interest too. Yet comparative analysis suggests that external pressures and Cardoso's enthusiasm for over-compliance, both unmistakeable features of this case, fail to account for the outcome. Argentina also came under considerable pressure and that country's leadership was similarly committed to over-compliance, but the outcomes in these two countries differed in substantially important ways. A key difference between the two countries was the extent to which coalitions for over-compliance were able to benefit from the support of exporters. Brazil's trade structure was such that threats of diminished market access were significantly more alarming and politically significant.

While over-compliance distinguishes Brazil from Argentina, the timing of this outcome sets Brazil apart from Mexico. Pharmaceutical patents were not introduced in Brazil until rather late in the 1990s. Of course, TRIPS allowed Brazil, as a developing country adopting pharmaceutical patenting, to wait until 2005, so there is no denying that this constitutes a sacrifice of much of the available transition period. But the fact that drug patents were not available for six years after the change was proposed is an important characteristic of the case, one that would turn out to have great significance too. The enduring resistance put forward by a surprisingly strong defensive coalition explains this dimension of the outcome. The conflict over the introduction of pharmaceutical patents in Brazil was part of a much larger conflict over questions

---

[2] Examples include Benjamin (1996), Caliari et al. (2013), Deere (2008), Harrison (2004), Flynn (2011; 2013; 2015), Nunn (2009), Sweet (2013). According to the preface to a four-hundred page publication proposing a revision of Brazil's patent law, the LPI "was drafted in English, under strong trade pressures from the US" (Centro de Estudos e Debates Estratégicos 2013, 19).

related to patents on biotechnology and the implications of a new patent system for the environment, biodiversity, and genetic resources.[3] The broad mobilization sparked by these issues provided allies for Brazil's pharmaceutical firms. Though the defensive coalition did not prevail in the final stages, its efforts meant that Brazil's over-compliant pharmaceutical patent regime came into effect years later than it otherwise might have—and much later than what we witnessed in Mexico.

In contrast to the first two cases where the key social structure conditions reinforced each other, with a robust defensive coalition complemented by a flaccid response by exporters to external pressures in Argentina and a tepid defensive coalition complemented by exporters' aggressive mobilization in Mexico, Brazil featured intensely committed and mobilized coalitions for and against over-compliance. This coalitional clash provided more opportunities for the Executive to shape the outcome, which it was able to do by exploiting exporters' palpable fears of trade sanctions. Ultimately, the Cardoso Government was able to secure the outcome it desired because Brazil's social structure enabled Executive agency.

This chapter has five sections. The first section examines the conflict between the US and Brazil over patents, leading to President Collor's proposal in April 1991, and the ensuing legislative process that, ultimately, produced the 1996 LPI. The second section places Brazilian over-compliance in comparative perspective, showing the trajectory of key provisions in the new patent law. The third section examines the cores of the rival coalitions in Brazil, focusing primarily on the preferences, capabilities, and strategies of the transnational and national pharmaceutical sectors. Though the interests of these two segments of industry were similar as observed elsewhere, both actors' political strategies and patterns of mobilization were shaped by distinct characteristics of the political process in Brazil. The fourth section examines the broad social mobilization in Brazil that was sparked by the potential introduction of patents in biotechnology. Pharmaceutical firms were able to integrate into this movement, and doing so helped this otherwise weak actor have more influence than we might otherwise expect. The fifth section shows how external pressures allowed the Executive to build a strong coalition in favor of over-compliance by using the country's vulnerability to trade sanctions to mobilize exporters in support of over-compliance.

---

[3] Alencar and Ree (1996), Assumpção (2001), Cavalcanti (1988), Carvalho et al. (1995), and Marques (1993), focus on these dimensions of the IP debate in the 1990s. Beyond the debates of the 1990s, analyses of Brazil's intellectual property policies in agricultural and human biotechnology include Filomeno (2014), Iacomini (2007), Mitre and Reis (2014), Octaviani (2010), Varella and Pereira (1996), Zucoloto and Freitas (2013).

EXTERNAL PRESSURES, LEGISLATIVE ACTIVISM, AND BRAZIL'S NEW PATENT LAW

Brazil was subject to intense external pressures in the 1980s to alter its patent regime, with particular focus on the introduction of pharmaceutical patents.[4] Pharmaceutical products had been non-patentable since 1945, and process patents were disallowed in the late 1960s. The size of the country and thus potential market for drugs, in combination with the country's international leadership in the Uruguay Round, and the fact that by the end of the 1980s, Brazil stood out among middle-income developing countries for not offering *any* type of pharmaceutical patents, neither product nor process, meant that for both material and symbolic reasons changing Brazil's patent regime was treated as a high priority by the transnational sector and foreign governments. Yet through most of the 1980s efforts to induce policy change in Brazil failed. Reporting on a United States Commerce Department delegation to Brazil in 1987 that pressed for the introduction of pharmaceutical patents, for example, one industry monitor concluded that "the mission got absolutely nowhere."[5]

In 1988 the United States Trade Representative (USTR) escalated pressures by increasing tariffs on Brazilian exports from twenty-two sectors.[6] These sanctions followed bilateral consultations dating from late 1986 and the launching of a formal Section 301 investigation in July 1987.[7] Brazil's initial reaction was adamant rejection of the US pressures. President José Sarney (1985–1990) defended the country's approach to pharmaceutical patents, both as matters of policy and international law, and insisted that trade sanctions would not alter Brazil's policies. The Sarney Government maintained that the denial of patent protection to pharmaceuticals made sense for a country with Brazil's characteristics, noting that as recently as the late-1970s developed countries such as Italy, Japan, and Switzerland still did not grant pharmaceutical patents, and concluded that Brazil should wait to do so until it reaching similar levels of economic and technological development.[8] Brazilian officials

---

[4] Previous analyses of US–Brazilian conflicts over patents in the 1980s include Arslanian (1994), Bayard and Elliott (1994), Deere (2008), Flynn (2011; 2015), Harrison (2004), Hirst (1998), Marques (1993), Richards (1988b), Serrano (2012), Tachinardi (1993). The dispute over patents was preceded by a US–Brazil dispute over informatics (Bastos 1994; Evans 1989).

[5] "US Fails in Patent Bid," *The Pharma Market Letter*, April 20, 1987.

[6] "US Imposes Trade Sanctions on Brazil Over Patents," *The Pharma Market Letter*, August 1, 1988.

[7] "Industry Files Section 301 Case against Brazil for Lack of Patent Protection," *Inside U.S. Trade*, June 12, 1987. Note that these investigations occurred under *Section 301*, not *Special 301*, as they pre-dated the reform of US trade law that established the IP-specific instrument. The first Special 301 review took place in 1989. The original complaint identified Brazil's intention to introduce a market reserve policy alongside other measures to essentially "nationalize" pharmo-chemical production. When those measures were relaxed, the conflict became consumed by the question of pharmaceutical patents.

[8] "Brazil Government Group Looks at Drug Patents," *The Pharma Market Letter*, May 1, 1989, p. 16.

also reminded their US counterparts that the country was fully compliant with prevailing international law; so long as Brazil's patent law was consistent with international rules, the Brazilians maintained, there was nothing to change (Arslanian 1994, 58; Harrison 2004, 108; Serrano 2012). In fact, the Brazilians asserted that it was the US that was violating international law, by unilaterally punishing a country that was in compliance with its international obligations. Sarney labeled the trade sanctions "unfair and outlandish" (Harrison 2004, 107) and indicated that Brazil would pursue a case against the US.[9]

Brazil's defiance subsided considerably under the Presidency of Fernando Collor de Melo (1990–92). During the electoral campaign Collor had indicated that he would review patent policy if elected, declaring that the denial of pharmaceutical patents was contrary to Brazil's national interests because it was drawing trade sanctions from the US (Marques 1993, 72), and soon after inauguration the new government announced that it would begin drafting a patent law that would allow for pharmaceutical patents, a pledge that prompted the US to remove the trade sanctions (USTR 1990). Having committed to altering Brazil's patent law, the Executive established an Inter-Ministerial Commission to prepare a proposal to send to Congress, and in April 1991 President Collor submitted the draft legislation to the Chamber of Deputies.[10]

Collor's proposal represented a more cautious approach than those drafted by Menem in Argentina and Salinas in Mexico. The Brazilian Executive's initiative called for the immediate introduction of pharmaceutical patents, but did not offer pipeline protection, so most drugs that were to come on the market in the years immediately following the change would not be protected in Brazil.[11] Reflecting a degree of continuity with Brazil's postwar patent policies, in which the state played an active role in brokering technology transfer, Collor's proposal also retained a wide array of measures to buttress

---

[9] "Brazil Calls for GATT Arbitration," *The Pharma Market Letter*, February 27, 1989. Brazil did attempt to challenge the legality of the sanctions, but the issue was never resolved at the multilateral level.

[10] During this period, once it became clear that Brazil would adopt a new patent law, a flurry of conflicting proposals were put forward by actors from across the political spectrum—some drafts submitted to the Inter-Ministerial Commission and others drafts submitted in Congress by politicians from opposition parties. For discussion and review of various proposals, see Gosain and Daniel (1991), Harrison (2004, 109), Reis (2015), Tachinardi (1993). The transcript of the Special Commission's hearings on November 19, 1991 includes discussion of these proposals CESP 1991a).

[11] In fact, the government's initial draft had called for transition periods, with process and product patents to be introduced two and three years, respectively, after the law entered into force. Yet following discussions with the US, the Executive removed transition periods from the proposal submitted to Congress. As a notable reflection of how this last-minute adjustment was introduced, the transition periods, though removed from the proposed legislation itself, remained in President Collor's formal letter that accompanied the initiative. When pressed, the Executive attributed the inconsistency to the frenetic process by which the legislation was drafted and revised—"an oversight... because so many hands were involved" (CESP 1991a, 57–8).

the rights of knowledge users.[12] For example the compulsory licensing provisions defined "local working" in a way that would have required patented products to be manufactured in Brazil. The comparatively tempered characteristics of Collor's approach toward pharmaceutical patents were reflected in the transnational sector's criticism, quoted at the top of this chapter (PMA 1992).

Each of these elements was subject to considerable debate in subsequent years, as the proposed law underwent extensive hearings in both the Chamber of Deputies and Senate. Aiming for light treatment, Collor submitted the original proposal with a petition that Congress treat it with "urgency," which would have restricted legislators' abilities to propose amendments and, it was anticipated, allow the new law to go into effect by the end of 1991. Instead, the initiative ended up traversing a long and complicated route to becoming a law in 1996. In contrast to the cautious approach reflected in Collor's proposal, the new patent law that was passed five years later was greeted with glee by the transnational pharmaceutical sector, as also indicated in a passage cited at the top of this chapter (PhRMA 1997).

While detailed step-by-step review is not the objective here, it is worth pointing to key moments of inflection in Brazil's path to over-compliance. Rejecting the Executive's request for light treatment, the Chamber of Deputies established a Special Commission that proceeded with hearings to work on modifying the proposed legislation. In 1992 the Special Comission's "rapporteur" (i.e. the deputy in charge of preparing a revised version on behalf of the Commission), Dep. Ney Lopes (PFL/RN), introduced revised drafts that altered key elements of Collor's proposal and, if passed, would have offered a level of patent protection more line with what the international pharmaceutical sector and the US Government demanded. When the Special Commission's proposal went to the full Chamber of Deputies, however, it was met with uproar by legislators and social movements who resisted the over-compliant provisions in Dep. Lopes' proposal. Congressional deliberation took place in the context of major political and economic crises in Brazil, as President Collor was impeached in October 1992 and replaced by Itamar Franco (1992–95), first as Acting President and then, and then, following Collor's resignation, as President. The country entered into a period of hyperinflation in this period too. As a result of these events, the patent law seemed to have been put aside. When the Chamber of Deputies eventually returned to the issue, it conducted yet more hearings and debates, and ultimately passed a revised version in June 1993. This version, which was prepared by the leaders of the legislative blocs in coordination with the Executive, and not the Special Commission itself, stripped out many of the over-compliant provisions and was closer to Collor's original proposal.

---

[12] Discussions of Brazilian science and technology policies include Adler (1987), Arruda (1985), Barbosa (2013), Bastos (1995), Mazzoleni and Póvoa (2010).

The patent law underwent further transformation in the Brazilian Senate, which also held hearings and engaged in extensive deliberation over the course of nearly three years.[13] The Chamber of Deputies' proposal was considered by two separate Committees in the Senate. First, the Constitution and Justice Committee passed a version that was largely consistent with that received by the lower house, but then the Economic Affairs Committee overrode this and passed an over-compliant version that was largely identical to what the Chamber of Deputies' Special Commission had drafted in 1992. Here too the legislative process was shaped by major political events, most importantly the national elections of October 1994 that put Fernando Henrique Cardoso, by that point an enthusiast for over-compliance, in the Presidency. These elections, which left Cardoso with a supportive legislature (Pereira et al. 2011; Power 1998), also meant that the Senate's Commissions responsible for the patent law would be recomposed. Indeed, one of Cardoso's political allies, Sen. Fernando Bezerra (PMDB-RN), became the rapporteur for the patent law in the Economic Affairs Committee and was responsible for assuring that the over-compliant provisions were restored in the final version. And it was Bezerra's version that was approved by the full Senate and returned to the Chamber of Deputies, where it passed and was subsequently signed into law by President Cardoso in May 1996.

To summarize, the path from the Executive's 1991 proposal to the 1996 LPI was anything but linear: relative to President Collor's original proposal the degree of over-compliance first increased under the direction of the Special Committee, only to be moderated by the full Chamber of Deputies, and then be ratcheted up again in the Senate.[14] Brazil went from leading resistance in the 1980s, to grudgingly accepting new global norms in the early 1990s, to over-complying by the middle of the decade.

BRAZILIAN OVER-COMPLIANCE
IN COMPARATIVE PERSPECTIVE

The most important way that the 1996 LPI differed from Collor's original proposal was the inclusion of pipeline patents. This meant that drugs that were

---

[13] The extent of legislative activism on the patent law has made it a focus of attention. Curiously, most analyses emphasize activities in the Chamber of Deputies, not the Senate. Tachinardi's (1993) account was published before the Senate even began to consider the Law. Harrison's (2004) analysis jumps from 1993 to 1996, skipping over events in the Senate. Nor does Reis's (2015) detailed analysis consider the twists and turns that the law underwent in the Senate. An exception is Fonseca and Bastos (2016, 432–5), which explicitly examines the events in the Senate.

[14] *Diário da Câmara dos Deputados* (April 2, 1996) presents detailed article-by-article comparisons of various versions.

still in clinical trial stage or awaiting marketing authorization could become patented in Brazil, immediately, for twenty years from the date of the first foreign application. The course of this specific provision reflects the larger trajectory observed in Brazil, from defiance to over-compliance.

The Brazilian Government adamantly opposed any efforts to mandate retroactive recognition of patents during the Uruguay Round negotiations, and, despite Collor's willingness to relax the country's opposition to pharmaceutical patents, pipeline protection remained a "red line" and was not offered in the 1991 proposal. Indeed, when pressed on this issue in Congress, the Executive left no doubt that a pipeline was out of the question, indicating that the issue had been rejected out of hand by the Inter-Ministerial Commission as not worthy of discussion.[15] Dep. Lopes inserted a pipeline provision in the Special Commission's draft, notwithstanding the Executive's wishes, only for this to be removed by the full Chamber of Deputies in 1993. By the time the Senate began working on the bill, the Uruguay Round's IP negotiations were completed and countries' alternatives under TRIPS were clear: there was no obligation to acknowledge already-granted patents, nor applications filed prior to 1995. In the spirit of minimalist compliance, the Senate's Constitution and Justice Committee included a "mailbox" for applications filed from January 1995 onwards, the minimum required by TRIPS, but no acknowledgement of applications filed or patents granted abroad prior to 1995. Yet the Economic Affairs Commission restored this over-compliant provision, and the final LPI included both the mailbox for applications submitted from January 1, 1995 to May 14, 1997, and a pipeline for pre-1995 applications. Applications filed abroad prior to 1995 but still pending could be registered in Brazil too, once the applicant showed that the first patent was granted. None of these would be examined by the patent office (*Instituto Nacional da Propriedade Industrial*, INPI-BR[16]), but rather "revalidated" in Brazil as granted in the first country of application.

On the key dimension of this time period, how countries introduced pharmaceutical patents, Brazil differs from both of the other countries examined in this book. In Argentina, pharmaceutical products became patentable later than in Brazil, in October 2000, and without a pipeline. Applications and patents that pre-date 1995 could not obtain protection in Argentina. In Mexico, patents were introduced nearly six years earlier than in Brazil, in June 1991, and also with a pipeline. Yet even here there is an important difference between the pipeline provisions in these two countries. In Mexico, pipeline protection was available so long as the products covered by the patents had not yet been launched on the Mexican market, while in Brazil

---

[15] Testimony from Maria Margarida Rodrigues Mittellbach, Director of Patents (INPI-BR), to the Special Commission, April 7, 1992 (CESP 1992a).

[16] The abbreviation INPI-BR is used to avoid confusion with Argentina's patent office.

this protection was only meant to be available for products that had not yet been launched anywhere in the world. Thus, on this dimension Brazil clearly over-complied, but in a less extreme fashion than Mexico.[17]

Brazil's provisions on compulsory licensing, which also drew exceptional degrees of attention and underwent repeated revisions in Congress, followed a similar trajectory. Brazil's pre-TRIPS patent law, from 1971, stipulated that failure to "work" a patent locally constituted a ground for a compulsory license, and, critically, defined "local working" as manufacturing in Brazil, not importation. Collor's initiative retained this provision and the 1996 LPI has a local working requirement too, but even this issue illustrates movement toward over-compliance. President Collor's proposal stipulated that importation could not count as working unless a set of conditions were met, and in drafting the bill the government went out of its way to use language that would make the conditions exceedingly difficult to meet, but the version that passed in 1996 made it easy to satisfy these conditions and thereby allow importation to constitute local working.

The details are worth reviewing, as they illustrates both the Collor Government's objectives and how significantly the LPI ended up differing from these objectives. The debate turned on whether demonstrating that manufacturing a patented product locally was not economically viable would be solely sufficient to allow importation to satisfy the local working requirement, or whether the demonstration of economic non-viability would have to be supplemented by other conditions. For most drugs, the non-viability of local production can be demonstrated easily, with reference to scale economies. Aware of this, the Executive established a set of conditions, only one of which was economic non-viability, and required that *each* condition would have to be met in order for importation to satisfy the local working requirement. This was intentional: in 1992, when questioned if requiring all conditions (rather than any single condition) to be met was, perhaps, a drafting error, the inadvertent use of "and" rather than "or," the Executive was emphatic that, to the contrary, that was the very purpose—to make it as difficult and as unlikely as possible that importation could be considered as locally working a patent. Here too, when pressed on this by the Special Commission, the Director of Patents at INPI-BR left no doubt as to the Collor Government's objective, noting that the provision under consideration

> was the subject of some criticism, because no one, trying as hard as they might, could find an example in which importation could be seen as working if you have to obey these three hypotheses in a cumulative manner.... The intent of the

---

[17] As a representative from the transnational sector exclaimed to Congress in 1993, demanding that Brazil adopt Mexico-like wording, "it is essential to recognize the pipeline, defined clearly as 'all products that have not yet been launched in the Brazilian market'—and I emphasize the word 'Brazilian'" (Câmara dos Deputados 1993, 11).

article is only to allow imports [to satisfy the local working requirement] in cases of real interest to the country and not let the question of whether to manufacture or introduce via imports remain the specific will of the patentee...(CESP 1992a).[18]

Yet by 1996 this requirement was relaxed: if local production of a product is not viable, the LPI allows importation to count as working.[19]

To be sure, the retention of any clause at all that could make failure to manufacture locally grounds for a compulsory license is noteworthy. Even in diluted form, Brazil is one of the few countries in the world with such a provision.[20] But the trajectory of the local working requirement, and the reactions within Brazil, are revealing. It was precisely the actors that fought for a strict local working clause that expressed disappointment. Representatives from the local pharmaceutical sector complained that inclusion of the exception for "economic non-viability," left alone and without the other conditions stipulated in earlier drafts, neutered the local working provision, leaving foreign firms with an "escape hatch to avoid this obligation," an interpretation shared by the Senate's legislative consultancy (Consultoria Legislativa do Senado 1994; 1995a; 1995b).[21] In contrast, an official from the organization representing transnational pharmaceutical firms expressed satisfaction with the outcome: diluting the local working provision was a high priority of transnational firms, and they achieved their objective (Interview, May 11, 2007a). In fact, scrutiny of the legislative process suggests that this provision was revised and drafted in such a way as to be toothless. According to a legislative consultant in the Chamber of Deputies assigned to the patent law, the local working provision was made useless by design, a compromise between those who were committed to retaining "safeguards," in principle, and those wanting to make sure that, in effect, compulsory licensing on

---

[18] The exchange went on. Dep. Goldman (President of the Special Commission): "So, in fact, this article could be translated as saying 'the rights conferred by a patent only apply if the patent is actually manufactured..." Mittelbach (INPI-BR): "In the country." Goldman: "In practice that's it?" Mittelbach: "Exactly." Goldman: "Importation must satisfy these conditions....Otherwise importation is not working?" Mittelbach: "Exactly. It is not working." Goldman: "That is the situation, at the end of the day?" Mittelbach: "Exactly."

[19] Think of the following logic: if X (failure to manufacture the patented product in Brazil), then Y (compulsory license), except in the case of Z. The debate was whether Z should be a rare event or a common event. If Z is a rare event, then Y is likely to follow most instances of X; if Z is a common event than the presence of X is unlikely to be sufficient for Y. The Executive's position in 1991 was clear, that Z should be a rare event, so that failure to manufacture locally should yield a compulsory license. The 1996 LPI makes Z a common event, since pharmaceutical firms can nearly always demonstrate the non-viability of local production in a given country.

[20] As we shall see in Chapter 8, the US would challenge this aspect of Brazil's law at the WTO. The case was dropped after the two sides reached a mutual understanding (Attaran and Champ 2002).

[21] The "escape hatch" quotation comes from "O desenho da nova lei," *ABIFINA Informa*, November 1995.

grounds of failure to manufacture the product locally would be exceptionally rare (Interview, November 23, 2006).

While the specific phrasing of Brazil's local working provisions were in the crossfire throughout this period, other important aspects of Brazil's compulsory licensing provisions received little attention in these debates. Compulsory licenses on grounds of public interest are most relevant for health issues, as they allow state officials to negotiate for price reductions from patent-holding firms. These sorts of compulsory licenses are also simpler, in principle, in that they are subject to fewer constraints under TRIPS. As we shall see in Chapter 8, the Brazilian Government would revise these provisions in the late 1990s and early 2000s, so to deploy them as instruments to lower the price of patented drugs to treat HIV/AIDS. In the LPI process of the 1990s, however, these received hardly any attention, and the reason why they had to be revised subsequently was that they were also drafted in such a way as would make them difficult to use. Brazil's 1996 patent law did not include the sort of language we observed in Argentina, which permits Ministry of Health officials to act relatively unencumbered in this regard (Barbosa 2000; Correa 2000a; Oliveira et al. 2004).

Before proceeding, it is also worth noting another dimension of Brazil's new patent system that would, in time, prove to be of great importance. Patents in Brazil (as elsewhere) last twenty years from the date of application, yet the LPI also includes a guarantee of ten years of protection for granted patents. While the twenty-year minimum is required by TRIPS, the guaranteed period of protection is not, and thus constitutes another illustration of over-compliance. Provided that examination is completed in ten years this provision has no consequences, but where examination takes more than ten years, periods of protection become extended by the additional time. The guarantee was not in Collor's original proposal either, but introduced late in the process. According to an official in the Ministry of Foreign Relations that was involved in these debates, the head of INPI-BR at the time insisted on this, with the Executive's support, as an insurance policy to protect applicants from a failure of the public sector to examine applications within ten years (Interview, July 9, 2015).

PHARMACEUTICALS, BIOTECHNOLOGY, AND POLITICAL COALITIONS

Support for over-compliance in Brazil was spearheaded by transnational pharmaceutical firms and their allies in the IP law community. The transnational sector was represented by the Association of the Research-Based Pharmaceutical Industry (*Associação da Indústria Farmacêutica de Pesquisa*, INTERFARMA), an organization founded in the late 1980s to deal explicitly with intellectual property issues. Though originally created as a unit within a broader sector-wide organization, INTERFARMA quickly emerged as the principal representative of the transnational pharmaceutical industry in Brazil, and worked closely with the Brazilian Association for Intellectual Property (*Associação Brasileira da Propriedade Intelectual,* ABPI) to push for over-compliance.

The transnational sector was unrelenting. INTERFARMA was a regular participant at hearings in both bodies of Congress, prepared numerous studies to promote the benefits of over-compliance, submitted countless documents to legislators and the congressional consultancies, and maintained close contact with officials in the Executive.[22] Brazil needed a strong IP law, according to INTERFARMA, one that offered investors protection and rights of exclusion comparable to that available in the US, "without decoys, disguised as 'safeguards,' that may harm or even eliminate the rights" (Câmara dos Deputados 1993, 9).

The transnational sector was particularly alarmed by the absence of pipeline protection in Collor's proposal. INTERFARMA's Vice President told the Special Commission that even the quick introduction of pharmaceutical patents, as suggested by Collor, was a hollow victory in the absence of a pipeline: "although the law enshrines the principle of immediate implementation, it excludes the patenting of products in development, and these products are extremely important to our industry." INTERFARMA thus demanded that the Special Commission "correct this injustice" by making protection available for patents associated with drugs still in product development.[23] Later in the process, following the amendment in the Senate that that would have replaced a pipeline with a mailbox, the transnational sector's mobilization was sharp and abrupt, accusing legislators of unfairly depriving research-intensive firms of subsequent revenue streams and demanding the restoration of pipeline protection. In the updated 1995 version of a report that INTERFARMA issued on essential modifications that, in the transnational sector's view, needed to be made, restoring the pipeline was now listed as the first and most urgent correction for the Senate to make (INTERFARMA 1995).

INTERFARMA worked tirelessly to revise the wording on compulsory licenses as well, to make sure that patent holders would enjoy unfettered rights of exclusion. Ideally, transnational firms would have preferred to see compulsory licensing clauses linked to local manufacturing removed altogether, and INTERFARMA representatives cited the specific language of the Mexican

---

[22] Examples of the transnational sector's studies include (INTERFARMA 1993a; 1993b; 1993c; 1993d; 1995).

[23] Testimony of Francisco Teixeira, Special Commission, December 10, 1991 (CESP 1991e). Teixeira made similar remarks in testimony to the full Chamber of Deputies (Câmara dos Deputados 1993).

law as a model to be emulated, but failing that they aimed to pare away the additional conditions so that demonstration of economic non-viability, by itself, would be sufficient to allow importation to count as local working.[24]

Brazil stands out from the other cases examined in this book on account of the prominence of debates over biotechnology in the process of introducing a new patent law. The core of the coalition for over-compliance in Brazil included not just the expected actors, international pharmaceutical firms operating in Brazil and their local IP lawyers, but also the emerging biotechnology industry, represented by the Brazilian Assoication of Biotechnology Firms (*Associação Brasileira das Empresas de Biotecnologia*, ABRABI). Brazil by the late 1980s had an accomplished agricultural biotechnology sector based on traditional forms of plant and animal breeding, and was regarded as one of the developing countries most likely to make the leap into "modern" biotechnology.[25] ABRABI, which maintained a consistent and visible presence in Brasília, argued that facilitating the patenting of microorganisms and genetic resources constituted an essential step for the sector's development.[26]

The local pharmaceutical sector resisted. Representatives from the sector's two main organizations, the Association of National Pharmaceutical Firms (*Associação dos Laboratórios Farmacêuticos Nacionais*, ALANAC) and the Brazilian Pharmo-Chemical Association (*Associação Brasileira das Indústrias de Química Fina, Biotecnologia e suas Especialidades*, ABIFINA), attempted to counter the arguments put forward by INTERFARMA and its allies. Brazilian firms expressed alarm at the possibility of allowing pipeline patents, for example, and they insisted that altering the language on compulsory licensing to allow economic non-viability to justify importation would make the provision unusable.[27]

In presenting this resistance local pharmaceutical firms received a modicum of support from the Brazilian health community, such as *Fiocruz*, a research and teaching institute linked to the Ministry of Health.[28] These health actors' participation were reflective of the broader activism of health professionals

---

[24] See, for example, testimony of INTERFARMA to the Special Commission, December 10, 1991 (CESP 1991e).

[25] See, for example, Carvalho et al. (1995), Furtado (1985), Marques (1993), OTA (1992).

[26] For but one example of ABRABI's testimony, calling on Congress to introduce a patent law that would allow patenting (and thereby, according to ABRABI, encourage investment) in "modern" biotechnology, see the statement of Antonio Paes de Carvalho to the Special Commission on December 4, 1991 (CESP 1991d).

[27] Examples include testimonies to the Special Commission by Dante Alario (CESP 1991a), Kurt Politzer (CESP 1991b), and Nelson Brasil (CESP 1991e). At the Chamber of Deputies' hearings in April 1993, Alario took the floor directly following Teixeira and offered a passionate point-by-point rebuttal of INTERFARMA's presentation (Câmara dos Deputados 1993). See also "O desenho da nova lei," *ABIFINA Informa*, November 1995.

[28] See, for example, testimony of Eloan Pinheiro to the Chamber of Deputies on May 13, 1992 (CESP 1992b).

(Falleti 2010; Flynn 2013; Nunn 2009), yet this is one of the few interventions in the entire period by actors from—even distantly from—the Ministry of Health. Indeed, a striking aspect of politics in the early-mid 1990s is that the Ministry of Health, which would become the most important player in patent politics later, after pharmaceutical patents were introduced and the country was dealing with their effects, was on the periphery of the Executive in this period. Though formally part of the Executive's Inter-Ministerial team to draft the new patent law and work with Congress on its passage, the archival record and interviews with participants demonstrate that health officials played an exceptionally marginal role in deliberations over the new law in the 1990s.

Brazilian pharmaceutical and pharmo-chemical firms were resisting from a position of weakness. As indicated by the comparative data presented in Chapter 2 (Table 2.3, p. 47), local firms accounted for a small share of drug sales in Brazil, Indeed, throughout most of the postwar period the Brazilian pharmaceutical market was dominated by foreign firms. As a Health Ministry official noted in the early 1980s, "there does not exist a Brazilian pharmaceutical industry, rather there simply exists a pharmaceutical industry in Brazil" (Saraiva 1983, 169).

The weakness of Brazilian pharmaceutical firms may seem surprising, but in Brazil the absence of pharmaceutical patents was not complemented by additional industrial policies to promote the sector. Brazil offers a clear illustration that disallowing patents, alone, is not sufficient for developing local pharmaceutical capabilities.[29] Whereas countries such as India (Chaudhuri 2005; Horner 2014b), Japan (Reich 1990), and Argentina (Chapter 3) combined the absence of patents with active promotion of their domestic pharmaceutical sectors, in Brazil such supplementary measures were largely absent.[30] Pharmaceuticals were not treated as a priority sector for national development during the course of the postwar industrialization effort. To the contrary, most policies and regulations in this period tended to discriminate against local firms and set incentives for importation.[31]

This scenario of neglect began to change in the 1980s, as the Brazilian Government, concerned by the high import dependence on active pharmaceutical ingredients (APIs), along with intermediates and other raw materials

---

[29] "The elimination of [product and] process patents for pharmaceuticals in Brazil has not yet showed significant effects on the structure of the industry" (UNCTAD 1981, 32). Kirim's (1985) analysis of Turkey makes similar observations.

[30] Promotional instruments, which obviously varied across countries, included, for example, restrictions on foreign ownership, discriminatory government purchasing and drug approval practices, sector-specific regulations on foreign exchange transactions, and investment in biochemistry research.

[31] Bermudez (1995); Büchler (2005); Evans (1976); Febrefarma (2007); Flynn (2015); Gereffi (1983); Mazzoleni and Póvoa (2010); Muzaka (2015); Queiroz (1997); Rebouças (1997); Vaitsman et al. (1991).

for chemical synthesis, started to introduce industrial policies for more up-stream pharmo-chemical production.[32] Rebouças' study of industrial policy toward the pharmo-chemical sector contrasts the period prior to the early 1980s, when the absence of patents coincided with "sparse measures" toward the sector, with the rest of the 1980s, when the non-patenting environment was complemented by "various connected instruments, including greater resources for R&D" (Rebouças 1997, 181).[33] These measures contributed to the emergence of a "nascent" pharmo-chemical sector (Queiroz 1997, 134), a phenomenon marked by the creation of ABIFINA in 1986. For the patent debate of the early 1990s, however, these incipient efforts were too little and too late to alter the balance of power.

The relative weakness of Brazil's pharmaceutical firms within national industry was reflected in broader patterns of business mobilization. In contrast to Argentina, where local pharmaceutical firms were able to bring the coun-try's leading business organizations on their side, in Brazil the opposite happened. The peak business organization, the National Confederation of Industry (*Confederação Nacional da Indústria*, CNI), actively participated in the coalition for over-compliance. The CNI expressed "complete agreement" with the transnational pharmaceutical sector and its allies in the biotech sector, advocating a new patent law that featured minimal transition periods, pipeline patents, and complex compulsory licensing rules (along with a wide scope for patenting of genetic resources). According to a CNI survey reported to Congress, 71 percent of the Confederation's members regarded a new patent system that gave owners of knowledge stronger and longer rights of exclusion as "a necessity for modernization" of the country's industrial base.[34] The differences between Argentina and Brazil could not be starker: in Argentina the main business organization (UIA) supported the local sector's campaign for minimalist compliance; in Brazil the CNI supported the trans-national sector's campaign for over-compliance.

Were the outcome in Brazil determined solely by a conflict pitting the dominant transnational pharmaceutical sector and the emerging biotechnol-ogy sector against the fledgling local pharmaceutical sector with its peripheral allies in the health community, it would be hard to understand why it took so long for the coalition for over-compliance to prevail. Moreover, looking at these actors alone cannot help us understand the trajectory, that by 1993, when the Chamber of Deputies passed its version of the law, the defensive

---

[32] Moreover, the introduction of product patents in Japan and Italy (in the 1970s) and Spain (1980s) threatened to curtail the supply of APIs (Queiroz 1997, 130).

[33] Other authors that also note the unprecedented attention paid to pharmo-chemicals in the 1980s include Bermudez (1995), Büchler (2005), Cassier and Corrêa (2007; 2008), Chamas (2005), Flynn (2015).

[34] See the CNI's testimony to the Plenary of the Chamber of Deputies on 14 April 1993 (Câmara dos Deputados 1993, 13–14).

coalition appeared to have the upper hand. The following sections examine, first, the coalition that the local pharmaceutical sector participated in that allowed it to punch well above its weight in the early part of the LPI process, and then, second, the broader coalition that came together to assure passage of the over-compliant patent law in 1996.

A WEAK PHARMACEUTICAL SECTOR IN A STRONG DEFENSIVE COALITION

Brazil's local pharmaceutical sector was able to compensate for its own weaknesses by riding the tidal wave of political mobilization that was sparked by President Collor's initiative for a new patent law. The breadth and extent of societal opposition to the patent law in this period was enormous. In its submission to the USTR for the first Special 301 in 1989, the Brazil–US Business Council suggested that, "in truth, there is less opposition in Brazil to improvements in intellectual property protection than the United States Government might at first perceive."[35] This observation turned out to be wrong—very wrong.

The early 1990s witnessed massive mobilization in Brazil over patents, both in Congress and throughout civil society. A dense network of nongovernmental and religious organizations allied with a range of parties in Congress, principally the Workers Party (*Partido dos Trabalhadores*, PT), Communist Party of Brazil, and the Brazilian Socialist Party, but also legislators from rural-based right-wing parties. These parties, united in the "Nationalist Parliamentary Front," resisted over-compliance at nearly every step along the way from 1991 to 1996. As an indicator of the degree of salience and legislative activism, consider that Deputies and Senators submitted over 1400 separate amendments over the course of debate.

In civil society, a central actor in the movement against the patent law was the Forum for the Freedom of Use of Knowledge (*Fórum pela Liberdade do Uso do Conhecimento*, FLUC), a network uniting diverse non-governmental organizations in opposition to the patent law.[36] FLUC, created in 1992, functioned as the coordinating organ for a broad swathe of groups that objected to the introduction of a new patent regime. For example, the Brazilian Society for the Progress of Science (*Sociedade Brasileira para o Progresso da Ciência*, SBPC) worked with FLUC in expressing opposition to biotechnology patenting. In contrast to the by-nomination only, Brazilian Academy of Sciences, which was more supportive of the new patent law, the SBPC was a

---

[35] Document on file with author.
[36] FLUC (1992; 1994) provide statements of this network's positions on key issues of debate, as well as overviews of civil society mobilization and activities against the patent law.

voluntary association and had come to represent a more "nationalist" tradition in the Brazilian scientific community (Tigre 1983). The SBPC participated regularly in hearings in Brasilia and submitted documents and analyses to the legislative consultancies in both houses. FLUC's campaign was also supported by the Brazilian labor movement, the association of university students, and countless other organizations with leftist or nationalist orientations. FLUC, SBPC, and actors associated with this network participated actively in the hearings in both the Chamber of Deputies and Senate, regularly submitted commentaries on aspects of the patent law to the legislative consultancies, and wrote opinion pieces in the media.

FLUC worked in tandem with the network of environmental- and biodiversity-oriented NGOs that had become active in Brazil in the run-up to the United Nation's 1992 "Earth Summit" in Rio de Janeiro. The Earth Summit, which would produce the UN's Convention on Biodiversity, raised awareness of and sparked extensive mobilization over the use and ownership of biological resources. In Brazil, the many organizations whose activism was sparked by the Earth Summit were not born with a focus specifically on patents, but quickly formed an alliance with FLUC on account of the overlap between patents and biodiversity. Thus, the National Forum of NGOs and Social Movements for the Environment and Development (*Fórum Brasileiro de ONGs e Movimentos Sociais para o Meio Ambiente e o Desenvolvimento*, FBOMS) also provided testimony in Congress and, more generally, remained active and visible in its opposition to the patent law.[37]

Perhaps FLUC's most influential ally was the Brazilian Confederation of Bishops (CNBB), which took visible positions in the debates.[38] The Church was alarmed by issues regarding biotechnology patenting, and in particular concerns of "patenting life." Describing patents on genetic resources as "highly questionable from an ethical perspective," the CNBB advised legislators to proceed with extreme caution.[39]

In addition to these non-state actors, the state-funded agricultural research agency, *Embrapa*, played an important role too. Concerned, at the time, about the patenting of transgenic organisms, not on religious and moral grounds but rather for how such patents might inhibit Brazilian agricultural scientists' access to frontier technologies, *Embrapa* sought to limit patents strictly to processes used in genetic engineering. *Embrapa*'s participation in the defensive coalition was in many ways parallel to that of *Fiocruz* discussed in the preceding

---

[37] For observations of a prominent activist who testified on various occasions to Congress in this period (CESP 1991d; 1992b; Câmara dos Deputados 1993), see David Hathaway, "Brazil About to Patent Life?" *Seedling*, October 25, 1993 (goo.gl/ghPs9Y). Newell (2008) reviews these activities too.

[38] The Church had historically been a progressive actor in Brazilian politics, regularly allied with left parties and social movements (Burdick 2004; Houtzager 1998; Mainwaring 1986).

[39] *Diario do Congreso Nacional (Seçao I)*, June 23, 1992, p. 14,149. See also, CNBB (1993).

section: in both instances an agency of the state was dissenting, and in both cases dissent was marginalized as the Executive came to present a unified position.[40] The breadth and orientation of societal mobilization in Brazil warrant emphasis. Observers of this period are nearly uniform in emphasizing the extent of societal opposition inspired by the patent law debate.[41] IP was not a technical issue being left to the experts, but something that generated intense passions throughout civil society and social movements. Importantly, however, these actors tended to direct their ire not toward pharmaceutical patents but rather broader sets of concerns related to patents in the field of biotechnology. Consider, as a simple illustration, testimony in the Senate by the union of water and sewage workers from the state of Bahia (SINDAE):

> The possibility of patenting life forms and biologic and biotechnological processes [in the proposal] presents a serious threat to national security and sovereignty, as well as to the food security of the Brazilian people who already live in situations of extreme poverty and hunger, situations that will surely expand with the approval of this law. For these reasons we thus demand the removal from the law of any form of patenting on life forms or biological or biotechnological processes.... [42]

Two aspects of this intervention are telling, both reflective of the breadth and orientation of societal mobilization in this period: that the union of water and sewage workers of a state in the northeast of Brazil was taking a position in a debate on a new patent law, and that the focus of its concern was on biotechnology patents and food security. It was these issues related to the feared effects of a new patent law on the environment, biodiversity and the ethics of "patenting life" that captured the movement and drove resistance to a new patent law in Brazil. Pharmaceutical patents did, of course, receive attention, but this topic was not the principal focus of civil society activism. FLUC, for example, widely distributed a "Manifesto to the National Congress for the Freedom of the Use of Knowledge," a one-page leaflet articulating the network's criticisms of the patent law (see Figure 5.1). The "Manifesto" listed eight points, of which just one (point 6) regarded pharmaceuticals.[43] In sum,

---

[40] While *Fiorcruz's* marginalization was a function of the Ministry of Health's peripheral role in this period, *Embrapa's* dissent was simply overwhelmed by the emphatic support of the Ministry of Agriculture and the Ministry of Science and Technology (*Ministério da Ciência e Tecnologia*, MCT). In subsequent conflicts over IP, *Embrapa* would become much more influential (Filomeno 2014).

[41] Caliari et al. (2013); Fonseca and Bastos (2016); Hirst (1998); Marques (1993), Marques (2003); Reis (2015), Tachinardi (1993).

[42] Letter from SINDAE to Senate, 19 October 1993 (on file with author).

[43] The SBPC dedicated an issue of its monthly journal to the topic, with a forty-page section entitled "Medicamentos: A indústria farmacêutica e as patentes" (*Ciência Hoje*, Vol. 15, No. 89, April 1993). See also, FLUC's open letter to President Cardoso, calling the restoration of pipeline patents "unacceptable, shameful, and economically harmful" ("Carta aberta ao Excelentíssimo Senhor Presidente da República Professor Fernando Henrique Cardoso," *Gazeta Mercantil*, September 26, 1995).

MANIFESTO AO CONGRESSO NACIONAL
PELA LIBERDADE DO USO DO CONHECIMENTO

O FÓRUM PELA LIBERDADE DO USO DO CONHECIMENTO DENUNCIA O PROJETO DE LEI 824/91 E OS SEUS SUBSTITUTIVOS COMO INSTRUMENTOS DE DOMINAÇÃO ESTRATÉGICA APLICADOS AOS PAÍSES EM DESENVOLVIMENTO PELOS DETENTORES INTERNACIONAIS DA TECNOLOGIA DE PONTA.

GOVERNOS DECLARADOS SUSPEITOS EM SUA CONDUTA DEVEM TER IMPEDIDOS OS PROJETOS DE SUPOSTA MODERNIDADE QUE NÃO FORAM DISCUTIDOS E APROVADOS PELA SOCIEDADE.

O PROJETO DE LEI DA PROPRIEDADE INDUSTRIAL E SEUS SUBSTITUTIVOS ESTÁ:

* patenteando todas as formas de vida, desde microorganismos, plantas, até animais superiores, não excluindo o próprio homem;

* privatizando e monopolizando a reprodução de todos os seres vivos, inclusive os que são utilizados como matérias-primas para a indústria;

* permitindo a monopolização e internacionalização da agro-indústria que representa 40% do PIB;

* permitindo a monopolização e provável desnacionalização da produção de energia através da biomassa, de importância estratégica;

* permitindo a monopolização da produção de alimentos industrializados;

* decretando o monopólio para medicamentos, encarecendo a assistência farmacêutica pública e ameaçando a indústria nacional;

* impedindo o livre uso do conhecimento com consequente inviabilização do desenvolvimento científico e tecnológico nacional;

* dificultando pesquisas pois produtos e processos estarão monopolizados através das PATENTES;

– **POR 20 ANOS** –

A SOCIEDADE QUER A AVALIAÇÃO CLARA DO CONGRESSO NACIONAL DAS CONSEQUÊNCIAS DE UMA LEI DE PROPRIEDADE INDUSTRIAL FRUTO DE IMPOSIÇÕES INTERNACIONAIS.

FÓRUM PELA LIBERDADE DO USO DO CONHECIMENTO
(Participa do Movimento pela ÉTICA na Política)

Figure 5.1. FLUC Manifesto

Note: Manifesto distributed as leaflet in October 1992 and reproduced in FLUC (1994, 14).

the defining feature of societal mobilization over patents in Brazil, in this period, is that it was *not* primarily focused on drugs and health.[44]

These characteristics of societal mobilization in Brazil stand in contrast to what we witnessed in Argentina. Where societal groups mobilized against Menem's proposal, they did so largely with regard to pharmaceutical patents, and their mobilization was explicitly in support of the Argentinean pharmaceutical sector. In Brazil, mobilization was spearheaded by actors concerned primarily with patents on genetic resources, and focused on the environmental effects and ethical implications of biotech patents. Brazilian pharmaceutical firms integrated into this broad movement, but unlike their counterparts in Argentina, they were not in the pilot's seat. The case of Brazil also differs from what we witnessed in Mexico, where the network of civil society organizations was entirely disengaged from debates over patents, focusing on neither the patent law itself nor the relevant provisions of NAFTA. In Brazil mobilization was consistent and active, and focused explicitly on intellectual property and knowledge (as made evident by FLUC's name).

Broad societal mobilization contributed emboldened Brazil's defensive coalition and thus delayed the introduction of pharmaceutical patents. In the absence of the opposition put forward by FLUC and like-minded legislators in Brasilia, it is likely that the Chamber of Deputies would have passed the Special Commission's over-compliant version of the patent law. With the support of sympathetic Deputies, however, FLUC and its allies, including the local pharmaceutical sector, were able to exploit the upheavals around Collor's impeachment in 1992 to alter the Special Commission's proposal and create the more tempered version that the full House sent to the Senate in 1993. However, while the FLUC-led coalition could delay passage of the LPI, the defensive coalition was ultimately unable to prevail. To understand the limitations of this resistance, we need to need to consider how international pressures helped widen the coalition for over-compliance.

EXTERNAL PRESSURES, EXPORTER MOBILIZATION, AND EXECUTIVE COALITION BUILDING

Throughout the period that a new patent law was under consideration, Brazil remained subject to unremitting international pressures. The US treated securing the introduction of pharmaceutical patents in Brazil as a high priority, and expressed frustration at the protracted process. Officials from the

---

[44] This changes by the early 2000s, as we shall see in Chapter 8. Flynn (2015), Fonseca and Bastos (2016), and Matthews (2011) make similar observations.

US Embassy in Brasilia attended legislative hearings, submitted materials to the legislative consultancies in both houses of Congress, and arranged meetings with deputies and senators. For example, the Embassy arranged for a senior economic advisor from the State Department (Carmen Suro-Bredie) to make a presentation on the LPI to the Senate in May 1995, offering to provide simultaneous translation. That month the Embassy also sent the 1995 "National Trade Estimate" report on Brazil to Senators, along with an explanation (in Portuguese) of the Special 301 process (USIS, n.d.), and then later that year a fifty-nine-page pamphlet on IP rights that extolled the importance—for the Brazilian economy and for Brazil's economic relationship with the US—of adopting the new patent law (USIS 1995).

Brazil was repeatedly targeted in the USTR's Special 301 reports too. Brazil remained on the Priority Watch List in 1991 and 1992, while hearings on President Collor's initiative were taking place. In 1993, with delayed passage of the law attributed to political and economic events, the USTR listed Brazil as a Priority Foreign Country and, later that year, with USTR Mickey Kantor exclaiming that "Brazil has to learn to walk and chew gum at the same time," initiated investigations into trade sanctions.[45] Following high-level talks between the two countries and the Brazilian Government's pledge of imminent passage of a new law, the sanctions were not imposed and Brazil was removed from the watch lists altogether in 1994, listed simply as a country of "concern" in the Special 301 report.[46] Yet the following year, the USTR again placed Brazil on the Priority Watch List, indicating an expectation that the new law would be passed by the end of the year, with a threat of being listed, again, as a Priority Foreign Country.

External pressures altered the Executive's orientation and inspired efforts to overcome resistance in Congress and society. US pressures had prompted Collor to commit to pharmaceutical patents in the first place,[47] and they nurtured Fernando Henrique Cardoso's embrace of over-compliance, first as Minister of Foreign Relations, then Minister of Finance, and, as of January 1995, as President. By the time the draft law was under consideration in the Senate in late-1993, the Executive in Brazil, as in Argentina and Mexico, was

[45] "EUA voltam a ameaçar o Brasil," *Jornal do Comercio*, October 29, 1993. Calling for Brazil to be elevated to the Priority Watch List, the PMA's submission to the 1993 Special 301 Report complained that the proposed law "remains flawed and would not offer the same protection found in other patent laws enacted recently, such as that of Mexico" (PMA 1993).

[46] This was front-page news in the business press ("EUA elogiam lei brasileira de patentes," *Gazeta Mercantil*, May 3, 1994).

[47] In one of the first hearings of the Special Commission, the President of the patent office, and head of the Inter-Ministerial Committee that drafted Collor's proposal, warned Deputies that countries that buck the global sea change "run the risk of missing the train of history and remaining marginalized from flows of investment and trade" (CESP 1991a), yet even then we will recall that the Brazilian Executive's position at this time was much less enthusiastic than we witnessed in Argentina and Mexico.

committed to over-compliance, no longer trying to evade external pressures, but rather working hand-in-hand with the US Government to secure rapid approval of a new patent law that satisfied the demands of the international pharmaceutical industry. In 1994, for example, the Foreign Ministry (*Itamaraty*) sent the Senate a list of forty-three amendments to be introduced, including, importantly, restoration of pipeline protection and dilution of the compulsory licensing provisions.[48]

The Brazilian Executive's pivot can be understood as part and parcel of a broader shift in development strategy at this time. Caliari et al. (2013) argue that over the course of three Presidencies (Collor, Franco, Cardoso), Brazilian leaders came to regard a new patent law as an instrument to attract foreign investors and alter the country's integration in the global economy. This view reached its apex under Cardoso, whose zeal is undeniable: the new patent law was a key dimension of his government's economic development strategy (Flynn 2015; Fonseca and Bastos 2016). The Executive's approach to patents is nicely illustrated by the detailed presentations by the Minister of Science and Technology (Vargas 1995) and the Minister of Foreign Relations (Lampreia 1995) to the Senate's Economic Affairs Committee in August 1995, both officials emphatically articulating the Cardoso Government's case for over-compliance.[49]

Yet Executive preferences for over-compliance are not sufficient to explain the outcome. Cardoso's enthusiasm and commitment to the cause were no more striking than Menem's in Argentina, and in that country we saw an Executive unable to secure its desired outcome. Nor was the Brazilian Executive consistently capable of pushing measures through Congress on its terms. The same globalizing zeal also led the Cardoso Government to negotiate a series of Bilateral Investment Treaties (BITs), but none of these were ever ratified, notwithstanding the President's generally favorable relationship with the Legislature (Campello and Lemos 2015; Kleinheisterkamp 2004). What distinguishes the case of patents in Brazil from Argentina, and, within Brazil, the case of the new patent law from the case of investment treaties, is the ability of the Executive to widen the coalition in support of the outcome it pursued.

Cardoso's success in constructing a winning coalition for over-compliance was rooted in the country's trade structure, in particular the vulnerability of exporters to US sanctions. The Executive could exploit exporters' intense concerns with market access to mobilize support for satisfying the US's demands. Exporters' alarm is evident throughout the period under study (Bayard and Elliott 1994, 198). When the US imposed trade sanctions in

---

[48] The Executive's proposed modifications are reviewed in an internal document prepared by the Senate's Legislative Consultancy (Consultoria Legislativa do Senado 1994).

[49] The Foreign Ministry's (Lampreia 1995) presentation also included an extended annex, with detailed explanations of the Executive's positions on the key points of debate.

1988, exporters from the targeted sectors pressured the government to alter course and introduce a new patent law (Arslanian 1994, 67). The National Association of Pulp and Paper Manufacturers lobbied President Collor's Inter-Ministerial Group to introduce pharmaceutical patents immediately, and, fearing sanctions, continued to push for rapid approval of a patent law that would satisfy the US.[50] The Brazilian Association of Exporters (*Associação Brasileira de Exportadores*, ABE) requested that Congress waste no time passing a new law, suggesting that Brazil's new LPI should be modelled on the proposal that President Menem had recently submitted to Congress in Argentina, offering pipeline protection and avoiding any requirements for local production.[51] Similarly, the Brazilian Shoe Industry Association explicitly linked its desire for "modern legislation" to be passed to its own "active participation in international trade."[52] Examples of this sort abound: Brazilian exporters, concerned about a loss of market access, sought over-compliance. Again, this constitutes "activating agnostics." These are not actors that we would expect to have strong preferences regarding patents, but the threat of reduced market access brought them to attention.

The activation of agnostics in Brazil is neatly illustrated by the mobilization of paper, cardboard, and cork producers. After the Chamber of Deputies passed its more moderated version of the patent law in 1993, the association representing these firms in the state of São Paulo (SIAPAPECO) presented the Senate with a fifty-four-page bound report on the damage being suffered by Brazil because of the country's patent system (SIAPAPECO 1993). The report listed nearly fifty "lost opportunities," including foreign and national inventions that allegedly were not being commercialized in Brazil due to the absence of a "modern" patent system, alerting Senators that the situation "urgently needs to be corrected" (p. 54). The examples, language, and argumentation deployed in this document are nearly identical to that used in documents also submitted to Congress by the Ad Hoc Group, a coalition of US investors in Brazil that was exceptionally active and visible in its lobbying Brasilia (Ad Hoc Group 1993). The reason for this, as the petitioners acknowledge (SIAPAPECO 1993, 3), is that the report was prepared with the assistance of American Chamber of Commerce in São Paulo. That this association relied on the Chamber of Commerce's lawyers to prepare a document to make the case for a new patent law is noteworthy. Although these firms' motivation for wanting a "modern" patent law may have been simply to preserve market access for exports, they sought to articulate a

---

[50] This submission was reported to the Special Commission in November 1991 (CESP 1991b).

[51] See testimony to the Special Commission (December 3, 1991) of Laerte Setúbal Filho, Vice President of the ABE (CESP 1991c).

[52] *Albicalçados*, letter to Senate, August 26, 1993 (on file with the author).

broader case that would present a new patent law as being beneficial to everyone. Yet industrialists in the paper, cardboard, and cork sectors have little experience with or knowledge of IP, other than the simple fact that their exports were under threat on account of the country not having acquiesced to the US's demands. While the organization has in-house staff with expertise on production, sales, financing, marketing distribution and so on, and even lawyers, there is no reason to expect a sectoral association of this sort to have expertise in—or ready access to expertise in—patent law. And it is impossible to put together a compelling case highlighting—and providing specific examples of—the purported benefits of a "modern" patent system without such knowledge and expertise. What to do? Contract the report. External pressures activated agnostics: threats of trade sanctions inspired actors to care about a topic that did not affect them directly, and to invest resources to secure policy change.

The structure of Brazil's trade allows us to understand exporters' concerns. Figure 5.2 presents data on Brazil's trade dependence on the US, from 1985 to 2000. Although Brazil's overall trade dependence decreased in the 1990s, as the LPI was being debated and as the US was renewing threats of trade sanctions, dependence on removable trade preferences remained at roughly 5 percent.

Brazilian officials were acutely aware of what the country's export structure meant for the politics of patents, and how to exploit this situation politically.

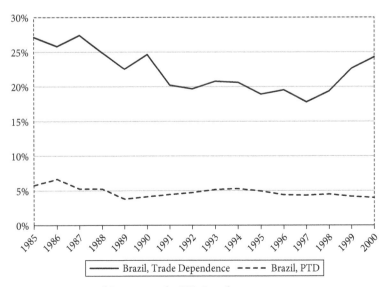

Figure 5.2. Structure of Exports to the US: Brazil

Note: Data on preferential exports to the US are from the United States International Trade Commission; data on overall exports to the US and global exports are from UN-COMTRADE.

Under Cardoso, the Executive, seeking over-compliance, explicitly used the threats of reduced market access to mobilize exporters, a political strategy that we do not observe under Cardoso's less enthusiastic predecessors. If the US were to apply sanctions against Brazilian exports, the government could have perhaps contested these in the newly created World Trade Organization. But *Itamaraty* officials downplayed such possibilities, choosing instead to emphasize the complex and time-consuming nature of such a process, the uncertainty of the outcome, and the costs incurred while doing so. These were chips that the Executive used to its advantage. In August 1995, with Brazil back on the Priority Watch List, Minister of Foreign Relations Luiz Felipe Lampreia made an impassioned plea to the Senate's Economic Affairs Committee to pass the patent law quickly to avoid punishment by the US (Lampreia 1995). Rather than dismiss or downplay the threats of sanctions, the Executive played these up, if anything exaggerating their imminence and likely effects. Detailing the history of the US-Brazil conflict over patents in twenty-two bullet points, Lampreia emphasized how easily the USTR could punish Brazil by removing the country's privileges under the Generalized System of Preferences, and presented a grave image of what the consequences would be. To buttress his case, the Minister provided the Senators with data on the country's dependence on preferences for exports to the US. Although Lampreia did not call this "political trade dependence," it is precisely what he was citing: according to the Minister, roughly 5 percent of Brazil's total exports ("a hardly insignificant level of differential treatment of Brazilian products") were likely to suffer were the US to impose trade sanctions.

The strategy worked. The rapporteur of the bill in the Economic Affairs Commission, Sen. Bezerra, himself an industrialist from the export sector, dispensed with the legislative consultants who had worked on the law to that point and replaced them with privately contracted consultants to prepare a better version (Interview, November 24, 2006).[53] Bezerra, who was also head of the National Confederation of Industry, was fiercely committed to over-compliance.[54] The Senate's in-house researchers had produced numerous evaluations of the patent law, consistently advising against Brazil taking measures that were not specifically required by TRIPS and advocating that the Senate pass a version close to that approved by the Chamber of Deputies in 1993 (Consultoria Legislativa do Senado 1993; 1994; 1995a). Sen. Bezerra, looking for a different sort of patent law and regarding the in-house staff to be

---

[53] Büchler (2005) and Fonseca and Bastos (2016) also emphasize the role played by Bezerra. See also, "Lei de Patentes poderá esbarrar nas reformas," *Correio Brasiliense*, July 24, 1995.

[54] Bezerra (1995) is an unpublished document from the Brazilian Senate. For a public statement, see Fernando Bezerra, "Patentes: Um assunto complexo," *Folha de São Paulo*, April 12, 1996.

overly "nationalistic," contracted his own advisers to deliver what the Executive sought.

Social structure enabled Executive agency. In the context of intense external pressures, Brazil's trade structure and the subsequent ability to mobilize exporters in the coalition for over-compliance allowed the President to secure his desired outcome. Again, the contrast with Argentina is useful. In both countries the Executives demonstrated unquestionable commitments to over-compliance, and both countries were on the receiving end of the US's threats of trade sanctions if they failed to deliver. Figure 5.3 plots political trade dependence in these two countries, with the spotlight on the key years of conflict. Argentina's lower levels of PTD meant that external pressures had little effect on coalitions, while Brazil's trade profile meant that exporters were available as partners in the campaign for over-compliance. Thus while Menem and his top officials were unable to introduce pharmaceutical patents in a way that satisfied the US and the transnational pharmaceutical sector, Cardoso and his team could do so. Indeed, Executives' political strategies reflected these conditions: while Argentinean authorities rarely invoked the US threats, instead going out of their way to make the case for over-compliance on its own terms, Brazilian officials constantly referred to the external pressures facing the country and warned of the dire consequences of failing to meet the US's demands, often exaggerating the likely impact.

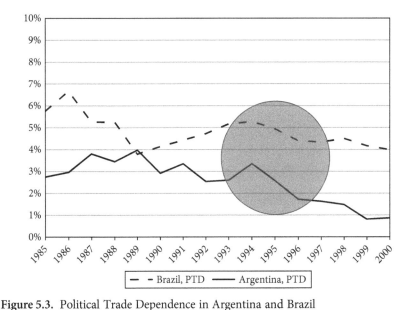

Figure 5.3. Political Trade Dependence in Argentina and Brazil

Note: Data on preferential exports to the US are from the United States International Trade Commission; data on global exports are from UN-COMTRADE.

CONCLUSION

In the 1980s, Brazil presented vociferous opposition to the integration of IP into negotiations on international trade rules, and then to the obligation for countries to make pharmaceuticals patentable. Once these international battles had been lost, Brazil accepted the new world order, but grudgingly. The Collor Government's initial proposal to Congress, lacking many of the elements of over-compliance noticeable in the initiatives submitted by Menem and Salinas, for example, still reflected ambivalence. By 1996, however, Brazil had adopted a patent system that left the US and the international pharmaceutical sector jumping for joy.

This chapter has examined Brazil's path from resisting to embracing the global sea change in IP, focusing on the changing preferences of the Executive and the rival coalitions opposing and supporting over-compliance. Brazil had an exceptionally robust and active defensive coalition—not because of but rather in spite of the local pharmaceutical industry. Brazil's pharmaceutical firms were economically and politically weak, surprisingly so given the country's industrial development, and left on their own would have been steam-rolled. ABIFINA and ALANAC were able to integrate into and benefit from broad and extensive resistance to the new patent law that was being waged by civil society, religious, environmental, and labor organizations in Brazil. While this defensive coalition was able to fight back against the transnational sector and its allies, it did not prevail. Brazil's export structure left the country vulnerable to trade preferences being removed, and this vulnerability created opportunities to widen the coalition for over-compliance. The Cardoso Government, deeply committed to over-compliance, deftly exploited the opportunity, playing up exporters' vulnerability and the dire consequences awaiting Brazil if it failed to satisfy the USTR. The Executive's efforts to activate agnostics kicked into higher gear with the patent law in the Senate in 1995, at which point the outcome of over-compliance was secured. In sum, integration into a broad coalition allowed the otherwise weak local pharmaceutical sector to punch well above its weight for a considerable period of time, but once the Executive mobilized exporters, the tide turned in favor of over-compliance.

The account of events given here needs to be complemented by attention to the changing relationship between the Executive and Legislature in Brazil. Importantly, change in the Executive's preferences was accompanied by a change in its power relative to the Legislature. Although President Collor's 1991 proposal to Congress did not reflect the same degree of enthusiasm for over-compliance as did the proposals submitted by Menem in 1991 and Salinas in 1990, within just a few years the Executive's preferences had changed. Under Cardoso's leadership, as Minister of Foreign Relations, Minister of Finance, and then as President, the Brazilian Government's fervor for over-compliance became was beyond dispute. And as President, Cardoso enjoyed substantial legislative support as well, with the 1994 elections producing a cohort of deputies and senators (not all from Cardoso's party, but acting in concert with the President) that were also committed to his economic policy agenda. With this "unbeatable alliance" (Power 1998, 61), the President could make sure that the new patent law, held up for years in Congress, passed at long last. Although it is correct that Cardoso was able to obtain the Legislature's support, by no means was it a foregone conclusion that the Executive would secure the outcome on such favorable terms. Again, we need to understand not just if countries introduced pharmaceutical patents, but *how* they introduced pharmaceutical patents. The changing nature of Executive-Legislature relations help us understand why Cardoso succeeded in getting a new patent law passed where previous Executives had failed, but the ability to get this passed with pipeline patents and the other elements of over-compliance that President Cardoso sought and promised to the international community is a function of the underlying social structure.

Comparative analysis, both cross-national and within-case, prompts us to look beyond electoral and institutional factors. In Argentina, President Menem and his team also pressed hard for over-compliance, and the Argentinean Executive also benefited from a seemingly propitious relationship with the legislature, but societal resistance was such that the ordinarily accommodating Congress restrained the Executive. Argentina did pass a new patent law, but not the sort of patent law demanded by the Executive. And even within Brazil, the same Cardoso Government could not prevail upon the legislature to pass any of the bilateral investment treaties. Although Campello and Lemos (2015) attribute the non-ratification of BITs to the Executive not caring enough and thus not using all means available to overcome Congressional resistance, the amount the Executive cared is not independent of social structure and the Executive's expectation of success. As these authors write, the Executive's "lack of resolve can be partly attributed to the absence of a constituency for BITs among important domestic and international economic groups" (Campello and Lemos 2015, 1056). Operating in the context of different social structure conditions, the Brazilian Executive may have pushed harder for these BITs and secured the outcome it sought, on its desired terms, as it was able to do in the case of the new patent law.

Finally, it is worth recalling that the way countries introduced pharmaceutical patents has two defining characteristics, one regarding substance and one regarding timing. With regard to substance, Brazil is clearly a case of over-compliance, as illustrated by the pipeline, most importantly, as well as cumbersome compulsory licensing provisions. As regards timing, however, the fact that Brazil's defensive coalition put up such extensive resistance to the new patent law meant that these provisions did not enter into effect until 1997. In the absence of this resistance it is reasonable to believe that the over-compliant patent law, such as that proposed by the Special Commission in 1992, would have passed much earlier. In that case the outcome in Brazil would have been much more similar to that observed in Mexico. The timing of Brazil's over-compliance turns out to be critically important, for it affected the possibilities for subsequently changing course in the 2000s. The significance of both aspects of the outcome analyzed in this chapter, introducing pharmaceutical patents in an over-compliant—yet comparatively delayed—fashion, will become evident in Chapter 8.

Part III

Modifying New Pharmaceutical Patent Systems

6

The Defensive Coalition on the Offensive

National Industry and Argentina's Market-Preserving Patent System

Argentina's patent policy in the 2000s continued the trajectory of the 1990s, when, after protracted debate, the country complied with the global sea change in a comparatively minimalist fashion. The patent system remained the subject of dispute in subsequent years, because of the dissatisfaction of actors that had sought over-compliance in the 1990s and their continued to push for desired changes, and also because of challenges that emerged once product patents became available. Argentina came under considerable external pressures to deliver more patent protection, but successive governments rebuffed such overtures, and in some instances Argentinean authorities further altered arrangements to the benefit of local firms. Argentina has pharmaceutical patents, and in that sense the country underwent a radical change, but the implementation of this radical change and subsequent modifications of the new arrangements were done in ways that helped local pharmaceutical firms preserve their strong position in the local market.

The analysis in this chapter points to the iterative and cumulative characteristics of patent politics. How countries reacted in the first period of conflict, to the new international obligation to allow pharmaceutical patents, conditions politics in the second period of conflict, over the functioning of their new patent systems. In Argentina, a set of conditions helped the national pharmaceutical sector shape the way patents were introduced, as analyzed in Chapter 3. What a representative from the sector refers to as the "intelligent implementation" of the country's TRIPS obligations, in turn, facilitated continued expansion and growth, and this accumulated muscle allowed the sector to remain a formidable political force.[1] Ultimately, the local pharmaceutical sector's resources contributed to the minimalist response to the global sea

---

[1] The reference to "intelligent implementation" comes from an interview with a CILFA official (Interview, December 9, 2014a).

change of the 1990s, and that initial minimalist response helped the sector retain the ability to prevail in subsequent conflicts in the 2000s.

Paradoxically, the deep economic crisis that Argentina experienced in the early 2000s helped the national pharmaceutical sector solidify its strength in the local political economy. One might expect the steep devaluation of the currency in December 2001 and subsequent default on sovereign debt to make the country more vulnerable to external pressures, and to isolate local actors seeking to resist such pressures. Yet even as Argentina negotiated with external creditors the government remained aligned with domestic drug firms on issues related to pharmaceutical patenting. The crisis, which led to sharp spikes in joblessness and poverty, and across-the-board cutbacks in spending, also prompted the Ministry of Health to declare a national health emergency. Whereas the Ministry of Health had been a peripheral actor in the debates of the 1990s, with concerns that health officials had about the possible effects of pharmaceutical patents on drug prices suppressed within the Executive, in this second period the Ministry of Health was at the forefront of state policy.[2] Concerned about the price of drugs and access to medicines in the context of economic crisis, the Ministry of Health and Argentinean pharmaceutical firms found common ground on the issue of patent protection.

While the explanation of Argentina's policy trajectory in the 2000s is rooted in the retained resources of the local pharmaceutical sector, one may, instead, be tempted to attribute the outcome to the character of the governments in power. After 2003, the country's leadership took marked turns to the left, under the leadership of Nestor Kirchner and Cristina Fernández de Kirchner (Etchemendy and Garay 2011; Manzetti 2016; Wylde 2011). Challenging international norms and bucking external pressures would seem consistent with the ideological thrust of *kirchnerismo*. Yet attributing pharmaceutical patent policies to the ideology and preferences of the Executive is problematic. In other areas where we might expect a rebellious and "anti-imperialist" Kirchner Government to try to subvert international norms, it was unable to do so without benefiting from a social structure that facilitated coalition building. President Fernández de Kirchner attempted to challenge Microsoft's dominance and promote non-proprietary software in both government and the private sector, for example, but such efforts were stymied by the absence of a local software sector to act analogously to what we observe in pharmaceuticals (Jones 2015).

The more fundamental problem with attributing the government's pharmaceutical patent policies to the identity and ideological orientations of the incumbent Executives is that the minimalist approach was established as state policy well before the before the rise of *kirchnerismo*. As discussed in Chapter 3,

---

[2] In 1999 the Ministry of Health became its own ministry, whereas before it had been the Ministry of Health and Social Action.

the Argentinean pharmaceutical sector prevailed in the first period of conflict, not just in terms of successfully resisting the push for over-compliance, but in terms of getting the Executive on its side. Since the late 1990s, the preferences of successive governments on key issues of pharmaceutical patenting remained aligned with those of local industry. Menem, in the final years of his presidency, stopped fighting against and came to ally with Argentina's mobilized and ever-vigilant pharmaceutical firms. As did Menem's successor, Fernando de la Rua (1999–2001) of the Radical Party, elected in an alliance with the center-left Front for a Country in Solidarity (*Frente País Solidario*, FREPASO). In 2001, with the economy in freefall, de la Rua resigned and was replaced by Eduardo Duhalde (2002–2003), from the Peronist Party.[3] Again, minimalism and defense of the local pharmaceutical sector remained state policy. And then came the Kirchners, Nestor Kirchner (2003–2007) succeeded by Cristina Fernández de Kirchner (2007–2015). In short, we witness continuity across a series of presidents with widely varying ideological roots: the "neo-liberal" wing of Peronism in the 1990s, the centrist and center-left UCR-FREPASO alliance at the turn of the century, the traditional wing of Peronism that took over imme-diately after the crisis, and the *kirchnerista* left wing of Peronism after 2003.

One way of disentangling the relationship between the preferences of the Executive and those of the national pharmaceutical sector is to look at areas of disagreement, as we did for the early-mid 1990s in Chapter 3. The Executive and local firms also found themselves at odds in the 2000s, over a set of issues related to the prescription of "generic" medicines and the controlling the price of drugs, including those sold by Argentinean firms. In these instances the local pharmaceutical sector also prevailed. Indeed, an important takeaway from the Argentinean case is that the same factors that allowed the country to resist intense external pressures for over-compliance in introducing pharma-ceutical patents also made it difficult to regulate the pharmaceutical market for health purposes and control the price of medicines.

The chapter consists of four sections. The first section examines the impact of Argentina's 1996 patent law on drug patenting and the phar-maceutical industry. The delayed and non-retroactive introduction of phar-maceutical patents meant that by the early 2000s the effects remained minimal, allowing the local sector to adjust to the eventual arrival of the new status quo. The second and third sections show how the local sector's resources allowed it to shape the Argentinean patent system in this period of patent politics, with conflict no longer over how to introduce pharmaceut-ical patents but rather how the new arrangements function. Section two

---

[3] Duhalde had been Peronist Party's candidate in the 1999 presidential elections, which were won by de la Rua. In December 2001 de la Rua resigned, and in January 2002, after a succession of interim replacements, Duhalde assumed the presidency for the remainder of the four-year term.

examines Argentina's response to external pressures, focusing on conflicts over the protection of test data and the procedures for issuing injunctions in cases of alleged infringement, and section three considers changes to the patent office's procedures for examining pharmaceutical patent applications. In both sets of conflicts we see Argentina's defensive coalition on the offensive. Section four considers a downside of persistent producer power in Argentina, showing how the same conditions that allow the government to build coalitions for reforming some aspects of the patent regime create challenges for reforming other aspects of the pharmaceutical market.

PATENTS, ADJUSTMENT, AND THE NEW POLITICAL ECONOMY OF PHARMACEUTICALS IN ARGENTINA

By the end of 2000 Argentina had just granted its first pharmaceutical product patents. This is in stark contrast with the substantial proliferation of patents that had already been issued in Mexico and Brazil, as we shall see in subsequent chapters. And even after the patent office began granting drug patents in October 2000, the pace of patenting picked up only slowly. As Argentina remained outside of the Patent Cooperation Treaty (PCT), the sheer quantity of applications received was less than elsewhere.[4] Examining a set of roughly 5200 international pharmaceutical applications deposited in multiple countries, Sampat and Shadlen (2017) found one-fifth of these to be filed in Argentina. In contrast, the filing propensities for Brazil and Mexico were 36 percent and 43 percent, respectively.[5] Figure 6.1 shows the number of pharmaceutical and pharmo-chemical applications received from 1990 to 2012, while Figure 6.2 provides data on product patents granted. Applications were filed in Argentina in the early 1990s, as firms awaiting change to the patent system allowing pharmaceutical products to be patented did not know when this would occur or how applications that had been filed would be treated, and the numbers increase substantially following the passage of the new patent law, the LPIMU, in the mid-1990s. At the time Argentina started granting patents in late 2000, the economy was already in

[4] The Patent Cooperation Treaty allows applicants to file one application centrally, and then, later, after it has undergone preliminary examination by a PCT-recognized "International Searching Authority," decide in which countries to file nationally for full examination by local patent offices. If a country is not a member of the PCT, applicants need to decide earlier in the process if they will file a national application.

[5] When we look only at the most "important" international applications, as measured by the number of countries where national versions are filed (i.e. "family size"), we see filing propensities in most countries approaching 100 percent, while in Argentina even at the top of the distribution the share of applications filed locally is only about 60 percent (Sampat and Shadlen 2017).

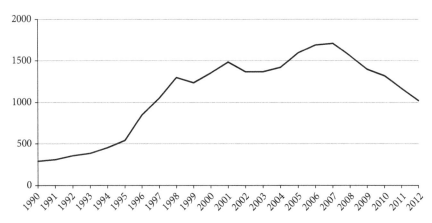

Figure 6.1. Pharmaceutical and Pharmo-Chemical Applications Filed in Argentina*
* Applications with first International Patent Classification of A61K or C07D.
Source: INPI-AR

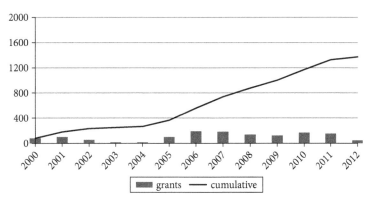

Figure 6.2. Granted Pharmaceutical Patents in Argentina, 2000–2012
Source: INPI-AR

recession and a deepening crisis, and the rate of applications first declined and then began increasing again only slowly. By the end of 2005 only 367 pharmaceutical patents had been issued in Argentina. Though the rate of patenting increased considerably after that, never were more than 200 pharmaceutical patents issued in a single year.

The effects of patenting on the pharmaceutical market were also slow to be felt. Argentina's refusal to introduce product patents retroactively, i.e. no pipeline, meant that drugs launched in the years after the new law was passed still lacked patent protection in Argentina. Only applications filed in Argentina from 1995 onwards were eligible. To appreciate the significance of these details, it is important to recall the significant lags between patent application and product launch that are characteristic of this sector. Even pharmaceutical patent applications filed during the transition period, and held in the mailbox to be examined as of October 2000, would be associated with products unlikely to come on to the market until well into the 2000s. The drugs that transnational pharmaceutical firms launched in the late 1990s and early 2000s, after the LPIMU was passed, typically had pre-1995 patent applications. Again, these products were in the pipeline at the time that the LPIMU was being debated in Argentina, and they provided the motive both for the transnational sector's intense preoccupation with making pharmaceutical patenting retroactive and for the local sector's equally intense preoccupation with avoiding pipeline patents. The local sector's victory on this point was decisive, for nearly all new drugs that were coming to market globally in the rest of the 1990s and still a majority of new drugs in the first decade of the 2000s had their first patent filing dates before 1995 (Sampat and Shadlen 2015a, Figure 2), and thus were not eligible for protection in Argentina. The only form of patent protection possible in Argentina for these drugs would be via process patents and "secondary" patents filed after 1995, topics we return to later in this chapter.

The impact of Argentina's new patent regime on both patenting outcomes and pharmaceutical markets are captured with comparative analysis of patent status of drugs across all therapeutic classes, as presented in Chapter 2 (Table 2.2, p. 41). Recall that this exercise consisted of identifying applications filed in Argentina, Brazil, and Mexico, associated with all new drugs launched in the United States from 1996 to 2004. Argentina had the fewest number of patents granted from this set, and the share of drugs receiving patents in Argentina was considerably lower too. In fact, as the note in Table 2.2 indicates, and consistent with the observations above, even the figure of 23 percent of the drugs in the sample receiving patents in Argentina needs to be interpreted with caution to avoid overstating the effects, as these patents were issued over time, beginning in late 2000 (the data reflect status as of the time the searching was conducted in 2016). As of the end of 2001, only nineteen of these drugs were protected by product patents in Argentina.

To illustrate how these issues regarding the introduction of product patents affected Argentina's pharmaceutical industry, consider that one comprehensive analysis of the topic could hardly find any cases of pharmaceutical patents affecting the Ministry of Health's procurement practices (Correa et al. 2011). The study was conducted by a research team that is known for its critical assessments of pharmaceutical patenting, yet even this group of authors, never shy to express reservations about pharmaceutical patents in developing countries, struggled to find problems to report in Argentina. The authors' research revealed that local health authorities still did not worry about patents in making procurement decisions (p. 24). The study presents one instance where a pharmaceutical patent created an obstacle for the Ministry of Health:

the government was obliged to suspend purchase of a particular formulation of an antiretroviral drug (didanosine) in 2006, on account of an injunction against the local provider obtained by the patent-holding firm. Even in this instance, however, the patent covered a specific formulation of the drug (400mg, slow release tablet), not the molecule itself, which was a pre-1995 invention and thus not eligible for a patent in Argentina—and in April 2007 the court of appeals revoked the injunction (Correa et al. 2011; Levis 2010, 378).

The patterns of patenting in Argentina discussed in this section were a function of the country's "intelligent implementation" of the new obligation to create a pharmaceutical patent system. Argentina complied with TRIPS, but it did so in a way that provided local labs with opportunities to adjust to the coming of a new status quo. With pharmaceutical patenting on the horizon, in the late 1990s Argentinean firms began to prepare for the onset of this new reality.

In thinking about adjustment to the introduction of pharmaceutical patents, it is important to underscore that this does not mean that local firms became innovation-focused, R&D-based enterprises. To be sure, some firms reacted to the new environment by investing in new production facilities and increasing expenditures on research;[6] as a sector Argentina's pharmaceutical producers invest more in R&D than they did in the past, and more than firms in most other industrial activities in Argentina. Yet these local efforts must be considered in the context of the enormous—orders of magnitude larger—investments that would be required to transition to business models based on discovery of new molecules, the launch of new products, and competing at the technological frontier. Officials in industry and government, as well as analysts of the sector, acknowledge that Argentinean firms are unlikely to break into the ranks of innovative originator pharmaceutical firms.[7] Not surprisingly, in Correa et al.'s (2011) analysis of pharmaceutical patenting, less than 2 percent of the patents granted had Argentinean inventors.[8]

The prevailing mode of adjustment by Argentinean pharmaceutical firms was to adapt their traditional *copista* model, of quickly launching their own versions of foreign-invented drugs, to the new context so to retain their abilities to compete with their own branded products. Abilities to do so benefited from these firms' strengths in product commercialization and their extended retail presence. Integration into dense networks of distributors and

---

[6] To give one example, Roemmers, Argentina's largest pharmaceutical firm, opened a new $65 million, state-of-the-art production facility in 2000.

[7] Bisang (2010); Fernández Bugna and Porto (2013); González García et al. (2005); Guzmán (2014); Sosa (2002).

[8] From this, the authors conclude that "the scarce participation of Argentinean patents indicates that the granting of patents since 2000 has not served as an incentive for innovation in the sector" (Correa et al. 2011, 25).

vendors, close relationships with doctors and pharmacists, and the prominence of brands, all helped local firms remain competitive.

These networks also made local firms attractive as licensing partners for foreign firms seeking to increase their presence in the Argentinean market, as many did in the 1990s and early 2000s (Bergallo and Ramón Michel 2014, 79; Bisang 2010; CEP 2009, 23). Market entry has costs, in that firms need to learn how to deal with registration processes and establish supplier and distribution relationships. Locational advantages of this sort were particularly important in Argentina, given the size of the local market, characteristics of distribution, insurance, and reimbursement systems, and the overall importance of brands. Transnational firms seeking to establish (or re-establish) a local presence would often rely on Argentinean firms to navigate the local terrain, and Argentinean firms knew that they could use their locational advantages to bargain for productive relationships with TNCs (Aulmann and Zuccherino 2014; Bisang 2010; CEP 2009; Fernández Bugna and Porto 2013). Locals' brand names, relationships with consumers, and control of distribution channels allowed them to keep competing in non-patented drugs, and where patents were issued these characteristics made it easier to obtain licensing agreements. Indeed, from the foreign firms' perspective, licensing to local firms made sense too, particularly in the context of a new pharmaceutical patent system that would allow them to control the production and distribution of their products and prevent export to other markets.[9] In sum, when transnational firms began to return to Argentina following the passage of the LPIMU and anticipation of a pharmaceutical patent regime, their best route into the Argentinean market was not to displace local producers but rather to collaborate with local producers (CEP 2009; Fernández Bugna and Porto 2013; Irigoyen 2006; Panadeiros 2002).

Pharmaceuticals are one of the few manufacturing sectors that transitioned successfully through the period of economic opening and liberalization in the 1990s.[10] Local firms' share of the domestic market continued to increase through the 2000s: by the end of the decade, Argentinean firms accounted for greater than 80 percent of sales in retail markets, and six of the top ten pharmaceutical firms and fourteen of the top thirty were locally owned (CEP 2009; González García et al. 2005). During this period Argentinean firms often purchased foreign firms' pharmaceutical manufacturing facilities (BMI 2014; Espicom 2012), precisely the opposite of the "denationalization" that many feared, and a process that stands in stark contrast with the general trend in the Argentinean manufacturing sector (Wainer and Schorr 2014). Indeed, only one pharmaceutical firm features in Wainer and Schorr's (2014) long list of large

---

[9] It is not uncommon to see transnational firms relying on Argentinean firms for distribution or licensed production of their products in the country.

[10] Bisang (2010); BMI (2014); CEP (2009); Fernández Bugna and Porto (2013); Sosa (2002).

local firms that were absorbed by transnationals, GlaxoSmithKline's purchase of Phoenix in 2010—and after that acquisition the Argentinean firm's brand continued to be used.

The strategies of adjustment were not equally available to all firms, however, and the patterns described here deepened asymmetries within the local sector. It was the largest Argentinean firms that succeeded, as they were the ones with the resources that facilitated alliances with, rather than displacement by, transnational firms. Where foreign firms gained or recovered ground, it was largely at the expense of smaller local firms (Boccanera 2005; CEP 2009; Fernández Bugna and Porto 2013). The same firms that dominated the market in the early 1990s continued to dominate: the top three Argentinean firms (Roemmers, Bagó, and Gador) accounted for nearly one-fifth of all retail pharmaceutical sales in 2010 (BMI 2014; Espicom 2012).[11]

The way conflicts of the 1990s over introducing a pharmaceutical patent system unfolded are crucial for understanding these market dynamics. Had pharmaceutical patents been made available immediately and retroactively, or had the data protection rules created barriers to market entry, the local sector would not have been able to continue its upward trajectory. Argentinean pharmaceutical firms would have had to stop selling the products they were selling and preparing to sell, and they would have faced greater challenges placing their own *copista* versions on the market quickly. Instead, rather than immediately disrupting the prevailing business model, the way pharmaceutical patenting was introduced allowed local firms to adapt and continue to grow, to use their resources to adjust to the coming onset of drug patenting, and by the end of the decade Argentinean firms still had considerable market power. The benefits that transition periods brought local firms were aided, indirectly, by the economic crisis too, for even after pharmaceuticals became patentable in 2000, the state of the economy, particularly high levels of unemployment and low demand, lessened the attractiveness of the Argentinean market and increased foreign firms' willingness to rely on local firms. The country's deep economic crisis served, effectively, to amplify the transition period, giving the national sector even more time to consolidate control of the market and prepare for the new world.

The fact that Argentina's leading pharmaceutical firms adjusted to the new status quo, and that adjustment includes production and distribution arrangements with transnational firms, "diluted the conflict over patents" (Bergallo and Ramón Michel 2014, 79; Bisang 2010; Katz 2001). Dilution of conflict is precisely what we would expect. The issues that gave rise to the intense and high-pitched conflicts of the 1990s, when and how to introduce pharmaceutical patents, were resolved, and as the new system set in actors

---

[11] Note that Roemmers has a minority stake in Gador.

did not continue to fight yesterday's fights. The introduction of a new status quo, and adjustment to this new status quo, do not mean that conflict is gone, however, but rather that the contours of conflict change. As in all countries with pharmaceutical patent regimes, originator and non-originator firms battle over the extent of patent protection and the conditions for market entry. In Argentina, as multiple informants from the pharmaceutical sector made clear, on many issues transnational firms in CAEME and local firms in CILFA have common interests and cooperate—they are all, ultimately, in the business of selling medicines—but on the policy issues where their interests do not coincide, the conflicts are as intense as ever. One of CILFA's officials used the analogies of "cold war" and "détente" to describe the relationship between Argentinean and transnational pharmaceutical firms: they have to accept the other and learn to tolerate and even work together, where possible, but on key issues they remain arch enemies (Interview, September 23, 2011a.). The remainder of this chapter examines these policy debates.

EXTERNAL PRESSURES AND ARGENTINEAN DEFIANCE, AGAIN

Argentina's new pharmaceutical patent regime remained subject to considerable external pressures. As we saw in Chapter 3, the US Government and the transnational sector regarded the LPIMU and the data protection law with abhorrence. With the trade sanctions imposed in 1997 having little effect, the US began preparing a complaint through the World Trade Organization's dispute settlement mechanism, charging that multiple dimensions of Argentina's new patent regime violated TRIPS. Argentina, with the active support of the local pharmaceutical industry, responded defiantly to these complaints, and on the most important issues prevailed. This section examines the two most salient and high-stakes issues in this conflict, both of which had immediate implications for market entry in Argentina: how health authorities treat test data submitted by pharmaceutical firms launching their products locally, and the procedures for granting preliminary injunctions in case of alleged patent infringement. In doing so we see how Argentina's defensive coalition helped the national government defend the minimalist and market-preserving approach to pharmaceutical patents.

The significance of data protection and preliminary injunctions in the second period of patent politics is a function of initial choices made over the introduction of pharmaceutical patents. As discussed, the decision not to recognize pre-1995 inventions (no pipeline) meant that most drugs launched in the late 1990s and early 2000s were not patent protected.

In this context, the transnational sector regarded more restrictive data protection, which would prevent health authorities from using the test data that originators generated and submitted as points of reference to make decisions about approving local firms' *copista* versions, as an alternative way of obtaining exclusivity in the local market. Argentinean firms, in contrast, feared that such steps would erect new barriers to entry and thus undermine their accomplishments in the debates over the introduction of pharmaceutical patents.[12] As regards preliminary injunctions, the debate centered on cases of alleged infringement of *process* patents. Recall that such patents, protecting laboratory methods of chemical synthesis and drug manufacturing, and not the molecular structures themselves, were never proscribed in Argentina, and in fact until late 2000 were the only form of patent protection available for drugs. The continued absence of patent protection for pharmaceutical products (again, a function of policy choices in the 1990s) increased the importance to originator firms of enforcing their process patents.

Before examining the resolution of these two specific issues, it should be noted that the formal bilateral consultations, which began outside the WTO and moved within the multilateral framework in 2000,[13] covered seven aspects of Argentina's new patent system. In addition to data protection and preliminary injunctions, the US also registered complaints about the system of system of exclusive marketing rights for pharmaceutical patent applications filed in the mailbox, procedures for granting compulsory licenses, a set of issues regarding the enforcement of process patents (again, until 2000 the only sort of patent protection available for drugs), and the scope of patentability in biotechnology.[14]

In 2002, following nearly three years of negotiations, the two countries reached a settlement that preempted the formation of a WTO dispute resolution panel. On some issues (treatment of applications in the mailbox, compulsory licenses, and biotechnology patents) Argentina's negotiators convinced their US

---

[12] Consider a drug with a patent in the US applied for in 1992 and subsequently granted, that after completing product development and receiving regulatory approval was to be launched in 2000. This drug's pre-1995 patent would not be available in Argentina, for the reasons discussed in the text, and local firms would be able to launch their own versions (provided they are not blocked by secondary patents, as shall be discussed in this section). However, if data exclusivity regulations obstructed local health authorities from authorizing these firms' *copista* products, this would constitute a new barrier to market entry. Thus, rules on test data, often about the effective duration of periods of market exclusivity (if the data period extends beyond the patent term), in the absence of patents can also affect the existence of exclusivity.

[13] As 2000 was the deadline for developing countries such as Argentina to enter into in full compliance with TRIPS, the US could not pursue a case on these grounds in the WTO until then.

[14] Bentolila (2002) and Czub (2001) review the issues driving the US complaint, though both articles were written before the conflict was resolved. Aulmann and Zucherino (2014), Bergallo and Ramón Michel (2014), and Negro (2006) provide detailed analyses of this bilateral dispute.

counterparts that Argentina was indeed in conformity with TRIPS and the US dropped the complaint. In the case of test data regulations the two countries agreed to disagree. And with regard to process patents, Argentina committed to revising the relevant aspects of the patent law. Inspection of the events in both of these latter issues reveal a case of the Argentinean Government, nourished by an active and committed local pharmaceutical sector, withstanding external pressures.

Data Protection

The US charged that the way Argentinean authorities handled test data submitted for the approval pharmaceutical products was in violation of TRIPS.[15] The data law, which in the 1990s was the final issue prompting the US to impose trade sanctions, remained a principle bone of contention. The US sought not just "data protection," but "data exclusivity," which would prohibit the health regulator, the National Administration for Drugs, Food, and Medical Technology (*Administración Nacional de Medicamentos, Alimentos y Tecnología Médica*, ANMAT) from relying on data provided by originator firms in authorizing local firms to enter the market with their own products. Argentina adamantly resisted this demand. The Ministry of Foreign Relations, working closely with CILFA, designed a detailed rebuttal of the US position and defense of Argentinean policy. Argentinean authorities maintained that the country's data rules were consistent with the country's obligations under the WTO, and that the US was demanding a level of protection that exceeded TRIPS. That is, Argentina insisted that TRIPS required protecting originator firms' test data against unfair use, but not treating data with "exclusivity," and regarded this request to adopt practices beyond what was required by TRIPS as another instance of the US demanding over-compliance.[16] In contrast with the conflicts of the 1990s, however, now the Argentinean Executive was defiant; rather than trying to push through the US's agenda, the Executive was allied with the local pharmaceutical sector in resistance.

Argentina prevailed. Formally, the two countries reached a settlement that amounted to "agreeing to disagree," with the US reserving the right to re-initiate dispute settlement proceedings at the WTO, but the US dropped the case and Argentina was not obligated to alter its laws or practices on test data.[17] From the perspective of CILFA and the Argentinean authorities, this is

[15] While the focus here is on pharmaceuticals, the US complaint also cited Argentina's treatment of test data in agrochemicals (Negro 2006, 153–5).

[16] The restrictive treatment of test data that the US demanded was what the US had sought in the TRIPS negotiations, but not what it obtained (Godoy 2013; Reichman 2004; Shadlen 2009a).

[17] The reason why the US dropped the case is not known with certainty, but it appears to be because it feared that a WTO ruling would favor Argentina's interpretation

clearly regarded as a victory, as a result of which local firms continue to be able to rely on data that producers of originator drugs supply to health regulators to place their products on the local market. From transnational sector's perspective this is a setback, and the use of test data, and more generally ANMAT's drug approval processes, has remained a principal grievance with regard to the Argentinean pharmaceutical patent system.[18]

As important as the outcome itself, of Argentina prevailing over the US on an international dispute, is the political mobilization by the defensive coalition that produced this outcome. Argentinean pharmaceutical firms worked closely with the government to respond to the external pressures.[19] Their commercial strategies were based on their abilities to launch imitation products, abilities that were a function of the test data rules and drug approval regime, so they invested considerable efforts in shaping policy to retain these conditions. CILFA's leadership was concerned that, without the active participation and input that the chamber's membership could provide, the Executive might, in the context of economic turmoil and vulnerability, take the path of least resistance and compromise with the US. To combat this, CILFA contracted two law firms, one in Argentina and one in Brussels, to help the Ministry of Foreign Relations develop and defend its legal interpretation of TRIPS that underscored the data protection system. CILFA even sent delegations to Geneva and Washington to support the diplomats' negotiations with the USTR.

Preliminary Injunctions

The US also complained that Argentina's rules on preliminary injunctions in instances of alleged infringement of process patents were not consistent with TRIPS. In this instance, Argentina accepted the US complaint and reformed the LPIMU to "fix" the problem. At first glance this appears to be an instance of the US securing a change in policy, but upon closer inspection this too is

---

of TRIPS, and the precedent set by losing in the multilateral body would undermine efforts to secure data exclusivity in other countries.

[18] That this is regarded was a victory for Argentinean firms and a defeat for transnational firms was abundantly clear in all interviews. Aulmann and Zuccherino (2014), Bensadon and Sánchez Echagüe (2009), Bergallo and Ramón Michel (2014), and Irigoyen (2006) reach this conclusion as well. Unable to secure change through diplomatic and trade pressures, foreign firms operating in Argentina have challenged the country's data protection rules in the courts.

[19] Collaboration between Argentinean negotiators and local pharmaceutical firms was noted almost universally by informants discussing these events. Most notably the influence and role of the local sector is stressed not just by actors from the pharmaceutical industry, but also by government officials, for example, a former Economy Minister lawyer on the "Permanent Working Group on Intellectual Property" who helped craft Argentina's response (Interview, November 22, 2007b).

a victory for Argentina, which converted the external challenge into an opportunity to tailor the new patent law in a way that would further benefit local producers.

In the absence of product patents, Argentinean pharmaceutical firms' modus operandi had been to develop new, non-infringing ways of manufacturing drugs, where the processes (but not the products) might be patented. Foreign firms regularly accused locals of infringing their process patents. Typically, when a patent holder accuses another actor of infringement, the owner may ask a judge to enjoin the alleged infringer from continuing its activities while legal proceedings take place (hence the term "preliminary injunction"). TRIPS requires countries to establish procedures for granting such injunctions, and the US charged that Argentina's 1996 LPIMU fell short of the WTO's requirements because, among other things, it provided too much discretion for judges. In revising the relevant provisions of the LPIMU to make the system of preliminary injunctions TRIPS-compliant, however, government officials worked closely with the local pharmaceutical industry to do so in a way that effectively made it more difficult to obtain preliminary injunctions.

To understand how Argentina converted defeat into victory, it is worth digging deeper into the details of the issue. Doing so illustrates the larger point of how the local pharmaceutical sector's accumulated resources allowed the defensive coalition of the 1990s to shape outcomes in the 2000s regarding how the pharmaceutical patent system functions. Although the formal rules on preliminary injunctions in Argentina's 1996 patent law did not satisfy TRIPS, in practice Argentinean judges had adopted an approach that was favorable toward granting such injunctions. Judges were applying an interpretation of the law that favored transnational firms over Argentinean firms.[20] The fact that preliminary injunctions were, in effect, easy to obtain in Argentina was a point of great consternation for local firms. After all, once a producer exits a market segment it is difficult to re-enter at a later period; even when a firm that had been subject to an injunction is found not to be infringing the process patent, and the injunction is lifted, the damage inflicted by being forced to exit the market can be long lasting. Reversing this tendency by creating a system that would make preliminary injunctions more difficult to obtain was thus a priority for CILFA (Levis 2005).

Paradoxically, the US challenge and the subsequent requirement to alter the rules on preliminary injunctions created an opportunity for Argentinean firms. They were able to prevail upon the government not just to eliminate the particular aspect of the preliminary injunction regime that violated TRIPS, but also to revise other aspects of the system that, de facto, made it easy for

---

[20] Genovesi and Kors (2005), Moncayo von Hase and Moncayo (2006) and Pardo (2003) discuss the jurisprudence and judicial practices.

transnational firms to obtain injunctions. Specifically, the new rules condition the granting of injunctions on the opinion of court-appointed experts, and make it standard for defendants to be heard in the course of proceedings. The new rules also relaxed a presumption of validity, requiring the complainant to demonstrate to the court that its patent would likely withstand a charge by the defendant that the patent in question should be annulled on grounds of invalidity. And the new rules require judges to consider not just the damages that delaying the injunction would cause the patent-holder, but also the damages to defendants that would be suffered were the injunction to remove the defendant's product from the market inappropriately. That is, the law requires judges to weigh harm to patent-holders against possible harm caused to alleged infringers if a preliminary injunction were granted and, then, subsequent hearings were to conclude that there was no infringement.[21] These extra obligations were not required by TRIPS, but nor were they prohibited. In fact, Argentina's new system is close to—indeed, modelled on—the US common law approach. None of the steps are insurmountable, so preliminary injunctions remained possible in Argentina, but as result of the reforms they were less likely to be granted than they had been.[22]

As with preservation of the regulations on data protection, the revised rules on preliminary injunctions constitute a triumph for the local pharmaceutical sector. While CILFA rejoiced in its accomplishment, the transnational sector and the Argentinean IP law community railed against the new arrangements. One informant called it "lousy writing" that prejudices foreign firms (Interview, November 21, 2007), for example, while a prominent Argentinean patent lawyer referred to it as "a clear effort to weaken patent rights" (Otamendi 2004).[23] And the reform was successful in achieving its goals. Whereas preliminary injunctions had been commonly granted, after the new arrangements were put in place these dropped off precipitously (and when judges did grant them they tended to be overturned on appeal on the basis of the new procedures). CILFA data indicate that over the period from

---

[21] Bensadon and Sánchez Echague (2009), Correa (2006), and Genovesi and Kors (2005) provide legal analyses. Bergallo and Ramón Michel (2014) and Irigoyen (2006) provide useful accounts of the events.

[22] As a prominent Argentinean lawyer who was consulted by the government on this reform put it, the US demanded that Argentina fix the rules on preliminary injunction to bring them into conformity with TRIPS, and that is exactly what Argentina did (Interview, September 23, 2011b).

[23] For a review of complaints from the IP community on the eve of the bill's passage, see "Patentes: el proyecto puede ser major," *La Nación*, September 24, 2003. Writing before the final version was passed, one lawyer close to the transnational sector lamented "that the proposed arrangements mean going back from advances made on the matter (Pardo 2003, 30). Correa (2006, 18, note 50) provides references to a series of articles by Argentinean lawyers criticizing the outcome.

2008 to 2012 only two injunctions were issued in the pharmaceutical sector, and of these just one was upheld on appeal.[24] So much did the tide turn that in 2009, when a preliminary injunction was issued, the IP community celebrated this, hopefully, as a "landmark" ruling.[25] As a CILFA lawyer put it, "If I were in private practice and had to live from defending local firms in litigation, I wouldn't survive" (Interview, December 9, 2014a).

The conflict over preliminary injunctions reflected a serious misjudgment on the part of the USTR, which challenged Argentina on the basis of an isolated case where an American firm failed to obtain an injunction to remove an alleged infringer from the market. This ruling was not consistent with prevailing trends, and thus an odd case upon which to press for alteration of the law in Argentina. Although Argentina's patent law was formally incon-sistent with TRIPS in a "black letter" sense, the status quo largely favored foreign firms because of how judges were interpreting and enforcing the law. The US stirred up a hornets' nest, unnecessarily—and counterproductively. In the words of a key CILFA director, "the grenade exploded in their own hands" (Interview, September 23, 2011a).[26]

It is important to put the USTR's error in comparative perspective, as this too reflects the nature of political coalitions in Argentina.[27] One might expect the USTR to consult the actors in the domestic legal profession with the best and most complete understanding of the state of play in the country, rather than rely on information from the lawyers advocating on behalf of a specific company that was hurt by a particular ruling. Indeed, as two prominent Argentinean lawyers who work with CAEME and the transnational sector lamented, had the USTR properly consulted with them, or with the local legal profession more generally, US officials would have been advised not to get involved. But the USTR proceeded, based on poor information, and suffered a serious setback (Interview, September 23, 2011c).[28] It is difficult to imagine this sort of poor communication between the USTR and the transnational pharmaceutical sector in Brazil or Mexico, for example, and the reason is not simply because these two countries are larger than Argentina and therefore receive

---

[24] Data provided by email from CILFA, February 2, 2015. On file with author.

[25] "Landmark decision issued on pharmaceutical patent enforcement," *International Law Office*, October 18, 2010 (goo.gl/jOwk8n). See also BMI (2014, 66). Note that in this case the defendant was not an Argentinean firm but rather the local affiliate of a major international generics producer (Sandoz).

[26] After the law was changed, the USTR, implicitly recognizing its error, complained that injunctions were difficult to obtain and urged Argentinean authorities to remedy the situation (USTR 2006).

[27] I am grateful to Duncan Matthews for discussions on this topic.

[28] Jorge Otamendi, another Argentinean lawyer who works with the transnational sector, is more scathing: "That a country [the US] that has always stood for strengthening the rule of law ends up accepting what it accepted, can, in the most generous explanation, only be attributed to the incompetence of its negotiator" (Otamendi 2004).

more attention, but because the transnational pharmaceutical sector's local subsidiaries have established much more presence. The low profile of foreign drug firms in Argentina gave less voice to their patent professionals and allowed individual firms and their lawyers to get the USTR's ear.[29] To be sure, subsidiaries of US firms in Brazil and Mexico relate their particular grievances to the USTR as well, but in those countries there is so much regular communication between the USTR, PhRMA, and the local associations that individual firms' particular grievances get subordinated. There can be no doubting that the USTR dropped the ball here, but the error is not independent of the social structure conditions of the time in Argentina. Nor was the USTR able to mobilize exporters on its behalf, given the low levels of dependence on the US market (see Table 2.4, p. 49).

To summarize this section, the US's challenge to Argentina's new pharmaceutical patent system was resolutely unsuccessful. On most issues the US ended up accepting Argentina's approach, either explicitly or implicitly, and even where it looked like the US won, it lost. In October 2002, following the settlement with the US, President Duhalde submitted revisions to Congress with the agreed reforms. In contrast to the 1990s, when introducing the patent law united Congress and the local pharmaceutical sector against the Executive, in this instance all three sets of actors were on the same page.[30] Indeed, the initiative, regarded as the outcome of a resounding diplomatic success, sailed smoothly through Congress, passed unanimously in both the Chamber of Deputies and Senate. As a congressional aid relayed the events, the Minister of Foreign Relations and Minister of Health "went to the Senate and in an informal meeting, with no attendance or minutes, they prepared the text. And that's how it turned out" (Interview, November 20, 2007). The defensive coalition prevailed.

LOCAL LABS, SECONDARY PATENTS, AND PATENT EXAMINATION GUIDELINES

The local pharmaceutical sector's mobilization and influence are evident not only in its collaboration with the government to ward off external challenges, but also campaigns to alter patent examination practices. Here too the defensive

---

[29] It is conceivable that the economic turmoil of the early 2000s also contributed to the poor coordination and communication between the USTR and the transnational sector.

[30] For a comparison of the simplicity and "peaceful" process of the 2000s with the intense conflict of the 1990s, see "Aprobaron cambios en la ley de patentes," *La Nación*, September 18, 2003.

coalition went on the offensive and secured favorable modifications of the new pharmaceutical patent system.

One area where Argentinean firms had cause for concern regarded new patents on existing drugs. As explained, most drugs launched in the late 1990s and early 2000s were not protected by patents in Argentina, as these drugs tended to rely on earlier, pre-1995 applications. Yet many of the drugs launched in the late 1990s and early 2000s also had additional "secondary" patents, on alternative forms of the molecules or distinct compositions, for-mulations, and uses. These applications for secondary patents, unlike those for primary patents, often were filed after the 1995 cut-off date. While an appli-cation for a drug's primary patent may have been filed globally in the early 1990s and thus not eligible in Argentina because of the decision not to allow pipeline patents, the secondary patent applications may have been filed in Argentina in the late 1990s and thus held in the mailbox to be examined after 2000. Were such drugs to become protected by these secondary patents, local producers could then find themselves restricted, notwithstanding the "intelli-gent implementation" of the 1990s.[31]

CILFA's concerns about secondary patents were accentuated by the transi-tional context, and the shock to the system represented by the introduction of pharmaceutical patents. Prior to 2000 the patent office (INPI-AR) did not examine applications for patents on pharmaceutical products. Doing so meant embarking on an entirely new form of work, developing and deploying scarce technical and human capabilities in this new endeavor.[32] And the workload was considerable, as made evident by the growth in pharmaceutical patent applications presented in Figure 6.1. Pharmaceuticals constituted roughly half of the applications received and examined after the transition period ended and examination commenced in October 2000 (Levis 2010, 389). Were secondary pharmaceutical patents to be granted liberally, their spread could reduce some of the benefits that local producers secured with their efforts to shape the creation of the new patent system in the 1990s. Lacking the legal infrastructure to invalidate granted patents through litigation, as is common in the US (Hemphill and Sampat 2012), Argentinean producers sought to prevent these from being granted in the first place.

CILFA initially focused its attention on a particular form of secondary patents, those on new uses of existing drugs. Seeking to prevent the increased workload being demanded from new pharmaceutical patent examination arrangements from allowing "new use" patents to slip through, CILFA worked

---

[31] The example discussed above, of a specific formulation of didanosine being patented despite the molecule not being patented, illustrates this possibility.

[32] According to an INPI-AR official in the patents division, in the early 2000s the patent office had just three examiners responsible for pharmaceuticals (Interview, September 27, 2011, and follow-up email, November 23, 2011).

with the patent office to tighten the procedures for vetting applications. In October 2001, responding to CILFA's requests, the Ministry of Economy instructed the patent office to prepare new examination guidelines. The following year, in consultation with CILFA and the Ministry of Health, INPI-AR complied, issuing instructions to examiners not to grant patents on second medical uses. Specifically, the patent office clarified that it would continue to grant new use patents, in general, but that patents of new medical uses of existing pharmaceutical substances would not be allowed (Bensadon and Sánchez Echagüe 2008; Witthaus 2003).[33] This prohibition did not constitute a formal reform of the LPIMU, but rather made by the patent office as an interpretation of the relevant provisions of the patent law, responding to CILFA's demands.

CILFA's concerns with secondary patents were not limited to patents on new uses of existing drugs. As indicated, it is common for originator firms to file for patents on alternative structural forms of molecules, new dosages, compositions, and formulations (Howard 2007; Kapczynski et al. 2012; Sampat and Shadlen 2017). While few drugs on the market in Argentina had primary patents on original molecules and compounds, because of the way pharmaceutical patents were introduced, or use patents, because of the revised guidelines, an increase in other types of secondary patents could, potentially, pose threats too. Over the course of the 2000s, as pharmaceutical patenting became more common in Argentina, these other forms of secondary patents became one of the principal points of concern for the local sector.

CILFA worked with academics at the University of Buenos Aires to analyze patterns of pharmaceutical patenting in Argentina. While the earlier revisions of INPI-AR's guidelines reduced the number of patents on second medical uses, the research team found a significant number of secondary patents that, with alternative examination procedures, could potentially have been avoided (Correa et al. 2011). The authors concluded that, despite the policy choices of the 1990s regarding the introduction of drug patents, the patent office's subsequent practices were allowing many secondary patents to be granted.[34] CILFA thus proposed new examination guidelines for all pharmaceutical patents. Citing as evidence the analysis of Correa et al. (2011) on INPI-AR outputs through 2007, and its own internal research for subsequent years,

---

[33] See also, "Patentability of Second Medical Uses," *International Law Office*, June 16, 2008 (goo.gl/ntnXhl).

[34] Because Correa et al.'s (2011) study only looks at granted patents, it does not tell us if the patent office also rejected applications for secondary patents. Nor does the study compare outcomes of given pharmaceutical patent applications in Argentina with other countries, so does not tell us if INPI-AR practices were more or less permissive than other patent offices. The purpose of the study simply was to demonstrate a high number of secondary patents in Argentina and thus serve as a call to action. For comparative analysis of pharmaceutical patent examination in Argentina and other countries, see Sampat and Shadlen (2017).

CILFA made the case to the Ministry of Health and the newly-created Ministry of Industry that the patent office's approach toward secondary patents should be revised.[35] The new guidelines that CILFA proposed were based closely on a set of recommendations that had been prepared by Carlos Correa and distributed widely by the United Nations (Correa 2007). In May 2012, following CILFA's invocations, the patent office issued new examination guidelines that made most forms of secondary pharmaceutical patents ineligible for protection in Argentina.

The introduction of new examination guidelines constitutes another victory for the national pharmaceutical sector in Argentina. While roughly 140 pharmaceutical patents were granted annually from October 2000 through May 2012, in the three years after the new guidelines entered into effect INPI-AR granted 159 pharmaceutical patents.[36] To repeat, this is a victory at the margins. Argentina has a pharmaceutical patent system and grants pharmaceutical patents; the global sea change introduced a new status quo. But within that new reality, representatives of the local sector regard the new guidelines as a major accomplishment that helps them retain their strong position in the market, while representatives from the transnational sector regard the new guidelines as yet another setback that dilutes some of the benefits they expected to gain with the country's adoption of pharmaceutical patents.[37]

In this instance, this is less a case of Argentinean officials seeking to tailor the patent system and searching for allies, than of private sector actors seeking change and finding allies in government to advance a tailoring project. Here it is also worth underscoring how, with the issue of the day no longer designing a new patent system but affecting how the new system functions, the different branches of the Executive acquired more autonomy and were able to take more initiative. The local pharmaceutical sector could take advantage of its extensive ties to different actors within the Executive to push its agenda forward. Indeed, one of the things that is most interesting about the Correa et al. (2011) study is that it was conducted by a combination of actors in academia and the state (Ministry of Health, Ministry of Industry), all with ties to the local pharmaceutical industry. By the mid-2000s all these actors were

---

[35] When the Ministry of Industry was created in 2007, out of what had been a Secretariat within the Ministry of Economy, management of the patent office moved to the new ministry.

[36] CILFA analysis, on file with the author. These data do not distinguish between primary and secondary patents. Correa (2014, 11) presents similar findings. Sampat and Shadlen (2017) also report a reduction in Argentina's secondary patent grant rate (and, importantly, an increase in non-grant final determinations) following the new guidelines in 2012.

[37] In 2014 an initiative was proposed to Congress to reform the LPIMU to incorporate the revised guidelines, though as of the time of writing this had not advanced. At the same time, CAEME and its legal allies filed a constitutional complaint that the patent office was overstepping its authority and that the guidelines were discriminatory.

working on the same page; the defensive coalition had become solidified, emboldened, and was fully on the offensive.

PHARMACEUTICAL PRODUCER POWER AND STATE REGULATORY CAPACITY

One of the abiding points of Argentinean case is that local pharmaceutical firms were able to use their considerable economic and political resources to shape national policy on patents. It is not surprising that international observers conclude that "government policy is heavily biased toward local drug producers" (BMI 2014, 9). Yet the Argentinean Government and the national pharmaceutical industry are not in agreement on all issues regarding drug regulation, however, and examining areas of conflict provides an opportunity to better understand state-society dynamics. One such area subject to conflict is the price of prescription medicines, for notwithstanding the country's cautious approach to patents, the market structure that local firms managed to preserve allows them to charge high prices for their products. The flipside of the local sector's strength is that it is hard to regulate; the same factors that facilitate tailoring the patent system—the local sector's impressive resources—also create barriers to designing and implementing regulations to control prices and the marketing of drugs.

In March 2002, with the country in deep economic crisis and public and private health plans under severe stress, Minister of Health Ginés González García declared a public health emergency. The Ministry agreed price freezes with leading labs on over two hundred drugs, created emergency programs to ensure access to essential treatments (e.g. immunizations, maternal and neo-natal care), and introduced a range of measures to control prices and increase access to medicines. One of these measures was a requirement that physicians use generic names of active principal ingredients, and not brand names of drugs, in writing patients' prescriptions.[38] The requirement to prescribe by generic name was first introduced as an emergency resolution by the Ministry of Health in 2002, and then later that year converted into national law.[39] The measure addressed the prescription of drugs, not production or marketing. That is, this was not about creating "generic" drugs, if generic is defined as

---

[38] Other elements of the National Medicines Policy included changes to the package of basic drugs that insurers are obligated to provide, and a program of pharmaceutical assistance to provide free essential medicines to under-served segments of the population (*Remediar*). See Homedes and Ugalde (2006), Tarragona and de la Puente (n.d.), Tobar (2008).

[39] Some of Argentina's provinces had already put this requirement in place locally.

having demonstrated bioequivalence or lacking a branded label, but rather requiring that doctors write prescriptions using non-proprietary names.[40]

The saga of the generics drug regulation in Argentina illustrates key dynamics of how the sector functions, and the power of local industry to shape its regulatory environment (Tobar and Godoy Garraza 2003). Where drugs have patents there is a single supplier, of course, but for drugs without patents, which remained the case in much of the Argentinean market, multiple firms can compete with their own products. In Argentina these products were "similars," i.e. drugs that have the same active pharmaceutical ingredients but were not required to demonstrate bioequivalence.[41] Brands allowed firms to distinguish their drugs from others. Indeed, promotion of brands and competition based on brands had always been the lifeblood of the sector, with Argentinean firms investing considerable resources in downstream activities to cultivate relationships and generate loyalty among doctors, pharmacists, and patients. These efforts only increased in the 1990s and 2000s, with the arrival of patents, for brands are what would allow local firms to preserve their share of the still large—but inevitably shrinking—non-patented segment of the market.[42] Firms thus worked tirelessly to create brand loyalties and differentiate their products from their competitors' seemingly identical products. As the director of one leading firm put it, discussing the importance of brands to local firms and consumers, medicines are selected based on brand preferences, just like other consumer products: "When you want chocolate you decide whose chocolate you like best and you buy their chocolate. You don't care who invented chocolate" (Interview, December 5, 2014a).[43]

Argentinean pharmaceutical firms had historically opposed initiatives to reduce the importance of brands, and with their increased importance in the new environment were as steadfast as ever in their opposition. CILFA resisted efforts to include more generalized requirements to demonstrate bioequivalence, and particularly restrictions on the use of brands. The former would raise costs (at least temporarily), while the latter would fundamentally

---

[40] Fonseca and Shadlen (2017) provide a framework for comparing national approaches to regulating and promoting "generic" drugs. Bioavailability measures the extent to which a drug is absorbed into the body and is available to act upon its intended target. Demonstrating "bioequivalence" means that it has been shown that there is no significant difference in the rate and extent of availability of two drugs over a period of time, at the same dose and under the same conditions.

[41] Bioequivalence is required in a few high-risk therapeutic segments.

[42] Virtually all analysts of the Argentinean pharmaceutical sector emphasize local firms' emphasis on brands (Bekerman and Sirlin 2001; Bergallo and Ramón Michel 2014; Bisang 2010; Hayden 2011; Katz 2001; Lakoff 2005; Sosa 2002). Indeed, this is unmissable for observers in the country, with pharmacies' windows and shelves visibly promoting specific firms' branded products.

[43] For more discussion of brand promotion, see "El negocio detrás de las recetas: El oscuro circuito de la prescripción de medicamentos," *La Nación*, December 27, 2014.

undermine leading firms' business model. The costs of these two regulations would be felt differently, depending on firm size. Larger firms would have an easier time meeting bioequivalence requirements than smaller firms, but larger firms also had more recognized brands and more invested in their brand reputations, so had more at stake in preserving the right to compete by brand name (CEP 2009). And it was the larger firms that drove CILFA's approach. As it was, the Ministry of Health was also concerned that introducing bioequivalence requirements in a time of crisis would reduce supply and increase prices, so did not push hard for this at the time. Thus the crux of the debate was over regulations on prescription practices, in particular the use of brands.[44]

The outcome of the 2002 "generics" law reflects CILFA's interests, and in particular its obsession with preserving large firms' abilities to compete on the basis of their brands. While the new law requires physicians to indicate the drug's non-proprietary name on all prescriptions, it allows doctors to continue to recommend particular branded products as well and for pharmacists to dispense the brands they are familiar with. Doctors are required to include the name of the molecule, but they are not prohibited from also indicating specific brand names. Pharmacists can offer alternative versions of prescribed drugs, and patients have the right to request alternatives, but pharmacists do not have the authority to decide which version of the medicine to supply. The law does not create a situation where patients provide pharmacists with a prescription indicating a "generic" drug and the pharmacist decides which version to provide; if the prescription indicates a particular brand, as most do, and the patient wants that product (as most tend to do, after being told by physicians what drug to take), the patient receives that brand. The objective here is not to analyze the "generic" policy itself, or the legislative process that produced this version of the law (Hayden 2011; Tobar and Godoy Garraza 2003), but rather to drive home the point that the way the legislation was crafted provides ample opportunities for pharmaceutical firms to subvert it. Alternative versions that would have de-emphasized the role of brands and thus been more threatening for the durability of local firms' business models were discarded. In fact, even the watered down legislation was largely circumvented: by the early 2010s only 20 percent of prescriptions were estimated to include non-proprietary names.[45]

In December 2014 I met with a top official in the health economics division of the Ministry of Health (Interview, December 9, 2014b). When we reached

---

[44] The transnational firms and their representatives, however, pushed strongly for more comprehensive bioequivalence testing, and in subsequent years continued to criticize health authorities for not including such requirements.

[45] "Genéricos y medicamentos públicos: el gobierno quema 'dos anchos' en una jugada cortoplacista," *Mirada Profesional*, November 7, 2014. My interviews with officials in the health sector uniformly stressed this point too.

the topic of brands, and measures to address the role of brands in the pharmaceutical market, in terms of prescription, promotion, and labeling, he paused, instructed his assistant to close the door, and then proceeded to articulate the political barriers to introducing such measures. Although the Ministry of Health would like to see such regulations, and was reported to be drafting proposed regulations, officials also know that that the local sector would fight tooth and nail with all its resources to block such measures. And they are almost certainly right: the president of one of Argentina's leading pharmaceutical firms, a former director of CILFA, stated emphatically that measures restricting the use of brand names would be intolerable (Interview, December 5, 2014b). Ultimately, health officials came to accept the central role of brands in the Argentinean pharmaceutical market as a reality they must adjust to, something they are unlikely to change. Indeed, the Health Ministry official concluded this section of our discussion, now behind a closed door, alone with his assistant and me, with frank resignation: "I don't see any future without brands here" (Interview, December 9, 2014b).[46]

The prominence of brands makes drugs more expensive than they might otherwise be, for they segment markets and reduce the substitutability of rival suppliers' versions of the same (or seemingly same) products. Reducing the role of brands, then, is an indirect way of reducing prices by promoting more competition. Not only has this been unsuccessful, but so too, not surprisingly, were more direct efforts to regulate prices (Bergallo and Ramón Michel 2014; Tobar 2008). Health economists and public health officials are united in expressing concern about the price of prescription drugs in Argentina and, critically, the local sector's ability to evade initiatives designed to control prices. Examples of the local sector's actions are abundant. A former Minister of the Economy, referring to the local sector as "untouchable," recounted an episode of his making public statements regarding drug pricing leading to a phone call from the President to change the topic (Interview, September 19, 2011b). In the late 2000s, a group of health policy professionals drafted proposed legislation on drug price regulation. After considerable difficulty arranging a meeting, they managed to meet with a collection of legislators, but the initiative received not one positive response in the Chamber of Deputies and never advanced.[47]

To summarize this section, the same resources that helped Argentina's local pharmaceutical firms shape the country's introduction of drugs patents, and that helped them adjust to the eventual onset of drug patenting, and that

---

[46] In 2016 a proposal to prohibit the naming of brands in prescriptions was proposed to the Chamber of Deputies ("Buscan modificar la Ley de Genéricos para prohibir la inclusión de marcas comerciales en las recetas," *Mirada Profesional*, March 22, 2016 [goo.gl/A8ZcmX]).

[47] Interview with leader of the group that proposing the legislation (Interview, September 19, 2011a).

helped them reform the patent system subsequently, also make these firms hard to regulate. In addition to pointing out this downside of the local sector's strength, the discussion plays an important analytic role in terms of the book's larger argument of the relative importance of Executive preferences and social structure in accounting for the outcomes we observe. As regards patents, since the late 1990s successive governments and the local pharmaceutical sector have been aligned, singing from the same hymn sheet in their resistance to overtures and demands for over-compliance. As regards health sector and drug market regulation, however, the Executive and this key societal actor often come into conflict, with the latter typically prevailing.

CONCLUSION

Since the mid-1990s, after the Menem Government at last came to accept that it would not get its way in the debate over the introduction of pharmaceutical patents in Argentina, the positions of successive governments have been constant. Presidents changed, from Menem to de la Rua, to Duhalde, and then the Kirchners, but the commitment to minimalist compliance with the new global order in pharmaceutical patenting did not. An important reason for this is that the local sector has been able to influence—at times drive—the government's position. The enduring strength of the local pharmaceutical sector allowed it help the government rebuff the US's demands, and also to secure revisions of the patent office's examination guidelines.

Although the emergence of new dimensions of conflict is common across all countries that introduced pharmaceutical patents in the 1990s, what happens within the new parameters varies. In Argentina, as actors adjusted to the presence of pharmaceutical patents, other aspects of the country's pharmaceutical patent system continued to be the subject of intense conflict. Rules over data protection, preliminary injunctions, and examination guidelines, for example, were all fought with the same level of intensity and acrimony in the 2000s, as the introduction of pharmaceutical patents had been contested in the 1990s. The battle over the introduction of pharmaceutical patents ended, but Argentinean and transnational firms continue to have divergent and incompatible interests over these other issues. And the local firms kept prevailing.[48] Indeed, the local pharmaceutical sector's ability to shape revisions to the pharmaceutical patent system is universally recognized. Discussions with lawyers and patent agents working for transnational pharmaceutical firms in

---

[48] Likewise, the local sector also sought to keep Argentina outside of the Patent Cooperation Treaty. Though not examined here, the outcome of this dispute was consistent with the analysis in this chapter.

Argentina illustrate this clearly: these actors have resigned themselves to what they regard as a lamentable fact, that they face an uphill battle in securing changes to the patent system on account of the local sector's economic and political power.[49]

It is tempting to attribute the outcomes observed in Argentina to the creative lawyering of Carlos Correa, a prominent Argentinean lawyer and academic who played a key role in the events analyzed in this chapter.[50] Correa's presence and fingerprints are undeniable: Correa helped prepare Argentina's defense against the US's demands for data exclusivity; Correa crafted the revision of the system for preliminary injunctions; Correa was the lead author of the study used to make the case for altering Argentina's pharmaceutical examination guidelines (Correa et al. 2011), and the new guidelines adopted were based largely on a study that Correa wrote for the International Center for Trade and Sustainable Development in conjunction with the United Nations (Correa 2007). Yet the influence that Correa may have exerted is certainly not independent of the underlying conditions. After all, his positions are well known by governments throughout the developing world, as are his services and availability to help craft legal provisions (and, of course, other countries also have legal experts with these abilities, even if not the same degree of international visibility). Quite simply, Argentina did not resist the US efforts to alter the data protection rules, subvert the US efforts on preliminary injunctions, and introduce restrictive pharmaceutical patent examination guidelines because of Carlos Correa, but, rather, Correa was able to help Argentina achieve these outcomes because of permissive social structure conditions.

Importantly, the local sector's continued influence is not just a reflection of the same factors that yielded the minimalist response to the global sea change in the 1990s, but was enhanced by and thus is also a consequence of the initial policy choices . The way pharmaceutical patents were introduced in Argentina allowed the local sector to continue accumulating resources. As conflicts moved from when and how to introduce patents, to the functioning of the pharmaceutical patent system, the local sector was able to work closely with the Executive to resist external pressures and push through changes to the

---

[49] In late 2015, the government of Mauricio Macri came to power, a change that has led many to expect changes to Argentina's pharmaceutical patent system. Consistent with expectations, in June 2016 Macri replaced the longtime president of the patent office with a lawyer from one of Argentina's law firms associated with the transnational sector. How these events will affect the direction of patent policy is of course to be seen.

[50] Consider a passage written by Otamendi, an Argentinean lawyer who works with the transnational sector and a consistent advocate of over-compliance, with reference to Correa's role in dispute with the US over data protection and the reform of the preliminary injunction system: "Our country was advised by someone who has inspired changes to patent laws in other Latin American countries that constitute a weakening of inventors' rights" (Otamendi 2004).

examination system. Argentinean pharmaceutical firms resisted the introduction of pharmaceutical patents, but that was a fight they were always going to lose; after that they succeeded in shaping how patents were introduced, and this success allowed them to continue to shape how the system functioned.

Ultimately, protecting and promoting the local pharmaceutical sector appears to be a thread that unites virtually all policy. Even when the government implements health policy reforms, e.g. "generic" prescription, it has done so in a way that preserves opportunities for local pharmaceutical firms to exploit their commercial strengths. Taking a step back, one can think of two distributive conflicts: between transnational and local firms, and between pharmaceutical firms and consumers. The power of the "untouchable" local pharmaceutical sector has allowed it to shape the patent system to prevail on the first dimension, and to shape the health regulatory system to prevail on the second dimension as well. As many authors have pointed out, and as many informants acknowledged, while extensive pharmaceutical patent protection can be threatening to public health, the absence of such does not necessarily translate into health benefits (Bergallo and Ramón Michel 2014; Hayden 2011; Lakoff 2005). Note, however, that it is not likely that the Argentinean state would be more successful in regulating the pharmaceutical sector were it dominated by transnational firms either (as the next chapter suggests). The implication of the Argentinean case is that having a strong national pharmaceutical sector that can lend political support may be essential for resisting external pressures for over-compliance and for tailoring the patent system, but other conditions are needed for a minimalist patent system to yield broader health benefits.

7

What's Good for Us is Good for You

The Transnational Pharmaceutical Sector and Mexico's Internationalist Patent System

The enthusiasm with which Mexico embraced the global sea change in the 1990s was reproduced in the 2000s, as Mexico continued to exceed its international obligations under both the World Trade Organization and the North American Free Trade Agreement. Much of Mexican politics was different after the end of seventy years of single-party rule, but in the area of pharmaceutical patents, continuity was the order of the day. This period witnesses the consolidation of an "internationalist" pharmaceutical patent system in Mexico, featuring consistent catering to the demands of the transnational pharmaceutical sector and seemingly open-ended adoption of global "best practices."

Analysis of Mexico's internationalist patent system highlights the iterative and cumulative characteristics of patent politics, and the enduring effects of initial choices. In the 2000s, even as desires to reform the patent system emerged, coalition building to achieve these reforms proved to be exceptionally difficult. The reasons for this are found in the transformation of industrial structure, a by-product of the way patents were introduced in the 1990s.

An explanation of patent policies based on social structure and the legacies of initial choices is to be contrasted with explanations based on international pressures and Executive preferences. One seemingly obvious explanation for Mexico's policy trajectory, for example, may be the country's relationship with the United States. After all, Mexico's northern neighbor has not only been the principal leader of the global campaign to increase IP protection, but the US is also Mexico's most important economic partner and its main export market. The close economic relationship between the two countries is solidified in the form of NAFTA, and this trade agreement includes a chapter dedicated to IP. Yet NAFTA itself is an inadequate explanatory factor for the events of the 2000s. After all, the changes to the pharmaceutical patent system that Mexico introduced, a decade after NAFTA entered into force, were not required by the agreement; nor were the changes that were contemplated but beaten back inconsistent with NAFTA.

Executive ideology and preferences are not sufficient to understand Mexican patent politics in this period either. To be sure, given the orientation of the Executive for the first twelve years of the twentieth century, with Presidents Vicente Fox (2000–2006) and Felipe Calderón (2006–2012) both from the conservative National Action Party (*Partido de Acción Nacional*, PAN), we would hardly expect radical policy shifts. Even in conservative and US-friendly Mexico, however, we witness efforts to tailor the patent system to address some of the consequences of over-compliance. Yet these efforts, all consistent with Mexico's international obligations, were uniformly unsuccessful.

The Mexico case helps place Executive ideology as an explanatory variable into context. Both of the other two countries examined in this book had Executives in the early 2000s from leftist governments. The Mexican experience suggests that left-orientation is not a necessary condition for health officials to seek to address challenges associated with having new pharmaceutical patent systems.[1] Motives to tailor the patent regime may be more structurally rooted: health officials care about the price of drugs and access to medicines, and to the extent that these appear to be affected by pharmaceutical patents, they may seek changes. That is likely to be the case regardless of the overall orientation of the Executive or the ideology of the President's party. Indeed, analysis of this period of Mexican political economy reveals divisions within the Executive, with health officials seeking to reform the pharmaceutical patent system.

It was not motives to make the Mexico's new pharmaceutical patent system more health-oriented that sets Mexico apart from Argentina and Brazil, but rather the absence of means to do so. Changes to social structure left the opponents of tailoring unrivaled in their economic and political strength, and thus made coalition building for modifying the patent system seemingly impossible. It is for understanding these structural changes that NAFTA is indeed of crucial importance—not as a set of legal obligations that prohibit or compel particular activities, but rather the broader political economy landscape which the agreement helped shape. In addition to patenting, the pharmaceutical sector was subject to further tariff reduction, building on the process started in the late 1980s, and, eventually, revisions to government procurement practices that had previously afforded special treatment to local firms. These shifts in policy, in combination with the early and retroactive introduction of pharmaceutical patents, also linked to NAFTA, induced changes to industrial structure that, by altering constellations of interests and affecting patterns of political mobilization, had important implications for politics. One effect was cementing the transnational sector's dominance in the Mexican pharmaceutical industry. Mexico's social structure restricted the realm of feasible policy alternatives in the 2000s.

---

[1] Fairfield and Garay (2017, forthcoming) and Garay (2016) also document efforts to expand social provision even under conservative governments.

Economic policies, once implemented, affect the landscape out of which coalitions are formed for subsequent policies.[2] The initial policy choices made in the early 1990s set Mexico on a path of increasing patent protection. Changes to the pharmaceutical sector induced by the way patents were introduced, as well as by the broader economic policies of the 1990s, altered the possibilities for subsequent coalition formation. The importance of timing is clear, particularly Mexico's early introduction of pharmaceutical patents: by the time tailoring the patent system emerged as a consideration, the new status quo had been in place for a considerable amount of time and the country's social structure had been fundamentally altered. When actors had motives to alter the new patent system in the 2000s, their abilities to do so were hemmed in by the social and political conditions created by the policies introduced in the 1990s.

The chapter has four sections. The first section provides an assessment of the impacts of the policy choices of the 1990s, pointing to the high level of pharmaceutical patenting in Mexico and the effects of the new policy environment on the pharmaceutical industry. The following sections then examine revisions to the new pharmaceutical patent regime, all to the benefit of patent-holders seeking greater rights of exclusion. Section two shows the perverse process by which efforts to alter the compulsory licensing system in Congress ended up making it more difficult to use this policy instrument. Section three examines the reshaping of the functioning of the new patent system by the courts that also allowed patent owners to extend effective periods of protection. Section four analyzes another legislative event, an initiative to introduce pre-grant opposition into the process of patent examination, which again yielded the outcome desired by the transnational sector. The within-case comparative analysis offered by these case studies provides variation on a range of important variables, including the preferences of health officials in the Mexican Executive, preferences and strategies of the local pharmaceutical sector, and sensitivity to US pressures. Yet the outcomes did not change: the transnational sector prevailed.

THE LEGACIES OF EARLY AND EXTREME
OVER-COMPLIANCE

The introduction of pharmaceutical patents implies that new drugs will become patented, and, for the duration of the patents, have single suppliers.

---

[2] Murillo's analysis of utilities regulation also shows how politicians can be constrained by earlier choices. When President Fox tried to promote market competition in the telecommunications sector, for example, these efforts were largely unsuccessful on account of the constraints established by the market structure created by earlier reforms of the 1990s (Murillo 2009, 219–20).

That new reality is common, or will become common, to all countries that introduced pharmaceutical patents, as required by TRIPS and the new international context.

The fact that Mexico introduced pharmaceutical product patents comparatively early, in 1991, meant that these effects came to be felt earlier than in other countries. Figure 7.1 illustrates the rapid increase in patent applications filed in Mexico in the 1990s. Because the 1991 patent law allowed patenting to begin immediately, Mexico did not adopt any provision akin to a "mailbox," where applications would be retained pending expiration of a transition period. Rather, these began to be granted without delay. Indeed, the early adoption of pharmaceutical patents meant that for years, when other countries still were not granting pharmaceutical patents, Mexico was; after the change of law in 1991, applications were filed and patents were granted in Mexico, but none of this was occurring, yet, in most other developing countries.

That Mexico not only introduced patents early, but retroactively as well, with a generous pipeline provision, exacerbated these effects. Pipeline protection meant that inventions from the 1980s, prior to the LFPPI, could become patent protected in Mexico too.[3] Mexico allowed more than 1600 patents via the pipeline, which meant that many drugs became patented immediately in

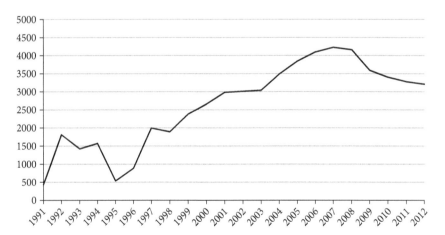

Figure 7.1. Pharmaceutical and Pharmo-Chemical Applications Filed in Mexico*
* Applications with first International Patent Classification of A61K or C07D.
Source: IMPI

---

[3] In 1994 the name of the patent law was changed to *Ley de Propiedad Industrial*. As this title, in Spanish, is the same as the Portuguese title of Brazil's *Lei de Propriedade Industrial*, to avoid confusion with identical acronyms I continue to refer to Mexico's patent law using LFPPI, the acronym derived from its original name.

the early 1990s.[4] Drugs with applications from the 1980s that were launched in the early 1990s, for example, could receive patents in Mexico and thus be protected from competition. And because the pipeline only excluded patents from eligibility if the associated product had already been launched on the *Mexican* market, even drugs that were already marketed outside of the country could subsequently enjoy patent protection—and thus single-supplier status— in Mexico.

As a result of the early and retroactive introduction of pharmaceutical patents, more drugs became patented than would otherwise be the case. In Argentina, for example, the first pharmaceutical patent was not granted until late 2000. By that time Mexico already had been granting pharmaceutical patents for nearly a decade, and thousands of pharmaceutical patents were in force. Brazil's new patent law included a pipeline as well, and, as we shall see, this also led to a surge of single-supplier, patent-protected drugs. But Brazil's pipeline was not introduced until 1997; for most of the decade Brazil remained free of pharmaceutical patents, while these were accumulating in Mexico. To illustrate, consider the sample of 159 new drugs launched from 1996 to 2004, presented in Chapter 2 (Table 2.2, p. 41). In identifying all the applications and patents associated with these drugs in Argentina, Brazil, and Mexico, of the three countries Mexico had by far the largest number of patents (granted or via pipeline) and, critically, the largest number of drugs protected by patents, with 89 percent of the drugs in the sample receiving patents.

Mexico's early and extreme over-compliance reconfigured the industrial sector. Whereas in Argentina we saw how a delayed and minimalist response to the global sea change allowed the local pharmaceutical sector to accumulate resources in the late 1990s and early 2000s, the effects in Mexico were nearly the opposite. By the end of the 1990s Mexican firms accounted for less than 15 percent of sales, with only a single firm featuring among the industry leaders (Moïse and Docteur 2007; Zúñiga and Combe 2002; BMI 2015b). Recall that Mexican firms traditionally had a low presence in local retail markets, with their sanctuary being selling to the state sector, but eventually they faced more competition in this segment too, the transition periods for implementing new (and less favorable) government purchasing arrangements expired in the early 2000s. And Mexico's drug manufacturers had to deal with trade liberalization too: the removal of barriers to imports, which began in the 1980s, was deepened at the same time as patents were introduced, as, in accordance with NAFTA, tariffs were reduced annually over ten years until eventually reaching zero by 2003 (International Trade Administration 2006). Upstream, the effects of these economic policy changes were even greater. Nearly two-thirds of the country's pharmo-chemical firms disappeared

---

[4] Becerra Ramírez (2009, 79) reports that Mexico received 2100 patents under the pipeline provision. My research, utilizing the patent office database, revealed 1612.

by 1998 (CEPAL 1999, 49; Jorge 2006). By 2005, only twenty-six firms in Mexico produced active pharmaceutical ingredients, compared to forty-eight such firms in 1994 (Enriquez 2013; Moïse and Docteur 2007; Secretaría de Salud 2005; Zúñiga and Combe 2002).[5]

The flipside of this reconfiguration is that transnational firms consolidated their power. The pharmaceutical industry, in its entirety, grew in Mexico in the 1990s, in terms of investment, employment, and share of output. Mexico had a larger pharmaceutical sector by the early 2000s than the 1980s, but transnational firms' domination was unprecedented.[6] As elsewhere, some local firms invested more in research and sought to become more innovative, and many sought licensing arrangements and collaborations with trans-nationals (Gonsen and Jasso 2000; Guzmán 2014; Solleiro et al. 2010; Zúñiga et al. 2007). Evidence of innovative outputs from national firms remained minimal in Mexico, however, and in stark contrast to what we witnessed in Argentina, where local firms' commercial and productive assets helped them establish co-production and commercialization relationships with foreign firms on favorable terms, Mexican firms that entered into such relationships did so as clear subordinates (BMI 2015b; Guzmán 2014; Zúñiga and Combe 2002). In fact, many firms that survived and adjusted to the changes unleashed by the opening of the economy and the introduction of patents tended to be absorbed by transnational firms, as Mexico experienced a wave of foreign acquisitions in the pharmaceutical sector (Espicom 2012; FUNSALUD 2013; Secretaría de Salud 2005).

Mexico's national pharmaceutical sector was not just weakened relative to the transnational sector, but also transformed. Those remaining firms tended to be smaller, specialized, and focused on producing and selling their own versions of drugs after originator firms' patents expired. Overall, the result of the new patent and economic policy changes introduced in the 1990s was not just a transnational-dominated pharmaceutical sector, but within that a residual national segment featuring a small number of firms concerned less about the existence of patents than about the sets of issues affecting how long periods of exclusivity last.

In addition to generating a shock to industry, the changes triggered by Mexico's early and extreme over-compliance in the 1990s presented substantial challenges to the health system too. The dense patenting landscape in Mexico makes it difficult to rely on competition to lower prices. While in other countries drugs could be secured from multiple sources, either locally from domestic firms that could produce their own versions of medicines lacking

---

[5] By the mid-2010s the number of Mexican firms producing active pharmaceutical ingredients was reported to be less than twenty (BMI 2015b, 76).

[6] BMI (2015b); Guerrero Castro (2012); Guzmán (2014); Jorge (2006); Torres Guerra and Gutiérrez (2009).

patent protection or imported from other countries where drugs were not patented either, in Mexico new drugs have single suppliers, either the patent holder or an authorized licensee. With regard to HIV/AIDS, for example, most key antiretroviral (ARV) drugs have enjoyed patent protection in Mexico. Among the medicines recommended by the World Health Organization for first-line treatment, all but one (zidovudine) received patents in Mexico (MPP n.d.). Not only did this mean that these patented drugs were more expensive, but not even generic fixed-dose combinations including zidovudine could typically be used in Mexico. To repeat, the density of patenting is greater than would otherwise be the case if Mexico had not introduced pharmaceutical patents so early and with pipeline protection for drugs coming on the market in the early 1990s.

Not surprisingly, ARV prices remained high in Mexico. The price of ARVs decreased throughout the developing world in the 2000s, as the attention brought by high prices and vibrant competition from Indian suppliers globally generated downward pressures on both originator and generic drugs (Kapstein and Busby 2013; MSF various years; Waning et al. 2010), and Mexico benefited from these global price reductions. Yet compared to peer countries Mexico continued to pay considerably more for ARVs—for some drugs up to six times more (Adesina et al. 2013; Gasman 2008, S424; Trout 2010). In the early 2000s Mexico began scaling up HIV/AIDS treatment through the public sector, but officials knew they needed to proceed with caution (Bautista-Arredondo et al. 2008; Adesina et al. 2013). After all, with the high price of ARVs, too much treatment would simply bankrupt the Health Secretariat's budget. The government's own National Center for HIV/AIDS prevention and control reported that a main obstacle to extending treatment was the "cost of acquiring medicines due to the fact that Mexico faces the highest prices in Latin America" (CENSIDA 2008, 22).

The high price of drugs in Mexico is not limited to ARVs, but is widely recognized as a broader phenomenon.[7] Drug prices in Mexico are high compared to other middle-income countries, and also relative to wealthier countries. Kanavos and Vandoros (2011) show that the average weighted price of patented drugs was 67 percent higher in Mexico than in five European countries (Britain, France, Germany, Italy, Spain) and 22 percent higher than in the US, while prices for non-patented drugs were more than two times higher than in the EU countries and roughly equivalent to the US. Among members of the Organization for Economic Cooperation and Development, which Mexico joined in 1994, the average share of health expenditures allocated to medicines in 2010 was 18.2 percent, while in Mexico drug spending

---

[7] See, for example, CESOP (2010), Comité de Competividad (2008), González Pier (2008), González Pier and Barraza-Lloréns (2011), Moïse and Docteur (2007), Molina-Salazar et al. (2008), Knaul et al. (2012), Secretaría de Salud (2005), Torres Guerra and Gutiérrez (2009).

accounted for 30.6 percent of overall health spending (OECD 2014).[8] The relationship between patents and prices is complex, as prices are a function of multiple factors, but there is little disagreement that Mexico has high drug prices and there are sound reasons to believe that the high level of pharmaceutical patenting contributes to this. Not only do patents appear to have significant price effects in Mexico, but data on prices of non-patented drugs suggest that leading firms are able to forestall competition even after legally sanctioned periods of exclusivity expire.[9]

The problems created by Mexico's response to the global sea change of the 1990s are not a secret. The government report cited above, for example, observing the obstacles that drug prices impose for HIV/AIDS treatment, lamented that Mexico "lacks policy instruments to improve the country's position in negotiating with the pharmaceutical industry and thus obtain prices that are appropriate for the level of development of the country" (CENSIDA 2008, 22). The expectation, then, might be to see tailoring of the pharmaceutical patent system. That is, if the patent system created by over-compliance in the 1990s did not contain policy levers that would allow health officials to combat high prices, we might expect to see steps undertaken to establish such levers. In fact, since the turn of the century, countless efforts to tailor Mexico's patent system have been proposed and attempted, but these have uniformly been unsuccessful, and at times further increased levels of pharmaceutical patent protection. The remainder of this chapter examines these events, showing how the transformations of industry impeded coalition building to tailor the patent system.

LEGISLATIVE PERVERSITY: REFORMING MEXICO'S COMPULSORY LICENSING PROVISIONS

In December 2002 the Mexican Green Party (*Partido Verde Ecologista de México*, PVEM) presented an initiative in the Chamber of Deputies to reduce pharmaceutical patent terms to ten years if deemed necessary to address the challenges of a "serious illness." As drafted, the initiative was problematic, legally, for shortening terms in this way would have violated the requirements in TRIPS and the North American Free Trade Agreement of twenty

---

[8] Drug spending as a share of health expenditures is an overly blunt measure, but the fact that the ratio is consistently high in Mexico—and consistently among the highest in the OECD—is telling. Among OECD countries only Hungary tends to allocate a higher share of health spending to pharmaceuticals.

[9] In 2016 Mexico's competition authorities announced an investigation into the high price of post-patent drugs. "Autoridad regulatoria investigará el mercado de medicamentos con patente vencida," *Expansión*, July 20, 2016.

years, a point that was recognized by virtually all observers. The initiative's origins also made it unlikely to advance: the PVEM, which had supported President Fox's candidacy in the 2000 elections, was no longer allied with Fox's National Action Party (PAN) but firmly in the political opposition. Furthermore, the initiative was made particularly toxic by the fact that the deputy who put this forward happened to be the nephew of Victor González Torres, the controversial owner and president of Farmacias Similares, a chain of pharmacies selling inexpensive off-patent medicines that emerged and took off in the 1990s (Chu and Garcia-Cuellar 2011; Hayden 2007). González Torres, a physician, pharmacist, and industrialist (he also owned his pharmacies' principal supplier, Laboratorios Best) who went by the nickname "*Dr. Simi*," had his own political ambitions too, which would include an effort to run for the Presidency of Mexico in 2006. González Torres waged a campaign in which he was purportedly empowering patients to take on a corrupt medical establishment. In doing so González Torres' attacks made little distinction between transnational or Mexican pharmaceutical firms, public or private clinics, hospitals, and medical professionals—these were all painted with the same brush, part of the problem that *Dr. Simi* offered to fix.[10] Thus, inconsistent with Mexico's international obligations, coming from an opposition party that had fallen out of alliance with the ruling PAN, and associated with a controversial political outsider who villainized virtually all key economic and political actors, the initiative to reform Mexico's compulsory licensing provisions seemed destined for a quick and quiet death.

Yet it did not die. The President of the Chamber's Science and Technology Commission, a deputy from the PAN, acknowledged the concerns expressed by the bill's sponsors and decided to rewrite the proposal (Interview, August 10, 2007).[11] For all its faults, the proposal's motivations and context were not to be ignored: escalating drug prices made access to medicines a growing problem, and, as the initiative itself emphasized, other developing countries were demonstrating the feasibility of reforming their pharmaceutical patent systems. Indeed, the initiative was clearly inspired by the Doha Declaration and broader changes occurring in the international political economy of IP. The preamble made this clear, specifically referencing other cases of patent reform to be emulated, such as Brazil (Cohen and Lybecker 2005; Shadlen 2009b). Mexico, too, could take such steps.

Instead of rejecting the PVEM's proposal out of hand, the Science and Technology Commission modified it. Whereas the PVEM's version limited the duration of patent protection, the Commission's revised reform addressed public interest compulsory licenses, an area where Mexico had discretion

---

[10] González Torres united the various commercial and political organizations he sponsored in the "Group for a Better Country" (*Grupo Por Un Pais Mejor*).

[11] See also, "Otorgan nuevo status a patentes médicas," *Reforma*, March 26, 2003.

under TRIPS and NAFTA. In March 2003 the Science and Technology Commission approved a reform that would increase the capacity of the Secretary of Health to issue compulsory licenses in the case of health emergencies. The key elements were to make a state of "serious illness" declared by health authorities a ground for compulsory licenses, to simplify the process by which "serious illness" is declared, and to assure that if a compulsory license is to be issued that this can occur rapidly and with low royalties.

The new version solved most of the problems that confounded the first: it was consistent with TRIPS and NAFTA, it was driven not by the PVEM but rather the PAN-led congressional committee, and it was no longer associated with *Dr. Simi*. As an illustration of changed ownership, at one point, as the reform was moving from the Commission to the full body of the Chamber, the Science and Technology Commission purchased space in *Reforma*, one of Mexico's leading newspapers, to update the public on the state of the legislation, underscoring the Commission's commitment to respond to "the urgent demands of wide sectors of the population" to alter Mexico's pharmaceutical patent system as a way of improving access to medicines.[12]

The Science and Technology Commission proposal drew a sharp reaction from the transnational pharmaceutical industry and its local legal representatives, who regarded this as a genuine threat (Interview, August 14, 2007a; Interview, August 16, 2007a). Government officials and legislators found themselves besieged by letters, faxes, emails, phone calls, and personal visits from the transnational sector's trade association (AMIIF), Mexico's leading IP law firms, the USTR, the US and European patent offices, and foreign embassies. The Director General of Eli Lilly, excoriating the deputies for lack of consultation, exclaimed that "this initiative is as bad or even worse for the health sector, in general, and the pharmaceutical industry in particular as the previous version." The Commission received virtually identical letters at this time from other firms, including Bristol-Myers Squibb, Pfizer, and Wyeth.[13] Beyond pharmaceutical firms themselves, AMIIF made appeals to all of the Mexican industrial community, indicating that the proposed reform to the compulsory licensing provision would dampen investment and, more generally, undermine the business environment in the country. On board with AMIIF, Mexico's peak business organization, the Business Coordinating Council (CCE) also assailed the proposal.[14]

Where the process gets most exciting is that the transnational sector did not just react defensively, but waged a counter-offensive. AMIIF had attempted to terminate the patent-reform project, though once it was kept alive by the

---

[12] This publicity (*desplegado*) was in *Reforma* on April 3, 2003.
[13] This correspondence is in the Science and Technology Commission's archive. Copies are on file with the author.
[14] "Critica el CCE política populista," *Reforma*, April 11, 2003.

Science and Technology Commission, AMIIF and its allies mobilized to secure a reform that was to their liking. Even better than making the proposal go away altogether, was reforming the patent law in such a way as to make the granting of compulsory licenses even less likely than under the 1991 law (Interview, August 14, 2007a). Thus AMIIF worked with its legal allies to prepare an alternative version, one that still addressed the conditions under which the Secretary of Health could issue a compulsory license, but did so in a way that would make it more difficult to do so.

The transnational sector's campaign to commandeer the initiative received the blessing of the Executive, which leaned on the *panista* deputies involved in the project. The Fox Government was never in support of altering Mexico's compulsory licensing provisions, and this was so even with the project being taken up by the PAN-led Commission. In the first regard, to the extent that political leaders were concerned by the price of drugs, health officials at this time did not, yet, regard IP reforms as the solution.[15] The Executive's position on this issue was also affected by Foreign Minister Jorge Castañeda's ambition to revise NAFTA to address immigration. Despite having trade preferences stabilized and locked in by the agreement, Mexico at this time remained especially sensitive and vulnerable to US concerns. Ordinarily we expect trade agreements like NAFTA to insulate countries from bilateral pressures. After all, a bilateral trade agreement alters the terms of preferential market access, so it is no longer a unilaterally granted concession that can be withdrawn at the US's discretion, but rather a non-removable, reciprocal commitment (Manger and Shadlen 2014; Shadlen 2008).[16] Yet in this instance, Mexico's quest to expand NAFTA, particularly to include a long sought-after clause on immigration, recreated vulnerability to US pressures. A letter from the US Embassy warned of "grave complications that might arise" if the legislation were approved, and interviews with former officials in the Mexican Executive reveal an acute awareness of this implicit linkage.[17]

In the same way that over-compliance in the 1990s was a condition for obtaining NAFTA, Mexican officials feared that securing a further agreement on immigration would only be made more difficult if the country were to buck the US in the 2000s and revise the compulsory licensing rules in the way that the Science and Technology Commission's proposal envisioned—and perhaps more likely if Mexico were to make AMIIF happy. Thus, not only did the Fox Government insist that the Commission's March 2003 version could not proceed, but its legislative liaison also provided Congress with a revised

---

[15] For the position of the Secretary of Health at the time, see "Defiende Julio Frenk las patentes," *Reforma*, March 27, 2003.

[16] This is reflected in Mexico's political trade dependence score, after NAFTA came into effect, being zero.

[17] Letter from U.S. Embassy (from the Science and Technology Commission archives, on file with author).

draft, written with the input of AMIIF's lawyers (Interview, August 14, 2007b). The new text *increased* the obstacles to issuing compulsory licenses by making the process by which "serious illness" was declared more complicated, removing "serious illness" alone as a ground for a compulsory license, and establishing a high minimum for royalty rates. And it was this version that was passed by the full Chamber of Deputies and Senate and then signed into law by President Fox in 2004.

While all this was going on, Mexico's local pharmaceutical sector essentially abstained from the debate. For these firms, left in a weakened position by the events of the 1990s, compulsory licensing was not regarded as a high priority and worthy of expending the minimal resources they had. We might expect organizations representing the national pharmaceutical sector to embrace a proposed reform that would simplify compulsory licensing or to oppose a proposed reform that would make compulsory licensing more complex, yet they never regarded themselves as potential winners or losers in these debates. To the contrary, ANAFAM and other associations representing local firms regarded the entire issue of compulsory licenses as peripheral to their members' interests. Even if the government were to issue a compulsory license, it would almost certainly be for a drug that local firms did not make and would need to be imported from India, such as an antiretroviral for treating HIV/AIDS. Here the effects that patenting and liberalization had on the local sector in Mexico loom large. In contrast to what we shall see in Brazil, where local firms could be mobilized to support the compulsory licensing revisions on account of specific wording that offered opportunities of supplying the state, coalition building of this type was not possible in Mexico because of the local sector's diminished capabilities.

ANAFAM's indifference illustrates how changes to industrial structure affect patent politics. The national sector was not just weakened by the way pharmaceutical patents were introduced in the 1990s, but its interests had been altered too. The introduction of pharmaceutical patents more than a decade earlier meant that the local sector had long-ceased producing or, frankly, even caring about copying and producing their own version of new, originator drugs while they were under patent. Instead, local firms cared more about issues that affect terms of exclusivity. As firms, at least still-existing firms, had adjusted to the new status quo, fights over compulsory licensing simply did not seem relevant any longer. With compulsory licensing not a priority, ANAFAM kept out of the fray, preserving its resources for more important matters.

Taking a step back, the result of the effort to make Mexico's compulsory licensing provisions more useful was, perversely, to make these provisions more complex. The Mexican government had not issued—nor threatened to issue—any compulsory licenses in the period since pharmaceutical patents were introduced, and the 2004 reform made such an event even less likely.

Quite simply, after this reform was made, were Mexican officials to want to issue a compulsory license, doing so would be more difficult, and the threat to do so would be less credible, than it had been under the 1991 LFPPI. Knowing they have little to fear, then, patent holders set prices as they see fit. Abbott, for example, priced its patented version of lopinavir/ritonavir ("Kaletra"), a key second-line treatment for HIV/AIDS, more than five times higher in Mexico than in Brazil. When the H1N1 epidemic swept through Mexico in 2009 and the Secretary of Health declared "swine flu" a serious illness, it was clear that compulsory licenses on drugs to treat either the virus itself (or other conditions experienced by those infected by the virus), were not perceived as feasible options (Alcarez Hernandez 2013).[18] The revised system for compulsory licensing simply creates too many barriers.[19]

EXTENDING PROTECTION THROUGH THE COURTS

At the same time as pharmaceutical patent holders' rights of exclusion in Mexico were strengthened by the rewriting of the country's compulsory licensing provisions, they also benefited from a series of judicial decisions. This section provides brief reviews of three changes to Mexico's pharmaceutical patent system, each constituting an example of the transnational sector's ability to secure further over-compliance. Importantly, in each instance actors within the Executive resisted strengthening protection, only to be overruled by the courts. Thus, in contrast to the case of compulsory licensing, where the outcome could be predicted by either social structure or Executive preferences, in these instances social structure—shaped by the way pharmaceutical patents were introduced in the 1990s—clearly overwhelmed and subordinated the Executive's preferences.

In 2003 the Fox Government declared that the country's recently-created health surveillance agency, the Federal Commission for Protection against Health Risks (*Comisión Federal para la Protección contra Riesgos Sanitarios,*

---

[18] See also the discussion in "Defiende COFEPRIS patentes de antivirales," *El Universal,* May 9, 2009.

[19] One legal analysis of the 2003–2004 reform offers an alternative interpretation, that this might lead to an increase in compulsory licenses (Rangel-Ortiz 2005), yet not only have subsequent events revealed that this is incorrect, even at the time both the reactions of the actors affected, as well as interviews with the participants, suggest that they did not see it this way. AMIIF celebrated this as a resounding victory, while advocates of compulsory licensing regarded this as a loss. See, for example, "Ven en los genéricos una batalla perdida," *Reforma,* September 30, 2003; "Limita el Senado el uso de patentes médicas en casos de emergencia," *La Jornada,* October 8, 2003.

COFEPRIS) would be required to consult with the patent office (IMPI) and withhold marketing authority from drugs where patents remain in effect.[20] Accordingly, IMPI would begin to publish a supplementary gazette of pharmaceutical patents in force in Mexico, and COFEPRIS was prohibited from granting marketing authorization to any drugs that might infringe the patents listed in the supplementary gazette.

This type of coordination, known as "linkage," was not in the original LFPPI, nor was it required by NAFTA, but had become a high priority of the US Government and the transnational pharmaceutical sector by the early 2000s (Sell 2010b; Shadlen 2009a). Although the introduction of any linkage system at all constitutes an example of Mexico exceeding its international obligations, it was not regarded that way by state officials at the time. In fact, Mexico's Secretary of Health expected that the new system, as originally designed, would clarify when patents expired and thus place limits on the "artificial extension of patents" (Interview, August 16, 2007c). That it did not do so is a function not just of the system itself but of the capacity of the transnational sector to convert these arrangements into an instrument for extending periods of patent protection.

To understand how this occurred, it is worth comparing Mexico's linkage system to the US system, which served as the model. While linkage in the US also prevents firms from receiving market authorization while patents on a given drug are in effect, the US system couples this with another provision that gives periods of shared market exclusivity to firms that successfully invalidate patents through legal challenges. That is, linkage protects the patent holder from infringement, and it also offers an incentive to challenge patents that should not have been granted.[21] The promise of shared exclusivity, what Hemphill and Sampat (2011) refer to as a "bounty," helps solve a collective action problem, avoiding a situation whereby challenging firms bear the costs and risks of litigation only for instances of success to put the knowledge in the public domain. In Mexico, however, the linkage system protects the originator firm without also providing the incentive to potential generic competitors. In the absence of a bounty, if a

---

[20] This was introduced via a presidential decree that revised the implementing directive to one article of the patent law. See Becerra Ramírez (2013), González Luna (2004), González Luna and Lazo Corvera (2003).

[21] Originator firms list their patents in the FDA's Orange Book. If another firm seeks market authorization of a drug before a patent listed in the Orange Book is set to expire, it files an "abbreviated new drug application" under Paragraph Four of the Hatch-Waxman Act. Once the originator firm is notified of this filing, it can then initiate litigation against the follow-on firm for alleged patent infringement, and in doing so receive an extension of the challenged patent's term. If the challenger wins in litigation, not only is the extension removed as the patent becomes invalidated, but, critically, the follow-on firm receives six months of shared exclusivity with the originator firm.

firm were to successfully challenge a patent it would have to share the benefits of prevailing with all firms.[22]

Were Mexico's linkage system to offer protection only to strong patents that are more likely to be upheld in litigation, or less likely to ever be subject to litigation, then the absence of an incentive to challenge patents would be less significant. Yet Mexico's unidirectional linkage system offers protection to secondary patents (e.g. alternative molecular forms, compositions and formulations, uses) that are typically more vulnerable on legal grounds. Empirical analyses of pharmaceutical litigation in the US, for example, demonstrate that secondary patents are more likely to be challenged, and challenges of secondary patents are more likely to result in the patents being ruled invalid or for owners to accept settlements (Hemphill and Sampat 2011; 2012). In Mexico the linkage system provides these patents with blocking power too.

The reason for this is that the transnational sector assured that IMPI includes *all* patents in the supplementary linkage gazette—not just patents on base molecules and compounds, but also patents on alternative molecular forms, formulations, and uses. If a patent is listed in the linkage gazette, then COFEPRIS is obliged to deny market authorization to any drugs that might infringe on these patents. The stakes of including secondary patents in the linkage gazette were further heightened in the context of the pipeline. Pipeline patents, we recall, were not examined in Mexico. Rather, these were transplanted into Mexico, after being granted in jurisdictions, like the US, a jurisdiction that has mechanisms to encourage challenges and invalidation. In Mexico, these same secondary patents could have high blocking power— more perhaps than in the US—on account of the unidirectional linkage system.

Whereas local pharmaceutical firms did not express much interest in the reform to compulsory licenses, the linkage system was regarded as a cause for concern. This is consistent with expectations. Once the new status quo of pharmaceutical patent protection had settled in, those firms that had been able to adjust and still existed (or new firms that emerged) cared about the terms of entry into the market for their own products; these terms of market entry would be greatly affected by arrangements that complicated and delayed their ability to receiving marketing authorization. ANAFAM thus opposed the introduction of the linkage system and, more critically, consistently resisted the inclusion of secondary patents in IMPI's supplementary gazette, arguing that including such patents gives them greater blocking power than they deserve. ANAFAM's position was that the gazette should

---

[22] Another difference with the US system, where patent-holding firms list their patents in the FDA's Orange Book, is that in Mexico the government (the patent office) publishes the list of protected drugs. Thus, state authority is not just providing a forum for the owners and users of proprietary knowledge to defend and advance their rights, but is being deployed on behalf of owners to protect their rights for them.

be limited to primary patents, i.e. patents on molecules, not on additional patents associated with drugs.

Health authorities resisted too. The Health Secretariat and COFEPRIS sought to minimize the impact of linkage from the start. Rather than consult the supplementary gazette, for example, COFEPRIS' approach was simply to ask IMPI if granting marketing authorization to a given drug would violate any patents, giving the patent office a short period to respond ("ten *calendar* days," the former director of COFEPRIS exclaimed, "not ten working days") before it interpreted a non-reply as a green light to go forward with authorization (Interview, August 9, 2007). And COFEPRIS was adamant that secondary patents should not be included, that doing so would undermine the purpose of the system, which was to provide clarity as to when patents expired, and instead create opportunities for the "artificial extension of patents" that health officials feared. The patent office also took the position that the supplementary gazette should only include primary patents, that listing secondary patents could extend periods of exclusivity, and when IMPI began publishing the supplementary gazette it omitted secondary patents (Interview, August 16, 2007b).

The treatment of secondary patents in the supplementary gazette subsequently became subject to extensive litigation, with transnational firms demanding that IMPI include them (and for ample time to be allowed for information regarding relevant patents to be provided by patent-holding firms) and that COFEPRIS use their inclusion as the basis for denying marketing authorization to follow-on products. Ultimately, as indicated, AMIIF prevailed: after a series of inconsistent judicial rulings over which patents should be listed, the Mexican Supreme Court sided with the transnational sector and declared that IMPI must publish all pharmaceutical patents—not just primary patents—in the linkage gazette.[23] This ruling, celebrated as a "victory for the leading pharmaceutical companies" (Espicom 2012, 6), raised significant obstacles to COFEPRIS' ability to authorize competitors' drugs and thus allows transnational firms to extend the periods of patent protection they enjoy. Once again, transnational firms managed to strengthen their rights of exclusion—this time in the courts and, importantly, over the opposition of increasingly wary state officials.

The courts also supported the transnational sector's demands—again, over resistance from local firms and within the Executive—to have terms of patents granted under the pipeline extended. The LFPPI stipulates that pipeline patents expire in Mexico on the same date as they expire in the first country where the patent was filed. But what happens, then, if the expiration date is

---

[23] "Cierran paso a los genéricos: Amplía Corte publicación de patentes," *Reforma*, January 14, 2010. For an update on the linkage system, Ivan Martinez, "Aplicación actual del sistema de vinculación (linkage) en México" (goo.gl/eALxMc).

extended in the first country, as commonly happens?[24] Consider a US patent with an application date in 1988 that was introduced in Mexico under the pipeline. The expiration date on the original US patent and the Mexican pipeline patent would be in 2008. If the patent-holder obtained an extension from in the US until 2010, does Mexico then extend its expiration date locally as well? This became a pressing topic in Mexico in the years prior to 2011, as patents introduced under the pipeline were reaching their expiration dates. Patent-holders seeking to retain exclusivity for as long as possible demanded that IMPI "correct" patent terms, while potential generic suppliers seeking market entry and health officials looking forward to competitive effects on prices expressed opposition to the "extension" of patent terms. Mexico's international obligations did not require the country to adjust patent terms in this way, and the IMPI was inclined to reject these requests, but the courts interpreted this provision of the LFPPI as committing Mexico to adjust (extend) expiration dates.[25]

On account of the large number of secondary patents in Mexico, both those imported via the pipeline and those granted by IMPI after 1991, their inclusion in the supplementary gazette, and the absence of useful system to invalidate patents through litigation, Mexico ends up with more pharmaceutical patents than would otherwise be the case, and these patents have stronger blocking power than would otherwise be the case. And by extending the terms of patents granted under the pipeline, the effect of this earlier decision became exacerbated in the 2000s. Assessing the consequences of these regulatory and judicial decisions is difficult, though it is estimated that more than 20 percent of patented drugs on the market in Mexico in the late 2000s had their periods of protection extended through the linkage system, and that as many as sixteen drugs had their periods of patent protection extended on account of adjustments to pipeline patents.[26]

Finally, and consistent with the pattern of health officials being overruled on matters regarding patents and competition in the pharmaceutical sector, the transnational sector also managed to secure effective periods of data exclusivity in the 2000s. Requirements for how countries treat test data in

---

[24] Pharmaceutical patent terms are extended in the US to compensate for regulatory delay (if the FDA takes longer than expected to approve the associated product for market launch), for example, and as rewards for pediatric formulations and treatments for rare diseases. Beyond pharmaceuticals, all patents granted prior to 1995 were subject to term adjustment on account of US compliance with TRIPS. Previously patents in the US lasted seventeen years from the date of concession, and in 1995 this was changed to twenty years from date of application.

[25] "La extensión de vigencia de las patentes En México," *Reyes Fenig Asociados-Propiedad Intelectual,* June 14, 2008 (goo.gl/k49Sbz); "Patent Term Extensions in Mexico Buck Latin American Trend," *IHS Global Insight,* January 2, 2008 (goo.gl/y2Hxdo).

[26] "Hay 'error' en extensión de patente," *Reforma,* December 1, 2009; "Disputan la ampliación de patentes," *Reforma,* September 17, 2009; "Aumentan prácticas de 'evergreening' en el mercado farmacéutico nacional," *El Financiero,* October 5, 2016.

NAFTA mirrored those in TRIPS, and TRIPS, as we have seen from the Argentina case, left countries a great deal of discretion. Countries were expected to "protect" test data against unfair use, but they were not obliged to provide periods of "data exclusivity" as transnational, originator firms and the US Government sought. Mexico, notwithstanding the otherwise over-compliant approach to introducing pharmaceutical patents in the 1990s, adhered closely to TRIPS/NAFTA obligations and did not offer data exclusivity. In the 2000s, as data exclusivity became a more pressing part of the international agenda for over-compliance, Mexican health authorities remained opposed. The transnational sector consistently complained about "insufficient" data protection in Mexico, asserting that this was an implicit violation of NAFTA and TRIPS, yet the Health Secretariat and COFEPRIS refused to revise their regulations and practices. Unable to secure data exclusivity through either legislative or regulatory channels, AMIIF pursued a legal case, arguing that the grant of marketing authorization based on an originator firm's data violated constitutional law, and, eventually, secured an injunction against COFEPRIS. The judicial order essentially established a five-year period of data exclusivity, and in 2012 the health surveillance agency subsequently revised its regulations to comply. Here again, even with health authorities clearly opposed to the strengthening of patent-holders' rights of exclusivity, such is the domineering power of the transnational pharmaceutical sector in Mexico that it continued to get its way.

UNFULFILLED AMBITION: INTRODUCING PRE-GRANT "OPPOSITION"

Mexico's patent law underwent another reform in 2010. The objective of the proposed reform was to introduce a system of pre-grant opposition, which would allow actors other than applicants (e.g. non-governmental organizations, health professionals, rival firms) to submit information to the patent office relating to whether an invention claimed in an application satisfies patentability criteria and thus whether the patent should be granted. Previously, such outside actors ("third parties" in legal parlance) had no input into patent examination; they could only challenge the patent office's decisions post-grant. The 2010 reform promised to offer the first opportunity for actors to influence—and not just react to—IMPI's decisions.

The proposal that reached the legislature in 2009–10 was driven by the leaders of Mexico's main political parties, particularly the PRI and PRD, and based on extensive collaboration with the local pharmaceutical sector. Pre-grant opposition was a high priority of the local sector, given the rate of patenting in Mexico and a concern that the IMPI had excessively permissive examination practices. Once patents are granted they are difficult to remove (Amin et al. 2009; Drahos 2010; Sampat et al. 2012), and local firms thus sought to secure a mechanism to reduce the rate at which IMPI granted pharmaceutical patents in the first place.

The backlash from the transnational sector against the proposed measures was intense. AMIIF, along with its allies in the legal community, warned of grave threats presented by pre-grant opposition. Their objections consisted of standard refrains: pre-grant opposition would slow patent examination, diminish the rate of innovation, and lead to new drugs being withheld from the market in Mexico (Gómez Violante 2010).[27] While the initiative was written specifically with pharmaceutical patents in mind, AMIIF campaigned to get all of industry on board, and to be sure many of Mexico's main business organizations also expressed concerns about the project. IMPI opposed the initiative too, regarding pre-grant opposition as likely to slow down the pace of patent examination and place extra burdens on the patent office.[28] And, of course, external pressures came into play as well, with the US Government and international pharmaceutical producers complaining about the proposed reforms.[29]

Once again the transnational sector's mobilization stymied efforts to modify Mexico's patent system. The final version was some distance from what had been envisioned and proposed by the reform's sponsors. The original proposal, modeled in part after the pre-grant opposition system in India (Amin et al. 2009; Kapczynski 2009; Sampat and Shadlen 2015b), would have created a legally "contentious" process, with inputs received in the opposition process constituting formal components of the examination process that the patent office becomes obligated to address. The outcome passed by Congress and signed into law by President Calderón in 2010, however, does not include these binding elements. As one pharmaceutical patent attorney put it, in a celebratory note to the international law community, "after much debate in congress, the final amendment to the law resulted in a fairly mild proceeding which should not affect patent prosecution in general" (*Lawyer Monthly* 2013).

---

[27] See, for example, "Complicarán el registro de patentes en el País," *Reforma* February 2, 2010. These same objections tend to be expressed against pre-grant opposition whenever and wherever it is proposed (Löfgren 2011).

[28] See, for example, the discussion in Alberto Aguilar, "Crece rechazo a oposición de patentes, daño a innovación en industria, IMPI en contra y mañana análisis en el Senado," *El Universal*, November 3, 2009.

[29] For example: "A considerable number of members of the Mexican Congress (in both houses) seem to be insufficiently informed on the importance of IP and inaccurately believe that pharmaceutical IP rights are a barrier to access to medicines in Mexico. This lack of understanding leads to the continued submission of bills that seek to undermine IP for pharmaceuticals in Mexico. This trend has manifested itself on issues including: compulsory licensing and pre-grant opposition on patent applications" (PhRMA 2009).

The differences between the form of pre-grant participation that was proposed and that which was passed merit attention. The formal status given to actors who submit information about applications' suitability and the obligations set on the patent office to use this information distinguish "opposition" from "observation" (Amin 2013; Amin et al. 2009). The version that was passed stripped the provisions that defined this as "opposition." Although the reformed law allows third parties to provide input into examination, it leaves IMPI unconstrained regarding whether and how it uses the input. That is, those who submit information are not party to the proceedings or able to intervene in the course of patent prosecution; IMPI is not obligated to consider the input, or even respond to it, as the revised law allows the patent office to consider this input where it wishes, leaving IMPI to decide if it wants to do so. IMPI is not obligated to notify the third party whether or not it is considering its input, and the reasons why it may decide that the concerns expressed are being dismissed. Third parties thus have little way of knowing if the information submitted is taken into account and has any input into the prosecution process. Some observers suggest that IMPI examiners may take the input received into account (Chagoya Cortes and González Vargas 2013), though my research suggests that few actors in industry or civil society are even filing oppositions.[30] In sum, what started as a proposal for pre-grant "opposition" became reduced to a meek form of "observation" that is unlikely to affect the rate at which Mexico grants patents.

The 2009–10 legislative process did not increase pharmaceutical patent protection, and in that sense is unlike the 2003–2004 episode analyzed above, but here too an effort to revise the patent system failed, with the result more favorable to the interests of knowledge owners than knowledge users. Each of these events elicited similar reactions, with the transnational sector claiming victory and advocates of reform licking their wounds. For example, the transnational sector and IP law community celebrated their success in warding off a more substantial opposition system. Notwithstanding the introduction of the pre-grant observation rules, the reform was regarded, as was the earlier case, as a victory for transnational sector: "all of the changes support the interests of the [transnational] pharmaceutical industry."[31]

---

[30] See, for example, "Challenging Patents in Mexico," *International Law Office,* September 9, 2013 (goo.gl/ZWnSUz). It is difficult to obtain systematic data on use of the system. There is no central database of applications "opposed" under this provision of the reformed law. IMPI's website includes documents related to granted patents, and one could, potentially, consult the documents posted for each granted patent and search for cases of input received (in that case being dismissed or, perhaps, used to alter the granted patent's claims). Yet even this laborious process would yield seriously incomplete information: we would not know about cases where input was submitted but ignored by the patent office, and nothing about rejected applications.

[31] "Reform for Pharmaceutical Patents: Fair Balance or Fresh Disputes?" *International Law Office,* February 7, 2011 (goo.gl/Mx8J3g).

In contrast, advocates of the pre-grant opposition project from the local pharmaceutical sector invariably express disappointment. In the words of one frustrated representative from ANAFAM, "the initial plan was to have a form of pre-grant opposition..., but it ended up as practically nothing."[32] According to a lawyer who advises ANAFAM and represents local firms in litigation, "Mexico does not have an opposition system." Following up, I expressed surprised at the strength of the statement, given the reform, albeit minor, that was introduced in 2010, to which the response was "we accomplished nothing so it's not worth talking about" (Interview, January 24, 2016).

The failed effort to introduce pre-grant opposition further illustrates how changes to the local pharmaceutical sector, and its subsequently altered policy priorities, affect patent politics. In stark contrast to the debates over compulsory licensing, from which the key actors in the local pharmaceutical sector distanced themselves, in this instance, with the focal point being a proposed change that could facilitate market entry for non-patented products, they were front and center of the project to reform the patent system. Obviously this mobilization was not sufficient to overcome the transnational sector's hostility toward the project, but the case nicely illustrates how the way pharmaceutical patents were introduced in the 1990s affects both capabilities and preferences in the 2000s.

In comparative perspective, the 2009–10 effort to alter the patent law appeared to benefit from many conditions that were absent in the earlier case of legislative reform. Whereas the 2003 proposal originated with a small party with ties to a fringe segment of the pharmaceutical sector, only to be revived by a PAN-led Commission led by an independent-thinking deputy, the second initiative came from the PRI and PRD, supported by the principal organizations representing the national pharmaceutical sector. The Chamber of Deputies conducted extensive research on the topic (CESOP 2010; Comité de Competividad 2008), and at the same time, and contributing to the knowledge base that underscored the Legislature's work, in 2007 Mexico's National Institute of Public Health (with support of the Ford Foundation) convened a conference to examine possibilities for health-oriented patent reforms in Mexico. External conditions differed as well. In the first episode, as discussed, Mexico was acutely sensitive to US demands because of the desire to revise NAFTA. Those concerns had subsided. Of course, Mexico remained sensitive to US concerns, as the Calderón Government was seeking cooperation and support for its "war on drugs," but there is little evidence that these issues were linked, or, importantly, perceived as linked.

Divisions within the Mexican Executive became more accentuated and prominent in this period too. Notwithstanding conservative orientations of

---

[32] Email, July 2, 2010 (follow-up to Interview, March 30, 2010).

the Fox (2000–2006) and Calderón (2006–2012) Governments, health officials became concerned about the price of drugs and the consequences that earlier choices on patenting and pharmaceutical policies were having for Mexican society. One observer refers to the publication of the Secretariat of Health's (2005) book on the pharmaceutical industry as "a milestone" in recent political history where, after many years of neglect, the government was beginning to care about these issues (Gasman 2008, S424). As a new national health insurance program (*Seguro Popular*) created earlier in the decade began to expand, for example, national and state governments all became increasingly concerned about the prices that health authorities across the country were paying for key medicines. Examples abound: the Health Secretariat established a commission to improve public procurement of drugs and negotiate price reductions, for example, searching for mechanisms to address the problems created by high prices, and the National Institute for Public Health launched a project entitled "Prices, Patents, and Policies" (Adesina et al. 2013; Gómez-Dantés et al. 2012; Knaul et al. 2012); officials in the Mexican Government, host of the 2008 International AIDS conference, were becoming alarmed by the price of drugs and attuned to the contributing role of the patent system, in ways that were clearly not the case in the earlier episode; the 2009 "swine flu" pandemic heightened concern with patents and the availability of affordable medicines in Mexico.[33] Indeed, as we have seen, health officials were never entirely on board with revisions to the patent system that threatened to delay the entry of lower-priced drugs into key therapeutic segments, such as the linkage system that protected secondary patents. The conjuncture of events in the 2000s witnessed health officials becoming increasingly outspoken, and not infrequently making the case for reducing the strength of pharmaceutical patent protection in Mexico. According to the head of COFEPRIS Miguel Ángel Toscano, for example, the extension of patents produced by the linkage system "demonstrates the need for a systematic and deep revision" of the relationship between the health surveillance agency and the patent office.[34] To be sure, what we witness in Mexico is not equivalent to the commitment to health-oriented patent reforms that we will observe in Brazil, but at least part of the Mexican Executive's orientation toward the pharmaceutical patent system was unquestionably different in this latter period. Yet the outcome of the second episode of legislative reform in Mexico looks much more like the outcome in the first episode than anything witnessed in Brazil.

In fact, even the bill that was debated in Congress was a considerably diminished version of the measures that were originally being proposed and

---

[33] Concerns on the part of the Executive in this period were complemented by increased civil society activism, particularly regarding HIV/AIDS treatment (Torres-Ruiz 2011).

[34] "Hay 'error' en extensión de patente," *Reforma*, December 1, 2009. See also, "Atoran a genéricos acuerdos globales," *Reforma*, January 5, 2010.

considered when this process was launched. At a 2007 meeting with an industry advisor who was actively engaged in this process, for example, I was shown a document with proposed wording for a reform to the patent law to define "novelty" and "inventive step" in ways that would lead to more secondary patents being rejected in Mexico. This restriction, which further discussion revealed was inspired by India's Section 3(d) and the examination guidelines written by Carlos Correa and disseminated by the United Nations (Correa 2007), was never seriously considered by Congress. Earlier proposals also included enhancing coordination between IMPI and Mexico's competition authorities to facilitate invalidation of patents where the market power conferred was being abused. Nor did the initiative combat the array of regulatory measures that served to extend periods of market exclusivity, such as the linkage system, despite the head of COFEPRIS' public criticisms and calls for reform. The analysis here has focused on what happened within the Legislature, but the entire project had already been limited even before the debates began. Indeed, for a legislative initiative that was motivated explicitly with a concern over effective patent terms (and the discussion of motives of the bill was clear, this was about nothing if not about concerns that extended patent terms can have on prices and health system), not to address these issues is revealing. What started out as a project to revamp the pharmaceutical patent system, in ways that were fully consistent with Mexico's international obligations, ended up dealing largely with administrative issues, with the only substantive issue being pre-grant "opposition"—and even this provision ended up significantly diluted.

CONCLUSION

Pharmaceutical politics in Mexico are marked by perpetual strengthening of patent-holders' rights of exclusion. Throughout the 2000s, even under conservative governments, health officials have increasingly shown concern with the effects of ever-increasing rights of exclusion and sought to reform the patent system to make it more attuned to health challenges. Yet efforts to modify the patent system have uniformly failed; the momentum for increasing protection has been too much to overcome.[35]

Comparison of the two legislative initiatives to revise Mexico's pharmaceutical patent system reveals differences on most conditions. The Executive never supported revising the compulsory licensing provisions, but health officials were moved to tailor the pharmaceutical patent system later in the

---

[35] Not just patents: Mexico's protection and enforcement of copyrights also increased in this period, with the 2003 reform of the copyright law (Haggart 2014, Chapter 8).

decade; external constraints were much less significant in the latter period than in the early 2000s when Mexico was seeking US cooperation to revise NAFTA; the local pharmaceutical sector was intensely concerned and mobilized with the objectives of the second project, obtaining opportunities for pre-grant opposition to minimize the grant of weak patents was a high priority; and civil society actors (both national and international) were more engaged in reforming the patent law in the case of introducing pre-grant opposition. Yet one condition—and just about only one condition—is common across these two cases, the transnational sector's staunch opposition, while the outcomes are markedly similar.[36] Indeed, throughout all of the policy debates analyzed in this chapter—the counterproductive effort to revise Mexico's compulsory licensing rules, the consolidation of a linkage system with significant blocking powers, judicial rulings that increase patent terms of exclusion, and the failed effort to introduce pre-grant opposition—runs a common theme: the transnational pharmaceutical industry gets its way.

We can understand the phenomenon of ever-increasing patent protection as a legacy of how pharmaceutical patents were introduced in the first place. The early and retroactive introduction of patents, along with broader economic policies introduced by NAFTA, fundamentally restructured the pharmaceutical industry in Mexico. Local firms closed, capabilities generated in the pre-TRIPS/NAFTA era were eliminated, and firms that survived were eventually taken over by foreign firms. In Chapter 5, a quote from a Brazilian health official of the early 1980s was invoked (p. 123), remarking that there was a pharmaceutical industry in Brazil but not a Brazilian pharmaceutical industry. That observation is even more appropriate for Mexico by the 2000s.

With the local sector neutered, economically and politically, transnational firms reign unrivalled. Early in the 2000s, AMIIF was able to do better than prevent Mexico's patent law from being reformed to simplify the procedures for compulsory licensing. The transnational sector engineered reforms to patent and health policies that strengthen their ability to control pharmaceutical markets. Then, later, when facing a seeming tidal wave behind a reform to introduce pre-grant opposition, the transnational sector was able to make sure that the most disagreeable proposals were taken off the table, and significantly dilute the final version. The local pharmaceutical sector in Mexico, or what is left of it, is too weak to secure revisions of the patent system, nor to stand in the way of the transnational sector's efforts to further strengthen the benefits they enjoy. Policies have consequences; once the first changes made in the

---

[36] In fact, these two legislative initiatives are the tip of the iceberg. Lindner (2010) reviews many of the proposals that were under consideration in Congress in the mid-2000s. The same pattern repeats in these cases as well: those seeking reform end up disappointed that they did not achieve what they desired, and those threatened by what was first proposed leave feeling victorious.

1990s had time to settle, Mexico became a country in which tailoring the patent system becomes exceptionally difficult.

Finally, it is worth asking what might have transpired in Mexico had less conservative governments been in power. The 2006 election was exceptionally close, had the PRD's candidate won, would Mexico's pharmaceutical patent system undergone more substantial tailoring? It is obviously impossible to answer that hypothetical question, though the analysis in this chapter suggests a negative answer. As we have seen, even under conservative leadership, health officials desired change—but they failed. Nor has the system undergone serious change since 2012, when the PRI's Enrique Peña Nieto won the Presidential elections. In sum, Mexico's internationalist pharmaceutical patent system does not look as it looks and function as it functions because health officials do not seek to modify it, but rather because those who seek to modify it lack the ability to overcome the immense—an constantly growing—resources of the coalition for over-compliance.

8

Patent Policy in the Shadows of Over-Compliance

Neo-Developmentalism in Brazil

Brazil altered course in the second period of patent politics, as successive governments introduced revisions to the new patent system to deal with the consequences of the initial policy choices made in the 1990s. Modifications of Brazil's pharmaceutical patent policies and practices have been the subject of extensive research.[1] Less noticed is another dimension of policy in this period: a broad array of innovation-industrial policies to build new capabilities in the pharmaceutical sector. The demands of the health sector meant that reforms to the patent system would not be sufficient in the absence of a more vibrant national pharmaceutical industry. Brazil's policies have thus been marked by complementary steps of revising how the patent regime functions, to reduce the burdens on the health sector, and also helping local firms acquire new production capabilities and adjust to the new status quo of pharmaceutical patents. I refer to this dual-pillared response as "neo-developmental."[2] This chapter analyzes both dimensions of Brazil's neo-developmental response, and the uneasy relationship between them.

Neo-developmentalism is not a partisan story. The Brazilian approach cannot be attributed to the ideological orientation of the political parties in power, as all of the efforts discussed in this chapter transcended such differences. The principal revisions of the patent system were initiated during the

---

[1] Analyses of Brazil's patent reforms include Cassier (2012), Centro de Estudos e Debates Estratégicos (2013), Chaves (2016), Chaves et al. (2008), Cohen and Lybecker (2005), Corrêa and Cassier (2010), Deere (2008), Eimer and Schüren (2013), Fonseca and Bastos (2016), Flynn (2011; 2013; 2015), Nunn et al. (2009), Oliveira et al. (2004), Olsen and Sinha (2013), Possas (2008), Sampat and Shadlen (2015b), Shadlen (2009b; 2011a; 2011b), Shaver (2010).

[2] The terms "neo-developmental" and "new developmental" have been invoked to refer to various aspects of Brazilian policy in the 2000s. Caliari et al. (2013) and Filomeno (2014) also characterize Brazilian IP and innovation policies as "neo-developmental."

government of Fernando Henrique Cardoso, the same president who pushed so hard for over-compliance in the 1990s, and continued by successive presidents from the Workers Party, Lula (2003–11) and Dilma Rousseff (2011–16).[3] Likewise, the complex of measures to support local pharmaceutical production, though clearly driven forward by Lula and Rousseff, were built on steps introduced by Cardoso's government too.

Rather than partisanship, understanding neo-developmentalism in Brazilian patent policy draws our attention to the legacies of early choices. The way pharmaceutical patents were introduced in the 1990s inspired and shaped subsequent policy changes. Both the modifications of the patent system and the new innovation-industrial policies were motivated by the challenges that emerged from over-compliance. Moreover, and in paradoxical ways, Brazil's initial policy choices both enabled coalition building and complicated coalition maintenance by mobilizing differing sets of actors with conflicting expectations and demands.

As elsewhere, the Ministry of Health was the driving force behind policy changes in this period. The nature of the government's health policies created an unsustainable demand for expensive, patented drugs, which subsequently made modification of the patent regime a priority. Because modifying the approach to pharmaceutical patenting generated fierce backlash from the same national and international actors that had successfully secured over-compliance in the 1990s, the ability of health officials to press forward depended on the construction of a coalition to overcome the considerable resistance that they faced. One factor that facilitated coalition building was a change to the country's trade structure, which made it more difficult for the advocates of over-compliance to secure the support of Brazil's export community. Another factor facilitating coalition building was the timing of the introduction of pharmaceutical patents. Although Brazil's response to the global sea change of the 1980s and 90s was marked by over-compliance, for example the inclusion of pipeline patents, it was also comparatively delayed. By the time that the Brazilian Government sought to alter course, the new pharmaceutical patent system had not been in place for long.

The importance of timing, particularly the timing of national policy decisions relative to global trends, is brought to light by comparing Brazil with the case of Mexico, analyzed in Chapter 7. Had debates over revising the patent regime emerged in Brazil a decade after the introduction of pharmaceutical patents, as was the case in Mexico, the result may have been similar, as the effects of over-compliance would have had considerable time to set in. In Mexico, by the time initiatives to reform the patent regime emerged in the early 2000s, more than a decade had passed since pharmaceutical patents had

---

[3] President Rousseff was elected to a second four-year term in 2014, but removed from office in August 2016 following impeachment proceedings.

been introduced and patented products came to dominate the market. The Mexican pharmaceutical sector had been fundamentally transformed, and local firms had lost nearly all ability to defend themselves or serve as useful allies for would-be reformers. In Brazil, by contrast, reforms began soon after the new patent law came into effect, before the potential effects of over-compliance were fully felt. Thus, while Mexico and Brazil both responded to the global sea change with over-compliant patent systems, that they did so at different times created different possibilities for subsequent coalition building and policy change.

While social structure has enabled coalition building in Brazil, it has also complicated coalition maintenance. The two dimensions of policy that constitute neo-developmentalism, modifying the patent regime to temper the effects of pharmaceutical patents on health policy and introducing innovation–industrial policies to build local pharmaceutical capabilities, sit uncomfortably. An important aspect of neo-developmentalism in Brazil is the considerable degree of conflict that it generated; it is anything but a stable equilibrium. Some actors in state and society regard measures to revise the patent system as antithetical to campaigns to strengthen the country's science and technology infrastructure, at the same time as measures to increase innovative capabilities alter some actors' perspectives regarding the merits of pharmaceutical patenting. Balancing these tensions has been an ongoing challenge in Brazil.

The chapter consists of five sections. The first section examines the effects of over-compliance on patenting in Brazil, and the implications of these new patterns of patenting for industrial structure and the health system. The second section reviews the most important changes to Brazil's new pharmaceutical patent system that the Cardoso and Lula Governments introduced, focusing on revisions to the compulsory licensing provisions and inclusion of health officials in the examination of pharmaceutical patent applications. The third section shows how the limitations of these revisions, which were revealed in the course of a conflicts over the prices of patented HIV/AIDS drugs, triggered the subsequent expansion of innovation–industrial policies to support the local pharmaceutical sector, the complementary branch of neo-developmentalism. The fourth section analyzes the conditions that enabled coalition building, noting the role of health activists within the state and changes to Brazil's export profile, as well as the important effects that the timing of Brazil's initial policy choices had on industrial structure. The fifth section illustrates the tensions of neo-developmentalism through analysis of conflict over the country's novel system for examining pharmaceutical patents. We see how the two dimensions of Brazilian patent policy have created distinct and rival sets of interests regarding the role of pharmaceutical patents in development, and how these conflicting interests create challenges for governments seeking to balance the dual objectives.

PATENTS, INDUSTRY, AND TREATMENT CHALLENGES: THE LEGACIES OF OVER-COMPLIANCE

An immediate effect of Brazil's over-compliance in the 1990s was to increase pharmaceutical patenting activity. In the years prior to the eventual passage of the 1996 patent law (LPI), as the details of pharmaceutical patenting were being debated in Congress, firms increasingly filed applications in anticipation of the forthcoming change. The left side of Figure 8.1, which presents data on pharmaceutical and pharmo-chemical patent applications filed from 1990–2012, shows the spike in filings in the run-up to the new patent law and immediately following its entering into effect in 1997.

The way pharmaceutical patents were introduced in Brazil allows us to think of three different types of applications: normal, mailbox, and pipeline. *Normal* applications are those were filed after May 1997, when pharmaceuticals became patentable in Brazil. *Mailbox* applications refer to applications that were filed in Brazil as of January 1995, when TRIPS came into effect, and then examined along with normal applications as of May 1997. The *pipeline* refers to applications filed prior to 1995, including those where the patents had already been granted abroad (obviously not in Brazil, since Brazil did not grant pharmaceutical patents at that time). These older pre-TRIPS applications and patents were "revalidated" in Brazil, so long as the products covered were not yet on the market. TRIPS did not require countries to acknowledge these older applications and patents, and as we saw in Chapter 5, the decision to do so was exceptionally controversial in Brazil.

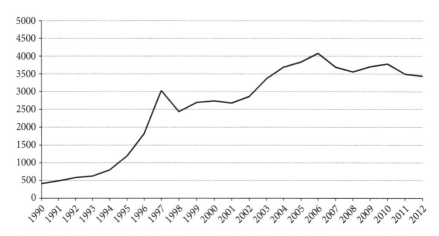

Figure 8.1. Pharmaceutical and Pharmo-Chemical Applications Filed in Brazil*
* Applications with first International Patent Classification of A61K or C07D.
Source: INPI-BR

The decision to allow pipeline patents had dramatic effects. Brazil received approximately 1200 requests for pipeline patents; more than three hundred different medicines became patented in Brazil on account of the pipeline, medicines that otherwise could have entered the market without patent protection (Hasenclever et al. 2010; Laforgia et al. 2008; Levis 2010; Sweet 2013). For comparative purposes, consider the sample of FDA-approved drugs discussed in Chapter 2 (Table 2.2, p. 41). Although the numbers of patents granted and drugs patented in Brazil are lower than in Mexico, the figures are remarkably higher than in Argentina, and this is because of the pipeline. More than half of the patents from this dataset that were granted in Brazil were granted via the pipeline. To see the effects of this provision the analysis distinguished, for each granted patent associated with each drug, whether the patent was issued via the pipeline. The data show that 80 percent of the drugs in the sample with patents in Brazil had at least one pipeline patent, and 60 percent of the drugs from this sample with patents granted had all of their patents granted via the pipeline. That is, in three-fifths of the cases, drugs became patented in Brazil because of the pipeline—*and only because of the pipeline.*

Importantly, because of timing, the introduction of pharmaceutical patents did not have the same devastating effect on industry in Brazil as witnessed in Mexico. The protracted period of debate over the new patent law served to buffer the considerable shock to the system provoked by over-compliance. Nearly two hundred new drugs were approved for launch in the United States in the period between 1991, when Mexico introduced pharmaceutical patents, and 1997, when Brazil did so (FDA n.d.). These drugs, which could not be patented in Brazil, remained available for local production. For most of the 1990s, as regarded patents, Brazilian firms could continue as if nothing had changed.

Nor did the country's industrial structure undergo as profound a transformation as in Mexico. The 1990s was a challenging period for the pharmaceutical sector, as many of the promotional policies introduced in the 1980s were retired as part of the Collor and Cardoso Governments' liberalization drives. Subsidies and tariff protection were reduced, for example, and government procurement practices revised in ways that curbed preferences for local suppliers.[4] Yet both the extent of the liberalization and its effects need to be placed in context. Trade liberalization in Brazil was much less significant than elsewhere in Latin America (Kingstone et al. 2008; Montero 2014). Tariffs were reduced, but nowhere nearly as steeply as in Mexico, for example, and as a result Brazil's pharmaceutical industry continued to benefit from considerably more import protection. Capabilities created in the 1980s allowed some firms to survive this period (Queiroz 1997, 158–61). In fact, when the government reintroduced industrial policies in the early 2000s, many of the recipients of

---

[4] Bermudez (1995), Chamas (2005), del Campo (2016), Flynn (2015), Queiroz (1997), Rebouças (1997), Sweet (2013).

support were the same firms that had benefited from promotional measures in the 1980s (BMI 2015a; del Campo 2016; Shadlen and Fonseca 2013). To be sure, Brazilian pharmaceutical firms had nothing like the resources of their counterparts in Argentina, which retained dominant market shares, but they did not end up in the state of their counterparts in Mexico either, where the local sector became entirely subordinate to—if not absorbed by—the transnational sector.

Though the effects of over-compliance on industrial structure may have been circumscribed by timing, the effects on—and implications for—the health system were nothing sort of awesome. The inflow of patent applications, and the abrupt move from a situation with no drugs covered by pharmaceutical patents to one with so many medicines having patent protection, sent shockwaves through the health sector. The reason for this is that the drugs with patents were of disproportionate importance to the health system. Brazil's 1988 constitution stipulates health as a constitutional right; the national health system (*Sistema Único de Saúde*, SUS), established in 1990, offers access to healthcare, including treatments, to all Brazilians.[5] Roughly 75 percent of Brazilians use the SUS, and even the quarter of the population with private healthcare coverage relies on the state system for many interventions, particularly more costly treatments. In the context of such extensive commitments, the spike in pharmaceutical patents was alarming.

The effects created by over-compliance in the 1990s were particularly acute with regard to HIV/AIDS medications. Brazil stands out for its early and comprehensive approach toward prevention and treatment. Importantly, a 1996 law guaranteed free anti-retroviral (ARV) treatment through the National HIV/AIDS Program, and intense mobilization by health activists working within the state (sometimes referred to as "*sanitaristas*") and in civil society further reinforced the government's obligations.[6] The law guaranteeing AIDS treatment was passed just a few months after the new patent law, seemingly with little consideration of how one might affect the other (Nunn 2009, Chapter 4).

Pipeline patents threatened to undermine the government's commitments to provide AIDS treatment. Many ARVs launched in the late 1990s and early 2000s received patents in Brazil, even if the original patent applications had been filed prior to 1995, and as a result had single suppliers. Older ARVs that had already been launched by 1996 were ineligible for patents in Brazil, and thus could be sourced locally. So long as treatment was based on older drugs, the demands of the National AIDS Program could be satisfied by local

---

[5] The SUS guarantees access to drugs on Brazil's essential medicines list. In the early 2000s the government also started to make inexpensive drugs, including those beyond the essential list— available through a system of "Popular Pharmacies" (Paim et al. 2011; Santos-Pinto et al. 2011; Yamauti et al. 2015).

[6] d'Adesky (2004); Biehl (2007); Flynn (2013; 2015); Galvão (2002; 2005); Gauri and Lieberman (2006); Levi and Vitória (2002); Rich (2013); Teixeira et al. (2003).

production from public laboratories, which had benefited from considerable investments to develop necessary capabilities for local production (Cassier and Corrêa 2003; Flynn 2008), and imports from manufacturers in other countries where the drugs were not produced. Even when AIDS treatment was based largely on unpatented, first-line drugs, it was expensive—just not as expensive as it would become.[7] As demand shifted from older drugs to newer drugs it became evident that the new patent regime was posing serious challenges for the AIDS treatment program.[8] Much of the politics of pharmaceutical patents in Brazil in the post-TRIPS era has been about responding to these challenges.

Before analyzing Brazil's subsequent reforms of the new, over-compliant pharmaceutical patent system, a few points about the relationship between patents and country's AIDS treatment program are in order. Because anti-retroviral drugs treat, but do not cure, HIV/AIDS, they need to be taken indefinitely. And for effectiveness to be maintained, patients need to change treatment regimens as resistance develops. By the late 1990s and early 2000s, AIDS treatment in Brazil came to depend increasingly on newer ARVs which, to repeat, were patented locally. Simply put, because Brazil was ahead of the curve internationally in terms of HIV/AIDS treatment, with more people receiving ARVs earlier than in many other countries, the migration from first-line regimens based on older—unpatented—drugs to second-line regimens including newer—patented—drugs came earlier in Brazil too. As more people began treatment, and as patients receiving treatment migrated to expensive second-line regimens based on drugs that were patented under the new LPI, the program risked becoming unsustainable.[9]

MODIFYING OVER-COMPLIANCE

The coverage of key ARVs by patents granted via the pipeline, and more generally the massive influx of pharmaceutical patent applications, alarmed

---

[7] As early as 1997 the Minister of Health complained that too much of the country's health spending was being allocated toward HIV/AIDS medicines (Flynn 2013, 10). Though the statement was met with outcry and the Minister was soon replaced, the episode illustrates sensitivity to concerns over prices even at this early date. It also points to a lack of coordination at this point between IP and health policies.

[8] Grangeiro et al. (2006), Hasenclever et al. (2010), Ministry of Health (2005), Nunn (2009), Nunn et al. (2007), Reis (2012), Serra (2004). Flynn (2015, Appendix 2) provides a breakdown of the ARVs used in Brazil and their patent status, including an indicator of whether each drug was protected by pipeline patents.

[9] This issue of timing certainly contributes to Brazil becoming a path-setter in polices toward patents on ARVs, because it faced problems before many other countries did. Not surprisingly, another country that found itself in the spotlight regarding compulsory licenses on second-line ARVs was Thailand, which also initiated treatment early (Ford et al. 2007; Krikorian 2009).

health officials. Since the late 1990s, both the Cardoso and Lula Governments attempted to modify the new patent system to address these concerns.

To improve the capacity of the National HIV/AIDS Program (and the SUS more generally) to acquire less-expensive versions of newer, patented drugs, the Cardoso and Lula Governments revised the LPI's provisions on compulsory licenses, particularly those regarding "public interest" and government use. Two Executive directives, one in 1999 and another in 2003, simplified the process for issuing compulsory licenses.[10] The modifications, designed to increase Brazil's ability to obtain price reductions, provided clearer definitions of what conditions constitute national emergency and public interest, and simplified the mechanism for issuing compulsory licenses by giving the Ministry of Health itself greater authority to act on behalf of the Executive (Barbosa 2000; 2013; Flynn 2015; Oliveira et al. 2004). The 2003 directive also stipulates that private firms supplying the government constitutes "public use" and is thus acceptable.

On numerous occasions in the early 2000s, the Ministry of Health negotiated price reductions by threatening to issue compulsory licenses on newer, patented ARVs that were essential to the National AIDS Program.[11] In 2001, when Brazil threatened compulsory licenses on Roche's nelfinavir and Merck's efavirenz, Roche responded by reducing the price by of its drug by 40 percent and Merck reduced its price by 59 percent. Similar episodes occurred with these two drugs as well as Abbott's lopinavir/ritonavir in 2003, and then, again with Abbott in 2005 in 2006. In 2007, following protracted negotiations with Merck, Brazil issued compulsory licenses on two patents covering efavirenz, which allowed it to obtain the drug at a 75 percent price reduction.

It is essential to underscore that the reforms to Brazil's compulsory licensing provisions, as well as their subsequent deployment to secure price reductions, were responses to challenges created by over-compliance. After all, the only reason why drugs such as nelfinavir, lopinavir/ritonavir, and efavirenz were patented in Brazil was because of the decision to allow pipeline patents. Had Brazil refused to acknowledge pre-1995 inventions, as permitted by TRIPS, these drugs would not have been patented in Brazil, and they could have been produced locally or secured from alternative suppliers in countries where they were not patented. Brazil needed to negotiate prices with single suppliers because the drugs were patented in Brazil, and the drugs were patented in Brazil because of the pipeline.

---

[10] Although Executive directives in Brazil are meant to establish implementation guidelines, and not to constitute formal reforms of laws, they are often substantive, as in this case.

[11] Among the many works that discuss the use of compulsory licenses in Brazil, see Cassier (2012), Cassier and Corrêa (2013), Cohen and Lybecker (2005), Fonseca and Bastos (2016), Flynn (2011, 2013, 2015), Nunn et al. (2009), Possas (2008), Ramani and Urias (2015), Rosenberg (2014), Shadlen (2009b), Sweet (2013), Urias (2015).

But even then, the 1999 and 2003 reforms that gave health authorities the ability to use the threat of a compulsory license to negotiate price reductions on patented drugs were only necessary because of another dimension of Brazil's over-compliance. Threatening a compulsory license is a bargaining tool used to entice patent holders to make their products available at lower prices; the effectiveness of the bargaining tool depends on the credibility of the threat. The wording of the compulsory licensing provisions in the 1996 patent law made their use overly complex, and thus would have made threats unproductive. The subsequent Executive directives constitute efforts to correct these earlier choices, enhancing the credibility of the government's threats by making compulsory licenses easier to issue and less vulnerable to appeal, and by increasing the government's ability to secure the relevant drugs from alternative suppliers. But, again, the Brazilian Government only found itself compelled to make these changes because of over-compliance in the first place: had Brazil adopted alternative phrasing in the 1996 LPI, health officials would have had the ability to threaten compulsory licenses and secure price reductions; reforming the patent law in this way would not have been necessary. In sum, over-compliance generated problems for health officials in Brazil, in the form of patents and high prices on key drugs, and also left them without a solution, in that compulsory licensing provisions were overly complex. Reforming this aspect of the patent system provided the Ministry of Health with a more useful instrument to address the problems created by over-compliance.

Brazil's compulsory licensing provisions regarding "local working" also drew attention in this period. As discussed in Chapter 5, the LPI made failure to manufacture a patented good within Brazil potentially a ground for compulsory licensing. Although the final version of this article passed in 1996 expressed the manufacturing requirement in much looser language than earlier drafts had, such that it was regarded in Brazil as having been neutered, the transnational pharmaceutical industry and the US Government remained upset by its inclusion in any form. After all, some countries' new patent laws explicitly indicated that importation constituted local working, and with the 2000 deadline for full TRIPS implementation in developing countries arriving, the existence of this clause, however weak and diluted, in the patent law of a leading country such as Brazil remained worrisome. Thus the transnational sector applied pressure on the USTR to challenge Brazil, and in 2000 the US initiated a complaint at the World Trade Organization. Brazil mobilized a defense of the provision and the right to define local "working" as local "manufacturing," and in June 2001 the two countries reached an agreement whereby the US dropped the case and Brazil promised to notify the US Government prior to issuing a compulsory license on these specific grounds of failure to manufacture locally, on any patents held by US firms (Attaran and Champ 2002; Dubowy 2003; Shadlen 2009a).[12]

Compulsory licensing is the aspect of Brazil's tailoring experience that has received the most attention from analysts, but these steps are not the only efforts made to respond to the challenges created by over-compliance. The decision to include pipeline patents presented Brazilian authorities with the question of how to deal with patent-holders' requests for extensions of their terms of protection. Patents that were allowed in Brazil under the pipeline were set to expire twenty years from the first date of foreign application, and when expiration dates were extended abroad, patent holders then sought that this adjustment be made in Brazil, too. As we saw in Chapter 7, this issue became salient in Mexico too, with important dimensions of policy that affect how new pharmaceutical patent systems function being made not through legislation, as in the 1990s, but also through administrative and judicial action. In contrast with what we witnessed in Mexico, however, Brazilian authorities tended not to adjust terms for patents granted under the pipeline mechanism. That is, if a patent had a 1990 priority date from its US application, for example, and was allowed in Brazil under the pipeline, the patent would be due to expire in both the US and Brazil on the same day in 2010. And even if the US patent office were to extend the expiry date by two years, so that the patent expired in 2012 in the US, it would still expire in 2010 in Brazil. The transnational sector pushed strongly for extending patent terms, and regularly demanded this in court, and as we have seen secured these extensions in Mexico, but not in Brazil.[13]

An important dimension of tailoring in Brazil was to involve the Ministry of Health in the examination of pharmaceutical patent applications. Since 2001, the government required all pharmaceutical applications approved by the patent office (INPI-BR) to be sent to the health regulatory agency, the National Agency for Health Surveillance (*Agência Nacional de Vigilância Sanitária*, ANVISA) for review.[14] According to the revised LPI, pharmaceutical patents can be issued only after ANVISA gives its "prior consent." The Prior Consent rule aimed to help the patent office deal with the deluge of pharmaceutical patent applications and to achieve

---

[12] In the episodes of compulsory licensing discussed above, threatened and issued, the "local working" requirement was not invoked; those negotiations and deliberations occurred in the context of the reformed provisions regarding compulsory licenses in situations of public interest.

[13] Barbosa (2012) discusses the legal conflicts. For illustrations of rulings, see "AGU impede prorrogação da patente de remédio contra câncer de mama e garante produção e venda mais barata por outros laboratórios" (goo.gl/rVXkVL); "INPI derruba no STJ extensão de patentes de remédios," *Inova Unicamp*. February 21, 2013 (goo.gl/O8oqfL).

[14] This was introduced by presidential decree (provisional measure) in 1999, but did not go into effect until 2001 when the LPI was formally revised.

coordination between patent policy and the broader set of health initiatives being put in place at the time.[15] Prior Consent could provide the health sector with an instrument to influence the patent examination process, influence that it would otherwise lack.

The Prior Consent system began operating in June 2001, after ANVISA created a division for executing its role. Since then Brazil had a dual examination system for pharmaceutical patents. In the first step, INPI-BR would examine the application. If the patent office determined that the patent should not be granted, then it was rejected and the process ended. However, if INPI-BR's examination concluded that the patent should be granted, the application was then passed to ANVISA, where it received a second examination. If ANVISA approved, i.e. issued its "consent," INPI-BR then could grant the patent. Though ANVISA lacks the legal authority to reject patents, INPI-BR can only grant patents where ANVISA has given its consent. As will be explained below, these arrangements were revised in 2012, with a new workflow introduced such that the first evaluation of pharmaceutical patent applications was conducted by ANVISA.

Table 8.1 presents data on the first ten years of the dual examination arrangements, from 2001 through 2010. Because the workflow in this period meant that ANVISA only received applications after they were approved by the patent office, the applications considered in the table are only those that would have been granted were ANVISA not involved. The data suggest that Prior Consent does not function as a block on pharmaceutical patenting. After all, nearly 75 percent of applications approved by INPI-BR passed the

Table 8.1. ANVISA's Prior Consent (June 2001–July 2010)

Decision	Number of Applications	Percentage
Approvals	1100	74.3
Denials of Consent	143	9.7
Rejected in Course*	79	5.3
Pending**	88	6.0
Other***	70	4.7
Total	*1480*	*100.0*

Source: ANVISA

* Rejected in Course refers to applications where, in the course of ANVISA's analysis, INPI-BR changed its original decision and rejected the application or declared it as withdrawn.

** Pending includes applications under analysis at ANVISA and where ANVISA's decision is under appeal.

*** Other includes applications returned to INPI-BR for further documentation or because determined not to be pharmaceutical patent applications.

[15] Basso (2006), Cassier (2012), Guimarães (2008), Guimarães and Corrêa (2012), Kunisawa (2009), and Silva (2008) discuss the origins of Prior Consent.

second hurdle too. But ANVISA was not a rubber stamp either: the health agency denied its consent to one in every ten of these applications that INPI-BR had approved, and in the case of another 5 percent, applications that had originally been approved ended up rejected or withdrawn after ANVISA's review pointed out irregularities in the patent office's analysis.[16]

Scrutiny of the dual examination arrangements reveal this to be a system to reduce granting of secondary patents (Sampat and Shadlen 2015b; 2017; Shadlen 2011b; Silva 2008). Where INPI-BR approved patent applications covering new molecules and compounds, the expectation is that these would be approved by ANVISA as well, and subsequently granted. Where the two agencies differed was specifically with regard to applications for patents on alternative structural forms of existing molecules, new formulations or dosages, and additional uses of existing drugs, i.e. secondary patents (Howard 2007; Kapczynski et al. 2012; Sampat and Shadlen 2015b; 2017). INPI-BR and ANVISA adopted different approaches toward assessing the merits of these sorts of applications.[17] The higher scrutiny of secondary applications promised by the dual examination system aims to control the price of drugs by stopping periods of exclusivity from being extended with the grant of new patents on already-existing molecules and drugs. The system is functionally similar to the measures discussed in the case of Argentina, such as prohibiting patents on second medical uses and the new examination guidelines that restrict secondary patents more widely, as well as measures taken by India that aim to reduce secondary pharmaceutical patents.[18]

Another set of measures that the Brazilian Government took to address the effects of having a pharmaceutical patent system was to regulate market entry at the time that patents expire. The "Generics Law" of 1999, which aimed to increase competition and improve quality of non-patented drugs, created a new category of interchangeable medicines and stipulated the conditions for establishing equivalence and substitutability (Fonseca 2014; Fonseca and Shadlen 2016). The Generics Law was complemented by introduction of an "early working" provision to facilitate generic market entry. The early working (sometimes called "Bolar") exception, included in the same 2001 reform of the patent law as Prior Consent, allows firms to use patented knowledge and produce generic versions of patented drugs to obtain marketing approval once patents expire. Without such a provision, firms might be

---

[16] In 40 percent of the applications that ANVISA approved through 2006, applicants first had to reduce the breadth of the patents' claims (Silva 2008).

[17] Basso (2006); Cassier (2012); Juca da Silveira e Silva and Vallini (2010); Kunisawa (2009); Sampat and Shadlen (2015b); Shadlen (2011b); Silva (2008).

[18] The dual examination arrangements can also be understood as a response to the challenges created by the pipeline. Previous analyses of Prior Consent indicate that ANVISA was less likely to grant its consent to secondary applications associated with drugs that had earlier patents granted under the pipeline (Sampat and Shadlen 2015b).

infringing patents by producing generic versions prior to the patents' expiration. Yet if firms must wait until patents expire to produce generic versions and apply to health authorities for authorization, patent terms are effectively extended by the amount of time it takes to complete these significant steps. And throughout this period, though Brazil offers exclusivity for test data in agricultural chemicals, the Ministry of Health resisted demands to apply this to drugs.

None of the measures discussed here reverse the global sea change of the 1990s. Brazil, like the other countries in this book (indeed, like nearly all developing countries) went from being a country without pharmaceutical patents to a country with pharmaceutical patents. The status quo changed, and remained changed. However, revisions to the compulsory licensing system, the bias against extending terms of patents granted under the pipeline, creation of a dual examination system, establishment of a regulatory framework for generic competition, all of these, collectively, affect the way Brazil's new pharmaceutical patent functions. Brazilian leaders, from Cardoso to Lula and Rousseff, incorporated health-oriented measures into the patent system to ameliorate the effects of over-compliance in the 1990s.

DISCOVERING AND CONFRONTING THE ACHILLES' HEEL

Tailoring the new patent system was insufficient to overcome the difficulties generated by Brazil's initial choices regarding the introduction of pharmaceutical patents. As the number of people receiving treatment through the National AIDS Program increased, and as more patients were being treated with newer, patented, and thus more expensive antiretroviral medicines, government expenditures on pharmaceuticals continued to increase.[19] The reforms instituted in this period risked being overwhelmed by the challenges that emerged from the increased demand for patented drugs.

Reviewing the Brazilian Government's interactions with transnational pharmaceutical firms over the price of patented AIDs drugs reveals the limitations of what could be achieved through revisions of the patent law. The ability of a government to use the threat of a compulsory license to elicit price reductions depends on the threats being credible. For the threats to be credible, two sets of

---

[19] The focus in this section is on AIDS drugs because of the significance of patents in this therapeutic area. For discussion of the broader relationship between the government's health commitments and subsequent policies toward the pharmaceutical sector, see Shadlen and Fonseca (2013).

conditions must be met, one legal and one material. First, as discussed, the patent law must allow the government to issue compulsory licenses under the relevant circumstances and not make the process overly complicated. Second, the government must be able to secure the product in question from alternative sources, foreign or domestic. The modifications introduced in 1999 and 2003 helped achieve the first condition, but legal changes by themselves could not generate the necessary supply.

Initially, when local firms were unable to supply the Ministry of Health, Brazil could import non-patented pharmaceutical products from India. As India delayed the introduction of pharmaceutical product patents until 2005, and did not acknowledge older, pre-1995 inventions, it emerged as an important supplier of non-patented drugs to developing countries (Chaudhuri 2005; Horner 2014a; 2014b; Waning et al. 2010).[20] When Brazil threatened to issue compulsory licenses, then, the government was doing so under the expectation that, were the patent-holding firm not to lower the price, drugs could be imported from India.

But Brazil would not be able to rely on India indefinitely. As of 2005 India also began granting pharmaceutical patents. While this change would not affect the patent status of drugs already being produced in India, i.e., drugs that were available from Indian suppliers as of 2005 continued to be, the introduction of pharmaceutical patents in India meant that, going forward, the supply of inexpensive non-patented products from Indian suppliers would become less reliable (Shadlen 2007). The changing nature of global supply, in turn, threatened to undermine the achievements made by Brazil's revisions of the new patent law.

In the absence of reliable external sources of supply, from India or elsewhere, the Ministry of Health would need to be able to source the drugs locally. Otherwise threats of compulsory licenses lacked credibility and would be less useful as tools to lower prices. In the case of some drugs, such as nelfinavir, the fact that the Ministry's principal public laboratory (*Farmanguinhos*) demonstrated an ability to produce and supply the drug at 60 percent of the price Brazil was paying enabled the government to obtain a price reduction from Roche. In the case of other drugs where local production capabilities were absent, such as efavirenz, the Ministry authorized *Farmanguinhos* to import the active pharmaceutical ingredient from India to learn how to reverse-engineer it.[21] Brazilian officials knew that, without

---

[20] India accepted post-1995 applications in the "mailbox," as required by TRIPS, and then began examining these after the transition period ended and patents became available for pharmaceutical products.

[21] Not surprisingly, Merck objected to this, claiming that its patent was being infringed, but the Ministry defended use for research as appropriate. Cassier (2012) and Corrêa and Cassier (2008; 2013) discuss this capability-building exercise, as well as Brazil's conflict with Merck.

capabilities to produce drugs locally, threats to issue compulsory licenses would become less effective over time.[22]

Understanding the relationship between compulsory licensing and the possibilities of local supply casts new light on Brazil's patent reforms of the 2000s. To be sure, compulsory licenses, threatened and in one instance issued, yielded savings and were indispensable to the sustainability of the Brazilian AIDS treatment program (Ford et al. 2007; Nunn et al. 2007). Yet these same episodes also provided signals that the strategy was insufficient. In the case of the lopinavir/ritonavir combination, the Ministry of Health took all the steps necessary to issue a compulsory license, yet ultimately settled with Abbott in 2005, with the latter guaranteeing supplies at an agreed price through 2011. One of the reasons why Brazil ultimately reached an agreement with Abbott, rather than circumvent the patent with a compulsory license, was concern that local laboratories could not satisfy the growing demand for this drug. Nor was importing from India, where this drug was not patented, regarded as sufficiently reliable at the time. Thus Brazil, even with a patent regime revised to help health officials in just these sorts of situations, had little choice but to come to terms with the patent holder. And though the agreement reduced the price, Brazil would still pay significantly more than Abbott's most discounted international price, a fact that drew widespread criticism from activists and health officials. Indeed, just as the transnational sector and the US Government complained about Brazil's threat to issue a compulsory license, many within Brazil (and abroad) assailed the Lula Government for *not* doing so and instead reaching an agreement with Abbott.[23]

In the case of efavirenz, where Brazil did issue a compulsory license, previous negotiations with the patent holder had yielded more substantial price reductions, but in terms of total expenditures the savings from lower unit prices were outweighed by the effects of higher demand. Eventually Merck

---

[22] Reflecting similar concerns, in 2007 health officials advised physicians in the National AIDS Program to refrain from prescribing the drug abacavir because of the high price and unreliability of alternative sources of supply (Hasenclever et al. 2010, 171).

[23] See the discussions in Cohen (2006), Flynn (2013), Grangeiro et al. (2006), and Possas (2008). For a critique from Brazilian civil society activists, see "Acordo do governo brasileiro com Abbott frustra expectativas dos brasileros, afirma ABIA" (goo.gl/OXk6hn). In negotiating with Abbott, the Ministry of Health claims to have received commitments from Abbott that it would transfer technology for lopinavir/ritonavir production to *Farmanguinhos*. Although the promise to transfer technology and help with production was reported in the press at the time (e.g. goo.gl/ FLn3UD), the formal agreement does not include any such provisions. To the contrary Clause 10 explicitly releases Abbott from obligations to assist with production. According to sources in *Fiocruz*, the promise of technology transfer was made in an informal "side agreement," though this version is also contested (see goo.gl/pRhWNJ). As it happened, according to an informant in ABIFINA, a local firm (Cristália) eventually developed the capabilities to produce the drug without Abbott's help, and the Ministry thus never needed to call on Abbott to make good on any such promise that may or may not have been made. Email from ABIFINA official, July 23, 2013 (follow-up to Interview, May 19, 2008a).

refused to lower the price further, and in 2007 the Ministry of Health responded with the compulsory license, exercising the revised provisions. In this instance the drug was available from Indian suppliers, and for the first two years after issuing the compulsory license Brazilian demand was satisfied by imports from India. This too can be interpreted as a successful use of the revised compulsory licensing provisions, but, again, it was obviously not a long-term solution, as Indian suppliers would not be available indefinitely for all drugs that would be needed for AIDs treatment in Brazil. Deficiencies in the country's pharmaceutical production capabilities were evident, and worrisome. Indeed, the health officials saw this coming: for years *Farmanguinhos* had been working on synthesizing efavirenz and developing its own version of the medication (Cassier 2012), but not until 2009, after a partnership with three private local firms, did *Farmanguinhos* deliver its first batch.[24]

The limits that changes in the *global* IP regime placed on the effects of tailoring in Brazil are also illustrated by the case of tenofovir. As with other essential ARVs, increased demand was burdening the health budget, and here too the Ministry negotiated for lower prices with the sole supplier, Gilead. In this instance, the application for the tenofovir patent had been filed after the LPI came into effect and thus, unlike other drugs discussed in this section, was not admitted in Brazil under the pipeline. The application would be examined by the patent office, and in 2008 it was rejected (Cassier 2012; Veras 2014). Here too, however, the Ministry of Health needed to import the drug, despite the absence of patent protection locally, as neither public nor private labs in Brazil could supply it. Foreign suppliers were only available because the application was denied in India too; had tenofovir received patent protection in India, in the absence of local production capabilities the rejection of Gilead's application in Brazil would have had little immediate effect on the country's ability to secure the drug at an affordable price. The Ministry cannot, however, rely on patent applications for important drugs routinely being rejected, locally or abroad; tenofovir was an exceptional case in that the application was vulnerable to legal challenges (Amin et al. 2009). Nor, as the data presented above indicate, was there reason to expect that the Prior Consent system would reliably lead to patent applications on new drugs being rejected.[25]

---

[24] Some observers have suggested that issuing a compulsory license in the case of efavirenz was feasible because of Brazilian labs' ability to produce the drug but, to the contrary, the government was handicapped by the absence of such abilities. In fact, in the course of negotiating efavirenz prices, the Ministry of Health also attempted, unsuccessfully, to secure technology transfer commitments from Merck to help build local production capabilities (Flynn 2011, 165).

[25] Again, the dual examination system targeted secondary patents, not new compounds. Where applied for, patents on new compounds are likely to be granted in all countries with pharmaceutical patent regimes. This is the fundamental shift introduced by the global sea change of the 1980s and 1990s.

The conflicts over these ARVs reinforced concerns regarding the ability of public and private laboratories to produce complex medicines. A clear take-away from these experiences is that even with the facilities to threaten and issue compulsory licenses on patented drugs, and even in the absence of a patent on a key drug, the country needed greater production capabilities. Deficiencies in local production capabilities constituted the "Achilles' heel" of the country's health system, and in the context of such deficiencies modi-fying the pharmaceutical patent system could achieve only so much. Indeed, even if, hypothetically, Brazil were to eliminate pharmaceutical patents altogether, in a world marked by single global suppliers, the ability to obtain price reductions by threatening to introduce competition via compulsory licensing would depend on existence of local production capabilities. Not necessarily capabilities to discover and launch new drugs, but capabilities to reverse engineer complex drugs and produce affordable versions of high quality at reasonable cost.[26]

With its ability to benefit from a reformed patent system to lower prices dependent on local (public and private) producers' having adequate supply capabilities, the government complemented the steps to tailor the new pharmaceutical patent system with innovation–industrial policies to build these capabilities. While the conflicts over ARVs discussed above provided a trigger for action, the industrial policies deployed were not developed from scratch. Pharmaceuticals had been identified as a "strategic" sector in the 2003 Industrial, Technological, and Foreign Trade Policy, with the government offering financial support for the local production of active pharmaceutical ingredients. Soon thereafter the National Development Bank (BNDES) launched a financing program to support the pharmaceutical sector, *Profarma*, and eventually the Lula Government introduced an array of programs toward the "Health Industry Complex" (*Complexo Industrial da Saúde*, CIS), all part of an integrated, trans-sectoral program to develop the strengthen the healthcare sector called "Greater Health" (*Mais Saúde*).[27]

The level of financing to support the pharmaceutical sector was unprece-dented in Brazil. *Profarma*, the BNDES-directed program to support local pharmaceutical firms, had lines of funding for production, innovation, and export (Capanema et al. 2008). In the first years of the program most of the lending was to improve existing production facilities. For example, resources were directed to help local firms adjust to the new generic drug

---

[26] Though early, because of the country's advanced HIV/AIDS treatment program, Brazil is not unique in reacting to these challenges. Imminent reduction in Indian supply has led to a wide array of initiatives to increase local pharmaceutical production in the developing world (African Union-UNIDO 2012; Anderson 2010; Mackintosh et al. 2016; Russo and Banda 2015).

[27] *Mais Saúde* was the overarching framework for healthcare strengthening. One of its principle axes is the Health Industry Complex. For a statement on the origins of this project, see Guimarães et al. (2006).

regulations, particularly to help them develop the capabilities to comply with requirements for demonstrating bioequivalence (Shadlen and Fonseca 2013).[28] Over time *Profarma* came to focus more on supporting innovation, and by 2011 innovation projects received the majority of *Profarma* funding.[29] Other instruments to encourage and subsidize local bio-medical innovation included tax incentives, direct public subsidies in private firms, and facilitating collaborations between private firms and public research institutions.[30]

Pharmaceutical industrial policy in Brazil aims to stimulate the local production of strategic medicines and medical devices, via the strategic use of government purchasing power and encouragement of public-private partnerships. In Brazil these partnerships are called "productive development partnerships" (*Parcerias para o Desenvolvimento Productivo*, PDPs). In putting together PDPs, the Ministry of Health identifies key inputs (e.g. drugs and medical devices) and then draws up plans to increase the local supply of these products (Chaves 2016; Chaves et al. 2015).[31] Where production capabilities are absent or inadequate, measures are taken to build capabilities by encouraging collaboration among public laboratories and private firms. And where collaboration among domestic actors alone is not sufficient, licenses are negotiated with foreign firms and joint-ventures launched for local production.

These efforts to promote the Brazilian pharmaceutical sector are part of a broader complex of innovation–industrial policies introduced in the 2000s, as the country's economic development strategy was redefined to focus explicitly on increasing competitiveness via innovation. Technological innovation became the guiding and uniting thread of economic policymaking in the 2000s, particularly under the Lula Government, systematically fused with sectoral industrial policies. Important measures to promote a shift toward innovation or "knowledge-based" growth include offering subsidized loans through the expansion of BNDES credit lines (as discussed above in the case of *Profarma*), providing tax incentives as well as direct subsidies for private firms' research and development activities, and a set of measures to simplify and

---

[28] Though not the principal focus of the analysis here, these measures to help develop a generic drug industry in Brazil contributed to local firms' acquiring growing shares of the retail market in the 2000s (BMI 2015a; del Campo 2016; Fonseca 2014; Shadlen and Fonseca 2013).

[29] Hochstetler and Montero (2013) provide more analysis of the Brazilian development bank's lending in this period.

[30] Analyses of these programs include Chaves (2016), Delgado (2008; 2013), Flynn (2015), Hasenclever et al. (2016), Muzaka (2017, forthcoming), Paranhos (2012), Schüren (2013).

[31] The template for Productive Development Partnerships emerged from the experience of creating public–private partnerships to produce efavirenz and tenofovir, with the state guaranteeing demand, local firms synthesizing the API, and public labs producing the final drug (Cassier 2012; Shadlen and Fonseca 2013, 570; Veras 2014, 97–9).

encourage increased university–industry collaborations.[32] Many of these measures required new legislation, for example the Good Law (*Lei do Bem*) was introduced to allow direct public subsidies to private firms, and the Law on Technological Innovation established new ground rules for interactions between private firms and public research institutions. Legislative changes were complemented by institutional reforms, including the reorganization of the Brazilian Innovation Agency (*Financiadora de Estudos e Projetos*, FINEP), and the creation of the Brazilian Industrial Development Agency (*Agência Brasileira de Desenvolvimento Industrial*, ABDI) as an overarching coordinating body.

The measures discussed in the previous paragraphs are notable, and without equivalents in the other countries examined in this book. The 1996 patent law transformed Brazil; intellectual property and innovation came to be regarded by the state as cornerstones of economic development. Governments have not just tailored the patent system to address specific problems created by the way pharmaceutical patents were introduced, but also taken steps to build a scientific, technological, and innovation infrastructure that is more suited for a new environment that features pharmaceutical patenting. Indeed, it is on account of this two-pronged response, both revising the new patent system in response to the country's needs and building capabilities to adjust to the pharmaceutical patent system's existence, that the term "neo-developmental" is used.

SOCIAL STRUCTURE, COALITION BUILDING, AND EXECUTIVE AGENCY

The key actor within the Executive pushing through revisions to the new pharmaceutical patent system was the Ministry of Health. As many observers have noted, a network of health professionals who had been active during the period of military rule took on important roles in the state bureaucracy in the course of the transition to democracy in the late 1980s.[33] These health professionals, many committed to a comprehensive, universalist, and rights-based vision of health, served as institutional activists within the state, not just keeping the Executive's feet to the fire in terms of its commitments on AIDS treatment, but pressuring to make the necessary revisions of the patent system.

---

[32] See, for example, Arbix (2007), CGEE-ANPEI (2009), Cruz and de Mello (2006), de Negri (2008), de Toni (2015), Doctor (2009), Hochstetler and Montero (2013), Lugones and Suárez (2007), Octaviani (2010), Schüren (2013).

[33] Arretche (2004); Biehl (2004); Escorel (1999); Flynn (2013; 2015); Fonseca and Bastos (2016); Gómez 2012; Nunn (2009); Nunn et al. (2009); Rich and Gómez (2012).

While the motives for revising the new pharmaceutical patent system are easily understood, inspired by the challenges that the policy choices made in the 1990s subsequently posed to the health system, the key analytic question is, once reformers in the Executive decided to try to alter course, what factors allowed them to succeed? After all, many of the same actors that had lobbied intensely for over-compliance in the 1990s reacted with abhorrence to—and attempted to block and undermine—the new tailoring measures. The transnational sector and the much of the IP law community vociferously opposed modifications of the compulsory licensing rules, for example, viewing them as an assault on the hard-won rights secured in the 1990s. INTERFARMA and ABPI also fought back against Prior Consent, seeking to block the involvement of health officials in patent examination by whatever means necessary, including legal challenges to the constitutionality of the new arrangements.[34] Externally, these measures were also viewed with disdain. Initially, the US Government expressed tolerance of the reforms to Brazil's public interest compulsory licensing provisions. Even as the US launched a case in the WTO against Brazil's "local working" rule, the US was explicit that the measures introduced to complement the country's health policies were uncontroversial (USTR 2000; 2001).[35] When the revised regulations were put into use, however, the full machinery of external pressures was again put into action, as the USTR and State Department exerted considerable efforts in trying to stop Brazil from threatening—let alone issuing—compulsory licenses (Flynn 2011; 2015). Likewise, international pharmaceutical firms assailed the Prior Consent arrangements, complaints that were regularly echoed in the USTR's Special 301 assessments of IP policies in Brazil.[36]

In contrast to what we observed in the 1990s, however, the advocates of over-compliance were unable to mobilize exporters on their behalf. During the debates over the introduction of pharmaceutical patents in the 1990s, Brazil's Political Trade Dependence (PTD), the share of the country's global exports that entered the US under removable, preferential schemes, had allowed the transnational

---

[34] "Mudanças na lei desagradam múltis," *Folha de São Paulo*, February 21, 2000. For discussions of the political and legal challenges to Prior Consent, see Basso (2006), Shadlen (2011a; 2011b).

[35] Referring to the dispute at the WTO over Brazil's local working requirement, the 2001 Special 301 Report included the following: "Brazil has asserted that the U.S. case will threaten Brazil's widely-praised anti-AIDS program, and will prevent Brazil from addressing its national health crisis. Nothing could be further from the truth. For example, should Brazil choose to compulsory license antiretroviral AIDS drugs, it could do so under Article 71 of its patent law, which authorizes complsory licensing to address a national health emergency, consistent with TRIPS, and which the United States is not challenging" (USTR 2001, 10).

[36] The international pharmaceutical industry described ANVISA's involvement as introducing a "fourth criterion" into patent examination (PhRMA 2003, 88). Kogan (2006) provides a scathing review of Brazilian policy from the perspective of IP rights-holders in the US.

sector and the Executive to mobilize exporters by presenting over-compliance as a pre-condition for retaining endangered market access. The subsequent diversification of trade, both in terms of export markets and types of goods, however, meant that exporters had become less dependent on the US market in the 2000s. Even where exporters focused on the US, their exports were less dependent on unilateral preferences that could be removed. As Figure 8.2 shows, Brazil's overall trade dependence on the US increased until 2002, and then decreased throughout the decade, reaching historically low levels. To be sure, fear that the US would revoke preferences mobilized some exporters to caution the Ministry of Health, but the share of exports that depended preferences that could be easily removed was much less important in this period. The diversification and subsequent reduced vulnerability of Brazilian exports are illustrated by the PTD measure, which declined in the late 1990s even as overall trade dependence increased, and continued to decline, such that by the middle of the decade it was at half the level witnessed in the 1990s, and by the end of the decade was roughly 1 percent (Figure 8.3). While Brazil's trade structure had helped widen the coalition for over-compliance in the 1990s by activating agnostics, changes to the trade structure altered the possibilities for coalition building in the 2000s. As an illustration, in 2011 a collection of Brazilian trade associations representing Brazilian exporters and internationalized industries submitted a detailed report to the USTR defending the countries' IP policies (BIC-CEBEU-CNI-FIESP 2011). Rather than join forces with the transnational pharmaceutical sector and support the crusade for over-compliance, now exporters were defending government against such demands—precisely the opposite sort of mobilization as witnessed in the 1990s.

In addition to benefiting from a more amenable trade structure, health officials had opportunities to build coalitions in support of their efforts. One source of support came from the dense network of IP- and health-focused civil

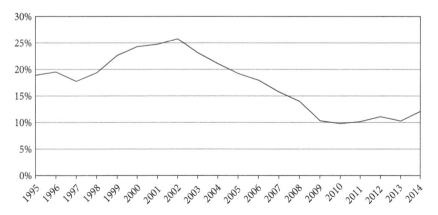

Figure 8.2. Brazil's Trade Dependence, 1995–2014

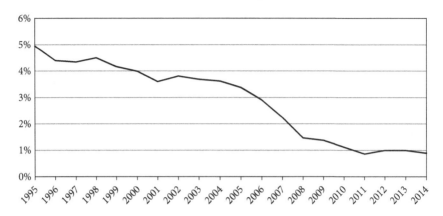

Figure 8.3. Brazil's Political Trade Dependence, 1995–2014

Note: Data on preferential exports to the US are from the United States International Trade Commission; data on overall exports to the US and global exports are from UN-COMTRADE.

society groups that emerged in this period (Biehl 2007; Matthews 2011; Nunn et al. 2009). Brazil had long histories of both IP-based and health-focused activism, but they tended to operate in separate spheres: IP-based activism had been oriented toward issues related to biotechnology and the environment rather than health, as discussed in Chapter 5, while civil society mobilization around health focused little on patents. The visible conflict with the US over Brazil's compulsory licensing provisions bridged this divide and triggered extensive IP-oriented activism by patients groups and health advocates, particularly with regard to HIV/AIDS.[37] For example, the "Intellectual Property Working Group" (*Grupo de Trabalho sobre Propriedade Intelectual*, GTPI), the leading coordinator of IP-related activism in Brazilian civil society, was founded in the aftermath of this conflict. Thus, while the defining characteristic of Brazilian civil society mobilization on patents in the 1990s had been that pharmaceuticals and drugs were not the main issue of concern, that was, emphatically, no longer the case in this second period of patent politics.

Health officials could also cultivate the support of the local pharmaceutical industry. Though Brazil's pharmaceutical and pharmo-chemical producers were unsuccessful in resisting over-compliance in the 1990s, they did not subsequently become absorbed by the transnational sector, economically or politically, as, for example, their counterparts did in Mexico. Rather, associations representing national firms, such as ABIFINA and ALANAC, continued to act in opposition to INTERFARMA, consistently presenting positions contrary to those of the transnational sector. They quickly transitioned from contesting

---

[37] Chaves (2016); Chaves et al. (2008); Flynn (2013); Matthews (2011); Muzaka (2017, forthcoming); Rosina et al (2010).

when and how pharmaceutical patents would be introduced to fighting over the details of how the new patent system functioned and imploring the government to make all necessary adjustments (ABIFINA-ALANAC 2001).

The existence of a national pharmaceutical sector with retained capabilities and interests distinct from the transnationals presented Brazilian officials with cooperative and supportive interlocutors. For example, the 2003 presidential directive that defined "public interest" in a broader way that made threats of compulsory licensing more credible was drafted by a lawyer working as an advisor to ABIFINA (Interview, May 18, 2008).[38] Throughout this period, the support of the local pharmaceutical industry was crucial in helping health officials overcome the resistance of transnational firms and their allies in the Brazilian legal community. When INTERFARMA and ABPI assailed the reforms introduced in this period, ABIFINA quickly came to the Ministry of Health's defense, defending the government's right to use compulsory licenses as a bargaining tool, for example, and, ultimately, the issuance of the compulsory license in 2007.[39] In sum, revising the patent system was made more feasible in Brazil because the government could elicit the support of local actors that had retained valuable economic and political resources.

Attributing the Brazilian government's ability to build a coalition for reform to the retained capabilities of the local pharmaceutical sector, and these capabilities to the timing of Brazil's introduction of patents in the 1990s, illustrates a central argument of this book: by shaping the universe of coalition possibilities for would-be reformers, the way pharmaceutical patents were introduced in the 1990s affected how patent systems were subsequently revised in the 2000s. Comparing Brazil with Mexico further illustrates the enduring effects of initial choices on subsequent coalitional possibilities. Both countries introduced pharmaceutical patents with pipeline provisions that allowed patents, retroactively, on older inventions, but in Mexico the change came much earlier. This difference meant that when the issue of revising Mexico's patent system emerged in the 2000s, the implications of over-compliance in the 1990s were much greater because the effects had had longer to settle. The local sector had been absorbed by the transnational sector, and reformers seeking to build alliances to overcome the transnational sector's intense mobilization against tailoring regularly found themselves frustrated. In Brazil, in contrast, where pharmaceutical patenting did not commence until 1997, notwithstanding the substantial effects of pipeline patents, the patent regime had not been in effect long enough to foreclose possibilities for the government

---

[38] For further illustration of the collaboration between ABIFINA and the Ministry of Health, see Eduardo Costa and Nelson Brasil, "A emancipação do programa anti-Aids," *Jornal de Brasília*, November 15, 2007.

[39] For a statement in defense of compulsory licensing by one of ABIFINA's directors, see Marcos Oliveira, "A falácia da quebra de patente," *Jornal do Comércio*, April 10, 2006.

to revise earlier policy choices. The comparison allows us to see what we otherwise miss with an exclusive focus on the role of health activists in the state and civil society. Brazil's ability to alter course was aided by the fact that the effects of over-compliance had not had much time to settle. Actors in the defeated coalition for minimalism in the first period of patent politics were still available to participate in coalitions for tailoring the new patent system in subsequent episodes of patent politics.

We witness similar coalition-building dynamics with regard to innovation– industrial policies. Beginning in the late 1990s under Cardoso and continuing through the 2000s under Lula and Rousseff, state officials built new forms of government–business interaction to help develop and sustain the countries' new health and innovation policies. The Ministry of Health encouraged local pharmaceutical firms to form an association to work with the government in the implementation of new generic medicines regulations (Fonseca 2014; Shadlen and Fonseca 2013), and the Ministry of Health gave ABIFINA significant input into the shaping and implementation of the measures that form the Health-Industry Complex.[40] The government also worked closely with Brazil's leading industry associations, e.g. the state federations of industry in Sao Paulo and Rio de Janeiro, and the National Confederation of Industry (CNI), to design and implement the array of innovation policies. Perhaps the most important coalition partner in this area was the business organization representing private-sector firms with in-house research and development in Brazil, the National Association for Research, Development, and Engineering in Innovative Firms (*Associação Nacional de Pesquisa e Desenvolvimento das Empresas Inovadoras*, ANPEI), which was actively involved in shaping innovation-industrial policies throughout this period.

TENSIONS WITHIN THE NEO-DEVELOPMENTAL PROJECT

Brazil's neo-developmental approach to pharmaceutical patents remained contested. At first glance, this appears to be a coordinated and self-reinforcing mission to address a set of problems from multiple angles, simultaneously modifying the patent regime to address the challenges of over-compliance, supporting the growth of the local pharmaceutical sector, and reorienting public and private actors toward innovation. Yet these efforts triggered conflicts, as sets of actors within state and society come to regard other actors as promoting agendas antithetical to

---

[40] In fact, Reinaldo Guimarães, one of the leading government officials who had promoted the CIS, eventually left the Ministry of Health and took a leadership position in ABIFINA.

their own. This section uses the conflicts over one policy instrument, the Prior Consent rule for examining pharmaceutical patent applications, to illustrate these tensions.

By the middle of the 2000s the relationship between the two organizations responsible for pharmaceutical patent examination in Brazil became acrimonious. Although INPI-BR welcomed ANVISA's assistance at the outset, when the patent office was overwhelmed by the tidal wave of applications it received in the new and complex area of pharmaceuticals, the patent office came to regard health agency's participation as an inappropriate intrusion. Having its judgments and decisions subjected to review by another agency in the Brazilian state was intolerable, and the patent office's approach to the division of labor between the two bodies was that it, solely, was responsible for patents, and ANVISA, as the country's health surveillance agency, should deal with health— and only health. As such, the patent office indicated that it would give credence to ANVISA's interventions when they were made on grounds related to health, but not when they appeared to be based on intellectual property criteria.[41] As part of its effort to marginalize, and ultimately eliminate, ANVISA from the process of examining pharmaceutical patent applications, the patent office filed a complaint to the Brazilian Attorney General, reiterating its insistence that it was singularly vested with the authority to examine patent applications and requesting that it be permitted to proceed without interference from the health agency (PGF 2009, 1–2).[42]

More than a turf war between two state agencies, the conflict between INPI-BR and ANVISA reflects tensions within the neo-developmental approach toward pharmaceutical patents. The Brazilian Government had become committed to increasing levels of innovation, but policymakers recognize that local firms are unlikely to be able to achieve technological breakthroughs systematically. Hence the emphasis has been on encouraging "incremental innovation," and indeed we see this reflected repeatedly in statements from the directors of the patent office and officials at the Ministry of Development and Trade, who constantly (in the press, in public forums, in legislative hearings, and in interviews) repeat the mantra: knowledge and innovation are the key to Brazilian development, and given the level of capabilities in the country the emphasis must be on encouraging *incremental* innovations. Yet "incremental innovation" in pharmaceuticals typically means new forms of existing molecules, or new formulations and new uses of existing drug, i.e., secondary patents, and secondary patents can extend periods of exclusivity and raise the price of medicines. Indeed, this is why ANVISA set up its guidelines for

---

[41] "Carta aberta ao Jornal *Estado de São Paulo*," April 30, 2010 (goo.gl/Vxb57y).

[42] Not only was the patent office the sole actor that could examine patent applications, INPI-BR noted, but the patent office would be acting illegally and failing to discharge its responsibilities were it to deny patents based on another agency's examination.

participation in the Prior Consent system to focus on these sorts of applications. In short, one arm of neo-developmental policy aims to encourage activities that another arm of neo-developmentalism aims to combat.

These contradictions are manifest within the Brazilian state. The Ministry of Health is the driving force behind reforms to the patent system and also the key player in the CIS. From the Ministry's perspective, eliminating ANVISA from patent examination simply does not make sense. Other actors within government, however, are more inclined to support the patent office. After all, state agencies across the board have been re-geared to promote innovation. The new patent law and the array of innovation policies has created an "innovation-IP complex" in Brazil, with state agencies and public research institutions coming to regard investing in innovation and obtaining patents as part of their mission, and encouraging private firms to act similarly. Not only is INPI-BR itself a key player in these areas, but its emphasis on using the patent system to encourage incremental innovation (i.e. the smaller steps that Brazilian firms, far from the technological frontier, are more likely to achieve) is reflected in the government's broader strategy. With actors throughout society increasingly committed to innovation as a means to enhance the Brazilian economy's international competitiveness, there is a palpable aversion within the Brazilian state to policies and practices that appear to go against the grain. A prominent official in the Brazilian Innovation Agency (FINEP) exclaimed that it would be "suicidal" to adopt a restrictive (i.e., ANVISA-like) position toward secondary patents in pharmaceuticals (Interview, November 2, 2009).

The uncertainties and reservations regarding Prior Consent are evident within industry too. As local pharmaceutical firms have adjusted to the new environment, many aided directly by the new innovation–industrial policies discussed in this chapter, some firms' perspectives toward patents have begun to change. Brazilian pharmaceutical firms engage increasingly in innovation-oriented activities, reinvesting greater shares of their sales revenues in research and development, for example, and participating in collaborations with universities (Paranhos 2012; Ryan 2010). Though pharmaceutical patent applications filed in Brazil come overwhelmingly from transnational firms,[43] local firms' shares have increased in absolute terms—and this growth is mostly in the area of secondary patents.

Capability growth within the pharmaceutical industry produced inconsistent public positions regarding Prior Consent. Because a bias against secondary patents could lead to some Brazilian firms' own applications being denied, many developed misgivings about ANVISA's role in patent examination. Indeed, the Brazilian pharmaceutical industry's support for ANVISA became

---

[43] Barbosa (2013); Caliari and Ruiz (2014); Caliari et al. (2013); Laforgia et al. (2008); Shadlen (2011b); Zucoloto (2011).

notably less visible over time. Reactions to legislative proposals are revealing. In 2008, for example, a proposal was introduced in the Chamber of Deputies that would have effectively eliminated ANVISA's role in patent examination, while in 2009 another proposal was introduced that would have forced the patent office to adopt examination practices closer to ANVISA's. With regard to the former, while ANVISA and the Ministry of Health submitted a detailed rebuttal (Ministério de Saúde 2008) and met with legislators in the Chamber of Deputies in Brasilia, legislators involved report minimal resistance from local firms and sector associations (Interview, June, 12, 2009; Interview, June 9, 2009a). Nor did local industry actively endorse a more restrictive approach in the hearings for the latter proposal (Interview, June 9, 2009b).[44]

It is not that organizations such as ABIFINA and ALANAC have become aligned with INTERFARMA, but rather that capability growth within the sector came to restrain—even paralyze—these organizations. In interviews, leaders of ABIFINA and ALANAC continued to express their support for Prior Consent and a restrictive approach to secondary patents, but their organizations' public postures largely stopped reflecting this. Reflecting what a director of ABIFINA referred to as "a lot of ambiguity" among members, at one point in 2010 the association adopted, after considerable internal debate and with some members abstaining, a statement in support of reinforcing ANVISA's role in patent examination. Yet then, out of fear that publicly supporting ANVISA would alienate Brazil's leading firms and potentially drive them from the organization, ABIFINA's leaders decided to engage in self-censorship and not publicize the statement.[45] And quiet ABIFINA remained, so quiet that ANVISA's officials were not even aware of the association's position. In an interview with *Intellectual Property Watch*, the then-director of patent examination in ANVISA publicly lamented the lack of support from the local pharmaceutical sector. When asked about reactions in industry, the outgoing director of patents at ANVISA contrasted the strong and resolute opposition put forward by the transnational sector with the waning and timid support of local industry.[46]

---

[44] In addition to the interviews with the deputies responsible for the legislative projects, I also consulted with the legislative researchers in the Chamber of Deputies. Cassier and Corrêa (2007) also point to the opposition of local pharmaceutical firms (and also scientific researchers) to legislative initiatives that limit opportunities for pharmaceutical patenting.

[45] I learned about this statement and the events related to its non-publicized adoption via email communication (June 22, 2011, follow-up to Interview, May 19, 2008a) with a member of ABIFINA's board of directors, where among other things I received the minutes of the meeting. The reference to "ambiguity" is from this email as well.

[46] "Inside News: Alto funcionário discute sobre renúncia ao seu cargo na ANVISA, no Brasil, devido à política sobre patentes," *Intellectual Property Watch*, August 11, 2011 (goo.gl/IBC5lU). Similarly, in Cassier's discussion of political mobilization around Prior Consent, the activities of the transnational sector and lawyers, on one side, and civil society health activists, on the other side, receive ample attention, but the position of the local pharmaceutical industry is not mentioned (Cassier 2012, 292–3).

Not all actors in the local sector are so inhibited, and ABIFINA's self-censorship did not achieve its goal. Brazil's leading pharmaceutical firms created a new organization in 2012, *Grupo Farma Brasil*, a statement of the growth of an indigenous, Brazilian innovative pharmaceutical sector that is more committed to patent protection (Interview, July 10, 2015a). *Grupo Farma Brasil*, led by the former director of the Brazilian Agency for Industrial Development, a parastatal unit at the heart of the innovation–IP complex, regularly articulates opposition to a more restrictive position on pharmaceutical patents, and, more generally, tailoring the patent regime.

The misgivings toward tailoring that we witness in the pharmaceutical sector are reflected more generally throughout Brazilian industry. Consider the case of ANPEI, the association for firms conducting research and development and the leading voice in Brazilian industry on matters related to innovation policy. Most of ANPEI's members are not directly affected by pharmaceutical patent policies, but measures such as Prior Consent are viewed with concern by ANPEI, as these appear to go against the grain of the new thrust toward innovation. The association's key position in innovation policy leads it inexorably toward suspicion vis-à-vis ANVISA, which it regards as threatening to undermine the "patent culture" that, according to the Association, is taking hold among Brazilian firms.[47] More broadly, with ANPEI working hand-in-hand with the National Confederation of Industry to reorient patterns of business mobilization around innovation, the nature of business politics in Brazil has been shaped by the quest for and acquisition of new, innovative capabilities. Within the CNI, the *Mobilização Empresearial pela Innovação* (MEI) has become increasingly active in calling for an approach to innovation and industrial policy based on increased patent protection.[48] For example, the MEI, and by extension CNI, lobbies extensively to reform legislation to facilitate commercial access to genetic resources and introduce a more permissive approach toward biotechnology patents. Although the MEI is not sector-focused, it adopts a position in the debate over pharmaceuticals supporting more patents, regarding Brazil's dual examination system as contrary to the country's emphasis on patenting (MEI 2015).[49] In short, the coalition within Brazilian industry of innovation-focused firms and organizations that seeks increased patent protection, a coalition inspired and nurtured by the government's new innovation–industrial policies, regards the efforts to tailor the patent law as

---

[47] Interview, May 11, 2007b. For more illustrations of ANPEI's orientation toward patents, see "INPI e Anpei assinam acordo para fortalecer cultura de PI no Brasil," (goo.gl/r8ewzq); "Sociedade precisa valorizar propriedade intelectual, diz Anpei" (goo.gl/0hIF9J); "Presidente da Anpei alerta sobre problemas da legislação em PI" (goo.gl/6UM9TR).

[48] For an illustration, see "Lei de Propriedade Industrial precisa ser atualizada para ampliar proteção ao conhecimento no Brasil" (goo.gl/DDVwwX).

[49] The MEI's position toward pharmaceutical patenting was also made clear in an interview July 2015 at the CNI's offices in Brasilia (Interview, July 10, 2015b).

misguided steps that move the country in the wrong direction (Barbosa 2013; Interview, July 10, 2015a).

The objective to here has been to illustrate the tensions at the heart of Brazil's neo-developmental approach to pharmaceutical patents, to show how the coalition-building projects attached to both policy dimensions contradict each other. To understand how the government has responded to these tensions, we can consider the "resolution" of the conflict over Prior Consent. In October 2009, the Attorney General published a report that supported the patent office's position almost in its entirety (PGF 2009). ANVISA would be allowed to participate in evaluating pharmaceutical patent applications, as the tailored patent law required, but in doing so ANVISA's interventions were to be limited to health-based assessments. That is, ANVISA was not to rule if an application satisfied the criteria of novelty or inventive step, for the patent office—and only the patent office—had the authority to examine patent applications on these grounds; ANVISA could only deny "prior consent" to applications when it judges that granting the patents would pose health risks. The Attorney General's ruling, in turn, was upheld by the Solicitor General (*Advocacia-Geral da União*, AGU) in January 2011.[50] When the AGU issued its ruling in 2011, the director of ANVISA's patent examination office resigned in protest, and it appeared that Prior Consent was effectively finished (Barbosa 2013; GTPI/Rebrip 2011; Shadlen 2011a).

The Executive could have exploited this opportunity to once and for all sideline ANVISA from patent examination. But, instead, rather than jump through this window, the government—at the Ministry of Health's insistence—went back to the drawing board and recreated Prior Consent. The Executive constituted a new Inter-Ministerial Working Group, which it commissioned with breaking the deadlock between ANVISA and the patent office and reaching a definitive resolution. In May 2012 the Working Group announced a new arrangement, according to which pharmaceutical patent applications were reviewed by ANVISA prior to being examined by INPI-BR. The health agency was expected to assess whether or not granting the patent would present a "health risk." If ANVISA grants prior Consent then the patent office examines the application and decides whether to grant or reject, but if ANVISA denies consent then INPI-BR is not supposed to examine these applications.

The new arrangement between INPI-BR and ANVISA had multiple ambiguities, and remained subject of conflict. Just as Prior Consent's apparent demise yielded both laments from health activists and cheers from the transnational sector, its subsequent resuscitation also yielded sharp reactions, though this time the mirror image (GTPI/Rebrip 2013; Mueller and Costa 2014). Ultimately, how the new arrangements will function is to be determined.

---

[50] "AGU restringe poder da Anvisa na concessão de patente de medicamento," *O Estado de São Paulo*, January 24, 2011.

The point is that by saving Prior Consent from what appeared to be its demise, Brazilian authorities were trying to tread a fine line and balance competing interests and demands. Reconciling these two rival and antagonistic coalitions is the challenge of neo-developmentalism.

CONCLUSION

Soon after introducing pharmaceutical patents in 1997, Brazil began to tailor the new patent system. By revising the compulsory licensing provisions and establishing new arrangements for examining patent applications, successive governments have sought to ameliorate the effects of over-compliance on the health sector. The analysis of these measures in this chapter illustrates the iterative and sequential dimensions of patent policy. The steps that were taken in this period of patent politics were responses to the challenges generated by the initial choices made as Brazil responded to the new international context of the 1980s and 1990s.

Importantly, the measures taken in the second period were not just motivated by earlier choices, but also enabled by them, for the ability of health officials to construct supportive coalitions for tailoring was a function of how and when pharmaceutical patents were introduced in the first place. Health officials seeking to revise aspects of Brazil's new patent system benefited from the support of local actors that had retained valuable economic and political resources. Brazil's pharmaceutical firms did not initiate the tailoring process (that is, the government did not change course in response to their demands), but the sector's economic and political characteristics enhanced the government's ability to carry out these initiatives. And this, in turn, is a function of timing: Brazil's over-compliant pharmaceutical patent regime had not been in effect long enough to wipe out this sector and thus foreclose possibilities for coalition building. Thus, whereas the effects of initial choices confounded reform in Mexico, they enabled Executive agency in Brazil.

In addition to being iterative and sequential, patent policies can also be generative. Tailoring, alone, was inadequate to address the immense challenges created by over-compliance. Recognizing this, the Brazilian Government complemented the health-oriented reforms of the patent system with a set of industrial and innovation policies to strengthen the local pharmaceutical industry. Hence the "neo-developmental" label: Brazil is not only exploiting opportunities in the global IP regime to adjust the patent system in accordance with the country's needs and conditions, but also attempting to create capabilities for local actors to compete in the new environment. Brazil is not unique in seeking to build capabilities and encouraging domestic innovation, elements of such measures can be witnessed throughout the developing world in the 2000s. Yet the extent of the Brazilian efforts, including considerable changes to legislation and restructuring of state institutions, as well as substantial resource allocations, sets Brazil apart from the other countries in this book.

In tying together the two elements of the Brazil's neo-developmental response, we have also seen the tensions that emerge. Policies can affect politics by triggering patterns of adjustment and thus shaping the universe of potential coalition partners. As the comparative case studies show, the nature of these effects depends on initial policies and the amount of time that the new policies have been in place. This is relevant not only for understanding the ability of health officials to build coalitions for tailoring Brazil's pharmaceutical patent system, but also for the difficulties that such measures encountered, domestically. The changes to state institutions and social structure triggered by the 1996 patent law and subsequent innovation–industrial policies had political effects too. Brazilian policy unleashed and nurtured two conflicting currents, one that seeks to reduce the quantity of pharmaceutical patents granted and the degree of protection that patents offer, and one that increasingly embraces the patent system and seeks a pharmaceutical sector that uses the patent system to spur and protect innovations. Balancing these two conflicting currents in state and society is the challenge for neo-developmentalism in Brazil.

Part IV

Conclusion

9

Patents and Development in the New Global Economy

The global political economy has undergone substantial change in the late twentieth and early twenty-first centuries, as new patterns of investment and international rules place new restrictions on national economic policy. These changes in transnational economic activities and international agreements, known as "globalization," engender convergence, as countries either choose or are compelled to adopt similar policies and practices. Yet national policies continue to differ. Persistent differentiation in the context of overarching convergence, and not uniformity, is the hallmark of globalization. Because countries' react differently to changing global environments, in any given policy area, one global change may yield multiple national responses. Compliance comes in many shapes and sizes.

Political coalitions underpin forms of compliance with the new international order. External shocks interact with social structure to yield different possibilities for building and maintaining political coalitions in support of particular policies. And once new policies are introduced, these trigger new patterns of economic activity and political mobilization that condition subsequent coalition-building experiences. Throughout the iterative process of responding to external pressures, changing characteristics of social structure establish the parameters for coalitional dynamics and, hence, policy.

In this book we have examined the processes of coalitional changes shaping compliance with a new international environment in the area of intellectual property (IP). Historically, countries had substantial autonomy in setting up their IP systems. Although international agreements in IP existed, they left countries considerable leeway in determining which types of knowledge and information could be privately owned, and how strong the rights of exclusion attached to ownership would be. Countries IP systems were allowed to vary, and did they vary; some countries opted for "stronger" IP systems (i.e. private ownership available over more types of knowledge and information, with owners having more extensive rights of exclusion and control over the use of their property), some countries opted for "weaker" IP systems (Park 2008).

The 1980s and 1990s witnessed the emergence of a profoundly altered global context for national IP policymaking, as the permissive environment that tolerated differentiation was replaced by a new set of rules that expected countries' IP systems to be more alike. The most visible manifestation of the shift from an international environment allowing differentiation to an international environment commanding harmonization was the inclusion of an agreement on intellectual property rights in the World Trade Organization, the TRIPS Agreement. To be a member of the WTO, and thus to participate on equal footing in international trade, countries needed to adapt their IP policies and practices, satisfying a new set of international conditions. TRIPS, which entered into effect in 1995, is the cornerstone of the new environment, but hardly its sole expression. The new rules on IP in the WTO had been preceded by the increased prominence of IP in trade policy of the United States and leading European countries since the 1980s, and they were supplemented by foreign assistance programs to encourage countries to increase their levels of IP protection, as well by the spread of bilateral trade agreements that also include restrictive provisions on IP. These events, collectively, constitute what has been referred to as a "global sea change" in IP, as the policy area went from being one where countries could essentially do as they wished to one where they faced dramatically reduced policy space. National IP policies since the late 1980s have been made in response to a vector of external forces that push for convergence around a global set of "best practices."

This book has analyzed national responses to these global changes in the most contentious area of IP, pharmaceutical patenting. As of the mid-1980s few developing allowed patents on pharmaceutical products, fearing that the costs of having private rights of exclusion over these sorts of inventions would outweigh the benefits. TRIPS, however, requires countries to do so, and the establishment of the WTO was followed by the global extension of pharmaceutical patenting: by 2005, pharmaceutical patents could be obtained in all but the poorest countries. Pharmaceutical patenting thus presents a clear opportunity to examine national responses to global changes. If not for the new international environment, few developing countries would have begun to allow drug patenting in the 1990s and early 2000s.

With this global change serving as trigger, the analysis has focused on two periods of politics. Initially, responding to global imperatives to allow patents on pharmaceutical products, countries needed to decide how to do so—when to start examining applications and granting patents, and whether to acknowledge inventions that occurred previously for products not yet commercialized. Then, having acquiesced to the new global order, many countries considered revising their new patent systems. While conflict in the first period regarded how to introduce drug patents, conflict in the second period concerns how these new patent systems should function. Throughout both periods, policies have been made in the context of intense global pressures not just to make pharmaceuticals patentable, the bare minimum, but to do so quickly, and in ways that offer the transnational firms that dominate this sector the greatest ability to place and keep their products on local markets without competition. That is, countries have been urged not to comply with new global rules, but to over-comply. Importantly, these two sets of conflicts are linked: how countries responded to external pressures for over-compliance in the first period affects how countries adjust their patent systems in the presence of on-going external pressures in the second period. Although initial policy choices over how to introduce pharmaceutical patents did not lock countries into paths from which deviation was impossible, policy choices at T_1, by inspiring distinct patterns of adjustment and generating new constellations of actors, condition subsequent political conflicts at T_2, over the functioning of new patent systems.

To explain variation in countries' forms of compliance with the new international order, we have examined how social structure shapes possibilities for coalition building, with a particular focus on the relative economic and political resources of rival segments of pharmaceutical industries within developing countries. The analyses have emphasized two sources of change to social structure: the process by which exporters become converted into IP enthusiasts that can be mobilized in support of more extensive patent protection, and the ways that new policies, once introduced, transform industrial structure, inspire new forms of economic behavior, and thus alter actors' preferences and capabilities. Throughout the book, process tracing has been used to adjudicate among alternative explanations for policy outcomes, particularly the importance of social structure relative to the direct effects of external pressures and the preferences of incumbent Executives.

This concluding chapter reviews the main findings from the case studies, synthesizes the main lessons, and looks at emerging challenges that countries face in adjusting their development strategies to the new global economy marked by the private ownership of knowledge. The first section synthesizes the key findings from the comparative case studies, illustrating the key dimensions of the cross-national and longitudinal variation in responses to the global sea change. The second section considers alternative explanations that may account for this variation, reviewing key points of comparison. The discussion highlights key lessons of the book's focus on social structure and coalitions for analyses of comparative and international political economy. In this section we also consider extensions of the explanatory framework beyond the political economy of pharmaceutical patents in the three Latin American countries. The third section looks forward, supplementing the book's analysis of the politics of pharmaceutical patents with discussion of additional ways that countries respond to the global sea change in IP. This broader focus underscores the immense economic and political challenges that countries face in adjusting to the new world order of privately owned knowledge, and points to asymmetries in global politics that reinforce these challenges.

THE POLITICAL ECONOMY OF PHARMACEUTICAL
PATENTS IN ARGENTINA, BRAZIL, AND MEXICO

Patent policy in larger developing countries came under the spotlight in the 1980s and 90s. Few allowed patents on drugs as of the mid-1980s, and the potential revenues promised by large populations in some countries made securing pharmaceutical patents a high priority for international firms. Thus, larger developing countries throughout the developing world became the subject of considerable pressure from the transnational pharmaceutical sector and, especially, the US Government (Gadbaw and Richards 1988a; Nogués 1990).

Among Latin America's three largest economies, Argentina most bucked the campaign for over-compliance, delaying the introduction of patents until 2000, and refusing to recognize earlier applications or patents associated with inventions that pre-dated the TRIPS Agreement. These policy choices, which meant that new products entering the market in the late 1990s and early 2000s would remain free of patent protection in Argentina, were accompanied by other measures that allowed Argentina's pharmaceutical firms to continue dominating the local market. The Argentinean case offers a clear illustration of the importance of social structure, and the conditional impact of external pressures and Executive pressures. Argentina came under relentless diplomatic and economic pressure to over-comply, and the government of President Menem aimed to please the US and the transnational pharmaceutical industry, but these efforts failed. Industrial structure allowed Argentinean firms to build a robust defensive coalition, not to block the introduction of drug patents but to make sure this was done in a minimally disruptive way, while the country's export profile inhibited expansion of the coalition for over-compliance. By the end of the 1990s, minimalism had become state policy in Argentina; the local pharmaceutical sector prevailed.

Argentina's trajectory continued in the 2000s, as pressures for over-compliance were consistently rebuffed, and on numerous occasions the new arrangements were revised in ways that dampened the impact of now having a pharmaceutical patent system. Central to understanding continuity in minimalist compliance in Argentina are the enduring economic and political capabilities of the local pharmaceutical sector. Argentina's largest national pharmaceutical firms retained considerable market shares and a domineering presence in the national health infrastructure, assets that they were able to use to assure that when patenting began and foreign firms returned to the local market, as would inevitably happen, this occurred in ways that were less disruptive than might otherwise be the case, and that created new opportunities. Health officials fearing the effects of providing strong rights of exclusion to foreign drug firms had available and active allies in local industry. Ultimately, Argentina's policy choices in the 1990s regarding the introduction of drug patents inspired patterns of adjustment that facilitated subsequent coalition building for revising how the patent system functions. However, the same resources that made the local sector a formidable ally for health officials seeking to combat the overtures of foreign governments and the transnational pharmaceutical industry had, from a public health perspective, a worrying flipside; Argentinean drug firms' power also encumbered health officials' efforts to regulate the drug market and control prices.

At the other extreme, Mexico acquiesced to the campaign for over-compliance in the earliest and most extreme fashion. In order to launch negotiations with the US for a trade agreement, Mexico introduced pharmaceutical patents early, in 1991, and with a pipeline provision that amplified the immediacy and shock of these effects. Here too external preferences shifted Executive preferences: a few years earlier the same state officials adopted a cautious approach toward drug patenting, insisting that this should not happen until the late 1990s; now President Salinas and his team demanded that patenting should begin as quickly as possible, that the owners of patents should have strong rights of exclusion and control over their privately owned knowledge, and that drug firms should be able to begin benefiting from these new property rights immediately. What Salinas sought is similar to what Menem sought in Argentina, but a differently configured social structure enabled Mexico's Executive to construct a winning coalition, a set of conditions that were significantly enhanced by the NAFTA context. Mexico's dependence on removable, preferential exports made the country vulnerable to US pressures, and the promise of converting the trading relationship to one with stable market access in the form of a reciprocal agreement mobilized exporters and prompted a restructuring of business politics; together these changes converted Mexican business, albeit indirectly, into enthusiastic advocates of over-compliance. In contrast, Mexico's local pharmaceutical sector, heavily reliant on sales to the state and worried that NAFTA would open state health providers' tendering to international firms, made a priority of securing favorable government purchasing rules in NAFTA. The local sector's relative demobilization over how Mexico would adopt drug patents contributed to a remarkably uneventful debate. The same issues that consumed political economies for years in other countries were resolved quickly, virtually without notice, and almost entirely to the Executive's liking in Mexico.

Mexico also experienced continuity in the second period of patent politics, with the political dynamics in many ways the mirror image of what we witnessed in Argentina. Extreme and early over-compliance transformed the local pharmaceutical industry in Mexico, exacerbating transnational firms' domination. Many local firms closed, while those that survived restructured their practices to adjust to the new order, largely to stay out of conflict with foreign firms. The new industrial structure triggered by the choices of the 1990s had substantial effects on coalition building in the 2000s: local firms were indifferent toward some efforts to tailor the new patent system, and where they were mobilized in support of other efforts they were too weak to serve as useful coalitional partners. Indeed, as health authorities concerned about the prices of essential drugs sought to temper the effects of Mexico's earlier choices, which they did, even under right-of-center Executives, they were unable to prevail in the face of the overwhelming resources of the coalition for over-compliance.

Brazil's response to the global sea change in the 1990s was over-compliance, introducing drug patents with a pipeline provision that offered protection to older inventions. Yet Brazil's over-compliance was less radical than Mexico's, in that this happened much later in the decade and in a form that made the immediate effects of policy choices less generalized and amplified. Brazil most likely would have over-complied early, and in a more extreme form, given the domineering position of the transnational pharmaceutical sector, buttressed by its alliances with other actors in industry such as the country's emerging biotechnology sector, and the comparative weakness of the local sector. Yet here coalitional dynamics were shaped by the groundswell of opposition that a new patent law engendered on the part of social movements, non-governmental organizations, and legislators who feared the environmental and ethical consequences of patents. Brazil's local firms joined this movement, and the defensive coalition was much more vibrant than one might expect from looking just at the pharmaceutical industry. Indeed, this resistance created a coalitional clash that contributed to an intense legislative conflict that went on for years in both bodies of Congress. Although the defensive coalition was able to fight back and delay the outcome, it could not prevail, as ultimately an Executive committed to satisfying the transnational sector's expansive demands was able to exploit Brazilian exporters' fears of US trade sanctions to construct a winning coalition for over-compliance.

The effects of over-compliance in Brazil threatened to undermine the country's health system, in particular its successful approach to addressing HIV/AIDS with universal treatment. Because so many of the HIV/AIDS drugs that were needed in Brazil became patented, precisely because of over-compliance (i.e. not because Brazil introduced pharmaceutical patents, but because of *how* Brazil did so), health officials found themselves motivated to revise the new system, and where tailoring alone was not sufficient, to launch a set of industrial and innovation policies to build pharmaceutical capabilities. Because, unlike Mexico, the new arrangements had not been in place long enough to transform the industrial structure, reformist health officials were able to rely on local firms as allies for these efforts. Thus, in Brazil, the way pharmaceutical patents were introduced both inspired subsequent reforms and facilitated subsequent coalition building to advance these reforms. But it also complicates reform: not only do the transnational sector and the patent community that were energized by over-compliance consistently oppose health officials' efforts to modify the new arrangements, but the programs put in place to increase productive and innovative capabilities in the local pharmaceutical sector served, over time, to dilute this actor's enthusiasm for tailoring as well. In sum, all efforts at reforming Brazil's patent system are constrained by the long shadow of over-compliance in the 1990s.

In synthesis, national differences in social structure affected how these three countries introduced pharmaceutical patents in the 1990s, and, by triggering patterns of adjustment in state and society, these choices, in turn, affected possibilities for tailoring in the 2000s. The result is persistent cross-national variation, even in the context of over-arching convergence. Taking a step back, it is undeniable that the room for variation is, in a historical sense, smaller in the second period. That is, the differences among these countries nearly two decades into the twenty-first century, at the end of the processes analyzed here, are less than the differences between any of them now and what their patent systems looked like in the 1980s. Neither Argentina, nor Mexico, nor Brazil had pharmaceutical patents; now each country does, and the subsequent conflicts that take place are about how these countries' new patent systems should function. This narrowing of the terrain of debate and conflict provide further illustration of how international politics have fundamentally changed national policies and political economies (Farrell and Newman 2014).

LESSONS AND EXTENSIONS

This book addresses one of the foundational issues in the study of comparative and international political economy: national responses to global change. In doing so, a number of important analytic themes are addressed, such as business power, the role of external pressures, and the importance of Executive ideology and partisanship. This section uses the lessons from the comparative analyses to speak to these themes, and to consider extensions of the analytic framework to additional cases.

Diversity in national coalition-building experiences affects the way that countries respond to changes in the global economy. In the first period of patent politics, with the international pharmaceutical industry and foreign governments treating the early and retroactive introduction of patents as a high priority (it was clear from the outset that merely introducing drug patents would not satisfy these actors), and with the bundling of IP and trade and integration in the global economy making it easy for Executives to justify radical policy changes, over-compliance was the default outcome. In that context, resisting the crusade for over-compliance depended on the presence of defensive coalitions, a condition that is a function first and foremost of legacies of industrial development in national pharmaceutical sectors. Could the national pharmaceutical sector defend itself? At its core, then, this is an analysis of the preferences and power of national firms in the increasingly internationalized pharmaceutical industry. While our starting point has been the position of rival segments of industry in the market, as is standard in political economy (Frieden 1991; Keohane and Milner 1996), understanding business actors' influence requires going beyond the countries' production profiles and considering their political strategies (Culpepper 2010; Fairfield 2015; Gourevitch 1986; Woll 2008). The comparative analyses demonstrate how national contexts create opportunities and challenges to rival segments of industry, as they attempt to cultivate allies and build coalitions in support of their desired responses to global shocks.

In Argentina, the local pharmaceutical sector's political influence was enhanced by extensive forward integration in the health community and retail sector, which helped it mobilize a wide range of allies, as well as by the long period of economic crisis and gutting of the country's technology infrastructure, which allowed it to dominate business politics. The intensity of the opposition Radical Party's long-standing conflict with the transnational pharmaceutical industry, and the links of key figures in that party to the public health community, also created fertile ground for the growth of a robust defensive coalition. And Argentina's local labs conserved no resources in their all-out campaign to exploit these opportunities and mobilize against the project for drug patenting advanced by the Menem Government. Thus, in Argentina the defensive coalition, which we already expect to be strong on account of the production profile, became yet stronger on account of these national contextual and political factors.

Postwar industrial development experiences left both Mexico and Brazil with weaker national pharmaceutical sectors, thus creating expectations of weak defensive coalitions, but in both cases these conditions were affected by national conjunctures as well. In Mexico, the political debility of the local pharmaceutical sector was exacerbated by sharp economic policy shifts of the late 1980s, which served as a preemptive strike that further weakened the sector. Coalitions were also shaped by the NAFTA context, which both isolated local pharmaceutical producers in business politics and prompted them to prioritize fighting about government purchasing practices over fighting to shape how drug patents would be introduced. The sector's political strategy, largely a withdrawn and inattentive acceptance of pharmaceutical patent protection as unavoidable, contributed to a remarkably feeble defensive coalition, with the result being that the advocates of over-compliance faced virtually no resistance and were able to achieve even more than they originally sought.

In Brazil, national context had the opposite effects on the defensive coalition. Here, mobilization throughout Brazilian society around the UN's Earth Summit and the attention given to the implications of extending IP to genetic resources and biotechnology inspired a movement that local firms could tap into to compensate for their own weakness. At the same time, deep economic and political crises of the early 1990s created opportunities for these actors to exploit. Thus, despite having a pharmaceutical industry that was similar to Mexico's in terms of market position and other indicators (see Table 2.3, p. 47), Brazil had a defensive coalition that was closer in breadth and vibrancy to Argentina's. While in Argentina we observe a capable and influential defensive coalition largely because of the characteristics of the local pharmaceutical industry, in Brazil we observed this despite the characteristics of the local pharmaceutical industry. In sum, the case studies show that analyses of business power can start with the market positions of rival segments of industry, but need to build on these core material conditions by examining national contexts and political strategies.

Another important theme addressed by this book is how external pressures can alter national policy trajectories, both by shifting the preferences of Executives and, most importantly, by altering social structure. The principal focus has been on the US Government's threats to remove trade preferences, and the extent to which such threats converted exporters into supporters of increased IP protection and thus available coalition allies for actors seeking over-compliance. Because we would not otherwise expect exporters to care one way or the other about the details of pharmaceutical patenting, this process of making partisans of over-compliance out of otherwise indifferent actors has been referred to as "activating agnostics." As a predictor of whether we expect to witness this phenomenon, we have looked at the share of countries' global exports that enter the US under removable, preferential schemes, a measure called "political trade dependence" (PTD).

In Mexico, high levels of PTD in the late 1980s and early 1990s converted exporters into enthusiasts of over-compliance, a situation that was amplified by the opportunities provided by NAFTA: over-compliance would not only avert US sanctions, but could stabilize the preferences upon which exporters depended by converting them from removable concessions provided at the discretion of the US into bound commitments. Of course the opportunities to stabilize trade preferences in this way were available to other countries too, and in fact the Menem Government expressed a desire for a similar NAFTA-like trade agreement with the US, but Argentina's trade structure meant that exporters' participation in patent politics was different than in Mexico. Threats of trade sanctions, actual trade sanctions, and promises of stabilizing preferences all certainly excited exporters, but low levels of PTD meant that these reactions had little effect on social structure and coalitional possibilities. Notwithstanding their considerable efforts, the transnational pharmaceutical firms and their allies in the Argentinean Executive were unable to widen the coalition for over-compliance via the mobilization of exporters. In Brazil, however, they were. PTD in Brazil was lower than in Mexico, but it was higher than in Argentina, a difference that became particularly acute at the moment when conflicts over new patent laws allowing for drug patents reached their peak in the mid-1990s. Here we observed an explicit effort by the Brazilian Executive and its allies in the coalition for over-compliance to bring exporters on board, efforts that succeeded.

In pointing to the limitations of external pressures, one potential objection is that the transnational pharmaceutical sector and the US Government may have cared more about what happened in Mexico and Brazil. It is reasonable to claim that external pressures were most intense in these two larger countries,[1] but Argentina was anything but neglected. As we saw in Chapter 3, the US Government and the transnational pharmaceutical sector were tireless in their aggressive pursuit of over-compliance, using a wide range of diplomatic and trade instruments to secure this outcome. But they failed. Indeed, throughout the 2000s the US continued to use virtually all means available to elicit changes to Argentina's pharmaceutical patent regime, and continued to fail. Argentina's persistent minimalism was not a function of external actors' lack of concern or effort, but rather, the inability of external pressures to alter social structure sufficiently to enable domestic allies to build coalitions for over-compliance. In sum, the comparative analyses suggest that, while external pressures may alter the preferences of Executives, to shift outcomes they need to alter social structure in ways that contribute to the formation of coalitions supportive of these new preferences.

Indeed, the advocates of over-compliance used external pressures differently, depending on the different ways that they altered social structure. Argentina's trade profile meant that external pressures would not mobilize exporters in a way that would alter the balance of power and coalitions, so it was not worth paying the price that would be associated with trying to doing so. Throughout the conflict with Congress over the new patent law, Menem and Cavallo consistently downplayed external pressures. The US Government's crusade for over-compliance gained considerable prominence in Argentina, but this was because those opposing these efforts constantly reminded all concerned about the US's activities, precisely in order to elicit nationalist backlash against a meddling foreign power. In contrast, Brazil's trade profile meant that external pressures could mobilize exporters, so the Cardoso Government regarded the payoffs as greater than the costs of triggering nationalist backlash among civil society actors and opposition legislators. Thus, the Brazilian Executive went out of its way to cite external pressures and threats of punishment as reasons why the country should alter course and introduce pharmaceutical patents in a way that pleased the transnational sector and US Government.

We also see how social structure conditioned the effectiveness of US pressures in the second period of patent politics. Countries' efforts to tailor

---

[1] The transnational sector created "Ad Hoc" groups on IP in Brazil and Mexico, for example.

their new pharmaceutical patent systems consistently elicited threats of trade sanctions, but these threats played a less important role than in the 1990s. The explanation for this is not just the constraining influence of international law (Morin and Gold 2014; Shadlen 2004b), but also different material conditions that diminished the ability of external pressures to reshape coalitions. With lower PTD, mobilizing exporters by threatening to impose trade sanctions did not have the same effects on social structure and political coalitions as in the 1990s. Here the research is consistent with a wide range of studies that have shown how features of the global economy of the early 2000s created new opportunities (Campello 2015; Gallagher and Porzecanski 2008; Levitsky and Roberts 2011; Yang 2006): increases in foreign exchange revenues earned from high commodity prices, diversification of exports away from the US market and toward China, and lower PTD insulated developing country governments from US pressures and left them with greater policy-making freedom.

What about the role of Executive preferences and partisanship? These too are common explanations of variation in policy choice in studies of political economy (Garrett and Lange 1991; Lichbach and Zuckerman 1997; Murillo 2002; 2009). In many ways, intellectual property, an exceptionally technical field that is reliant on experts and where the distributive effects depend heavily not just on policy choice but implementation and subsequent regulation, would appear to be a policy domain particularly suited to explanations based on the preferences of Executives. Yet the analyses in this book consistently reveal, in contrast, that Executives' abilities to secure their desired outcomes depended on how social structure affected their abilities to construct winning coalitions. The cross-national comparisons of the 1990s illustrate this clearly: social structure frustrated Menem in Argentina but enabled Salinas in Mexico and Cardoso in Brazil. The within-case comparison of patents and investment treaties in Brazil tells a similar story: social structure allowed Cardoso to build a coalition for over-compliance in the introduction of pharmaceutical patents, but, notwithstanding similarities in terms of preferences and in-stitutional context, prevented the President from doing so in the case of ratifying the bilateral investment treaties that Brazil had negotiated. And the research also speaks to the inverse scenario, of social structure compel-ling Executives to pursue outcomes they may otherwise not pursue. Of course it is exceptionally difficult to know politicians' genuine preferences, and when laws are passed Executives typically take ownership, but the case of Argentina appears to offer an example of Executive preferences being altered by social structure: policies that Menem's Government fought adamantly against and regarded, initially, as defeats, became accomplish-ments, and, ultimately, the approach toward pharmaceutical patenting advanced by Argentina's defensive coalition became state policy that the Executive proceeded to defend.

The uncertain relationship between Executive preferences and policy outcomes is also brought out by examination of the second period of patent politics. As this period is marked by reforming, administrating, and regulating laws, rather than drafting entirely new laws, it provides a setting where we might expect there to be greater scope for Executive agency. To be sure, the comparative analyses do reveal more tailoring in left-governed Argentina and Brazil than in right-dominated Mexico, yet the apparent association between partisanship and policy outcome is misleading in two ways. First, patent policies that we might think of as corresponding to the "left" were present in pre-Kirchner Argentina and pre-Lula Brazil. Indeed, Argentina's resistance to US pressures for data exclusivity and reform of the guidelines for the examination of drug patents began under Presidents Menem and de la Rua, and the initial reforms to Brazil's compulsory licensing provisions and the introduction of the health agency in the examination of pharmaceutical patents occurred in President Cardoso's second term. Second, though unable to alter the country's trajectory of over-compliance, we also witnessed efforts to tailor the patent system in conservative Mexico, as health officials became alarmed by the effects of the first set of choices on prices, access to drugs, and health budgets. Though certainly pursued with less vigor than in the two South American countries, and also less successful, here too health officials became concerned about the effects of strong patent protection. It was not Executive ideology or partisanship that inhibited tailoring in Mexico, but an inhospitable social structure—a legacy of the way patents were introduced in the 1990s.

An important takeaway from the comparative analyses, then, is that the motives for tailoring are rooted not in ideology or partisan biases of Executives, but the costs imposed by pharmaceutical patenting and burdens on health systems. And regardless of what Executives want, motives must be matched by means. In Argentina, when health officials seek to revise the pharmaceutical patent system to reduce the benefits to foreign firms, the existence of a powerful and mobilized local pharmaceutical sector is an asset, but when health officials attempt to regulate marketing practices in the drug sector to control prices, these same social structure conditions are a hindrance. In Brazil, social structure enabled the government to tailor the patent system and also introduce a range of new policies to build capabilities in the local pharmaceutical industry, but these conditions—a function of both the way patents were introduced in the 1990s and the subsequent policies put in place in response to the ensuing problems created by pharmaceutical patenting—make coalition maintenance exceptionally difficult.

All in all, the central lessons of how social structure sets the parameters for coalitional alternatives and thus forms of compliance with the new international order apply across the three countries examined in the two time periods. An obvious question to consider is how these lessons might travel to other developing countries that also experienced aggressive external pressures to over-comply with new international rules. As regards pharmaceutical patents, an obvious comparator case is India. India eliminated product patents for pharmaceuticals in the early 1970s, and in the ensuing years developed the most advanced pharmaceutical industry in the developing world (Chaudhuri 2005; Horner 2014a; 2014b). In the international arena, India was one of the leaders among developing countries in resisting TRIPS and the obligation to allow patents on drugs, and, once defeated on that front, led the charge to push back and assure that countries would have a range of policy options in how they went about establishing new pharmaceutical patent systems (Watal 2011). Bringing India into the world of pharmaceutical patenting was, not surprisingly, one of the prize objectives of the transnational pharmaceutical industry and US Government during the 1980s and 1990s, and India consistently came under pressures that are similar to what we observed in the case of the three Latin American countries. To illustrate, in the USTR's annual Special 301 Reports, India has been placed on the Priority Watch List or identified as a Priority Foreign Country in every year since the process started in 1989. Yet, in the face of these pressures, while India has complied with the new international order, it has done so in a consistently minimalist fashion.

The explanatory framework used in this book allows us to understand India's trajectory. The accumulated resources of the large domestic pharmaceutical sector and its ties to civil society organizations generated a robust coalition to resist over-compliance. At the same time, the structure of India's trade, in particular the scarce utilization of the US's removable import preferences, meant that threats of sanctions failed to widen the transnational sector's allies within the country. The combined result of these two social structure conditions meant that efforts by the Indian Executive to over-comply were consistently frustrated, and the defensive coalition prevailed. Indeed, India's introduction of pharmaceutical patents arguably reflected the least degree of over-compliance of any country in the developing world: product patents did not become available until 2005, and without retroactive acknowledgement of pre-TRIPS inventions, such that even after drug patents began to be issued most new drugs on the market remained free of patent protection (Sampat and Shadlen 2015a; 2015b). While the initial decisions regarding the introduction of drug patents were made in the 1990s, as India acquiesced to the global sea change, here too further measures regarding how the new patent system should function were introduced in a subsequent period of patent politics. And, as expected, the local sector was able to use its accumulated resources to secure a range of measures designed to further reduce the impact of the new status quo (Chaudhuri et al. 2010; Kapczynski 2009; 2013). In both periods, and in the relationship between the two periods, India's experience is similar to what we observed in Argentina.

In both Figures 2.4 and 2.5 on coalitional dynamics (p. 50 and p. 56), India would be placed in the same positions as Argentina.[2]

Future research could examine countries in the upper-right cell in Figure 2.5, countries that introduced patents comparatively early but without retroactivity, such as Chile or Thailand. Because these countries introduced patents early, the effects of initial choices had considerable time to settle and alter social structure before subsequent conflicts emerged in the 2000s. Yet because these countries did not allow pipeline protection and avoided over-compliance on other dimensions, the disruptive effects of initial choices were attenuated. While no case with this combination of conditions is analyzed in this book, the expectation is that the dynamics would be similar to that witnessed in Brazil (the mirror image, with more delayed but more disruptive introduction of drug patents): Executives that seek to revise the patent system should be relatively enabled by social structure, but also constrained by the legacies of the initial choices. That said, while the similarity of these two pathways is plausible, it is also plausible that the effects of the two different dimensions of "how" countries introduce patents, the substance and the timing, are not equivalent. It may be the case that the feasibility of subsequent tailoring of the patent system, and the constraints that reformers face, are different in countries that introduced patents early but non-retroactively. Examining such cases thus offers a fruitful avenue for research.

LOOKING FORWARD

The world has changed. Developing countries did not grant pharmaceutical patents; now all but the poorest do. Regardless of the merits of this monumental change in terms of its effects on innovation, prices, and health—topics that continue to be intensely debated—restoring the earlier global order is unlikely. For better or worse, the globalization of pharmaceutical patenting appears to be here to stay. Laws that allow for drug patenting in developing countries have the characteristics of "super-statutes" (Eskridge and Ferejohn 2001), in that removing them is scarcely contemplated and their presence frames all subsequent debates about the politics of knowledge. Debates over patents, innovation, health, and access to medicines take place within these

---

[2] The case of India also speaks to a larger point about the iterative nature of patent politics in countries that, in acquiescence with the global sea change, accepted the obligation to allow pharmaceutical patents. Even in India, one of the few countries that used the full transition period available under TRIPS and waited until 2005 to begin granting pharmaceutical patents, policymaking was sequential: first, a decision to wait until 2005 to introduce pharmaceutical patents was made in the mid-1990s, and then, the details about how the patent system would function were established in the 2000s.

boundaries; they focus on resolving disagreements about how pharmaceutical patent systems should function, not, any longer, over whether or not they should exist. Again, this is an important way that changes in the global political economy have transformed national politics.

In the presence of this new status quo, the analysis in Chapters 6-8 has been about efforts to modify how new patent systems function to make them more compatible with local conditions, a process called "tailoring." The word is carefully chosen, as a metaphor for what one might do with an item of clothing that does not fit. The global sea change replaced a world where countries adopted patent systems in accordance with their own needs and conditions with a world where countries adopt similar types of patent systems—as if all countries had legal institutions, regulatory capabilities, and innovation systems that are more common across the "global north." Variation in how countries introduced pharmaceutical patents, the subject of Chapters 3-5, is important, but even minimalist compliance to the global sea change leaves countries with patent regimes that are of questionable fit. Hence the efforts to tailor patent regimes, efforts that are common at a general level (if not the specifics of the issues addressed) across all countries.

The contemporary politics of patents consists of more than tailoring, however. Another response to having a patent system that does not fit national conditions is to try to alter national conditions—or, to continue with the metaphor, another response to having an item of clothing that does not fit might be to change diet and lift weights in order to put on bulk and grow into the clothing. To that end, countries may invest in improving national scientific, technological, and innovative capabilities, and buttressing regulatory strength and state capacity. Countries may attempt to raise public and private expenditures in research and development, and improve linkages between private industries and publicly funded scientific research communities, for example, and, they may create new regulatory agencies endowed with additional responsibilities. We can think of this response as "aspiring," in that policy and regulatory changes are made with the objective of altering characteristics of the country in the hope that, eventually, the fit of the new patent regime will improve. Seen this way, arrangements to provide more rights of exclusion over more types of knowledge, which ultimately is what TRIPS and the global sea change are all about establishing, are not just burdens that generate subsequent efforts to introduce modifications, but they are also sources of aspiration for countries to change their science, technology, and regulatory infrastructures.

Brazil, as discussed in Chapter 8, went furthest in terms of "aspiring," creating new lines of funding and tax incentives for private firms to dedicate resources to R&D, restructuring the legal framework that affects the relationship between public sector research institutions (and researchers) and private industry, and establishing an array of new state institutions and agencies to drive these efforts.[3] The reorientation of economic development toward science, technology and innovation is unmistakable, and directly linked to the challenges created by the new patent system introduced in the late 1990s. Indeed, the former head of the patent office commented that he regarded the subsequent obsession with technology and innovation as the single most important effect of the 1996 patent law (Interview, May 19, 2008b).[4] But Brazil is not unique. Similar measures, or at least pronouncements, are visible in other countries. Argentina significantly increased expenditures on science and technology in the 2000s, and also put in place a number of programs to finance private sector R&D and encourage public–private collaborations. Argentina even created a new Ministry of Science and Technology and Productive Innovation to coordinate and sustain these efforts.[5] Though with less vigor, similar steps are evident in Mexico. The Science and Technology Law of 2003 reorganized the structure of the national science body to facilitate support of private sector research, for example, and this period witnessed the established a public–private forum for elaborating science and technology policy, as well as the announcement of a flurry of programs and initiatives to encourage and support innovative activities.[6] In sum, though these three countries reacted differently to the global sea change, each adopted a patent system of questionable fit, and in each country different experiences in tailoring have been complemented by different experiences in aspiring.

While it is not the intent here to explain cross-national differences in aspiring, it is important to underscore some of the political challenges countries face in trying to grow into their new patent systems. At first blush, the politics of aspiring would appear to be simpler than the politics of tailoring, on account of the motives for the former being universally shared. While debates over modifying patent regimes are exceptionally combustible, debates over growing into new patent regimes are not. Increasing science and technology infrastructures, improving linkages between researchers and industry, buttressing regulatory capabilities, improving legal systems, and so on—these are

---

[3] Arbix (2007); CGEE-ANPEI (2009); Cruz and de Mello (2006); de Negri (2008); de Toni (2015); Delgado (2008); Doctor (2009); Hochstetler and Montero (2013); Lugones and Suárez (2007); Paranhos (2012).

[4] Note that Brazilian responses to the challenges created by the new patent system also includes measures to strengthen the judicial system and antitrust authorities, so to prevent the abuse of dominant rights that patents confer (Martinez 2013; Rosenberg et al. 2012; Salgado et al. 2012).

[5] Chudnovsky et al. (2006); Dvorkin (2011); Etchichury and Pacheco (2014); Lugones and Suárez (2007); Morero (2013); Thomas (2004).

[6] Although Mexico's National Council for Science and Technology (*Consejo Nacional de Ciencia y Tecnología*, CONACYT) is not a Secretariat, its reorganization endowed it, in formal terms, with many of the same competencies as the MCT and FINEP in Brazil. In 2009 some of CONACYT's functions were transferred to a division within the Secretariat of Economy. For discussions of science, technology, and innovation policies in Mexico, see Amigo Castañeda (2009), Garrido et al. (2009), OECD (2009), Sanz Menéndez (2007), Shadlen (2012), Villavicencio (2009).

goals that have few detractors. And the external environment is more supportive too, at least rhetorically, as countries are encouraged by multilateral actors such as the World Bank and OECD, as well as by foreign governments, to undertake such steps.

Yet designing and implementing effective aspiring strategies to grow into new patent regimes is challenging. Consider, for example, the objective of increasing levels of spending on research and development. Accomplishing this, directly through subsidies and indirectly through tax incentives, calls for resource expenditures. Of course building capabilities involves many steps, including the design of new science and technology programs, introducing new legal frameworks for regulating interactions between public-sector researchers and private firms, creating or expanding competition authorities and relevant regulatory agencies, even perhaps establishing new ministries. Not all of these steps require money to do, but they all require money to do meaningfully. Without sufficient funding behind these endeavors, a country's aspiring strategy is likely to amount to little more than announcing new programs and institutions, grabbing headlines but making little impact. And budgetary reallocations are always complex and contested matters; though most actors will agree that spending larger shares of national income on R&D is a noble objective, few are prepared to allow resources be transferred from their area without putting up a fight.

The challenges that are created by conflicts over resources are exacerbated by the temporal dimensions of aspiring. Growing into a patent regime is inherently a long-term process; even if amply funded, these initiatives are unlikely to produce visible and tangible benefits in the short or even medium term. While tailoring patent systems consists typically of discrete acts (by Congress, Executives, regulators, or judges) that generate immediate effects, building capabilities can only be achieved over long periods of time; efforts to alter the characteristics of the country in these ways take years—perhaps generations—to manifest their effects (Pritchett et al. 2013).[7]

The budgetary and temporal challenges reinforce each other, in that the paucity of positive results in the short-term can make conflicts over resources that much more acute, as it is difficult to defend particular programs and patterns of expenditure. Here again, then, for motives to be accompanied by sufficient means, countries need enduring political coalitions to create and sustain aspiring strategies. Reliable and consistent societal allies are essential for preventing these sorts of measures involved in trying to grow into the new patent regime from falling prey to the normal pitfalls of long-term

---

[7] Indeed, if we think of the generation of science, technology, and regulatory capabilities as *outcomes* of development processes, then to grow into a patent regime means, essentially, to make the country more developed. One might even express concern that, in the new world of privately owned knowledge, the key to development is development.

development projects (Doner and Schneider 2016).[8] Without political coalitions to sustain aspiring strategies, the apparent enthusiasm and fervent activity is unlikely to amount to more than press releases and self-congratulatory ceremonies to celebrate the launch of new programs and agencies.

To this point we have considered tailoring and aspiring as complementary responses. That may be misleading. Consider that one commonly adopted "innovation policy" is to introduce measures that facilitate and encourage the patenting and exclusive licensing of publicly funded research outputs, a readily available "off-the-shelf" solution that promises to convert scientific capabilities into commercial outputs (Graff 2007; So et al. 2008). Yet this policy amounts to strengthening patent protection by expanding the scope of knowledge that can be privately owned, increasing the rights of owners to exclude, and most generally encouraging the treatment of knowledge as property. To the extent that innovation policy consists of increasing patent protection, aspiring and tailoring may be contradictory—rather than mutually reinforcing—approaches.

A broader concern is that aspiring can undermine tailoring by weakening coalitions for the latter. After all, actors that benefit from state efforts to build capabilities, particularly science, technology, and innovative capabilities, may push for stronger intellectual property rights, either to protect their own innovations or participate in partnerships with foreign investors. Together, constituencies in state and society that were mobilized by the introduction of new patent systems plus actors mobilized by subsequent aspiring strategies can create growing coalitions for increased patent protection, and regard tailoring as a threat. That aspiring is not just difficult but can undermine tailoring is illustrated by the analysis of Brazil in Chapter 8. As we saw, successive governments throughout the 2000s made efforts both to modify the new pharmaceutical patent system to address the challenges created by over-compliance, and build new capabilities to grow into the new patent regime; to make the patent system more appropriate for Brazil's conditions and to make Brazil more appropriate for the patent regime. New state agencies were created, new funding channels established, laws passed to encourage and reward technological development—all contributing to the emergence of an "innovation-IP complex." While the material impact of these efforts are mixed,[9] the political effects are clear: resistance to tailoring comes not just from actors unleashed by Brazil's over-compliant response to

---

[8] To illustrate, at the time this book was going to press, new governments in Argentina and Brazil both announced substantial reductions in science and technology spending (and in Brazil, as part of the government's fiscal tightening, the Ministry of Science and Technology was fused with the Ministry of Communication).

[9] de Negri and Turchi 2007; de Negri et al. (2009); del Campo (2016); Delgado (2013); Kasahara and Botelho (2016); Schüren (2013); Shadlen and Fonseca (2013).

the global sea change in the 1990s, but also from actors created and energized by the country's subsequent aspiring initiatives.

This potentially contradictory relationship between aspiring and tailoring prompts concerns of a trap. The premature adoption of strong patent regimes, a function of the global sea change of the 1980s and 1990s, may have salutary effects of encouraging more focus on strengthening national science and technology infrastructures and buttressing regulatory capabilities, but the effects of these subsequent efforts can also be perverse, in that they may create political obstacles to taking advantage of opportunities in the global regime for countries to modify their new patent systems. If measures to strengthen national capabilities have the effect of thinning coalitions for tailoring, developing countries may find themselves with the worst of both worlds: lacking the capabilities to make the benefits of their new patent regimes greater than the costs, and lacking the political conditions to tailor it to reduce the costs. That would be a trap, and another way that changes in the international environment reconfigure domestic political economies.

These observations on the relationship between different dimensions of national responses to the global sea change have important implications for global politics. The potential benefits and costs of allowing pharmaceutical products to be patented are well-known,[10] with the balance between these two forces in any given country a function of a range of national characteristics. Importantly, the characteristics and capabilities that determine countries' abilities to harness the benefits and mitigate the costs are unevenly distributed. Indeed, this sense that the likely costs of granting patents exceeded the likely benefits is why most developing countries, prior to the global sea change and when able to decide this autonomously, opted not to allow pharmaceutical products to be patented. Yet while pharmaceutical patenting has since become globalized, the underlying asymmetries in capabilities remain. In the new world order marked by privately-owned knowledge, most developing countries still lack the capabilities to make the patent system a net positive.

These enduring capability gaps have been largely disregarded in international politics. The global push since the 1980s has been to encourage—indeed, require—countries to increase the level of patent protection they make available. Other than short transition periods and rather vague commitments to technology transfer, the global campaign to get countries—of whatever their national characteristics—to grant more patents has not been accompanied by efforts to help them develop the necessary ancillary capabilities. Countries are left to develop these capabilities on their own, to leave the store with

---

[10] Kyle and McGahan (2012); Kyle and Qian (2014); Maskus (2014); Mazzoleni and Nelson (1998); Nogués (1993).

clothing that does not fit and do what it takes to grow into it. This asymmetry in global politics demands attention. If patenting is here to stay, then foreign governments and international organizations need to help countries build regulatory capabilities and improve science and technology infrastructures. Doing so should not be left to the countries themselves. Rather, the global campaign to get countries to adopt new patent systems must be complemented by a global campaign to help countries grow into these new patent systems.

Fieldwork Appendix

See List of Abbreviations for full meaning of organizations

	Argentina	Brazil	Mexico
*Location and Periods**	Buenos Aires (city and province) June 2003, November 2007, March–April 2008, May 2008, September 2011, December 2014	Brasilia, Rio de Janeiro, São Paulo (city and state) November 2006, May 2007, May 2008, April 2009, June 2009, November 2009, May 2015, July 2015	Mexico (city and state), Monterrey March 2004, July 2007, August 2007 March 2010, October 2010
Pharmaceutical Sectors	CAEME CEDIQUIFA CILFA + National and transnational firms	INTERFARMA ALANAC ABIFINA *Grupo Farma Brasil* + National and transnational firms	AMIIF AMEGI ANAFAM CANIFARMA + National and transnational firms
Lawyers	Representatives of national firms Representatives of transnational firms Law academics	Representatives of national firms Representatives of transnational firms Law academics	Representatives of national firms Representatives of transnational firms Law academics
Industry (non-pharma)	UIA	ANPEI CNI FIESP MEI	CCE COECE
Government	ANMAT Ministry of Economy Ministry of Health Ministry of Science, Technology and Productive Innovation Ministry of Industry INPI-AR Permanent Working Group on Intellectual Property Legislative staff	Ministry of Health *Fiocruz* Ministry of Development and Trade Ministry of Science and Technology INPI-BR ANVISA São Paulo Research Foundation FINEP ABDI	Secretariat of Economy (formerly SECOFI) Secretary of Health IMPI COFEPRIS CONACYT Deputies Legislative staff

(*continued*)

	Argentina	Brazil	Mexico
		Inter-Ministerial Working Group on Intellectual Property Deputies Legislative staff Legislative researchers	
Civil Society	*Fundación Grupo Efecto Positivo*	ABIA *Grupo de Incentivo à Vida* GTPI	RMALC *Grupo Por Un Pais Mejor*

* Research was also conducted in Washington D.C., at the offices of the United States Trade Representative (USTR), in September 2003 and November 2006.

References

Abbott, Frederick M. 2005. "The WTO Medicines Decision: World Pharmaceutical Trade and the Protection of Public Health." *American Journal of International Law* 99 (2): 317–58.

ABIFINA-ALANAC. 2001. "Propriedade intelectual: soberania e interesses nacionais." Unpublished manuscript.

Acemoglu, Daron, Philippe Aghion, and Fabrizio Zilibotti. 2006. "Distance to Frontier, Selection, and Economic Growth." *Journal of the European Economic Association* 4 (1): 37–74.

Ad Hoc Group. 1993. "Pelo progresso tecnológico do Brasil: comentários sobre o Projeto de Lei 824-D." Submission to Senate, Brazil.

Adesina, Adebiyi, Veronika J. Wirtz, and Sandra Dratler. 2013. "Reforming Antiretroviral Price Negotiations and Public Procurement: The Mexican Experience." *Health Policy and Planning* 28 (1): 1–10.

Adler, Emanuel. 1987. *The Power of Ideology: The Quest for Technological Autonomy in Argentina and Brazil.* University of California Press.

African Union-UNIDO. 2012. "Pharmaceutical Manufacturing Plan for Africa: Business Plan." United Nations Industrial Development Organization.

ALADI. 1985. "Los mercados farmacéuticos de la región." *Integración latinoamericana* 10 (98): 67.

Alcarez Hernandez, Gustavo. 2013. "Necesidad de licensias obligatorias en materia de medicamentos en México." In *Propiedad intelectual y farmacéutica: hacia una política de estado*, edited by Manuel Becerra Ramírez. México, D.F.: Instituto de Investigaciones Jurídicas, UNAM.

Alencar, G.S. de, and M.C. van der Ree. 1996. "1996: An Important Year for Brazilian Biopolitics?" *Biotechnology and Development Monitor* 27: 21–2.

AMIF. 1990. *Las Patentes y la modernización de la industria químico-farmacéutico (versón ampliada).* México, D.F.: Asociación Mexicana de Industriales Farmacéuticos.

Amigo Castañeda, Jorge. 2009. "Scientific and Technological Policy in Mexico and Intellectual Property." In *Knowledge Generation and Protection: Intellectual Property, Innovation and Economic Development*, edited by Jorge Mario Martínez-Piva. Springer Verlag.

Amin, Tahir. 2013. "Re-Visiting the Patents and Access to Medicines Dichotomy: An Evaluation of TRIPS Implementation and Public Health Safeguards in Developing Countries." In *The Global Governance of HIV/AIDS*, edited by Obijiofor Aginam, John Harrington, and Peter K. Yu. Edward Elgar Publishing.

Amin, Tahir, Rahul Rajkumar, Priti Radhakrishnan, and Aaron S. Kesselheim. 2009. "Expert Review of Drug Patent Applications: Improving Health in the Developing World." *Health Affairs* 28 (5): w948–56.

Anderson, Tatum. 2010. "Tide Turns for Drug Manufacturing in Africa." *The Lancet* 375 (9726): 1597–8.

Andia, Tatiana. 2015. "The Inverse Boomerang Pattern: The Global Kaletra Campaign and Access to Antiretroviral Drugs in Colombia and Ecuador." *Studies in Comparative International Development* 50 (2): 203–27.

Arbix, Glauco. 2007. *Inovar ou inovar: a indústria brasileira entre o passado e o futuro*. São Paulo: Editora Papagaio.

Arretche, Marta. 2004. "Toward a Unified and More Equitable System: Health Reform in Brazil." In *Crucial Needs, Weak Incentives: Social Sector Reform, Democratization, and Globalization in Latin America*, edited by Robert R. Kaufman and Joan M. Nelson. Woodrow Wilson Center Press.

Arriola, Carlos. 1994. *Testimonios sobre el TLC*. México, D.F.: Miguel Ángel Porrúa.

Arrow, Kenneth. 1962. "Economic Welfare and the Allocation of Resources for Invention." In *The Rate and Direction of Inventive Activity: Economic and Social Factors*, edited by Universities-National Bureau Committee for Economic Research, Committee on Economic Growth of the Social Science Research Council. Princeton University Press.

Arruda, Mauro F.M. 1985. "Brazil: Latest Position of INPI." *Les Nouvelles* 20 (3): 128–33.

Arslanian, Regis Percy. 1994. *O recurso à seção 301 da legislação de comércio norte-americana e a aplicação de seus dispositivos contra o Brasil*. Brasília Instituto Rio Branco.

Assumpção, Eduardo. 2001. "Nota sobre patentes e biotecnologia." Memória Técnica MT0067. Rio de Janeiro: INPI.

Attaran, Amir, and Paul Champ. 2002. "Patent Rights and Local Working under the WTO TRIPS Agreement: An Analysis of the U.S.-Brazil Patent Dispute." *Yale Journal of International Law* 27 (November): 365–93.

Aulmann, Federico, and Daniel Zuccherino. 2014. "Patentes y protección de los datos de prueba u otros no divulgados en la república Argentina." Contribution to the worskhop, "La vigencia del tratado OMC/ADPIC: sus contribuciones a la investigación y la salud." CEDIQUIFA.

Azpiazu, Daniel. 1997. *La industria farmacéutica argentina ante el nuevo contexto macroeconómico, 1991–1996*. Cuadernos de Economía, No. 28. Ministerio de Economía de la Provincia de Buenos Aires.

Baldwin, David Allen. 1985. *Economic Statecraft*. Princeton University Press.

Barbosa, Denis Borges. 2000. "Licenças compulsórias: abuso, emergência nacional e interesse público." *Revista da ABPI* 45: 3–22.

Barbosa, Denis Borges. 2004. "TRIPs e a experiência brasileira." In *Propriedade intelectual e desenvolvimento*, edited by Marcelo Dias Varella. São Paulo: Lex Editora.

Barbosa, Denis Borges. 2013. "Patents and the Emerging Markets of Latin America: Brazil." In *Emerging Markets and the World Patent Order*, edited by Frederick M. Abbott, Carlos M. Correa, and Peter Drahos. Edward Elgar Publishing.

Barbosa, Pedro Marcos Nunes. 2012. "A Brief Note Concerning Pipeline Patents in Brazil." In *Research Papers from the WIPO-WTO Colloquium for Teachers of Intellectual Property* Word Intellectual Property Organization-World Trade Organization.

Barton, John H. 2003. "Non-Obviousness." *IDEA: The Journal of Law and Technology* 43 (3): 475–508.

Basso, Maristela. 2006. "Intervention of Health Authorities in Patent Examination: The Brazilian Practice of the Prior Consent." *International Journal of Intellectual Property Management* 1 (1/2): 54–74.

Bastos, Maria Inês. 1994. "How International Sanctions Worked: Domestic and Foreign Political Constraints on the Brazilian Informatics Policy." *Journal of Development Studies* 30 (2): 380–404.

Bastos, Maria Inês. 1995. "State Autonomy and Capacity for S&T Policy Design and Implementation in Brazil." In *The Politics of Technology in Latin America*, edited by Maria Inês Bastos and Charles Cooper. Routledge.

Bautista-Arredondo, Sergio, Tania Dmytraczenko, Gilbert Kombe, and Stefano M. Bertozzi. 2008. "Costing of Scaling up HIV/AIDS Treatment in Mexico." *Salud Pública de México* 50 (January): S437–44.

Bayard, Thomas O., and Kimberly Ann Elliott. 1994. *Reciprocity and Retaliation in U.S. Trade Policy*. Institute for International Economics.

Beall, Reed, and Randall Kuhn. 2012. "Trends in Compulsory Licensing of Pharmaceuticals Since the Doha Declaration: A Database Analysis." *PLoS Med* 9 (1): e1001154.

Becerra Ramírez, Manuel. 2009. "La protección de la propiedad industrial para los productos farmoquímicos. ¿Un sistema ad hoc en favor de las empresas transnacionales?" In *Textos de la nueva cultura de la propiedad intelectual*, edited by Manuel Becerra Ramírez. México, D.F.: Instituto de Investigaciones Jurídicas.

Becerra Ramírez, Manuel. 2013. *Propiedad intelectual y farmacéutica: hacia una política de estado*. México, D.F.: Instituto de Investigaciones Jurídicas.

Bekerman, Marta, and Pablo Sirlin. 2001. "Static and Dynamic Impacts of MERCOSUR: The Case of the Pharmaceutical Sector." *CEPAL Review* 75: 217–32.

Benjamin, César. 1996. "Lei de patentes: como o Brasil foi vencido." *Atençao* 2 (4): 6–15.

Bennett, Andrew, and Jeffrey T. Checkel, eds. 2014a. *Process Tracing: From Metaphor to Analytic Tool*. Cambridge University Press.

Bennett, Andrew, and Jeffrey T. Checkel. 2014b. "Process Tracing: From Philosophical Roots to Best Practices." In *Process Tracing: From Metaphor to Analytic Tool*, edited by Andrew Bennett and Jeffrey T. Checkel. Cambridge University Press.

Bensadon, Martín, and Ignacio Sánchez Echagüe. 2008. "Criterios de patentabilidad en el ámbito químico-farmacéutico: un análisis comparativo." *Derechos Intelectuales* 14: 17–71.

Bensadon, Martín, and Ignacio Sánchez Echagüe. 2009. "A Review of Patent Litigation in Argentina." In *Innovating in Times of Crisis: Innovation, Technology and Its Protection*. Argentine-German Chamber of Industry and Commerce.

Bentolila, Hernan L. 2002. "Lessons from the United States Trade Policies to Convert a 'Pirate': The Case of Pharmaceutical Patents in Argentina." *Yale Journal of Law and Technology* 5 (March): 57–102.

Bergallo, Paola, and Agustina Ramón Michel. 2014. "The Recursivity of Global Lawmaking in the Struggle for an Argentine Policy on Pharmaceutical Patents." In *Balancing Wealth and Health: The Battle Over Intellectual Property and Access to Medicines in Latin America*, edited by Rochelle Cooper Dreyfuss and César Rodríguez-Garavito. Oxford University Press.

Bermudez, Jorge. 1995. *Indústria farmacêutica, estado e sociedade: crítica da política de medicamentos no Brasil*. São Paulo: Editora Hucitec.

Bermudez, Jorge, and Maria Auxiliadora Oliveira, eds. 2004. *Intellectual Property in the Context of the WTO TRIPS Agreement: Challenges for Public Health*. Rio de Janeiro: FIOCRUZ.

Bezerra, Fernando. 1995. "Propriedade industrial: pontos polémicos-conceitos." Unpublished manuscript.

BIC-CEBEU-CNI-FIESP. 2011. "Re: 2011 Special 301 Review." Submission to the USTR's hearings on Special 301. February 15.

Biehl, João Guilherme. 2004. "The Activist State: Global Pharmaceuticals, AIDS, and Citizenship in Brazil." *Social Text* 22 (3): 105–32.

Biehl, João Guilherme. 2007. *Will to Live: AIDS Therapies and the Politics of Survival*. Princeton University Press.

Birle, Peter. 1997. *Empresarios y la democracia en la Argentina*. Buenos Aires: Fundacion Editorial de Belgrano.

Bisang, Roberto. 1991. "Derechos de propiedad intelectual e industria farmacéutica." *Revista CAUCE* 3 (6).

Bisang, Roberto. 2010. "Perfil actual y evolución reciente de la industria Argentina en medicamentos." In *Propiedad intelectual y medicamentos*, edited by Carlos María Correa and Sandra Cecilia Negro. Buenos Aires: Editorial B de F.

Bleich, Erik, and Robert Pekkanen. 2013. "How to Report Interview Data: The Interview Methods Appendix." In *Interview Research in Political Science*, edited by Layna Mosley. Cornell University Press.

BMI. 2014. *Argentina Pharmaceuticals & Healthcare Report*. Business Monitor International.

BMI. 2015a. *Brazil Pharmaceuticals & Healthcare Report*. Business Monitor International.

BMI. 2015b. *Mexico Pharmaceuticals & Healthcare Report*. Business Monitor International.

Boas, Taylor C. 2007. "Conceptualizing Continuity and Change: The Composite-Standard Model of Path Dependence." *Journal of Theoretical Politics* 19 (1): 33–54.

Boccanera. 2005. "El acuerdo TRIP. La ley de patentes y la industria farmacéutica argentina." In *Industria farmacéutica y propiedad intelectual: los países en desarrollo*, edited by Alenka Guzmán and Gustavo Viniegra. México, D.F.: Editorial Porrúa.

Bohle, Dorothee, and Byla Greskovits. 2012. *Capitalist Diversity on Europe's Periphery*. Cornell University Press.

Boldrin, Michele, and David K. Levine. 2008. *Against Intellectual Monopoly*. Cambridge University Press.

Brady, Henry E., and David Collier, eds. 2004. *Rethinking Social Inquiry: Diverse Tools, Shared Standards*. Rowman & Littlefield Publishers.

Braithwaite, John, and Peter Drahos. 2000. *Global Business Regulation*. Cambridge University Press.

Braun, Johanna von. 2012. *The Domestic Politics of Negotiating International Trade: Intellectual Property Rights in US-Colombia and US-Peru Free Trade Agreements*. Routledge.

Brodovsky, Joan. 1997. "Industria farmacéutica y farmoquímica mexicana en el marco regulatorio de los años noventa." In *Apertura económica y desregulación en el mercado de medicamentos: la industria farmacéutica y farmoquímica de Argentina, Brasil y México en los años 90*, edited by Jorge M. Katz. Buenos Aires: Alianza Editorial.

Brooks, Sarah M. 2008. *Social Protection and the Market in Latin America: The Transformation of Social Security Institutions*. Cambridge University Press.

Brooks, Sarah M., and Marcus J. Kurtz. 2012. "Paths to Financial Policy Diffusion: Statist Legacies in Latin America's Globalization." *International Organization* 66 (1): 95–128.

Bruhn, Kathleen. 1997a. *Taking on Goliath: The Emergence of a New Left Party and the Struggle for Democracy in Mexico*. Pennsylvania State University Press.

Bruhn, Kathleen. 1997b. "The Seven-Month Itch? Neoliberal Politics, Popular Movements, and the Left in Mexico." In *The New Politics of Inequality in Latin America: Rethinking Participation and Representation*, edited by Douglas A. Chalmers, Carlos M. Vilas, Katherine Hite, Scott B. Martin, Kerianne Piester, and Monique Segarra. Oxford University Press.

Büchler, Maryann. 2005. "A câmara setorial da indústria farmoquímica e farmaceutica: uma experiencia peculiar." Dissertação de Mestrado, Universidade Federal do Rio de Janeiro.

Budish, Eric, Benjamin N. Roin, and Heidi Williams. 2015. "Do Firms Underinvest in Long-Term Research? Evidence from Cancer Clinical Trials." *American Economic Review* 105 (7): 2044–85.

Burachik, Gustavo, and Jorge M. Katz. 1997. "La industria farmacéutica y farmoquímica argentina en los años 90." In *Apertura económica y desregulación en el mercado de medicamentos: la industria farmacéutica y farmoquímica de Argentina, Brasil y México en los años 90*, edited by Jorge M. Katz. Buenos Aires: Alianza Editorial.

Burdick, John. 2004. *Legacies of Liberation: The Progressive Catholic Church in Brazil at the Start of a New Millennium*. Ashgate.

Buscaglia, Edgardo, and Clarisa Long. 1997. *U.S. Foreign Policy and Intellectual Property Rights in Latin America*. Hoover Press.

Caliari, Thiago, Roberto Mazzoleni, and Luciano Martins Costa Póvoa. 2013. "Innovations in the Pharmaceutical Industry in Brazil post-TRIPS." In *TRIPS Compliance, National Patent Regimes and Innovation: Evidence and Experience from Developing Countries*, edited by Sunil Mani and Richard R. Nelson. Edward Elgar Publishing.

Caliari, Thiago, and Ricardo Machado Ruiz. 2014. "Brazilian Pharmaceutical Industry and Generic Drugs Policy: Impacts on Structure and Innovation and Recent Developments." *Science and Public Policy* 41 (2): 245–256.

Calvo, Ernesto. 2014. *Legislator Success in Fragmented Congresses in Argentina: Plurality Cartels, Minority Presidents, and Lawmaking*. Cambridge University Press.

Cámara de Diputados. 1991. *Diario de Los Debates* 3 (16). México, D.F.

Cámara de Senadores. 1987. "Decreto por el que se reforma y adiciona la Ley de Invenciones y Marcas." In *Diario de Los Debates*, 576–724. México, D.F.

Cámara de Senadores. 1990. *Diario de Los Debates*. 13th ed. México, D.F.

Câmara dos Deputados. 1993. "Sessão plenária transformada em comissão geral para debate acerca do projeto de Lei No. 824, de 1991, que regula direitos e obrigações relativos a propriedade industrial (14 de Abril de 1993)." Brasília: Diário do Congresso Nacional.

Cameron, Maxwell A., and Brian W. Tomlin. 2002. *The Making of NAFTA: How the Deal was Done.* Cornell University Press.

Campello, Daniela. 2015. *The Politics of Market Discipline in Latin America: Globalization and Democracy.* Cambridge University Press.

Campello, Daniela, and Leany Lemos. 2015. "The Non-Ratification of Bilateral Investment Treaties in Brazil: A Story of Conflict in a Land of Cooperation." *Review of International Political Economy* 22 (5): 1055–86.

Campo, Maria Victoria del. 2016. "Escaping An Institutional Middle-Income Trap: Upgrading in Brazil's Pharmaceutical Industry." PhD Dissertation, MIT.

CANIFARMA. 1988. *La industria farmacéutica en cifras, 1978-1987.* México, D.F.: Cámara Nacional de la Industria Farmacéutica.

Capanema, Luciana Xavier de Lemos, Pedro Lins Palmeira Filho, and João Paulo Pieroni. 2008. "Apoio do BNDES ao Complexo Industrial da Saúde: a experiência do Profarma e seus desdobramentos—BNDES." Rio de Janeiro: Banco Nacional de Desenvolvimento Econômico e Social.

Capoccia, Giovanni, and R. Daniel Kelemen. 2007. "The Study of Critical Junctures: Theory, Narrative, and Counterfactuals in Historical Institutionalism." *World Politics* 59 (3): 341–69.

Carey, John M., and Matthew Soberg Shugart. 1998. *Executive Decree Authority.* Cambridge University Press.

Carvalho, Antonio P. de, Daniel Goldstein, Isaias Raw, and Glaci T. Zancan. 1995. "Third-Generation Biotechnologies." *História, Ciências, Saúde-Manguinhos* 1 (2): 101–16.

Casar, Ma. Amparo. 2002. "Executive-Legislative Relations: The Case of Mexico (1946-1997)." In *Legislative Politics in Latin America*, edited by Scott Morgenstern and Benito Nacif. Cambridge University Press.

Cassier, Maurice. 2008. "Patents and Public Health in France. Pharmaceutical Patent Law In-the-making at the Patent Office between the Two World Wars." *History and Technology* 24 (2): 135–51.

Cassier, Maurice. 2012. "Pharmaceutical Patent Law in-the-Making: Opposition and Legal Action by States, Citizens, and Generics Laboratories in Brazil and India." In *Ways of Regulating Drugs in the 19th and 20th Centuries*, edited by Jean-Paul Gaudillière and Volker Hess. Palgrave Macmillan.

Cassier, Maurice, and Marilena Corrêa. 2003. "Patents, Innovation and Public Health: Brazilian Public-Sector Laboratories' Experience in Copying AIDS Drugs." In *Economics of AIDS and Access to HIV-AIDS Care in Developing Countries: Issues and Challenges.* Agence nationale de recherches sur le SIDA (ANRS).

Cassier, Maurice, and Marilena Corrêa. 2007. "Propriedade intelectual e saúde pública: a cópia de medicamentos contra HIV/Aids realizada por laboratórios farmacêuticos brasileiros públicos e privados." *Revista eletrônica de comunicação, informação & inovação em saúde* 1 (1): 83–91.

Cassier, Maurice, and Marilena Corrêa. 2008. "Scaling-up and Reverse Engineering: Acquisition of Industrial Knowledge by Copying Drugs in Brazil." In *The Political Economy of HIV/AIDS in Developing Countries: TRIPS, Public Health Systems and Free Access*, edited by Benjamin Coriat. Edward Elgar Publishing.

Cassier, Maurice, and Marilena Corrêa. 2013. "Nationaliser l'efavirenz: licence obligatoire, invention collective et néo-développementisme au Brésil (2001–2012)." *Autrepart* 63 (1): 107–22.

Castañeda, Jorge G. 1990. "Salinas's Internatinal Relations Gamble." *Journal of International Affairs* 43 (2): 407–22.

Cavalcanti, Ana Regina de Holanda. 1988. "A aplicação de legislações de propriedade às formas vivas: patentes en biotecnologia." Memória Técnica MT0005. Rio de Janeiro: INPI.

CEDIQUIFA. 1990. "Resumen de la propuesta de CEDIQUIFA en materia de patentes de invención." Buenos Aires: Centro de Estudios para el Desarrollo de la Industria Químico-Farmacéutica Argentina.

CENSIDA. 2008. *Informe UNGASS Mexico 2008.* Mexico, D.F.: Centro Nacional para la Prevención y el Control del VIH/SIDA.

Centeno, Miguel Angel. 1997. *Democracy Within Reason: Technocratic Revolution in Mexico.* Pennsylvania State University Press.

Centro de Estudos e Debates Estratégicos. 2013. *A revisão da Lei de Patentes: inovação em prol da competitividade nacional.* Brasília: Câmara dos Deputados.

CEP. 2009. "La industria farmacéutica en la Argentina: goza de buena salud." Síntesis de la economía real, 58. Buenos Aires: Centro Estudios para la Producción, Ministerio de Producción.

CEPAL. 1987. *La industria farmacéutica y farmoquímica: desarrollo histórico y posibilidades futuras. Argentina, Brasil y México.* Serie de Estudios 65. Santiago de Chile: CEPAL.

CEPAL. 1999. "Las industrias farmacéutica y farmoquímica en México y el Distrito Federal." LC/MEXL.400. Mexico, D.F.

CESOP, ed. 2010. *Situación del sector farmacéutico en México.* México, D.F.: Centro de Estudios Sociales y de Opinión Pública, Cámara de Diputados.

CESP. 1991a. *Transcript from Congressional Hearing on Patent Law, 19/11/1991.* Brasília: Comisão Especial sobre Propriedade Industrial, Câmara dos Deputados.

CESP. 1991b. *Transcript from Congressional Hearing on Patent Law, 25/11/1991.* Brasília: Comisão Especial sobre Propriedade Industrial, Câmara dos Deputados.

CESP. 1991c. *Transcript from Congressional Hearing on Patent Law, 3/12/1991.* Brasília: Comisão Especial sobre Propriedade Industrial, Câmara dos Deputados.

CESP. 1991d. *Transcript from Congressional Hearing on Patent Law, 4/12/1991.* Brasília: Comisão Especial sobre Propriedade Industrial, Câmara dos Deputados.

CESP. 1991e. *Transcript from Congressional Hearing on Patent Law, 10/12/1991.* Brasília: Comisão Especial sobre Propriedade Industrial, Câmara dos Deputados.

CESP. 1992a. *Transcript from Congressional Hearing on Patent Law, 7/04/1992.* Brasília: Comisão Especial sobre Propriedade Industrial, Câmara dos Deputados.

CESP. 1992b. *Transcript from Congressional Hearing on Patent Law, 13/05/1992.* Brasília: Comisão Especial de Propriedade Industrial, Câmara dos Deputados.

CGEE-ANPEI. 2009. *Os novos instrumentos de apoio à inovação: uma avaliação inicial.* Brasília: Centro de Gestão e Estudos Estratégicos (Ministério da Ciência e Tecnologia)-Associação Nacional de Pesquisa e Desenvolvimento das Empresas Inovadoras.

Challú, Pablo. 1991a. "The Consequences of Pharmaceutical Product Patenting." *World Competition* 15 (2): 65–126.

Challú, Pablo. 1991b. *Patentamiento de productos farmacéuticos: consecuencias.* Buenos Aires: Mercado.

Challú, Pablo. 1995. "Effects of the Monopolistic Patenting of Medicine in Italy since 1978." *International Journal of Technology Management* 10 (2/3): 237–51.

Challú, Pablo, and Mirta Levis. 1996. *Adecuacion de la ley Argentina de patentes.* Buenos Aires: Abeledo—Perrot.

Chamas, Claudia. 2005. "Developing Innovative Capacity in Brazil to Meet Health Needs." Commission on Intellectual Property Rights, Innovation and Public Health. Geneva: World Health Organization.

Chang, Ha-Joon. 2002. *Kicking Away the Ladder: Development Strategy in Historical Perspective.* Anthem Press.

Chaudhuri, Sudip. 2005. *The WTO and India's Pharmaceuticals Industry: Patent Protection, TRIPS, and Developing Countries.* Oxford University Press.

Chaudhuri, Sudip, Chan Park, and K. M. Gopakumar. 2010. *Five Years into the Product Patent Regime: India's Response.* New York: United Nations Development Program.

Chaves, Gabriela Costa. 2016. "Interfaces entre a produção local e o acesso a medicamentos no contexto do acordo TRIPS da organização mundial do comércio." Phd Thesis, Rio de Janeiro: Escola Nacional de Saúde Pública.

Chaves, Gabriela Costa, Lia Hasenclever, Claudia Garcia Serpa Osorio-de-Castro, and Maria Auxiliadora Oliveira. 2015. "Strategies for Price Reduction of HIV Medicines under a Monopoly Situation in Brazil." *Revista de saúde pública* 49 (86).

Chaves, Gabriela Costa, Marcela Fogaça Vieira, and Renata Reis. 2008. "Access to Medicines and Intelectual Property in Brazil: Reflections and Strategies of Civil Society." *Sur. International Journal of Human Rights* 5 (8): 170–98.

Chen, Yongmin, and Thitima Puttitanun. 2005. "Intellectual Property Rights and Innovation in Developing Countries." *Journal of Development Economics* 78 (2): 474–93.

Chorev, Nitsan. 2012. "Changing Global Norms through Reactive Diffusion the Case of Intellectual Property Protection of AIDS Drugs." *American Sociological Review* 77 (5): 831–53.

Chorev, Nitsan. 2015. "Narrowing the Gaps in Global Disputes: The Case of Counterfeits in Kenya." *Studies in Comparative International Development* 50 (2): 157–86.

Chu, Michael, and Regina Garcia-Cuellar. 2011. "Farmacias Similares: Private and Public Health Care for the Base of the Pyramid in Mexico." Harvard Business School Case 307–092.

Chudnovsky, Daniel. 1979. "The Challenge by Domestic Enterprises to the Transnational Corporations' Domination: A Case Study of the Argentinean Pharmaceutical Industry." *World Development* 7 (1): 45–58.

Chudnovsky, Daniel, Andrés López, Martín Rossi, and Diego Ubfal. 2006. "Evaluating a Program of Public Funding of Private Innovation Activities: An Econometric Study of FONTAR in Argentina." Office of Evaluation and Oversight, Inter-American Development Bank.

CILFA. 2014. *50 aniversario.* Buenos Aires: Cámara Industrial de Laboratorios Farmacéuticos Argentinos.

CNBB. 1993. "As patentes e as exigências éticas." Submission to Senate, Brazil.

Cohen, Jillian Clare, and Kristina M. Lybecker. 2005. "AIDS Policy and Pharmaceutical Patents: Brazil's Strategy to Safeguard Public Health." *World Economy* 28 (2): 211–30.

Cohen, Jon. 2006. "Ten Years After." *Science* 313 (5786): 484–7.

Collier, David, Henry E. Brady, and Jason Seawright. 2010. "Sources of Leverage in Causal Inference: Toward an Alternative View of Methodology." In *Rethinking Social Inquiry: Diverse Tools, Shared Standards*, edited by Henry E. Brady and David Collier, Second Edition. Rowman & Littlefield Publishers.

Collier, Ruth Berins, and David Collier. 1991. *Shaping the Political Arena: Critical Junctures, the Labor Movement, and Regime Dynamics in Latin America*. Princeton University Press.

Colombatto, Enrico. 2004. *The Elgar Companion to the Economics of Property Rights*. Edward Elgar Publishing.

Comité de Competividad. 2008. "Foro para impuslar la competitividad del sector farmacéutico en México." México, D.F.: Cámara de Diputados.

Commission on Intellectual Property Rights. 2002. *Integrating Intellectual Property Rights and Development Policy*. London: Commission on Intellectual Property Rights.

Consultoria Legislativa do Senado. 1993. "Contribuão à comprensão do PLC-115/93, sobre propriedade intelectual." Internal Document.

Consultoria Legislativa do Senado. 1994. "Projeto de Lei da Câmara No. 115/93: comentários às emendas do Executivo." Internal Document.

Consultoria Legislativa do Senado. 1995a. "Lei de Patentes: hora de ajustar o projeto." Internal Document.

Consultoria Legislativa do Senado. 1995b. "Subsídios à votação pelo Senado Federal." Internal Document.

Coriat, Benjamin. 2008. *The Political Economy of HIV/AIDS in Developing Countries: TRIPS, Public Health Systems and Free Access*. Edward Elgar Publishing.

Corigliano, Francisco. 2000. "La dimensión bilateral de las relaciones entre Argentina y los Estados Unidos durante la década de 1990: el ingreso al paradigma de 'relaciones especiales.'" In *Historia general de las relaciones exteriores de la república argentina*, edited by Carlos Escudé and Andrés Cisneros. Vol. 15. Buenos Aires: Grupo Editor Latinoamericano.

Corrales, Javier. 2002. *Presidents without Parties: The Politics of Economic Reform in Argentina and Venezuela in the 1990s*. Pennsyvlania State University Press.

Corrales, Javier. 2004. *Technocratic Policy Making and Parliamentary Accountability in Argentina, 1983–2002*. Democracy, Governance and Human Rights Programme Paper. Geneva: United Nations Research Institute for Social Development (UNRISD).

Correa, Carlos M. 1991. "Nuevas tendencias sobre patentes de invención en América Latina." *Revista del derecho industrial* 13 (39): 417–57.

Correa, Carlos M. 1999. "Intellectual Property Rights and the Use of Compulsory Licenses: Options for Developing Countries." Geneva: South Centre.

Correa, Carlos M. 2000a. "Reforming the Intellectual Property Rights System in Latin America." *World Economy* 23 (6): 851–72.

Correa, Carlos M. 2000b. *Intellectual Property Rights, the WTO and Developing Countries: The TRIPS Agreement and Policy Options*. Zed Books.

Correa, Carlos M. 2006. *Medidas cautelares en el régimen de patentes.* Buenos Aires: Lexis Nexis.

Correa, Carlos M. 2007. *Guidelines for the Examination of Pharmaceutical Patents: Developing a Public Health Perspective.* Geneva: Internatinoal Center for Trade and Sustainable Development (ICTSD), World Health Organization (WHO), and United Nations Conference on Trade and Development (UNCTAD).

Correa, Carlos M. 2014. "Tackling the Proliferation of Patents: How to Avoid Undue Limitations to Competition and the Public Domain." Research Paper 52. Geneva: South Centre.

Correa, Carlos M., Cynthia Balleri, Marina Giulietti, Federico Lavopa, Carola Musetti, Gastón Palopoli, Tomás Pippo, Catalina De la Puente, and Vanesa Lowenstein. 2011. "Patentes, suministro de medicamentos y protección de la salud pública." *Revista argentina de salud pública* 2 (7): 19–27.

Corrêa, Marilena, and Maurice Cassier, eds. 2010. *Aids e saúde pública: contribuições à reflexão sobre uma nova economia política do medicamento no Brasil.* Rio de Janeiro: EdUERJ.

Cruz, Carlos H. de Brito, and Luiz de Mello. 2006. "Boosting Innovation Performance in Brazil." Economics Department Working Paper 532. Paris: Organisation for Economic Co-operation and Development.

Culpepper, Pepper D. 2010. *Quiet Politics and Business Power: Corporate Control in Europe and Japan.* Cambridge University Press.

Czub, Kimberly A. 2001. "Argentina's Emerging Standard of Intellectual Property Protection: A Case Study of the Underlying Conflicts Between Developing Countries, TRIPS Standards, and the United States." *Case Western Reserve Journal of International Law* 33: 191–231.

d'Adesky, Anne-christine. 2004. *Moving Mountains: The Race to Treat Global AIDS.* Verso.

David, Paul A. 1993. "Intellectual Property Institutions and the Panda's Thumb: Patents, Copyrights, and Trade Secrets in Economic Theory and History." In *Global Dimensions of Intellectual Property Rights in Science and Technology,* edited by Mitchel B. Wallerstein, Mary Ellen Mogee, and Roberta A. Schoen. National Academy Press.

de Toni, Jackson. 2015. "Uma nova governança no padrão de relacionamento público-privado da política industrial brasileira." *Revista de Sociologia e Política* 23 (55): 97–117.

Deere, Carolyn. 2008. *The Implementation Game: The TRIPS Agreement and the Global Politics of Intellectual Property Reform in Developing Countries.* Oxford University Press.

Delgado, Ignacio José Godinho. 2008. "A política industrial brasileira para setores selecionados e a experiencia internacional." Brasília: Agência Brasileira de Desenvolvimento Industrial (ABDI).

Delgado, Ignacio José Godinho. 2013. "Saúde e indústria farmacêutica: apontamentos para uma análise comparativa entre Brasil, Argentina e Gra-Bretanha." In *Saúde, cidadania e desenvolvimento,* edited by Amélia Cohn. Rio de Janeiro: Centro Internacional Celso Furtado de Políticas para o Desenvolvimento.

Dion, Michelle. 2010. *Workers and Welfare: Comparative Institutional Change in Twentieth-Century Mexico.* University of Pittsburgh Press.

Doctor, Mahrukh. 2009. "Furthering Industrial Development in Brazil: Globalization and the National Innovation System." Paper prepared for delivery at the 2009 Congress of the Latin American Studies Association. Rio de Janeiro.

Dominguez, Jorge I., ed. 1997. *Technopols: Freeing Politics and Markets in Latin America in the 1990s.* Pennsylvania State University Press.

Doner, Richard F. and Ben Ross Schneider. 2016. "The Middle-Income Trap: More Politics than Economics." *World Politics* 68 (4): 608–644.

Drahos, Peter. 1995. "Global Property Rights in Information: The Story of TRIPS at the GATT." *Prometheus* 13 (1): 6–19.

Drahos, Peter. 2001. "Bits and Bips." *The Journal of World Intellectual Property* 4 (6): 791–808.

Drahos, Peter. 2008. "'Trust Me': Patent Offices in Developing Countries." *American Journal of Law & Medicine* 34 (2/3): 151.

Drahos, Peter. 2010. *The Global Governance of Knowledge: Patent Offices and Their Clients.* Cambridge University Press.

Dreyfuss, Rochelle Cooper, and César Rodríguez-Garavito. 2014. *Balancing Wealth and Health: The Battle Over Intellectual Property and Access to Medicines in Latin America.* Oxford University Press.

Dubowy, Irene Ribeiro. 2003. "Subsidies Code, TRIPS Agreement, and Technological Development: Some Considerations for Developing Countries." *Journal of Technology, Law & Policy* 8 (1): 33–67.

Dutfield, Graham. 2003. *Intellectual Property Rights and the Life Science Industries: A Twentieth Century History.* Ashgate.

Dutfield, Graham. 2009. *Intellectual Property Rights and the Life Science Industries: Past, Present and Future.* 2nd ed. World Scientific.

Dutfield, Graham, and Uma Suthersanen. 2005. "Harmonisation or Differentiation in Intellectual Property Protection? The Lessons of History." *Prometheus* 23 (2): 131–47.

Dvorkin, Eduardo N. 2011. "Argentina: The Development of Science Based Technology." In *ISTIC-UNESCO-WFEO Workshop on Science, Engineering and Industry: Innovation for Sustainable Development,* edited by Pablo J. Bereciartua and Guillermo A. Lemarchand. Science Policy Studies and Documents in LAC, Vol. 3. Montevideo: UNESCO.

Eimer, Thomas, and Susanne Lütz. 2010. "Developmental States, Civil Society, and Public Health: Patent Regulation for HIV/AIDS Pharmaceuticals in India and Brazil." *Regulation & Governance* 4 (2): 135–53.

Eimer, Thomas R., and Verena Schüren. 2013. "Convenient Stalemates: Why International Patent Law Negotiations Continue Despite Deadlock." *New Political Economy* 18 (4): 533–54.

El-Said, Mohammed. 2005. "The Road from Trips-Minus, to Trips, to Trips-Plus." *The Journal of World Intellectual Property* 8 (1): 53–65.

El Said, Mohammed. 2007. "Surpassing Checks, Overriding Balances and Diminishing Flexibilities—FTA-IPRs Plus Bilateral Trade Agreements: From Jordan to Oman." *Journal of World Investment & Trade* 8: 243.

Elliott, Kimberly Ann, and J. David Richardson. 1996. "Determinants and Effectiveness of 'Aggressively Unilateral' U.S. Trade Actions." In *The Effects of U.S. Trade*

Protection and Promotion Policies, edited by Robert C. Feenstra. University of Chicago Press.

Enriquez, Gerardo. 2013. 'El impacto de tratados internacionales en salud pública y la industria farmacéutica en México'. In *Propiedad intelectual y farmacéutica: hacia una política de estado*, edited by Manuel Becerra Ramírez. México, D.F.: Instituto de Investigaciones Jurídicas.

Eren-Vural, Ipek. 2007. "Domestic Contours of Global Regulation: Understanding the Policy Changes on Pharmaceutical Patents in India and Turkey." *Review of International Political Economy* 14 (1): 105–42.

Escorel, Sarah. 1999. *Reviravolta na saúde: origem e articulação do movimento sanitário*. Rio de Janeiro: Editora FIOCRUZ.

Eskridge, William N., and John Ferejohn. 2001. "Super-Statutes." *Duke Law Journal* 50: 1215–76.

Espicom. 2012. *Pharmaceutical Market Intelligence Reports: Latin America*. Espicom Business Intelligence.

Etchemendy, Sebastián. 2011. *Models of Economic Liberalization: Business, Workers, and Compensation in Latin America, Spain, and Portugal*. Cambridge University Press.

Etchemendy, Sebastián, and Candelaria Garay. 2011. "Argentina: Left Populism in Comparative Perspective, 2003–2009." In *The Resurgence of the Latin American Left*, edited by Steven Levitsky and Kenneth M. Roberts. Johns Hopkins University Press.

Etchichury, H. J., and M. C. Pacheco. 2014. "Global Forces and Local Currents in Argentina's Science Policy Crossroads: Restricted Access or Open Knowledge." *Revista de pensamiento e investigación social* 14 (3): 105–27.

Evans, Peter B. 1976. "Foreign Investment and Industrial Transformation: A Brazilian Case Study." *Journal of Development Economics* 3 (2): 119–39.

Evans, Peter B. 1989. "Declining Hegemony and Assertive Industrialization: U.S.-Brazil Conflicts in the Computer Industry." *International Organization* 43 (02): 207–38.

Fairbrother, M. 2007. "Making Neoliberalism Possible: The State's Organization of Business Support for NAFTA in Mexico." *Politics & Society* 35 (2): 265–300.

Fairfield, Tasha. 2013. "Going Where the Money Is: Strategies for Taxing Economic Elites in Unequal Democracies." *World Development* 47 (July): 42–57.

Fairfield, Tasha. 2015. *Private Wealth and Public Revenue in Latin America: Business Power and Tax Politics*. Cambridge University Press.

Fairfield, Tasha, and Andrew Charman. 2017, forthcoming. "Explicit Bayesian Analysis for Process Tracing: Guidelines, Opportunities, and Caveats." *Political Analysis*.

Fairfield, Tasha, and Candelaria Garay. 2017, forthcoming. "Redistribution under the Right in Latin America: Electoral Competition and Organized Actors in Policy-making." *Comparative Political Studies*.

Falleti, Tulia G. 2010. "Infiltrating the State: The Evolution of Health Care Reforms in Brazil, 1964–1988." In *Explaining Institutional Change: Ambiguity, Agency, and Power*, edited by James Mahoney and Kathleen Thelen. Cambridge University Press.

Falleti, Tulia G. 2005. "A Sequential Theory of Decentralization: Latin American Cases in Comparative Perspective." *American Political Science Review* 99 (03): 327–46.

Falleti, Tulia G., and Julia F. Lynch. 2009. "Context and Causal Mechanisms in Political Analysis." *Comparative Political Studies* 42 (9): 1143–66.

Falleti, Tulia G., and James Mahoney. 2015. "The Comparative Sequential Method." In *Advances in Comparative-Historical Analysis*, edited by James Mahoney and Kathleen Thelen. Cambridge University Press.

Farrell, Henry, and Abraham L. Newman. 2014. "Domestic Institutions Beyond the Nation-State: Charting the New Interdependence Approach." *World Politics* 66 (2): 331–63.

FDA. n.d. "Drug Approvals and Databases." United States Food and Drug Administration (http://www.fda.gov/Drugs/InformationOnDrugs/).

Febrefarma. 2007. *Origens e trajetória da indústria farmacêutica no Brasil*. São Paulo: Narrativa Um.

Fernández Bugna, Cecilia, and Fernando Porto. 2013. "La industria farmacéutica en la Argentina." In *La industria argentina frente a los nuevos desafíos y oportunidades del siglo XXI*, edited by Giovanni Stumpo and Diego Rivas. Santiago de Chile: CEPAL.

FIEL. 1990. *Protección de los derechos de propiedad intelectual: el caso de la industria farmacéutica en la Argentina*. Buenos Aires: Manantial S.R.L., Ediciones.

Filomeno, Felipe Amin. 2014. *Monsanto and Intellectual Property in South America*. Palgrave Macmillan.

Fink, Carsten, and Patrick Reichenmiller. 2005. "Tightening TRIPS: The Intellectual Property Provisions of Recent US Free Trade Agreements." Report 32111. Washington, D.C.: World Bank.

Flores-Macias, Gustavo A. 2012. *After Neoliberalism? The Left and Economic Reforms in Latin America*. Oxford University Press.

FLUC. 1992. *Dossiê das patentes: uma análise do projeto No. 824 do governo federal sobre a questão da propriedade industrial*. São Paulo: Fórum pela Liberdade do Uso do Conhecimento.

FLUC. 1994. *II Dossiê das patentes: uma análise do projeto No. 824 do governo federal sobre a questão da propriedade industrial*. São Paulo: Fórum pela Liberdade do Uso do Conhecimento.

Flynn, Matthew B. 2008. "Public Production of Anti-Retroviral Medicines in Brazil, 1990–2007." *Development and Change* 39 (4): 513–36.

Flynn, Matthew B. 2011. "Corporate Power and State Resistance: Brazil's Use of TRIPS Flexibilities for Its National AIDS Program." In *Intellectual Property, Pharmaceuticals and Public Health: Access to Drugs in Developing Countries*, edited by Kenneth C. Shadlen, S. Guennif, Alenka Guzmán, and N. Lalitha. Edward Elgar Publishing.

Flynn, Matthew B. 2013. "Origins and Limitations of State-Based Advocacy Brazil's AIDS Treatment Program and Global Power Dynamics." *Politics & Society* 41 (1): 3–28.

Flynn, Matthew B. 2015. *Pharmaceutical Autonomy and Public Health in Latin America: State, Society, and Industry in Brazil's AIDS Program*. Routledge.

Fonseca, Elize Massard da. 2014. *The Politics of Pharmaceutical Policy Reform: A Study of Generic Drug Regulation in Brazil*. Springer.

Fonseca, Elize Massard da, and Francisco Inácio Bastos. 2016. "Implementing Intellectual Property of Pharmaceuticals in Middle-Income Countries: A Case Study of

Patent Regulation in Brazil." *Journal of Health Politics, Policy and Law* 41 (3): 423–50.

Fonseca, Elize Massard da, and Kenneth C. Shadlen. 2017. "Promoting and Regulating Generic Medicines: Brazil in Comparative Perspective." *Pan American Journal of Public Health* 41: e5.

Ford, Nathan, David Wilson, Gabriela Costa Chaves, Michel Lotrowska, and Kannikar Kijtiwatchakul. 2007. "Sustaining Access to Antiretroviral Therapy in the Less-Developed World: Lessons from Brazil and Thailand": *AIDS* 21 (Suppl 4): S21–9.

Foweraker, Joe. 1990. *Popular Movements and Political Change in Mexico*. Lynne Rienner Publishers.

Frank, Roberto. 1989. "Ideas para la reforma de la ley argentina sobre patentes de invención." *Derechos intelectuales* 4 (189–97).

Frieden, Jeffry A. 1991. "Invested Interests: The Politics of National Economic Policies in a World of Global Finance." *International Organization* 45 (4): 425–51.

FUNSALUD. 2013. *Descripción del sector farmacéutico en México, 2012*. México, D.F.: Fundación Mexicana para la Salud.

Furtado, João Salvador. 1985. "Patentes en biotecnologia: capacitar-se ou perecer." In *Biotecnologia e sociedade: o caso brasileiro*, edited by Cláudio de Moura Castro and George Martine. Campinas: Ed. da UNICAMP.

Gadbaw, R. Michael, and Timothy J. Richards, eds. 1988a. *Intellectual Property Rights: Global Consensus, Global Conflict?* Westview Press.

Gadbaw, R. Michael, and Timothy J. Richards, eds. 1988b. "Introduction." In *Intellectual Property Rights: Global Consensus, Global Conflict?*, edited by R. Michael Gadbaw and Timothy J. Richards. Westview Press.

Gallagher, Kevin, and Roberto. Porzecanski. 2008. "China Matters: China's Economic Impact in Latin America." *Latin American Research Review* 43 (1): 185–200.

Galvão, Jane. 2002. "Access to Antiretroviral Drugs in Brazil." *The Lancet* 360 (9348): 1862–5.

Galvão, Jane. 2005. "Brazil and Access to HIV/AIDS Drugs: A Question of Human Rights and Public Health." *American Journal of Public Health* 95 (7): 1110–16.

Garay, Maria Candelaria. 2016. *Social Policy Expansion in Latin America*. Cambridge University Press.

Garrett, Geoffrey, and Peter Lange. 1991. "Political Responses to Interdependence: What's 'Left' for the Left?" *International Organization* 45 (4): 539–64.

Garrido Noguera, Celso, Ricardo Padilla Hermida, and Rogério Dias de Araújo. 2009. "Multinational Enterprises and Technological Innovation in Mexican Manufacturing." In *Technological Innovation in Brazilian and Mexican Firms*, edited by João Alberto de Negri, Bruno César Araújo, and Sérvulo Vicente Moreira. Brasília: Instituto de Pesquisa Econômica Aplicada.

Gasman, Nadine. 1995. "Drifting through Time: Pharmaceutical Policies in Mexico." *Development Dialogue* 1: 223–56.

Gasman, Nadine. 2008. "Políticas farmacéuticas en México: que 20 años no es nada." *Salud pública de México* 50 (Sup 4): 423–6.

Gaudillière, Jean-Paul. 2008. "How Pharmaceuticals Became Patentable: The Production and Appropriation of Drugs in the Twentieth Century." *History and Technology* 24 (2): 99–106.

Gauri, Varun, and Evan S. Lieberman. 2006. "Boundary Institutions and HIV/AIDS Policy in Brazil and South Africa." *Studies in Comparative International Development* 41 (3): 47–73.

Genovesi, Luis Mariano. 1995. *Patentes y medicamentos: un tema para debatir.* Buenos Aires: Fundación Argentina y el Mundo.

Genovesi, Luis Mariano, and Jorge Kors. 2005. "Medidas cautelares." In *Patentes de invención: diez años de jurisprudencia: comentarios y fallos,* edited by Jorge Kors. Buenos Aires: La Ley.

Gereffi, Gary A. 1978. "Drug Firms and Dependency in Mexico: The Case of the Steroid Hormone Industry." *International Organization* 32 (1): 237–86.

Gereffi, Gary A. 1983. *The Pharmaceutical Industry and Dependency in the Third World.* Princeton University Press.

Gerschenkron, Alexander. 1962. *Economic Backwardness in Historical Perspective: A Book of Essays.* Harvard University Press.

Ghafele, Roya, and Jakob Engel. 2012. "Intellectual Property Related Development Aid: Is Supply Aligned with Demand?" MPRA Paper No. 36584, Munich Personal RePEc Archive.

Gilligan, Michael J. 1997. *Empowering Exporters: Reciprocity, Delegation, and Collective Action in American Trade Policy.* University of Michigan Press.

Godoy, Angelina. 2013. *Of Medicines and Markets: Intellectual Property and Human Rights in the Free Trade Era.* Stanford University Press.

Gold, E. Richard, and Danial K. Lam. 2003. "Balancing Trade in Patents." *The Journal of World Intellectual Property* 6 (1): 5–31.

Golob, Stephanie R. 1997. "'Making Possible What Is Necessary': Pedro Aspe, the 'Salinas Team', and the next Mexican 'Miracle'." In *Technopols: Freeing Politics and Markets in Latin America in the 1990s,* edited by Jorge I. Dominguez. Pennsylvania State University Press.

Gómez, Eduardo Jesus. 2012. "Pursuing Centralization amidst Decentralization: The Politics of Brazil's Innovative Response to HIV/AIDS." *Journal of Politics in Latin America* 3 (3): 95–126.

Gómez Violante, Amando. 2010. "Competitividad y patentes." In *Situación del sector farmacéutico en México,* edited by CESOP. México, D.F.: Centro de Estudios Sociales y de Opinión Pública, Cámara de Diputados.

Gómez-Dantés, Octavio, Veronika J. Wirtz, Michael Reich, Paulina Terrazas, and Maki Ortiz. 2012. "A New Entity for the Negotiation of Public Procurement Prices for Patented Medicines in Mexico." *Bulletin of the World Health Organization* 90: 788–92.

Gonsen, R., and J. Jasso. 2000. "The Pharmaceutical Industry." In *Developing Innovation Systems: Mexico in a Global Context,* edited by Mario Cimoli. Continuum.

González García, Ginés, Catalina de la Puente, and Sonia Tarragona. 2005. *Medicamentos: salud, política y economía.* Buenos Aires: Ediciones Granica S.A.

González Luna, Santiago González. 2004. *Los medicamentos genéricos: un acierto patente.* México, D.F.: Editorial Porrúa.

González Luna, Santiago González, and Alberto Lazo Corvera. 2003. *Patentes y medicamentos genéricos: en búsqueda de un sano balance.* México, D.F.: Editorial Porrúa.

González Pier, Eduardo. 2008. "Healthy Pharmaceutical Policy." *Salud pública de México* 50 (January): S488–95.

González Pier, Eduardo, and Mariana Barraza-Lloréns. 2011. "Trabajando por la salud de la población: propuestas de política para el sector farmacéutico." México, D.F.: Fundación Mexicana para la Salud.

Gosain, Rana, and Denis Allan Daniel. 1991. "Brazil's New Draft Patent Law: The Main Features." *Patent World*, October: 42–6.

Gourevitch, Peter. 1978. "The Second Image Reversed: The International Sources of Domestic Politics." *International Organization* 32 (4): 881–912.

Gourevitch, Peter. 1986. *Politics in Hard Times: Comparative Responses to International Economic Crises.* Cornell University Press.

Grabowski, Henry. 2002. "Patents, Innovation and Access to New Pharmaceuticals." *Journal of International Economic Law* 5 (4): 849–60.

Graff, Gregory D. 2007. "Echoes of Bayh-Dole: A Survey of Intellectual Property and Technology Transfer Policies in Emerging and Developing Economies." In *Intellectual Property Management in Health and Agricultural Innovation: A Handbook of Best Practices*, edited by Anatole Krattiger. MIHR-USA.

Grangeiro, Alexandre, Luciano Teixeira, Francisco Bastos, and Paulo Teixeira. 2006. "Sustentabilidade da política de acesso a medicamentos anti-retrovirais no Brasil." *Revista de saúde pública* 40 (Supplement): 60–9.

Grillo, O. J. 1990. "Politicas publicas y la industria farmacéutica Argentina (1983–1989)." Serie informes de investigación 2. Buenos Aires: Centro Latinoamericano para el Análisis de la Democracia.

Gruber, Lloyd. 2001. "Power Politics and the Free Trade Bandwagon." *Comparative Political Studies* 34 (7): 703–41.

Gruner Kronheim, Enrique. 1991. "Pharmaceuticals: Mexican Perspective." In *U.S.-Mexican Industrial Integration: The Road to Free Trade*, edited by Sidney Weintraub, Luis Rubio, Luis Rubio-Freidberg, and Alan Dennis Jones. Westview Press.

Grzymala-Busse, A. 2011. "Time Will Tell? Temporality and the Analysis of Causal Mechanisms and Processes." *Comparative Political Studies* 44 (9): 1267–97.

GTPI/Rebrip. 2011. "Os interesses privados e a conivência do estado: o caso das patentes farmacêuticas e a atuação da ANVISA." Rio de Janeiro: Grupo de Trabalho sobre Propriedade Intelectual da Rede Brasileira pela Integração dos Povos.

GTPI/Rebrip. 2013. "A Anuência Prévia da Anvisa sobrevive: impactos políticos da nova regulamentação." Rio de Janeiro: Grupo de Trabalho sobre Propriedade Intelectual da Rede Brasileira pela Integração dos Povos.

Guerrero Castro, Rodrigo A. 2012. *La industria farmacéutica mexicana y el TLCAN.* Editorial Académica Española.

Guimarães, Eduardo Ribas De Biase. 2008. "Direito à saúde e propriedade intelectual de medicamentos no Brasil: a Anuência Prévia da Agência Nacional de Vigilância Sanitária." Master's Thesis, Universidade do Estado do Rio de Janeiro.

Guimarães, Eduardo Ribas De Biase, and Marilena Corrêa. 2012. "Propriedade intelectual e saúde pública: o papel da Agência Nacional de Vigilância Sanitária no patenteamento farmacêutico no Brasil." *Revista eletrônica de comunicação, informação & inovação em saúde* 6 (3).

Guimarães, Reinaldo, Leonor Maria Pacheco Santos, Antonia Angulo-Tuesta, and Suzanne Jacob Serruya. 2006. "Defining and Implementing a National Policy for

Science, Technology, and Innovation in Health: Lessons from the Brazilian Experience." *Cadernos de Saúde Pública* 22 (9).

Guzmán, Alenka. 2014. *Propiedad intelectual y capacidades de innovación en la industria farmacéutica de Argentina, Brasil y México.* Mexico, D.F.: Gedisa.

Gwynn. 1988. "Mexico." In *Intellectual Property Rights: Global Consensus, Global Conflict?*, edited by R. Michael Gadbaw and Timothy J. Richards. Westview Press.

Haggart, Blayne. 2014. *Copyfight: The Global Politics of Digital Copyright Reform.* University of Toronto Press.

Hancke, Bob, ed. 2008. *Beyond Varieties of Capitalism: Conflict, Contradictions, and Complementarities in the European Economy.* Oxford University Press.

Harrison, Christopher Scott. 2004. *The Politics of the International Pricing of Prescription Drugs.* Greenwood Publishing Group.

Hasenclever, Lia, Rodrigo Lopes, Gabriela Costa Chaves, Renata Reis, and Marcela Fogaça Vieira. 2010. "O instituto de patentes pipeline e o acesso a medicamentos: aspectos econômicos e jurídicos deletérios à economia da saúde." *Revista de direito sanitário* 11 (2): 164–88.

Hasenclever, Lia, Maria Auxiliadora Oliveira, Julia Paranhos, and Gabriela Costa Chaves, eds. 2016. *Desafios de operação e desenvolvimento do Complexo Industrial da Saúde.* Rio de Janeiro: E-papers Editoriais.

Haunss, Sebastian, and Kenneth C. Shadlen, eds. 2009. *Politics of Intellectual Property: Contestation over the Ownership, Use, and Control of Knowledge and Information.* Edward Elgar Publishing.

Hayden, Cori. 2007. "A Generic Solution? Pharmaceuticals and the Politics of the Similar in Mexico." *Current Anthropology* 48 (4): 475–95.

Hayden, Cori. 2008. "Vinculaciones: Pharmaceutical Politics and Science." In *A Companion to Latin American Anthropology*, edited by Deborah Poole. Blackwell.

Hayden, Cori. 2011. "No Patent, No Generic: Pharmaceutical Access and the Politics of the Copy." In *Making and Unmaking Intellectual Property: Creative Production in Legal and Cultural Perspective*, edited by Mario Biagioli, Peter Jaszi, and Martha Woodmansee. University of Chicago Press.

Hemphill, C. Scott, and Bhaven N. Sampat. 2011. "When Do Generics Challenge Drug Patents?" *Journal of Empirical Legal Studies* 8 (4): 613–49.

Hemphill, C. Scott, and Bhaven N. Sampat. 2012. "Evergreening, Patent Challenges, and Effective Market Life in Pharmaceuticals." *Journal of Health Economics* 31 (2): 327–39.

Henisz, Witold J. 2002. "Henisz, W.J., 2002. The Political Constraint Index (POLCON) Dataset." The Wharton School, University of Pennsylvania (http://www-management.wharton.upenn.edu/henisz/).

Hilty, Reto M., and Kung-Chung Liu. 2014. *Compulsory Licensing: Practical Experiences and Ways Forward.* Springer.

Hirschman, Albert O. 1945. *National Power and the Structure of Foreign Trade.* University of California Press.

Hirst, Monica. 1998. "Strategic Coercion, Democracy, and Free Markets in Latin America." In *Strategic Coercion: Concepts and Cases*, edited by Lawrence Freedman. Oxford University Press.

Hitchings, A. W., E. H. Baker, and T. K. Khong. 2012. "Making Medicines Evergreen." *BMJ* 345 (nov29 3): e7941–e7941.

Ho, Cynthia. 2011. *Access to Medicine in the Global Economy: International Agreements on Patents and Related Rights.* Oxford University Press.

Hochstetler, Kathryn, and Alfred P. Montero. 2013. "The Renewed Developmental State: The National Development Bank and the Brazil Model." *Journal of Development Studies* 49 (11): 1484–99.

Hoen, Ellen 't. 2002. "TRIPS, Pharmaceutical Patents, and Access to Essential Medicines: A Long Way from Seattle to Doha." *Chicago Journal of International Law* 3 (1): 27–46.

Homedes, Núria, and Antonio Ugalde. 2006. "Improving Access to Pharmaceuticals in Brazil and Argentina." *Health Policy and Planning* 21 (2): 123–31.

Horner, Rory. 2014a. "The Impact of Patents on Innovation, Technology Transfer and Health: A Pre- and Post-TRIPs Analysis of India's Pharmaceutical Industry." *New Political Economy* 19 (3): 384–406.

Horner, Rory. 2014b. "Strategic Decoupling, Recoupling and Global Production Networks: India's Pharmaceutical Industry." *Journal of Economic Geography* 14 (6): 1117–1140.

Houtzager, Peter P. 1998. "State and Unions in the Transformation of the Brazilian Countryside, 1964–1979." *Latin American Research Review* 33 (2): 103–42.

Howard, Leighton. 2007. "Use of Patents in Drug Lifecycle Management." *Journal of Generic Medicines: The Business Journal for the Generic Medicines Sector* 4 (3): 230–6.

Hudson, John, and Alexandru Minea. 2013. "Innovation, Intellectual Property Rights, and Economic Development: A Unified Empirical Investigation." *World Development* 46 (6): 66–78.

Iacomini, Vanessa, ed. 2007. *Propriedade intelectual e biotecnologia.* Curitiba: Jurua Editora.

IFPMA. 1995. "GATT, TRIPs and the Pharmaceutical Industry: A Review." *Patent World* 75 (September): 29–33.

Immergut, Ellen M. 2008. "Institutional Constraints on Policy." In *The Oxford Handbook of Public Policy,* edited by Michael Moran, Martin Rein, and Robert E. Goodin. Oxford University Press.

INTERFARMA. 1993a. "Aspectos relevantes para uma boa Lei de Propriedade Industrial." São Paulo: Associação da Indústria Farmacêutica de Pesquisa.

INTERFARMA. 1993b. "O direito à propriedade industrial no Brasil: quem tem medo das patentes?" São Paulo: Associação da Indústria Farmacêutica de Pesquisa.

INTERFARMA. 1993c. "Patentes farmacêuticas: modificações sugeridas ao PLC 115/93 para atrair investimentos privados em pesquisas." São Paulo: Associação da Indústria Farmacêutica de Pesquisa.

INTERFARMA. 1993d. "Patentes farmacêuticas: os cinco pontos fundamentais a corrigir no PLC 115/93 que dispõe sobre propriedade industrial." São Paulo: Associação da Indústria Farmacêutica de Pesquisa.

INTERFARMA. 1995. "Patentes farmacêuticas: modifacações sugeridas ao PLC 115/93 para atrair investimentos privados em pesquisas. Edicao revista, ampliada e atualizada." São Paulo: Associação da Indústria Farmacêutica de Pesquisa.

International Trade Administration. 2006. "Drugs and Pharmaceuticals: Mexico." Industry Sector Analysis. Washington, DC: Department of Commerce.

Irigoyen, Alberto. 2006. "Hacia una nueva ley de protección de la propiedad intellectual: el caso de la industria farmacéutica argentina." PhD Dissertation, Universidad Torcuato di Tella.

Jacoby, Wade. 2006. "Inspiration, Coalition, and Substitution: External Influences on Postcommunist Transformations." *World Politics* 58 (4): 623–51.

Jaffe, Adam B., and Josh Lerner. 2004. *Innovation and Its Discontents: How Our Broken Patent System Is Endangering Innovation and Progress, and What to Do About It.* Princeton University Press.

Jalife Daher, Mauricio. 2009. "Análisis de aspectos legales y comerciales de las patentes de medicamentos en México." In *Textos de la nueva cultura de la propiedad intelectual,* edited by Manuel Becerra Ramírez. Mexico, D.F.: Instituto de Investigaciones Jurídicas.

Jauregui, Lisandro Luis. 2003. *La constitución nacional y la participación del poder legislativo en la formulación de la política exterior argentina.* Buenos Aires: Senado de la Nacion, Centro de Capacitación Superior.

Jones, Ivor. 2015. "Open or Closed? The Politics of Software Licensing in Argentina and Brazil." Phd Thesis, London School of Economics and Political Science (LSE).

Jones, Mark P. 1997. "Evaluating Argentina's Presidential Democracy: 1983-1995." In *Presidentialism and Democracy in Latin America,* edited by Scott Mainwaring and Matthew Soberg Shugart. Cambridge University Press.

Jones, Mark P. 2002. "Explaining the High Level of Party Discipline in the Argentine Congress." In *Legislative Politics in Latin America,* edited by Scott Morgenstern and Benito Nacif. Cambridge University Press.

Jorge, María Fabiana. 2006. "Efectos de la globalización en la industria farmacéutica en México." In *La industria farmacéutica mexicana,* edited by ANAFAM. México, D.F.: Editorial Porrúa.

Juca da Silveira e Silva, Ana Paula, and Juliana Veira Borges Vallini. 2010. "Patentes de productos y procesos farmacéuticos y la Anuência Prévia de la Agência Nacional de Vigilância Sanitária de Brasil." In *Propiedad intelectual y medicamentos,* edited by Carlos M. Correa and Sandra C. Negro. Buenos Aires: Editorial B de F.

Kaempfer, William H., James A. Lehman, and Anton D. Lowenberg. 1987. "Divestment, Investment Sanctions, and Disinvestment: An Evaluation of Anti-Apartheid Policy Instruments." *International Organization* 41 (3): 457–73.

Kalaycı, Elif, and Teoman Pamukçu. 2014. "Assessing the Drivers of R&D Activities of Firms in Developing Countries: Evidence from Turkey." *European Journal of Development Research* 26 (5): 853–69.

Kale, Dinar. 2010. "The Distinctive Patterns of Dynamic Learning and Inter-Firm Differences in the Indian Pharmaceutical Industry." *British Journal of Management* 21 (1): 223–38.

Kanavos, Panos G., and Sotiris Vandoros. 2011. "Determinants of Branded Prescription Medicine Prices in OECD Countries." *Health Economics, Policy and Law* 6 (3): 337–67.

Kapczynski, Amy. 2008. "The Access to Knowledge Mobilization and the New Politics of Intellectual Property." *The Yale Law Journal* 117 (March): 804–85.

Kapczynski, Amy. 2009. "Harmonization and Its Discontents: A Case Study of TRIPS Implementation in India's Pharmaceutical Sector." *California Law Review* 97: 1571–1649.

Kapczynski, Amy. 2013. "Engineered in India: Patent Law 2.0." *New England Journal of Medicine* 369 (22): 497–9.

Kapczynski, Amy, Chan Park, and Bhaven Sampat. 2012. "Polymorphs and Prodrugs and Salts (Oh My!): An Empirical Analysis of 'Secondary' Pharmaceutical Patents." *PLoS ONE* 7 (12): e49470.

Kapstein, Ethan B., and Joshua W. Busby. 2013. *AIDS Drugs For All: Social Movements and Market Transformations*. Cambridge University Press.

Kasahara, Yuri, and Antonio José Junqueira Botelho. 2016. "Catching up and Falling Behind: An Appraisal of Brazilian Industrial Policy in the Twenty-First Century." *European Review of Latin American and Caribbean Studies* 101: 97–109.

Katz, Jorge M. 1981. "Estadios de desarrollo e industria químicofarmacéutica." *Desarrollo económico* 21 (83): 291–320.

Katz, Jorge M. ed. 1997a. *Apertura económica y desregulación en el mercado de medicamentos: la industria farmacéutica y farmoquímica de Argentina, Brasil y México en los años 90*. Buenos Aires: Alianza Editorial.

Katz, Jorge M. 1997b. "Los países latinoamericanos con capacidad farmoquímica propria: Argentina, Brasil y México." In *Apertura económica y desregulación en el mercado de medicamentos: la industria farmacéutica y farmoquímica de Argentina, Brasil y México en los años 90*, edited by Jorge M. Katz. Buenos Aires: Alianza Editorial.

Katz, Jorge M. 2001. "Innovación farmacéutica, regulación y patentes." *Revista medicos* 4 (20): 6–7.

Katzenstein, Peter J. 1977. *Between Power and Plenty: Foreign Economic Policies of Advanced Industrial States*. University of Wisconsin Press.

Katznelson, Ira. 1997. "Structure and Configuration in Comparative Politics." In *Comparative Politics: Rationality, Culture, and Structure*, edited by Mark Irving Lichbach and Alan S. Zuckerman. Cambridge University Press.

Kaufman, Robert R. 2011. "The Political Left, the Export Boom, and the Populist Temptation." In *The Resurgence of the Latin American Left*, edited by Steven Levitsky and Kenneth M. Roberts. Johns Hopkins University Press.

Kawaura, Akihiko, and Sumner La Croix. 1995. "Japan's Shift from Process to Product Patents in the Pharmaceutical Industry: An Event Study of the Impact on Japanese Firms." *Economic Inquiry* 33 (1): 88–103.

KEI. 2014. "Recent United States Compulsory Licenses." KEI Research Note. Washington, D.C: Knowledge Ecology International.

Keohane, Robert O., and Helen V. Milner. 1996. *Internationalization and Domestic Politics*. Cambridge University Press.

Kim, Yee Kyoung, Keun Lee, Walter G. Park, and Kineung Choo. 2012. "Appropriate Intellectual Property Protection and Economic Growth in Countries at Different Levels of Development." *Research Policy* 41 (2): 358–75.

Kingstone, Peter R., Aline Diniz Amaral, and Jonathan Krieckhaus. 2008. "The Limits of Economic Reform in Brazil." In *Democratic Brazil Revisited*, edited by Peter R. Kingstone and Timothy J. Power. University of Pittsburgh Press.

Kirim, Arman S. 1985. "Reconsidering Patents and Economic Development: A Case Study of the Turkish Pharmaceutical Industry." *World Development* 13 (2): 219–36.

Kleinheisterkamp, Jan. 2004. "Brazil and Disputes with Foreign Investors." In *Comércio internacional e desenvolvimento: uma perspectiva brasileira*, edited by R. Di Sena Jr and M.T. Costa Souza Cherem. São Paulo: Saraiva.

Klug, H. 2008. "Law, Politics, and Access to Essential Medicines in Developing Countries." *Politics & Society* 36 (2): 207–45.

Knapp, Inti. 2000. "The Software Piracy Battle in Latin America: Should the United States Pursue Its Aggressive Bilateral Trade Policy Despite the Multilateral Trips Enforcement Framework." *University of Pennsylvania Journal of International Law* 21 (1): 173.

Knaul, Felicia Marie, Eduardo González-Pier, Octavio Gómez-Dantés, David García-Junco, Héctor Arreola-Ornelas, Mariana Barraza-Lloréns, Rosa Sandoval, et al. 2012. "The Quest for Universal Health Coverage: Achieving Social Protection for All in Mexico." *The Lancet* 380 (9849): 1259–79.

Kogan, Lawrence A. 2006. "Brazil's IP Opportunism Threatens U.S. Private Property Rights." *Inter-American Law Review* 38: 1–139.

Krikorian, Gaëlle. 2009. "The Politics of Patents: Conditions of Implementation of Public Health Policy in Thailand." In *Politics of Intellectual Property: Contestation over the Ownership, Use, and Control of Knowledge and Information*, edited by Sebastian Haunss and Kenneth C. Shadlen. Edward Elgar Publishing.

Krikorian, Gaëlle, and Amy Kapczynski. 2010. *Access to Knowledge in the Age of Intellectual Property*. Zone Books.

Krikorian, Gaëlle P., and Dorota M. Szymkowiak. 2007. "Intellectual Property Rights in the Making: The Evolution of Intellectual Property Provisions in US Free Trade Agreements and Access to Medicine." *The Journal of World Intellectual Property* 10 (5): 388–418.

Kuanpoth. 2008. "Intellectual Property Protection after TRIPS: An Asian Experience." In *Interpreting and Implementing the TRIPS Agreement: Is It Fair?*, edited by Justin Malbon and Charles Lawson. Edward Elgar Publishing.

Kumar, Nagesh. 2002. "Intellectual Property Rights, Technology and Economic Development: Experiences of Asian Countries." Working Paper RIS DP #25-2002. Research and Information System for Non-Aligned and Other Developing Countries.

Kunisawa, Viviane Yumy Mitsuuchi. 2009. "Patenting Pharmaceutical Inventions on Second Medical Uses in Brazil." *The Journal of World Intellectual Property* 12 (4): 297–316.

Kyle, Margaret, and Yi Qian. 2014. "Intellectual Property Rights and Access to Innovation: Evidence from Trips." NBER Working Paper No. 20799. National Bureau of Economic Research.

Kyle, Margaret K., and Anita M. McGahan. 2012. "Investments in Pharmaceuticals Before and After TRIPS." *The Review of Economics and Statistics* 94 (4): 1157–72.

La Croix, Sumner, and Ming Liu. 2008. "Patents and Access to Essential Medicines." In *Intellectual Property, Growth and Trade, Volume 2,* edited by Keith E. Maskus. Emerald Group Publishing Limited.

La Croix, Sumner, and Ming Liu. 2009. "The Effect of GDP Growth on Pharmaceutical Patent Protection, 1945–2005." *Brussels Economic Review* 52 (3/4): 355–75.

Labaké, Juan Gabriel. 2003. El *ocaso de los dioses.* Buenos Aires: Editorial Reconquista.

Laforgia, Francesco, Fabio Montobbio, and Orsenigo. 2008. "IPRs and Technological Development in Pharmaceuticals: Who Is Patenting What in Brazil after TRIPS?" In *The Development Agenda: Global Intellectual Property and Developing Countries,* edited by Neil Weinstock Netanel. Oxford University Press.

Lake, David A. 2009. "Open Economy Politics: A Critical Review." *The Review of International Organizations* 4 (3): 219–44.

Lakoff. 2005. "Numbers: Pharmaceutical Marketing in Post-Welfare Argentina." In *Global Assemblages: Technology, Politics, and Ethics as Anthropological Problems,* edited by Aihwa Ong and Stephen J. Collier. John Wiley & Sons.

Lamoreaux, Naomi R., Daniel M. G. Raff, and Peter Temin. 1999. *Learning by Doing in Markets, Firms, and Countries.* University of Chicago Press.

Lampreia, Luis Felipe. 1995. "Projeto de Lei de Propriedade Industrial (PL115/93)." Testimony to Senate, Brazil.

Lanoszka, Anna. 2003. "The Global Politics of Intellectual Property Rights and Pharmaceutical Drug Policies in Developing Countries." *International Political Science Review* 24 (2): 181–97.

Lashman Hall, Karen. 1986. "Pharmaceuticals in the Third World: An Overview." PHN Technical Note 86-31. Population, Health and Nutrition Department, World Bank.

Laveaga, Gabriela Soto. 2009. *Jungle Laboratories: Mexican Peasants, National Projects, and the Making of the Pill.* Duke University Press.

Lawyer Monthly. 2013. "Protecting Pharmaceutical Patents: Mexico" (Interview with Rodrigo Calderón). *Lawyer Monthly,* July.

Lerner, Josh. 2000. "150 Years of Patent Protection." NBER Working Paper 7478. National Bureau of Economic Research.

Levi, Guido Carlos, and Marco Antonio A. Vitória. 2002. "Fighting Against AIDS: The Brazilian Experience." *AIDS* 16 (18): 2373–83.

Levin, Richard C., Alvin K. Klevorick, Richard R. Nelson, Sidney G. Winter, Richard Gilbert, and Zvi Griliches. 1987. "Appropriating the Returns from Industrial Research and Development." *Brookings Papers on Economic Activity* 1987 (3): 783–831.

Levis, Mirta. 2005. "Role, Perspectives and Challenges of the Generic Pharmaceutical Industry in Latin America." In *Negotiating Health: Intellectual Property and Access to Medicines,* edited by Pedro Roffe, Geoff Tansey, and David Vivas-Eugui. Earthscan.

Levis, Mirta. 2010. "La visión de la propiedad intelectual por la industria farmacéutica nacional lationamericana." In *Propiedad intelectual y medicamentos,* edited by Carlos María Correa and Sandra Cecilia Negro. Buenos Aires: Editorial B de F.

Levitsky, Steven, and Maria Victoria Murillo. 2005. "Building Castles in the Sand? The Politics of Institutional Weakness in Argentina." In *Argentine Democracy: The Politics of Institutional Weakness,* edited by Steven Levitsky and Maria Victoria Murillo. Pennsylvania State University Press.

Levitsky, Steven, and Kenneth M. Roberts. 2011. *The Resurgence of the Latin American Left.* Johns Hopkins University Press.

Levitsky, Steven, and Lucan A. Way. 2015. "Not Just What but When (and How): Comparative-Historical Approaches to Authoritarian Durability." In *Advances in Comparative-Historical Analysis,* edited by James Mahoney and Kathleen Thelen. Cambridge University Press.

Lichbach, Mark Irving, and Alan S. Zuckerman. 1997. *Comparative Politics: Rationality, Culture, and Structure.* Cambridge University Press.

Lindner, Heidi. 2010. "Propiedad industrial." In *Situación del sector farmacéutico en México,* edited by CESOP. México, D.F.: Centro de Estudios Sociales y de Opinión Pública, Cámara de Diputados.

Liu, Ming, and Sumner La Croix. 2015. "A Cross-Country Index of Intellectual Property Rights in Pharmaceutical Inventions." *Research Policy* 44 (1): 206–16.

Llanos, Mariana. 2001. "Understanding Presidential Power in Argentina: A Study of the Policy of Privatisation in the 1990s." *Journal of Latin American Studies* 33 (1): 67–99.

Löfgren, Hans. 2011. "The Trans-Pacific Partnership Agreement: A Threat to Affordable Medicines and Public Health." *Southern Med Review* 4 (2): 2–3.

Löfgren, Hans, and Owain David Williams, eds. 2013. *The New Political Economy of Pharmaceuticals: Production, Innnovation and TRIPS in the Global South.* Palgrave.

López, Andrés. 2010. "Innovation and IPR in a Catch-Up-Falling-Behind Process: The Argentine Case." In *Intellectual Property Rights, Development, and Catch-Up: An International Comparative Study,* edited by Hiroyuki Odagiri, Akira Goto, Atsushi Sunami, and Richard R. Nelson. Oxford University Press.

Lugones, Gustavo, and Diana Suárez. 2007. "National Innovation Systems in Brazil and Argentina: Key Variables and Available Evidence." In *Technological Innovation in Brazilian and Argentine Firms,* edited by João Alberto de Negri and Lenita Maria Turchi. Brasília: Instituto de Pesquisa Econômica Aplicada.

Lustig, Nora. 1992. *Mexico: The Remaking of an Economy.* Brookings Institution Press.

Lynch, Julia. 2013. "Aligning Research Goals and Sampling Procedures in Interview Research." In *Interview Research in Political Science,* edited by Layna Mosley. Cornell University Press.

Mackintosh, Maureen, Geoffrey Banda, Watu Wamae, and Paula Tibandebage. 2016. *Making Medicines in Africa: The Political Economy of Industrializing for Local Health.* Palgrave.

Mahoney, James. 2000. "Path Dependence in Historical Sociology." *Theory and Society* 29 (4): 507–48.

Mahoney, James. 2001. *The Legacies of Liberalism: Path Dependence and Political Regimes in Central America.* Johns Hopkins University Press.

Mahoney, James. 2010. "After KKV: The New Methodology of Qualitative Research." *World Politics* 61 (1): 120–47.

Mahoney, James, and Dietrich Rueschemeyer, eds. 2003. *Comparative Historical Analysis in the Social Sciences.* Cambridge University Press.

Mahoney, James, and Kathleen Thelen, eds. 2015. *Advances in Comparative-Historical Analysis.* Cambridge University Press.

Mainwaring, Scott. 1986. *The Catholic Church and Politics in Brazil, 1916-1985.* Stanford University Press.

Mainwaring, Scott, and Matthew Soberg Shugart. 1997. *Presidentialism and Democracy in Latin America*. Cambridge University Press.

Malerba, Franco, and Luigi Orsenigo. 2015. "The Evolution of the Pharmaceutical Industry." *Business History* 57 (5): 664–87.

Manger, Mark S., and Kenneth C. Shadlen. 2014. "Political Trade Dependence and North–South Trade Agreements." *International Studies Quarterly* 58 (1): 79–91.

Mani, Sunil, and Richard R. Nelson, eds. 2013. TRIPS *Compliance, National Patent Regimes and Innovation: Evidence and Experience from Developing Countries*. Edward Elgar Publishing.

Mansfield, Edwin. 1986. "Patents and Innovation: An Empirical Study." *Management Science* 32 (2): 173–81.

Mansfield, Edwin, Mark Schwartz, and Samuel Wagner. 1981. "Imitation Costs and Patents: An Empirical Study." *The Economic Journal* 91 (364): 907.

Manzetti, Luigi. 2016. "Renationalization in Argentina, 2005–2013." *Latin American Politics and Society* 58 (1): 3–28.

María y Campos, Mauricio de. 1991. "Industrial Modernization, Technological Development, and Industrial Property: Mexico vis-à-vis the Challenges of the New Technological Revolution." In *The Dynamics of North American Trade and Investment: Canada, Mexico, and the United States*, edited by Clark Winton Reynolds, Leonard Waverman, and Gerardo M. Bueno. Stanford University Press.

Marques, Ivan da Costa. 2003. "Reverse Engineering and Other Respectful Enough Accounts: Creating New Spaces of Possibility for Technological Innovation under Conditions of Global Inequality." Centre for STS Studies, Department of Information & Media Studies.

Marques, Marilia Bernardes. 1993. *Patenting Life: Foundations of the Brazil-United States Controversy*. Série Política de Saúde 13. Rio de Janeiro: Ministério de Saúde: FIOCRUZ.

Marron, Donald B., and David G. Steel. 2000. "Which Countries Protect Intellectual Property? The Case of Software Piracy." *Economic Inquiry* 38 (2): 159–74.

Martinez, Ana Paula. 2013. "Abuse of Dominance: The Third Wave of Brazil's Antitrust Enforcement." *Competition Law International* 9: 169–82.

Maskus, Keith E. 2000. *Intellectual Property Rights in the Global Economy*. Institute for International Economics.

Maskus, Keith E. 2012. *Private Rights and Public Problems: The Global Economics of Intellectual Property in the 21st Century*. Peterson Institute for International Economics.

Maskus, Keith E. 2014. "The New Globalisation of Intellectual Property Rights: What's New This Time?" *Australian Economic History Review* 54 (3): 262–84.

Matthews, Duncan. 2002. *Globalising Intellectual Property Rights: The* TRIPS *Agreement*. Routledge.

Matthews, Duncan. 2011. *Intellectual Property, Human Rights and Development: The Role of NGOs and Social Movements*. Edward Elgar Publishing.

Matthews, Duncan, and Viviana Muñoz-Tellez. 2006. "Bilateral Technical Assistance and TRIPS: The United States, Japan and the European Communities in Comparative Perspective." *The Journal of World Intellectual Property* 9 (6): 629–53.

May, Christopher. 2000. *The Global Political Economy of Intellectual Property Rights: The New Enclosures?* Routledge.

May, Christopher. 2004. "Capacity Building and the (Re)production of Intellectual Property Rights." *Third World Quarterly* 25 (5): 821–37.

May, Christopher. 2007a. "The Hypocrisy of Forgetfulness: The Contemporary Significance of Early Innovations in Intellectual Property." *Review of International Political Economy* 14 (1): 1–25.

May, Christopher. 2007b. "The World Intellectual Property Organization and the Development Agenda." *Global Governance* 13 (2): 161–70.

May, Christopher. 2013. *The Global Political Economy of Intellectual Property Rights: The New Enclosures?* Second Edition. Routledge.

May, Christopher, and Susan K. Sell. 2006. *Intellectual Property Rights: A Critical History*. Boulder: Lynne Rienner Publishers.

Mazzoleni, Roberto, and Richard R. Nelson. 1998. "Economic Theories about the Benefits and Costs of Patents." *Journal of Economic Issues* 32 (4): 1031–52.

Mazzoleni, Roberto, and Luciano Martins Costa Póvoa. 2010. "Accumulation of Technological Capabilities and Economic Development: Did Brazil's IPR Regime Matter?" In *Intellectual Property Rights, Development, and Catch-Up: An International Comparative Study*, edited by Hiroyuki Odagiri, Akira Goto, Atsushi Sunami, and Richard R. Nelson. Oxford University Press.

McManis, and Jorge L. Contreras. 2014. "Compulsory Licensing of Intellectual Property: A Viable Policy Lever for Promoting Access to Critical Technologies?" In *TRIPS and Developing Countries: Towards a New IP World Order?*, edited by Gustavo Ghidini, Rudolph J. R. Peritz, and Marco Ricolfi. Edward Elgar Publishing.

MEI. 2015. *O estado da inovação no Brasil*. Brasília: Confederação Nacional da Indústria.

Mercurio, Bryan Christopher. 2006. "TRIPS-Plus Provisions in FTAs: Recent Trends." SSRN Scholarly Paper ID 947767. Social Science Research Network.

Merrien, François-Xavier. 2013. "Social Protection as Development Policy: A New International Agenda for Action." *Revue internationale de politique de développement* (2): 89–106.

Meyerhof Salama, Bruno, and Daniel Benoliel. 2010. "Pharmaceutical Patent Bargains: The Brazilian Experience." *Cardozo Journal of International and Comparative Law* 18 (3): 633–82.

Ministério de Saúde. 2008. "Dispõe sobre alteração do Artigo 229-C, da Lei 9.279, de 14.05.1996, e dá outras providências." Nota Técnica. Brasília: Ministério da Saúde.

Ministry of Health. 2005. "The Sustainability of Universal Access to Antiretroviral Medicines in Brazil." Brasília: Ministério da Saúde.

Mitre, Maya, and Bruno P. W. Reis. 2014. "Science and Politics in the Regulation of Genetically Modified Organisms in Brazil." *Review of Policy Research* 31 (2): 125–47.

Moïse, Pierre, and Elizabeth Docteur. 2007. "Pharmaceutical Pricing and Reimbursement Policies in Mexico." 25. OECD Health Working Papers. Paris: Organisation for Economic Co-operation and Development.

Molina-Salazar, Raúl E., Eloy González-Marín, and Carolina Carbajal-de Nova. 2008. "Competencia y precios en el mercado farmacéutico mexicano." *Salud pública de México* 50 (January): S496–503.

Moncayo von Hase, Andrés, and Guillermo R. Moncayo. 2006. "Las medidas precautorias y las patentes de invención a la luz de la reforma introducida por la Ley 25.859: un complejo caso de interacción entre el derecho internacional y el derecho interno." In *Medidas cautelares en el régimen de patentes*, edited by Carlos María Correa. Buenos Aires: Lexis Nexis.

Montero, Alfred P. 2014. "Why Developmentalism Persists in Democratic Brazil." Brazilian Studies Association, London, August 20–23, 2014.

Moreno-Brid, Juan Carlos, and Jaime Ros. 2009. *Development and Growth in the Mexican Economy: A Historical Perspective*. Oxford University Press.

Morero, Hernan Alejandro. 2013. "Internacionalizacion y Sistema Nacional de Innovacion argentino: una perspectiva de tramas productivas. Los casos automotriz y siderurgico." Munich Personal RePEc Archive.

Morgenstern, Scott, and Benito Nacif. 2002. *Legislative Politics in Latin America*. Cambridge University Press.

Morin, Jean-Frederic. 2006. "Tripping up TRIPS Debates: IP and Health in Bilateral Agreements." *International Journal of Intellectual Property Management* 1 (1): 37–53.

Morin, Jean-Frédéric. 2009. "Multilateralizing TRIPs-Plus Agreements: Is the US Strategy a Failure?" *The Journal of World Intellectual Property* 12 (3): 175–97.

Morin, Jean-Frédéric. 2014. "Paradigm Shift in the Global IP Regime: The Agency of Academics." *Review of International Political Economy* 21 (2): 275–309.

Morin, Jean-Frederic, and Edward Richard Gold. 2014. "An Integrated Model of Legal Transplantation: The Diffusion of Intellectual Property Law in Developing Countries." *International Studies Quarterly* 58 (4): 781–92.

Mosley, Layna. 2003. *Global Capital and National Governments*. Cambridge University Press.

Mosley, Layna, ed. 2013. *Interview Research in Political Science*. Cornell University Press.

Mosley, Paul. 2001. "Attacking Poverty and the 'post-Washington Consensus'" *Journal of International Development* 13 (3): 307–13.

MPP. n.d. "Patent Status Database." Geneva: Medicines Patent Pool.

MSF. various years. "Untangling the Web of Antiretroviral Price Reductions." Medecins Sans Frontieres.

Mueller, Lisa L, and Silvia Moreira Taketsuma Costa. 2014. "Should ANVISA Be Permitted to Reject Pharmaceutical Patent Applications in Brazil?" *Expert Opinion on Therapeutic Patents* 24 (1): 1–4.

Murillo, M. Victoria. 2002. "Political Bias in Policy Convergence: Privatization Choices in Latin America." *World Politics* 54 (4): 462–93.

Murillo, Maria Victoria. 2009. *Political Competition, Partisanship, and Policy Making in Latin American Public Utilities*. Cambridge University Press.

Murillo, Maria Victoria, Virginia Oliveros, and Milan Vaishnav. 2011. "Economic Constraints and Presidential Agency." In *The Resurgence of the Latin American Left*, edited by Steven Levitsky and Kenneth M. Roberts. Johns Hopkins University Press.

Murphy, Tomás Eric. 1997. "Un análisis económico del proceso de formación de leyes: El caso de la ley de patentes en la Argentina." Departamento de Economía, Universidad de San Andres.

Musungu, Sisule F., and Cecilia Oh. 2006. "The Use of Flexibilities in TRIPS by Developing Countries: Can They Promote Access to Medicines?" Geneva: South Centre and World Health Organization.

Muzaka, Valbona. 2011a. "Linkages, Contests and Overlaps in the Global Intellectual Property Rights Regime." *European Journal of International Relations* 17 (4): 755–76.

Muzaka, Valbona. 2011b. *The Politics of Intellectual Property Rights and Access to Medicines*. Palgrave.

Muzaka, Valbona. 2017, forthcoming. "Interrupted Constructions: The Brazilian Health-Industrial Complex in Historical Perspective." *Latin American Perspectives*.

Nadal, Alejandro. 1995. "Harnessing the Politics of Science and Technology Policy in Mexico." In *The Politics of Technology in Latin America*, edited by Maria Inês Bastos and Charles Cooper. Routledge.

Negri, João Alberto de. 2008. *Políticas de incentivo à inovação tecnológica no Brasil*. Brasília: Instituto de Pesquisa Econômica Aplicada.

Negri, João Alberto de, Bruno César Araújo, and Sérvulo Vicente Moreira, eds. 2009. *Technological Innovation in Brazilian and Mexican Firms*. Brasília: Instituto de Pesquisa Econômica Aplicada.

Negri, João Alberto de, and Lenita Maria Turchi, eds. 2007. *Technological Innovation in Brazilian and Argentine Firms*. Brasília: Instituto de Pesquisa Econômica Aplicada.

Negro, Sandra Cecilia. 2006. "Organización Mundial de Comercio y solución mutuamente convenida: el caso 'Argentina-patentes'." In *Medidas cautelares en el régimen de patentes*, edited by Carlos María Correa. Buenos Aires: Lexis Nexis.

Newell, Peter. 2008. "Trade and Biotechnology in Latin America: Democratization, Contestation and the Politics of Mobilization." *Journal of Agrarian Change* 8 (2–3): 345–76.

Nogués, Julio J. 1990. *Patents and Pharmaceutical Drugs: Understanding the Pressures on Developing Countries*. Policy, Research, and External Affairs Working Paper WPS502. Washington, D.C.: World Bank.

Nogués, Julio J. 1993. "Social Costs and Benefits of Introducing Patent Protection for Pharmaceutical Drugs in Developing Countries." *The Developing Economies* 31 (1): 24–53.

Noland, Marcus. 1997. "Chasing Phantoms: The Political Economy of USTR." *International Organization* 51 (3): 365–87.

Nunn, Amy. 2009. *The Politics and History of AIDS Treatment in Brazil*. Springer.

Nunn, Amy S., Elize Massard da Fonseca, Francisco I. Bastos, Sofia Gruskin, and Joshua A Salomon. 2007. "Evolution of Antiretroviral Drug Costs in Brazil in the Context of Free and Universal Access to AIDS Treatment." *PLoS Med* 4 (11): e305.

Nunn, Amy S., Elize Massard da Fonseca, and Sofia Gruskin. 2009. "Changing Global Essential Medicines Norms to Improve Access to AIDS Treatment: Lessons from Brazil." *Global Public Health* 4 (2): 131–49.

O'Donnell, Guillermo A. 1994. "Delegative Democracy." *Journal of Democracy* 5 (1): 55–69.

Octaviani, Alessandro. 2010. "Biotechnology in Brazil: Promoting Open Innovation." In *Access to Knowledge in Brazil: New Research on Intellectual Property, Innovation and Development*, edited by Lea Shaver. Bloomsbury Publishing.

Odagiri, Hiroyuki, Akira Goto, Atsushi Sunami, and Richard R. Nelson, eds. 2010. *Intellectual Property Rights, Development, and Catch-Up: An International Comparative Study.* Oxford University Press.

OECD. 2009. *OECD Reviews of Innovation Policy: Mexico.* Paris: Organisation for Economic Co-operation and Development.

OECD. 2013. *Supporting Investment in Knowledge Capital, Growth and Innovation.* Paris: Organisation for Economic Co-operation and Development.

OECD. 2014. "Pharmaceutical Spending Database." OECD (goo.gl/n4o5BY)

Okedjii, Ruth L. 2004. "Back to Bilateralism? Pendulum Swings in International Intellectual Property Protection." *University of Ottawa Law and Technology Journal* 1 (1–2): 125–47.

Oliveira, Maria Auxiliadora, Gabriela Costa Chaves, and Ruth Epsztejn. 2004. "Brazilian Intellectual Property Legislation." In *Intellectual Property in the Context of the WTO TRIPS Agreement: Challenges for Public Health,* edited by Jorge Antonio Zepeda Bermudez and Maria Auxiliadora Oliveira. Rio de Janeiro: FIOCRUZ.

Oliveira, Maria Auxiliadora, Jorge Antonio Zepeda Bermudez, Gabriela Costa Chaves, and German Velasquez. 2004. "Has the Implementation of the TRIPS Agreement in Latin America and the Caribbean Produced Intellectual Property Legislation That Favours Public Health?" *Bulletin of the World Health Organization* 82 (11): 815–21.

Olsen, Tricia D., and Aseema Sinha. 2013. "Linkage Politics and the Persistence of National Policy Autonomy in Emerging Powers: Patents, Profits, and Patients in the Context of TRIPS Compliance." *Business and Politics* 15 (3): 323–56.

Ordover, Janusz A. 1991. "A Patent System for Both Diffusion and Exclusion." *The Journal of Economic Perspectives* 5 (1): 43–60.

Orsi, Fabienne, and Benjamin Coriat. 2006. "The New Role and Status of Intellectual Property Rights in Contemporary Capitalism." *Competition & Change* 10 (2): 162–79.

Ortiz Mena, Antonio. 2004. "Mexico's Trade Policy: Improvisation and Vision." In *The Strategic Dynamics of Latin American Trade,* edited by Vinod K. Aggarwal, Ralph H. Espach, and Joseph S. Tulchin. Stanford University Press.

OTA. 1992. *Biotechnology in a Global Economy.* Washington, D.C.: Office of Technology Assessment.

Otamendi, Jorge. 2004. "La reforma a la Ley de Patentes de Invención y Modelos de Utilidad: tan mala como innecesaria. Referencia a La Ley 25.859 publicada en el B.O. el 14/1/2004." *La Ley,* no. 1117.

Paim, Jairnilson, Claudia Travassos, Celia Almeida, Ligia Bahia, and James Macinko. 2011. "The Brazilian Health System: History, Advances, and Challenges." *The Lancet* 377 (9779): 1778–97.

Paine, Lynn Sharp, and Michael A. Santoro. 1992. "Pfizer: Global Protection of Intellectual Property." Harvard Business School Case 392-073.

Panadeiros, Mónica. 1991. "Patentamiento en la industria farmacéutica argentina." *Derechos intelectuales* 5: 53–61.

Panadeiros, Mónica. 2002. "Nuevas estrategias competitivas en la industria farmacéutica argentina y reconocimiento de la propiedad intelectual." FIEL Working Paper 74. Buenos Aires: Fundación de Investigaciones Económicas Latinoamericanas.

Paranhos, Julia. 2012. *Interação entre empresas e instituições de ciência e tecnologia: o caso do sistema farmacêutico de inovação brasileiro*. Rio de Janeiro: EdUERJ.

Pardo, Dámaso. 2003. "Argentine Contradiction: Amendments to the Patent Act in Argentina." *Patent World* 154 (July/August): 26–30.

Park, Walter G. 2008. "International Patent Protection: 1960–2005." *Research Policy* 37 (4): 761–6.

Pechman, Robert J. 1998. "Seeking Multilateral Protection for Intellectual Property: The United States 'TRIPs' over Special 301." *Minnesota Journal of Global Trade* 7 (1): 179–210.

Pemberton, Gretchen A., and Mariano Soni. 1992. "Mexico's 1991 Industrial Property Law." *Cornell International Law Journal* 25 (1): 103–130.

Pereira, Carlos, Shane P. Singh, and Bernardo Mueller. 2011. "Political Institutions, Policymaking, and Policy Stability in Latin America." *Latin American Politics and Society* 53 (1): 59–89.

Peterson, Kristin. 2012. "Intellectual Property Designs: Drugs, Governance, and Nigerian (Non) Compliance with the World Trade Organization." In *Rethinking Biomedicine and Governance in Africa: Contributions from Anthropology*, edited by Wenzel Geissler, Richard Rottenburg, and Julia Zenker. Bielefeld: Transcript-Verlag.

PGF. 2009. "Atribuições INPI & ANVISA." Brasília: Procuradoria-Geral Federal.

PhRMA. 1996. "Submission of the Pharmaceutical Research and Manufacturers of America for the 'Special 301' Report on Intellectual Property Barriers, 1996." Washington, D.C. Pharmaceutical Research and Manufacturers of America.

PhRMA. 1997. "Submission of the Pharmaceutical Research and Manufacturers of America for the 'Special 301' Report on Intellectual Property Barriers, 1997." Washington, D.C. Pharmaceutical Research and Manufacturers of America.

PhRMA. 1998. "Submission of the Pharmaceutical Research and Manufacturers of America for the 'Special 301' Report on Intellectual Property Barriers, 1998." Washington, D.C. Pharmaceutical Research and Manufacturers of America.

PhRMA. 2000. "Submission of the Pharmaceutical Research and Manufacturers of America for the 'Special 301' Report on Intellectual Property Barriers, 2000." Washington, D.C. Pharmaceutical Research and Manufacturers of America.

PhRMA. 2003. "Submission of the Pharmaceutical Research and Manufacturers of America for the 'Special 301' Report on Intellectual Property Barriers, 2003." Washington, D.C. Pharmaceutical Research and Manufacturers of America.

PhRMA. 2009. "Submission of the Pharmaceutical Research and Manufacturers of America for the 'Special 301' Report on Intellectual Property Barriers, 2009." Washington, D.C. Pharmaceutical Research and Manufacturers of America.

Pierson, Paul. 1993. "When Effect Becomes Cause: Policy Feedback and Political Change." *World Politics* 45 (4): 595–628.

Pierson, Paul. 2000. "Increasing Returns, Path Dependence, and the Study of Politics." *American Political Science Review* 94 (2): 251–67.

Pierson, Paul. 2003. "Big, Slow-Moving, and…Invisible: Macro-Social Processes in the Study of Comparative Politics." In *Comparative Historical Analysis in the Social Sciences*, edited by James Mahoney and Dietrich Rueschemeyer. Cambridge University Press.

Pierson, Paul. 2004. *Politics in Time: History, Institutions, and Social Analysis*. Princeton University Press.

PMA. 1989. "Submission of the Pharmaceutical Manufacturers Associaton, Special 301 Review." Washington, D.C. Pharmaceutical Manufacturers Association.

PMA. 1991. "Submission of the Pharmaceutical Manufacturers Associaton, Special 301 Review." Washington, D.C. Pharmaceutical Manufacturers Association.

PMA. 1992. "Submission of the Pharmaceutical Manufacturers Associaton: Identification of Priority Foreign Countries, Priority Watch, and Watch Countries." Washington, D.C. Pharmaceutical Manufacturers Association.

PMA. 1993. "Submission of the Pharmaceutical Manufacturers Associaton, Special 301 Review." Washington, D.C. Pharmaceutical Manufacturers Association.

Possas, Cristina de Albuquerque. 2008. "Compulsory Licensing in the Real World: The Case of ARV Drugs in Brazil." In *The Political Economy of HIV/AIDS in Developing Countries: TRIPS, Public Health Systems and Free Access*, edited by Benjamin Coriat. Edward Elgar Publishing.

Powell, Walter W., and Kaisa Snellman. 2004. "The Knowledge Economy." *Annual Review of Sociology* 30: 199–220.

Power, Timothy J. 1998. "Brazilian Politicians and Neoliberalism: Mapping Support for the Cardoso Reforms, 1995–1997." *Journal of Interamerican Studies and World Affairs* 40 (4): 51.

Pritchett, Lant, Michael Woolcock, and Matt Andrews. 2013. "Looking Like a State: Techniques of Persistent Failure in State Capability for Implementation." *Journal of Development Studies* 49 (1): 1–18.

Puente, Catalina de la, Sonia Tarragona, Carola Musetti, Diego Slucki, and Nicolás Rosenfeld. 2009. *Propiedad intelectual y medicamentos: el caso de la república argentina*. Serie de Estudios ISALUD N° 9. Buenos Aires: Universidad ISALUD.

Puga, Cristina. 1993. *Organizaciones empresariales y Tratado de Libre Comercio*. México, D.F: Facultad de Ciencias Políticas y Sociales.

Pugatch, Meir Perez. 2004. *The International Political Economy of Intellectual Property Rights*. Edward Elgar Publishing.

Putnam, Robert D. 1988. "Diplomacy and Domestic Politics: The Logic of Two-Level Games." *International Organization* 42 (3): 427–60.

Qian, Yi. 2007. "Do National Patent Laws Stimulate Domestic Innovation in a Global Patenting Environment? A Cross-Country Analysis of Pharmaceutical Patent Protection, 1978–2002." *Review of Economics and Statistics* 89 (3): 436–53.

Queiroz, Sérgio. 1997. "La industria farmacéutica y farmoquímica brasileña en los años 90." In *Apertura económica y desregulación en el mercado de medicamentos: la industria farmacéutica y farmoquímica de Argentina, Brasil y México en los años 90*, edited by Jorge M. Katz. Buenos Aires: Alianza Editorial.

Ramanna, Anitha. 2005. "Shifts in India's Policy on Intellectual Property: The Role of Ideas, Coercion and Changing Interests." In *Death of Patents*, edited by Peter Drahos. Lawtext Publishing Limited.

Ramani, Shyama V., and Eduardo Urias. 2015. "Access to Critical Medicines: When are Compulsory Licenses Effective in Price Negotiations?" *Social Science & Medicine* 135 (June): 75–83.

Rangel-Ortiz, Horacio. 1981. "Working of Patents and Compulsory Licensing in Mexico." *Licensing Law and Business Report* 4 (2): 121–32.

Rangel-Ortiz, Horacio. 1988. "Analisis de las reformas de 1986 a la Ley de Invenciones y Marcas de 1975 en materia de patentes." *Cuadernos del Instituto de Investigaciones Jurídicas, UNAM* 3 (9): 857–76.

Rangel-Ortiz, Horacio. 2005. "The New Law Governing Pharmaceutical Patents in Mexico." *International Review of Intellectual Property and Competition Law* 36 (4): 434–44.

Rathbun, Brian C. 2008. "Interviewing and Qualitative Field Methods: Pragmatism and Practicalities." In *The Oxford Handbook of Political Methodology*, edited by Janet M. Box-Steffensmeier, Henry E. Brady, and David Collier. Oxford University Press.

Rebouças, Mariana Martins. 1997. "A industria de química fina no Brasil: um estudo de política industrial." Phd Thesis, Instituto de Economia, Campinas: UNICAMP.

Reich, Michael. 1990. "Why the Japanese Don't Export More Pharmaceuticals: Health Policy as Industrial Policy." *California Management Review* 32 (2): 124–50.

Reichman, Jerome H. 1996. "From Free Riders to Fair Followers: Global Competition under the TRIPS Agreement." *New York University Journal of International Law & Politics* 29 (January): 11–93.

Reichman, Jerome H. 2004. "Undisclosed Clinical Trial Data Under the TRIPS Agreement and Its Progeny: A Broader Perspective." UNCTAD-ICTSD Dialogue on moving the pro-development IP agenda forward: Preserving Public Goods in Health, Education and Learning. Bellagio, 29 November–3 December 2004.

Reichman, Jerome H. 2009a. "Compulsory Licensing of Patented Pharmaceutical Inventions: Evaluating the Options." *The Journal of Law, Medicine & Ethics: A Journal of the American Society of Law, Medicine & Ethics* 37 (2): 247–63.

Reichman, Jerome H. 2009b. "Intellectual Property in the Twenty-First Century: Will the Developing Countries Lead or Follow?" *Houston Law Review* 46: 1115–85.

Reichman, Jerome, and Frederick Abbott. 2007. "The Doha Round's Public Health Legacy: Strategies for the Production and Diffusion of Patented Medicines under the Amended TRIPS Provisions." *Journal of International Economic Law* 10 (January): 921–87.

Reis, Renata. 2015. "Redes invisíveis: grupos de pressão na Câmara dos Deputados – o processo de aprovação da Lei de Propriedade Industrial brasileira." Phd Thesis, Instituto de Economia, Rio de Janeiro: Universidade Federal do Rio de Janeiro.

Reis, Roberto Silveira. 2012. "Panorama patentário dos medicamentos antirretrovirais no Brasil." Phd Thesis, Instituto de Economia, Rio de Janeiro: Universidade Federal do Rio de Janeiro.

Rich, Jessica A. J. 2013. "Grassroots Bureaucracy: Intergovernmental Relations and Popular Mobilization in Brazil's AIDS Policy Sector." *Latin American Politics and Society* 55 (2): 1–25.

Rich, Jessica A. J., and Eduardo J. Gómez. 2012. "Centralizing Decentralized Governance in Brazil." *Publius: The Journal of Federalism* 42 (4): 636–61.

Richards, Timothy J. 1988a. "Argentina." In *Intellectual Property Rights: Global Consensus, Global Conflict?*, edited by R. Michael Gadbaw and Timothy J. Richards. Westview Press.

Richards, Timothy J. 1988b. "Brazil." In *Intellectual Property Rights: Global Consensus, Global Conflict?*, edited by R. Michael Gadbaw and Timothy J. Richards. Westview Press.

Robert, Maryse. 2000. *Negotiating NAFTA: Explaining the Outcome in Culture, Textiles, Autos, and Pharmaceuticals.* University of Toronto Press.

Rodriguez-Franco, Diana. 2012. "Globalising Intellectual Property Rights: The Politics of Law and Public Health." In *Lawyers and the Construction of Transnational Justice*, edited by Yves Dezalay and Bryant Garth. Routledge.

Roemer-Mahler, Anne. 2013. "Business Conflict and Global Politics: The Pharmaceutical Industry and the Global Protection of Intellectual Property Rights." *Review of International Political Economy* 20 (1): 121–52.

Roffe, Pedro, and Christoph Spennemann. 2006. "The Impact of FTAs on Public Health Policies and TRIPS Flexibilities." *International Journal of Intellectual Property Management* 1 (1–2): 75–93.

Roffe, Pedro, David Vivas-Eugui, and Gina Vea. 2007. "Maintaining Policy Space for Development: A Case Study on IP Technical Assistance in FTAs." Issue Paper 19. Geneva: International Center for Trade and Sustainable Development.

Rogowski, Ronald. 1990. *Commerce and Coalitions: How Trade Affects Domestic Political Alignments.* Princeton University Press.

Rosenberg, Barbara, Luis Bernardo Coelho Cascao, and Jose Carlos da Matta Berardo. 2012. "Antitrust Assessment of IP-Related Matters in Brazil: Recent Developments." *Competition Law International* 8: 28–33.

Rosenberg, Stephanie T. 2014. "Asserting the Primacy of Health over Patent Rights: A Comparative Study of the Processes That Led to the Use of Compulsory Licensing in Thailand and Brazil." *Developing World Bioethics* 14 (2): 83–91.

Rosina, Monica Steffen Guise, Daniel Wei Liang Wang, and Thana Cristina de Campos. 2010. "Access to Medicines: Pharmaceutical Patents and the Right to Health." In *Access to Knowledge in Brazil: New Research on Intellectual Property, Innovation and Development*, edited by Lea Shaver. Bloomsbury Publishing.

Rowat, Malcolm D. 1993. "An Assessment of Intellectual Property Protection in LDCs from Both a Legal and Economic Perspective: Case Studies of Mexico, Chile and Argentina." *The Denver Journal of International Law and Policy* 21 (2): 401–29.

Rudra, Nita. 2008. *Globalization and the Race to the Bottom in Developing Countries: Who Really Gets Hurt?* Cambridge University Press.

Russo, Giuliano, and Geoffrey Banda. 2015. "Re-Thinking Pharmaceutical Production in Africa; Insights from the Analysis of the Local Manufacturing Dynamics in Mozambique and Zimbabwe." *Studies in Comparative International Development* 50 (2): 258–81.

Ryan, Michael P. 2010. "Patent Incentives, Technology Markets, and Public–Private Bio-Medical Innovation Networks in Brazil." *World Development* 38 (8): 1082–93.

Ryan, Michael Patrick. 1998. *Knowledge Diplomacy: Global Competition and the Politics of Intellectual Property.* Brookings Institution Press.

Saiegh, Sebastián M. 2011. *Ruling by Statute: How Uncertainty and Vote Buying Shape Lawmaking.* Cambridge University Press.

Salgado, Lucia Helena, Denis B. Barbosa, and Graziela F. Zucoloto. 2012. "Study on the Anti-Competitive Enforcement of Intellectual Property (IP) Rights: Sham Litigation." Brasília: Instituto de Pesquisa Econômica Aplicada.

Salomón, Alfre. 1997. "La industria farmacéutica en tiempos de competencia." *Comercio exterior* 47 (3): 203–7.

Sampat, Bhaven N., and Frank R. Lichtenberg. 2011. "What Are The Respective Roles Of The Public And Private Sectors In Pharmaceutical Innovation?" *Health Affairs* 30 (2): 332–9.

Sampat, Bhaven N., and Kenneth C. Shadlen. 2015a. "Drug Patenting in India: Looking Back and Looking Forward." *Nature Reviews Drug Discovery* 14: 519–20.

Sampat, Bhaven N., and Kenneth C. Shadlen. 2015b. "TRIPS Implementation and Secondary Pharmaceutical Patenting in Brazil and India." *Studies in Comparative International Development* 50 (2): 228–57.

Sampat, Bhaven N., and Kenneth C. Shadlen. 2017. "Secondary Pharmaceutical Patenting: A Global Perspective." *Research Policy* 46 (3): 693–707.

Sampat, Bhaven N., Kenneth C. Shadlen, and Tahir M. Amin. 2012. "Challenges to India's Pharmaceutical Patent Laws." *Science* 337 (6093): 414–15.

Santoro, Federico M. 2000. "Innovación y sendero evolutivo en la industria farmacéutica: los casos de Argentina y España." Cadernos de Gestão Tecnológica, No. 48. São Paulo: USP.

Santos-Pinto, Cláudia Du Bocage, Nilson do Rosário Costa, and Claudia Garcia Serpa Osorio-de-Castro. 2011. "Quem acessa o programa Farmácia Popular do Brasil? aspectos do fornecimento público de medicamentos." *Ciência & saúde coletiva* 16 (6): 2963–73.

Sanz Menéndez, Luis. 2007. "Evaluación de la política de I+D e innovación de México 2001–2006." Unpublished Manuscript.

Saraiva, José Leite. 1983. "Politica nacional de medicamentos." Revista brasileira de educação médica 7 (3): 167–78.

Scherer, F.M. 2001. "The Innovation Lottery." In *Expanding the Boundaries of Intellectual Property: Innovation Policy for the Knowledge Economy*, edited by Rochelle Cooper Dreyfuss, Diane Leenheer Zimmerman, and Harry First. Oxford University Press.

Scherer, F. M., and Jayashree Watal. 2002. "Post-TRIPS Options for Access to Patented Medicines in Developing Nations." *Journal of International Economic Law* 5 (4): 913–39.

Schiff, Eric. 1971. *Industrialization without National Patents: The Netherlands, 1869–1912; Switzerland, 1850–1907.* Princeton University Press.

Schlager, Edella, and Elinor Ostrom. 1992. "Property-Rights Regimes and Natural Resources: A Conceptual Analysis." *Land Economics* 68 (3): 249–62.

Schneider, Ben Ross. 2004. *Business Politics and the State in Twentieth-Century Latin America*. Cambridge University Press.

Schüren, Verena. 2013. "What a Difference a State Makes: Pharmaceutical Innovation after the TRIPs Agreement." *Business and Politics* 15 (2): 217–243.

Scotchmer, Suzanne. 2004. *Innovation and Incentives*. MIT Press.

SECOFI. 1990. "Programa Nacional de Modernización Industrial y de Comercio Exterior, 1990–1994." *Comercio exterior* 40 (2): 164–77.

Secretaría de Salud. 2005. *Hacia una política farmacéutica integral para México.* México, D.F.: Secretaría de Salud.

Sell, Susan K. 1995. "Intellectual Property Protection and Antitrust in the Developing World: Crisis, Coercion, and Choice." *International Organization* 49 (2): 315–49.

Sell, Susan K. 1998. *Power and Ideas: North-South Politics of Intellectual Property and Antitrust.* SUNY Press.

Sell, Susan K. 2003. *Private Power, Public Law: The Globalization of Intellectual Property Rights.* Cambridge University Press.

Sell, Susan K. 2007. "TRIPS-Plus Free Trade Agreements and Access to Medicines." *Liverpool Law Review* 28 (1): 41–75.

Sell, Susan K. 2010a. "The Rise and Rule of a Trade-Based Strategy: Historical Institutionalism and the International Regulation of Intellectual Property." *Review of International Political Economy* 17 (4): 762–90.

Sell, Susan K. 2010b. "TRIPs Was Never Enough: Vertical Forum Shifting, FTAS, ACTA, and TPP." *Journal of Intellectual Property Law* 18: 447.

Sell, Susan K., and Aseem Prakash. 2004. "Using Ideas Strategically: The Contest between Business and NGO Networks in Intellectual Property Rights." *International Studies Quarterly* 48 (1): 143–75.

Senado de la Nación. 1993. *Ley de patentes y modelos de utilidad: investigación a cargo de la Comisión de Industria, Tomo 1.* Buenos Aires: Senado de la Nación, Secretaria Parlamentaria, Dirección Publicaciones.

Senado de la Nación. 1994a. *Ley de patentes y modelos de utilidad: investigación a cargo de la Comisión de Industria, Tomo 2.* Buenos Aires: Senado de la Nación, Secretaria Parlamentaria, Dirección Publicaciones.

Senado de la Nación. 1994b. *Ley de patentes y modelos de utilidad: investigación a cargo de la Comisión de Industria, Tomo 3.* Buenos Aires: Senado de la Nación, Secretaria Parlamentaria, Dirección Publicaciones.

Senado de la Nación. 1995. *Ley de patentes y modelos de utilidad: investigación a cargo de la Comisión de Industria, Tomo 4.* Buenos Aires: Senado de la Nación, Secretaria Parlamentaria, Dirección Publicaciones.

Serra, Jose. 2004. "The Political Economy of the Brazilian Struggle Against AIDS." Institute for Advanced Study.

Serrano, Omar. 2012. "Emerging Markets and Intellectual Property Rights: Comparing Brazilian, Chinese and Mexican Responses to US Demands." International Studies Association San Diego, April 1–4, 2012.

Seuba, Xavier. 2013. "Intellectual Property in Preferential Trade Agreements: What Treaties, What Content?" *The Journal of World Intellectual Property* 16 (5–6): 240–61.

Shadlen, Kenneth C. 2004a. *Democratization without Representation: The Politics of Small Industry in Mexico.* Pennsylvania State University Press.

Shadlen, Kenneth C. 2004b. "Patents and Pills, Power and Procedure: The North-South Politics of Public Health in the WTO." *Studies in Comparative International Development* 39 (3): 76–108.

Shadlen, Kenneth C. 2005. "Exchanging Development for Market Access? Deep Integration and Industrial Policy under Multilateral and Regional-Bilateral Trade Agreements." *Review of International Political Economy* 12 (5): 750–75.

Shadlen, Kenneth C. 2007. "The Political Economy of AIDS Treatment: Intellectual Property and the Transformation of Generic Supply." *International Studies Quarterly* 51 (3): 559–81.

Shadlen, Kenneth C. 2008. "Globalisation, Power and Integration: The Political Economy of Regional and Bilateral Trade Agreements in the Americas." *Journal of Development Studies* 44 (1): 1–20.

Shadlen, Kenneth C. 2009a. "Harmonization, Differentiation, and Development: The Case of Intellectual Property in the Global Trading Regime." In *Knowledge in the Development of Economies: Institutional Choices under Globalisation*, edited by Silvia Sacchetti and Roger Sugden. Edward Elgar Publishing.

Shadlen, Kenneth C. 2009b. "The Politics of Patents and Drugs in Brazil and Mexico: The Industrial Bases of Health Policies." *Comparative Politics* 42 (1): 41–58.

Shadlen, Kenneth C. 2011a. "The Rise and Fall of 'Prior Consent' in Brazil." *WIPO Journal* 3 (1): 103–12.

Shadlen, Kenneth C. 2011b. "The Political Contradictions of Incremental Innovation: Lessons from Pharmaceutical Patent Examination in Brazil." *Politics & Society* 39 (2): 143–74.

Shadlen, Kenneth C. 2012. "The Mexican Exception: Patents and Innovation Policy in a Non-Conformist and Reluctant Middle Income Country." *European Journal of Development Research* 24 (2): 300–18.

Shadlen, Kenneth C., and Elize Massard da Fonseca. 2013. "Health Policy as Industrial Policy Brazil in Comparative Perspective." *Politics & Society* 41 (4): 561–87.

Shadlen, Kenneth C., Guennif, Samira, Alenka Guzmán, and N. Lalitha. 2011. *Intellectual Property, Pharmaceuticals and Public Health: Access to Drugs in Developing Countries*. Edward Elgar Publishing.

Shadlen, Kenneth C., Andrew Schrank, and Marcus J. Kurtz. 2005. "The Political Economy of Intellectual Property Protection: The Case of Software." *International Studies Quarterly* 49 (1): 45–71.

Shaffer, Gregory. 2014. "How the WTO Shapes Regulatory Governance." *Regulation & Governance* 9 (1): 1–15.

Shaver, Lea. 2010. *Access to Knowledge in Brazil: New Research on Intellectual Property, Innovation and Development*. Bloomsbury Publishing.

Sherwood, Robert, Sidney Weintraub, Luis Rubio, Luis Rubio-Freidberg, and Alan Dennis Jones. 1991. "Pharmaceuticals: U.S. Perspective." In *U.S.-Mexican Industrial Integration: The Road to Free Trade*, edited by Sidney Weintraub, Luis Rubio, Luis Rubio-Freidberg, and Alan Dennis Jones. Westview Press.

Shugart, Matthew Soberg, and John M. Carey. 1992. *Presidents and Assemblies: Constitutional Design and Electoral Dynamics*. Cambridge University Press.

SIAPAPECO. 1993. "Patentes: onde o Brasil perde." Submission to Senate, Brazil.

Silva, Helen Miranda. 2008. "Avaliação da análise dos pedidos de patentes farmacêuticas feita pela Anvisa no cumprimento do mandato legal da anuência prévia." Master's Thesis, Escola Nacional de Saúde Pública.

Smith, Raymond A., and Patricia D. Siplon. 2006. *Drugs into Bodies: Global AIDS Treatment Activism*. Greenwood Publishing Group.

Smith, William C., Juan Pablo Luna, M. Victoria Murillo, Andrew Schrank, Evelyne Huber, John D. Stephens, Fernando Limongi, et al. 2014. "'Special Section: Political

Economy and the Future of Latin American Politics." *Latin American Politics and Society* 56 (1): 1–33.

So, Anthony D, Bhaven N Sampat, Arti K Rai, Robert Cook-Deegan, Jerome H Reichman, Robert Weissman, and Amy Kapczynski. 2008. "Is Bayh-Dole Good for Developing Countries? Lessons from the US Experience." *PLoS Biol* 6 (10): e262.

Solingen, Etel. 2009. "The Global Context of Comparative Politics." In *Comparative Politics: Rationality, Culture, and Structure*, Second Edition, edited by Mark Irving Lichbach and Alan S. Zuckerman. Cambridge University Press.

Solleiro, José Luis, López Martínez, Roberto E., Gabriela Sánchez, Yissel Inurrueta, Ana L. Sánchez, Antonia Terán, and Jorge I. Castillo. 2010. "Innovation strategies of Mexican pharmaceutical firms." *Revista CENIC: Ciencias Biológicas* 41.

Sosa, Mario Roberto. 2002. "Análisis sectorial: la industria farmacéutica." Centro de Estudios para la Producción. Buenos Aires: Ministerio de la Producción.

Stacy, Nathan E. 2004. "The Efficacy and Fairness of Current Sanctions in Effecting Stronger Patent Rights in Developing Countries." *Tulsa Journal of Comparative & International Law* 12: 263.

Sweet, Cassandra. 2013. "The Political Economy of Pharmaceutical Production in Brazil." In *The New Political Economy of Pharmaceuticals: Production, Innnovation and TRIPS in the Global South*, edited by Hans Löfgren and Owain David Williams. Palgrave.

Swift, Anne. 2006. "Discerning Manifestations of Continental Governance in the North American Pharmaceutical Industry in the Context of Intellectual Property Rights." Paper Prepared for Delivery at the 78th Annual Meeting of the Canadian Political Science Association, York University, Toronto, Ontario, June 1–3.

Szelényi, Iván. 2015. "Capitalisms after Communism." *New Left Review* 96 (November-December): 39–51.

Tachinardi, Maria Helena. 1993. *A Guerra das patentes: o conflito Brasil x EUA sobre propiedade intelectual*. São Paulo: Paz e Terra.

Tarragona, Sonia, and Catalina De la Puente. n.d. "La política nacional de medicamentos: ¿Qué se hizo? ¿Qué queda por hacer?" Unidad de Análisis Económico En Salud. Buenos Aires: Ministerio de Salud.

Teixeira, Paulo, Marco Antonio A. Vitória, and Barcarolo. 2003. "The Brazilian Experience in Providing Universal Access to Antiretroviral Therapy." In *Economics of AIDS and Access to HIV-AIDS Care in Developing Countries: Issues and Challenges*, edited by Jean-Paul Moatti. Agence nationale de recherches sur le SIDA (ANRS).

Ten Kate, Adriaan. 1992. "Trade Liberalization and Economic Stabilization in Mexico: Lessons of Experience." *World Development* 20 (5): 659–72.

Thacker, Strom C. 2000. *Big Business, the State, and Free Trade: Constructing Coalitions in Mexico*. Cambridge University Press.

Thelen, Kathleen. 1999. "Historical Institutionalism in Comparative Politics." *Annual Review of Political Science* 2 (1): 369–404.

Thelen, Kathleen. 2003. "How Institutions Evolve: Insights from Comparative-Historical Analysis." In *Comparative Historical Analysis in the Social Sciences*, edited by James Mahoney and Dietrich Rueschemeyer. Cambridge University Press.

Thelen, Kathleen, and James Mahoney. 2015. "Comparative-Historical Analysis in Contemporary Political Science." In *Advances in Comparative-Historical Analysis*, edited by James Mahoney and Kathleen Thelen. Cambridge University Press.

Thomas, Hernán. 2004. "Las políticas de ciencia y tecnología: La reflexión crítica y su relación con la dinámica innovativa local (Argentina, 1960–2003)." Technical Report. Buenos Aires: CONICET.

Tigre, Paulo Bastos. 1983. *Technology and Competition in the Brazilian Computer Industry*. Frances Pinter.

Tobar, Federico. 2008. "Economy of Generic Drugs in Latin America." *Revista panamericana de salud pública* 23 (1): 59–67.

Tobar, Federico, and Lucas Godoy Garraza. 2003. "Un vademécun necesario: alternativas en la formulación de medicamentos." *Gestión en salud* 2 (5): 32–41.

Torres Guerra, Sandra, and Juan Pablo Gutiérrez. 2009. 'Mercado farmacéutico en México: tamaño, valor y concentración'. *Revista panamericana de salud pública* 26 (1): 46–50.

Torres-Ruiz, Antonio. 2011. "HIV/AIDS and Sexual Minorities in Mexico: A Globalized Struggle for the Protection of Human Rights." *Latin American Research Review* 46 (1): 30–53.

Trout, Clinton H. 2010. "Public Price Trends for Innovator and Generic AIDS Medicines in Latin America and the Caribbean 2005–2008." Presentation at the XVIII International AIDS Conference, Vienna, Austria.

UNCTAD. 1981. *Examination of the Economic, Commercial and Developmental Aspects of Industrial Property in the Transfer of Technology to Developing Countries: Review of Recent Trends in Patents in Developing Countries*. TD/B/C.6/AC.5/3. Geneva: United Nations Conference on Trade and Development.

UNCTAD-ICTSD. 2005. *Resource Book on TRIPS and Development*. Cambridge University Press.

Urias, Eduardo. 2015. "Improving Access to HIV/AIDS Treatment in Brazil: When Are Compulsory Licenses Effective in Price Negotiations?" PhD Dissertation, Maastricht University/United Nations University.

USIS. 1995. "Direitos de Propriedade Intelectual." Submission to Senate, Brazil.

USIS. n.d. "'Medida Especial 301' da lei de comércio e proteção à propriedade intelectual dos Estados Unidos." Submission to Senate, Brazil.

USITC. 1990. "Review of Trade and Invesetment Liberalization Measures by Mexico and Prospects for Future United States-Mexican Relations." USITC Publication 2275. Washington, DC: United States International Trade Commission.

USTR. 1989a. "1989 Special 301 Report." Washington, D.C: United States Trade Representative.

USTR. 1989b. "U.S. and Argentina Engage in Productive Talks on Intellectual Property Protection." Press Release 89–50. Washington, D.C: United States Trade Representative.

USTR. 1990. "Brazilian Legislation to Protect Intellectual Property Prompts U.S. to Lift Sanctions." Press Release 90–40. Washington, D.C: United States Trade Representative.

USTR. 1995. "1995 Special 301 Report." Washington, D.C: United States Trade Representative. Washington, D.C: United States Trade Representative.

USTR. 2000. "2000 Special 301 Report." Washington, D.C: United States Trade Representative.

USTR. 2001. "2001 Special 301 Report." Washington, D.C: United States Trade Representative.

USTR. 2006. "2006 Special 301 Report." Washington, D.C: United States Trade Representative. Washington, D.C: United States Trade Representative.

Vaitsman, Jeni, Andre Cunha Tavares, Ivan Bonfim Silva, Geraldo Lucchesi, and Andreia Fernandes Cabral. 1991. *Representacao de interesses privados e formulacao de politicas: o caso da industria farmaceutica.* Washington, DC: Organizacion Panamericana de la Salud.

Varella, Marcelo Dias, and Márcia Cristina Pereira. 1996. "Propriedade intelectual sobre produtos da biotecnologia." *Revista de informação legislativa* 33 (130): 209–17.

Vargas, José Israel. 1995. "Ciência, tecnologia e propridade industrial." Testimony to Senate, Brazil.

Vázquez, Adolfo R. 1991. "Patentes farmacéuticas: derecho argentino y comparado." *Derechos intelectuales* 5: 37–51.

Veras, Juliana. 2014. "Making Tenofovir Accessible In the Brazilian Public Health System: Patent Conflicts and Generic Production." *Developing World Bioethics* 14 (2): 92–100.

Vicente, Wendy. 1998. "A Questionable Victory for Coerced Argentine Pharmaceutical Patent Legislation." *University of Pennsylvania Journal of International Law* 19 (4): 1101.

Villareal Gonda, Roberto. 1991. "La nueva ley mexicana en materia de propiedad industrial." *Comercio exterior* 41 (11): 1057–65.

Villavicencio, Daniel. 2009. "Recent Changes in Science and Technology Policy in Mexico: Innovation Incentives." In *Knowledge Generation and Protection: Intellectual Property, Innovation and Economic Development*, edited by Jorge Mario Martínez-Piva. Springer.

Wainer, Andrés, and Martín Schorr. 2014. "Concentración y extranjerización del capital en la Argentina reciente: ¿Mayor autonomía nacional o incremento de la dependencia?" *Latin American Research Review* 49 (3): 103–25.

Wallerstein, Mitchel B., Mary Ellen Mogee, and Roberta A. Schoen. 1993. *Global Dimensions of Intellectual Property Rights in Science and Technology.* National Academy Press.

Walter, Andrew. 2008. *Governing Finance: East Asia's Adoption of International Standards.* Cornell University Press.

Walter, Andrew. 2014. "The Political Economy of Post-Crisis Regulatory Response: Why Does 'Over-Compliance' Vary?" Unpublished manuscript. University of Melbourne.

Waning, Brenda, Ellen Diedrichsen, and Suerie Moon. 2010. "A Lifeline to Treatment: The Role of Indian Generic Manufacturers in Supplying Antiretroviral Medicines to Developing Countries." *Journal of the International AIDS Society* 13: 35.

Ward, Peter M. 1986. *Welfare Politics in Mexico: Papering over the Cracks.* Unwin Hyman.

Watal, Jayashree. 1999. "Implementing the TRIPS Agreement on Patents: Optimal Legislative Strategies for Developing Countries." In *Competitive Strategies for the Protection of Intellectual Property*, edited by Owen Lippert. The Fraser Institute.

Watal, Jayashree. 2000. "Pharmaceutical Patents, Prices and Welfare Losses: Policy Options for India under the WTO TRIPS Agreement." *World Economy* 23 (5): 733–52.

Watal, Jayashree. 2001. *Intellectual Property Rights in the WTO and Developing Contries*. Kluwer Law International.

Watal, Jayashree. 2011. "From Punta Del Este to Doha and Beyond: Lessons from the TRIPS Negotiating Processes." *WIPO Journal* 3 (1): 24–35.

Weir, Margaret. 2006. "When Does Politics Create Policy? The Organizational Politics of Change." In *Rethinking Political Institutions: The Art of the State*, edited by Ian Shapiro, Stephen Skowronek, and Daniel Galvin. New York University Press.

Weldon, Jeffrey. 1997. "The Political Sources of Presidencialismo in Mexico." In *Presidentialism and Democracy in Latin America*, edited by Scott Mainwaring and Matthew Soberg Shugart. Cambridge University Press.

Wellhausen, Rachel L. 2014. *The Shield of Nationality: When Governments Break Contracts with Foreign Firms*. Cambridge University Press.

White, Eduardo. 1983. "Cooperation among National Drug Manufacturers: Asociación Latinoamericana de Industrias Farmacéuticas (ALIFAR)." *World Development* 11 (3): 271–9.

Whiting, Van R. 1992. *The Political Economy of Foreign Investment in Mexico: Nationalism, Liberalism, and Constraints on Choice*. Johns Hopkins University Press.

WHO. 1988. *The World Drug Situation*. Geneva: World Health Organization.

WHO. 1997. *The Uruguay Round and Drugs*. Geneva: World Health Organization.

Wionczek, Miguel S. 1983. "Research and Development in Pharmaceuticals: Mexico." *World Development* 11 (3): 243–50.

Wise, Timothy A., Hilda Salazar, and Laura Carlsen. 2003. *Confronting Globalization: Economic Integration and Popular Resistance in Mexico*. Kumarian Press.

Witthaus, Mónica. 2003. "Patentes de segundo uso." *Actas de derecho industrial y derecho de autor* 24: 385–96.

Woll, Cornelia. 2008. *Firm Interests: How Governments Shape Business Lobbying on Global Trade*. Cornell University Press.

Wylde, Christopher. 2011. "State, Society and Markets in Argentina: The Political Economy of Neodesarrollismo under Néstor Kirchner, 2003–2007." *Bulletin of Latin American Research* 30 (4): 436–52.

Yamauti, Sueli Miyuki, Silvio Barberato-Filho, and Luciane Cruz Lopes. 2015. "Elenco de medicamentos do programa Farmácia Popular do Brasil e a Política de Nacional Assistência Farmacêutica." *Cadernos de saúde pública* 31 (8): 1648–62.

Yang, Yongzheng. 2006. "China's Integration into the World Economy: Implications for Developing Countries." *Asian-Pacific Economic Literature* 20 (1): 40–56.

Yu, Peter K. 2009. "A Tale of Two Development Agendas." *Ohio Northern University Law Review* 35: 465–572.

Zeng, Ka. 2002. "Trade Structure and the Effectiveness of America's 'Aggressively Unilateral' Trade Policy." *International Studies Quarterly* 46 (1): 93–115.

Zucoloto, Graziela Ferrero, and Rogerio Edivaldo Freitas. 2013. *Propriedade intelectual e aspectos regulatòrios em biotecnologia.* Brasília: Instituto de Pesquisa Econômica Aplicada.

Zucoloto, Graziela Ferrero. 2011. "Panorama do patenteamento brasileiro." *Radar: tecnologia, produção e comércio exterior* 16: 37–46.

Zúñiga, Maria Pluvia, and Emmanuel Combe. 2002. "Introducing Patent Protection in the Pharmaceutical Sector." *Region et developpement* 16: 191–221.

Zúñiga, María Pluvia., Alenka. Guzmán, and Flor.Brown Grossman. 2007. "Technology Acquisition Strategies in the Pharmaceutical Industry in Mexico." *Comparative Technology Transfer and Society* 5 (3): 274–96.

Cited Interviews

These are the interviews that are cited in the text, referenced by date. Chapter 1 and the Fieldwork Appendix provide a full overview of the research conducted.

November 23, 2006. Legislative researcher in Chamber of Deputies (Brazil). Brasilia.

November 24, 2006. Legislative researcher in Senate (Brazil). Brasilia.

May 11, 2007a. President, INTERFARMA. São Paulo.

May 11, 2007b. President and ex-President, ANPEI. São Paulo.

August 9, 2007. Former Director of COFEPRIS. Mexico City.

August 10, 2007. Former PAN Deputy, President of the Commission of Science and Technology in the 2000–2003 Legislature (Mexico). Mexico City.

August 14, 2007a. Executive Director, AMIIF. Mexico City.

August 14, 2007b. Legislative liaison, Secretary of Government (Mexico). Mexico City.

August 16, 2007a. Private sector lawyer representing local subsidiaries of transnational pharmaceutical firms in Mexico. Mexico City.

August 16, 2007b. Director General, IMPI (Mexico). Mexico City.

August 16, 2007c. Former Secretary of Health (Mexico). Mexico City.

August 21, 2007. Chief Executive Officer of Mexican pharmaceutical firm and former President of ANAFAM. Mexico City.

November 20, 2007. Legislative assistant, Chamber of Deputies (Argentina). Buenos Aires.

November 21, 2007. Coordinator of CEDIQUIFA and Consultant to CAEME. Buenos Aires.

November 22, 2007a. Former Executive Director of CILFA. Buenos Aires.

November 22, 2007b. Government lawyer, former member of the "Permanent Working Group on Intellectual Property" in Ministry of Economy (Argentina). Buenos Aires.

May 18, 2008. Private sector lawyer representing Brazilian pharmaceutical firms and legal advisor to ABIFINA. Rio de Janeiro.

May 19, 2008a. Vice-President, ABIFINA. Rio de Janeiro.

May 19, 2008b. President, INPI. Rio de Janeiro.

November 2, 2009. FINEP official. São Paulo.

June 9, 2009a. PT Deputy (Brazil); rapporteur on proposed legislation regarding ANVISA's role in patent examination. Brasilia.

June 9, 2009b. PMDB Deputy (Brazil); rapporteur on proposed legislation revising INPI's patentability criteria. Brasilia.

June 12, 2009. Former Coordinator of Intellectual Property, ANVISA. Rio de Janeiro.

March 23, 2010. Former PRI Deputy, and Secretary of CPFI in 1988–1991 Legislature (Mexico). Mexico City.

March 30, 2010. Vice-President of Mexican pharmaceutical firm and former Managing Director of ANAFAM. Mexico City.

September 19, 2011a. Health economist and former advisor to Minister of Health (Argentina). Buenos Aires.

September 19, 2011b. Former Minister of Economy (Argentina). Buenos Aires.

September 23, 2011a. CILFA official. Buenos Aires.

September 23, 2011b. Patent lawyer consulted by Argentinean Government on 2003–2004 reform. Buenos Aires.

September 23, 2011c. Private sector lawyers representing local subsidiaries of transnational pharmaceutical firms in Argentina. Buenos Aires.

September 27, 2011. Former Patent Controller, INPI-AR. Buenos Aires.

December 5, 2014a. General Manager of Argentinean pharmaceutical firm. Province of Buenos Aires.

December 5, 2014b. Director of Argentinean pharmaceutical firm and former President of CILFA. Buenos Aires.

December 9, 2014a. CILFA official. Buenos Aires.

December 9, 2014b. Health Economist, Ministry of Health (Argentina). Buenos Aires.

July 9, 2015. Official in Ministry of Foreign Relations. Brasilia.

July 10, 2015a. Executive President, *Grupo Farma Brasil*. Brasilia.

July 10, 2015b. Director, MEI/CNI. Brasilia.

January 24, 2016. Private sector lawyer representing Mexican pharmaceutical firms and legal advisor to ANAFAM. New York City.

Index

Note: Tables, figures and footnotes are indicated by an italic t, f and n following the page number. Foreign language terms are indexed under their English translation.

Abbott 180, 200, 207
activating agnostics 9–10, 19–20, 48, 53, 235–7
  Argentina 82–3
  Brazil 132–3, 136, 213
  Mexico 102
active pharmaceutical ingredients (APIs) 43–4
  Argentina 76–7
  Brazil 123–4, 206, 210n
  Mexico 98, 173
Ad Hoc Group (Brazil) 132, 236n
Ad Hoc Group on Mexican Industrial Property 91, 236n
Agreement on Trade-Related Aspects of Intellectual Property Rights *see* TRIPS
AIDS *see* HIV/AIDS
Alario, Dante 122n
Alfonsín, Raul 64n, 81n
alienation, rights of 30–1
American Chamber of Commerce 132
Argentinean Association for Technological Development 79
Argentinean Chamber of Specialist Medicines (CAEME) 73–4, 78, 82, 84, 150, 156, 160n
Argentinean Council of Industry 78, 82
Argentinean Doctors Association 80
Argentinean Industrial Union (UIA) 78–9, 124
Argentinean League of Housewives 80–1
Association of Argentinean Inventors 74n
Association of Brazilian Exporters (ABE) 132
Association of National Pharmaceutical Firms (Brazil, ALANAC) 122, 136, 214–15, 219
Association of the Research-Based Pharmaceutical Industry (Brazil, INTERFARMA) 120–2, 212, 214–15, 219

Bagó 75n
Bezerra, Fernando 116, 134–5
bilateral investment treaties 131, 137, 237
bilateral trade agreements *see* trade agreements

bioequivalence 162–3, 210
biotechnology
  Argentina 151
  Brazil 112, 122–9, 214, 220, 232, 234
  Bolivia 57n
Brady Plan 83n
brand (and branded) drugs 32n
  Argentina 77, 147–9, 161–4
Brazilian Academy of Sciences 125
Brazilian Association for Intellectual Property (ABPI) 121, 212, 215
Brazilian Association of Biotechnology Firms (ABRABI) 122
Brazilian Confederation of Bishops (CNBB) 126
Brazilian Industrial Development Agency (ABDI) 211
Brazilian Innovation Agency (FINEP) 211, 242n
Brazilian Pharmo-Chemical Association (ABIFINA) 119n, 122, 124, 136, 207n, 214–16, 219–20
Brazilian Shoe Industry Association 132
Brazilian Socialist Party (PSB) 125
Brazilian Society for the Progress of Science (SBPC) 125–6, 127n
Bristol-Myers Squibb 177
Brown, Ron 84
Bush, George H.W. 84n
Business Coordinating Council (Mexico, CCE) 103, 177
Business Mobilization for Innovation (Brazil, MEI) 220

Calderón, Felipe 169, 186, 188–9
Canada 8n, 35t, 88, 90, 94n
capacity-building programs *see* technical assistance and capacity-building
Cardoso, Fernando Henrique 110–12, 116, 127n, 130–1, 134–7, 194, 195, 197, 200, 205, 216, 236–8
Castañeda, Jorge 178
Cavallo, Domingo 63, 69–70, 84–7, 236
Center for Studies for the Development of the Argentinean Pharmo-Chemical Industry (CEDIQUIFA) 73–4

Challú, Pablo 74*n*
Chamber of Argentinean Exporters
   (CERA) 82
Chamber of Argentinean Pharmaceutical
   Industries (CILFA) 74–5, 77–81, 86,
   141*n*, 150, 152–6, 158–60, 162–4
Chamber of Deputies, Argentina *see* Congress,
   Argentina
Chamber of Deputies, Brazil *see* Congress,
   Brazil
Chamber of Deputies, Mexico *see* Congress,
   Mexico
Cheek, James 68, 84
Chile 240
China 47, 53, 75, 237
civil society actors and activism 26, 54, 239
   Brazil 125–9, 136, 198, 207*n*, 213–16,
      219*n*, 236
   Mexico 100–1, 187, 189*n*, 191
Clinton, Bill 16*n*
Collor de Melo, Fernando
   introduction stage 110, 112, 114–15,
      117–18, 120–1, 125, 129–32,
      136, 197
Communist Party of Brazil 125
compulsory licenses
   Argentina 68, 70–2, 80, 84–5, 151
   Brazil 115, 118–22, 124, 131, 137, 195,
      199–202, 205–9, 212, 214–15,
      222, 238
   general and comparative 41–5, 71*n*, 120,
      199*n*
   Mexico 93, 96–7, 103–5, 170, 175–80, 182,
      186*n*, 190–1
   see also local working requirements
Confederation of Argentinean
   Pharmacists 80
Congress, Argentina 63–5, 67–72, 74, 77,
   79–82, 84–6, 157, 160n, 164, 236
   see also Peronist Party (Argentina, PJ);
      Radical Party (Argentina, UCR)
Congress, Brazil 110–11, 114–32, 134, 136–7,
   196, 219, 232, 236
   see also Special Commission on Industrial
      Property (Brazil)
Congress, Mexico 89, 91–2, 93n, 94–5, 97,
   104–9, 170, 175–9, 186, 188–90, 191n
   see also Institutional Revolutionary Party
      (Mexico, PRI); National Action Party
      (Mexico, PAN); Party of the Democratic
      Revolution (Mexico, PRD); Science and
      Technology Commission (Mexico)
Cooperative of Argentinean Specialized
   Medicines Firms (COOPERALA) 74
Coordinator of Foreign Trade Business
   Organizations (Mexico, COECE) 103

copyright 4, 8*n*, 12, 23, 108*n*, 190*n*
Cristália 207*n*

data protection (and data exclusivity)
   Argentina 64–5, 72–3, 84, 86, 144, 149,
      150–3, 155, 165–6, 238
   Brazil 205
   general and comparative 45, 152, 185
   Mexico 184–5
de la Madrid, Miguel 91–3, 95
de la Rua, Fernando 73, 86, 143, 165, 238
dependence on preferential exports
   see political trade dependence
      (PTD)
di Tella, Guido 70, 73, 86
Doha Declaration on TRIPS and Public
   Health 53, 176
Dr. Simi 176–7
Duhalde, Eduardo 143, 157, 165

Eli Lilly 177
Embrapa 126–7
European Community 36, 38*n*
European Union (EU) 13, 14, 68*n*, 174
exporters (and export profiles, export
   structures)
   Argentina 65–6, 73, 82–4, 86, 157, 230–1
   Brazil 111–13, 131–6, 194–5,
      212–14, 232
   general and comparative 5, 9–11, 19–20,
      22, 24, 27, 29, 48–9, 53, 112, 229–32,
      235–7
   Mexico 88, 90, 93–4, 101–3, 108, 168, 231
   see also activating agnostics; political trade
      dependence

Farmacias Similares 176
   see also *Dr. Simi*
Farmanguinhos 206, 207*n*, 208
Federal Commission for Protection against
   Health Risks (Mexico, COFEPRIS)
   180–3, 185, 189–90
Fernandez, Roqué 87
Fernández de Kirchner, Cristina 142–3,
   165, 238
Finland 35*n*, 35*t*
Fiocruz 122, 126–7, 207*n*
Food and Drug Administration (US,
   FDA) 41*t*, 181*n*, 182*n*, 184*n*, 197
Ford Foundation 188
Forum for the Freedom of Use of Knowledge
   (Brazil, FLUC) 125–7, 128*f*, 129
Foundation for Latin American Economic
   Research (Argentina, FIEL) 74
Fox, Vicente 169, 170*n*, 176, 178–80, 189
France 33–4, 35*t*, 174

Franco, Itamar 115, 131
Front for a Country in Solidarity (Argentina, FREPASO) 143
Fujimori, Alberto 70

Gador 75*n*, 149
General Confederation of Industry 78
General Economic Federation 78
Generalized System of Preferences (GSP) 18–19
  Argentina 73, 82–3
  Brazil 134
  Mexico 93–4
  trade sanctions 18
generic drugs (and generic drug laws and regulations) 21, 32*n*, 181
  Argentina 143, 156*n*, 161–4, 167
  Brazil 204–5, 209–10, 216
  Mexico 174, 181, 184
Germany 33–4, 35*t*, 174
Gilead 208
GlaxoSmithKline 95*n*, 149
Global Intellectual Property Academy 14
  see also technical assistance and capacity-building
González García, Ginés 161
González Torres, Victor 176–7
  see also *Dr. Simi*
Good Law (Brazil, *Lei do Bem*) 211
Gore, Al 84
government drug purchasing (and procurement) 7, 32*n*, 46*n*, 58
  Argentina 147
  Brazil 123*n*, 210
  Mexico 90, 98–100, 108–9, 172, 231, 234
Grondona, Julio Maria 79*n*
Group for a Better Country (Mexico) 176*n*
Grupo Farma Brasil 220
Guimarães, Reinaldo 216*n*

H1N1 pandemic 180, 189
Hatch-Waxman Act (USA) 181*n*
Health Industry Complex (Brazil, CIS) 209, 216, 218
Health Ministers/Ministries and Secretariats/Secretaries (and health officials)
  Argentina 70, 80*n*, 142, 146, 157, 159–61, 163–4
  Brazil 71*n*, 120, 122–3, 127*n*, 194–5, 199*n*, 200–2, 205–8, 210–11, 213–16, 218–19, 221–3
  general and comparative 9, 11, 20–1, 26, 42–3, 45, 51–2, 56–9, 230–2, 238
  Mexico 96, 169–70, 174–5, 177–8, 180–1, 183, 185, 189–92
health regulatory agencies

Argentina *see* National Agency for Drugs, Food, and Medical Technology (ANMAT)
Brazil *see* National Agency for Health Surveillance (ANVISA)
Mexico *see* Federal Commission for Protection against Health Risks (COFEPRIS)
Hills, Carla 66*n*, 107
HIV/AIDS 7, 54, 120, 174–5, 179–80, 189, 195, 198–200, 205, 207, 209*n*, 211, 212*n*, 214, 232

IMS Health 46*n*
India
  global supply of drugs 174, 179, 206–8, 209*n*
  in comparative perspective 239–40
  Patent Act (2005) 71*n*, 204
  Pharmaceutical Manufacturers of America 24
  pharmaceutical production capabilities 47, 75, 123
  pre-grant opposition 186
  secondary patents 190, 204
  Section 3(d) 190
  Tenovovir 208
industrial secrets 23
Industry Ministry, Argentina 160
innovation 4, 6, 29–30, 32–3, 54, 147, 186, 188, 194–5, 209–11, 216–18, 220, 222–3, 232, 240–2, 244
Institute for Security and Social Services for State Employees (Mexico) 98
Institutional Revolutionary Party (Mexico, PRI) 89, 92–3, 97, 104–6, 108, 185, 188, 192
Intellectual Property Working Group (Brazil, GTPI) 214, 221
Inter-American Development Bank 83*n*
International Federation of Inventors 74*n*
International Federation of Pharmaceutical Manufacturers (IFPMA) 39
International Monetary Fund (IMF) 83*n*
Italy 35*t*, 113, 124*n*, 174
Itamaraty 131, 134

Japan 13–14, 33–4, 35*t*, 38*n*, 113, 123, 124*n*

Kantor, Micky 16*n*, 84, 130
Kirchner, Nestor 142–3, 165

Laboratorios Best 176
Lampreia, Luiz Felipe 131, 134
Law on Inventions and Trademarks (Mexico, LIM) 91–5, 97, 102, 104

Law on Technological Innovation (Brazil) 211
legal transplantation 4, 13n, 18
linkage system
  Mexico 181–4, 189–91
  USA 181–2
local working requirements
  Argentina 70, 84
  Brazil 115, 118–20, 122, 132, 201–2,
    212, 214
  general and comparative 43–4
  Mexico 44, 93, 96–7, 105
  see also compulsory licenses
Lopes, Ney 115, 117
  see also Special Commission on Industrial
    Property (Brazil)
Lula da Silva, Luiz Inácio 194–5, 200, 205,
  207, 209–10, 216, 238

Macri, Mauricio 166n
mailbox 36–7, 39–40, 206n,
  Argentina 44, 70–2, 146, 151, 158
  Brazil 117, 121, 196
  Mexico 39, 95n, 171
  and pipeline patents, distinction
    between 39–40
  transition periods 36, 37
Mais Saúde 209
Medical Confederation of Argentina 80
Menem, Carlos 63–74, 75–6, 78, 80–2, 84–7,
  114, 129, 131–2, 135–7, 143, 165, 230–1,
  234–8
Menem, Eduardo 82
Merck 200, 206n, 207–8
Mexican Action Network on Free Trade
  (RMALC) 101
Mexican Business Council for Foreign Affairs
  (CEMAI) 102
Mexican Green Party (PVEM)
  175–7
Mexican Institute for Intellectual Property
  (IMPI) 96, 181–7, 190
Mexican Institute for Social Security 98
Mexican Intellectual Property Association
  (AMPPI) 96–7
Mexican Pharmaceutical Industry Association
  (AMIF)/Mexican Pharmaceutical
  Research Industry Association
  (AMIIF) 96–8, 106n, 177–9, 180n, 183,
  185–6, 191
Microsoft 142
Mossinghoff, Gerald 66n
most-favored nation treatment (MFN)
  17–19

National Action Party (Mexico, PAN) 169,
  176–8, 188

National Agency for Drugs, Food, and
  Medical Technology (Argentina,
  ANMAT) 72, 84, 152–3
National Agency for Health Surveillance
  (Brazil, ANVISA) 202–4, 212n,
  217–21
National Association for Research,
  Development, and Engineering in
  Innovative Firms (Brazil, ANPEI)
  216, 220
National Association of Drug Manufacturers
  (Mexico, ANAFAM) 98, 100, 105, 179,
  182–3, 188
National Association of Importers and
  Exporters (Mexico, ANIERM) 102
National Association of Pulp and Paper
  Manufacturers (Brazil) 132
National Chamber of the Pharmaceutical
  Industry (Mexico, CANIFARMA) 100
National Confederation of Industry (Brazil,
  CNI) 124, 216, 220
National Council for Science and Technology
  (Mexico, CONACYT) 242n
National Development Bank (Brazil,
  BNDES) 209–10
National Forum of NGOs and Social
  Movements for the Environment and
  Development (Brazil, FBOMS) 126
National Health System (Brazil, SUS)
  198, 200
National Institute for Industrial Property
  (Argentina, INPI-AR) 144–5, 158–60,
  165, 166n
National Institute for Industrial Property
  (Brazil, INPI-BR) 117–18, 119n, 120,
  202–4, 208, 217–19, 221
National Institute of Public Health
  (Mexico) 188–9
new use patents *see* secondary patents
North American Free Trade Agreement
  (NAFTA) 14, 38, 48, 88–90, 94–5, 96n,
  99–108, 129, 168–9, 172, 175–8, 181, 185,
  188, 191, 231, 234–5
  see also trade agreements

Organization for Economic Cooperation and
  Development (OECD) 174–5, 243

Pan-American Health Organization 52
Party of the Democratic Revolution (Mexico,
  PRD) 104–6, 185, 188, 192
Patent Cooperation Treaty (PCT) 144, 165n
patent offices
  Argentina *see* National Institute for
    Industrial Property (Argentina,
    INPI-AR)

Brazil *see* National Institute for Industrial
Property (Brazil, INPI-BR)
Mexico *see* Mexican Institute for
Intellectual Property (IMPI)
path dependence 10–11, 28
Peña Nieto, Enrique 192
Peronist Party (Argentina, PJ) 69–70, 81,
86, 143
Peru 70
Pfizer 177
Pharmaceutical Manufacturers of America
(PMA)/Pharmaceutical Research and
Manufacturers of America (PhRMA) 24,
63, 66*n*, 72, 88, 91, 92, 96, 110, 115, 130*n*,
157, 186, 212*n*
Phoenix 75*n*, 149
pipeline patents
and mailbox, distinction between 39–40
Argentina 63–5, 67–8, 70–2, 74, 77, 79–81,
84–5, 143, 145–6, 149–50, 158
Brazil 110–11, 114, 116–18, 121–2, 124,
127*n*, 131–2, 137, 172, 194, 196–200, 202,
204*n*, 205, 208, 215
general and comparative 37–41, 44, 55,
230–2, 239–40
Mexico 88, 95–7, 101, 103–4, 107, 118*n*,
169, 171–2, 174, 182–4, 191, 215
political trade dependence (PTD)
Argentina 82–3, 135
Brazil 133–5, 212–14
general and comparative 48–9, 235–7
Mexico 101–2, 178*n*,
see also exporters (and export profiles,
export structures)
pre-grant opposition 170, 185–91
preliminary injunctions (Argentina) 144,
150–1, 153–7, 165–6
Prior Consent system (Brazil) 202–4, 208,
212, 217–22
see also National Agency for Health
Surveillance (ANVISA)
process patents (for pharmaceuticals) 5,
35, 91–2, 113, 114*n*, 123*n*, 146, 151–2,
154–5
process tracing 25–7, 229
productive development partnerships (Brazil,
PDPs) 210
Profarma 209–10
public sector drug purchases *see* government
drug purchasing (and procurement)

Radical Party (Argentina, UCR) 69, 81, 84*n*,
86, 143, 234
regional trade agreements *see* trade
agreements
replication of drugs, ease of 31–2, 42

research and development 21, 24*n*, 29, 31–2,
80*n*, 96*n*, 124, 147, 173, 210, 216, 218,
220, 241–4
retroactive protection *see* pipeline patents
Roche 200, 206
Roemmers 75*n*, 81*n*, 147*n*, 149
Rousseff, Dilma 194, 205, 216
Rozanski, Felíx 74*n*

Salinas de Gortari, Carlos 88–92, 94–5, 97,
100–1, 104–9, 114, 136, 231, 237
Salinas Lozano, Raul 91–2
Sandoz 156*n*
Sarney, José 113–14
Science and Technology Commission
(Mexico) 176–9, 188
Science and Technology Law (Mexico,
2003) 242
secondary patents 32, 45
Argentina 146, 151*n*, 157–60
Brazil 204, 208*n*, 217–19
India 190, 204
Mexico 182–4, 189–90
Secretariat of Trade and Industrial
Development (Mexico, SECOFI) 93, 95,
100, 104–5, 107–8
Section 301 113
Seguro Popular 189
Senate, Argentina *see* Congress, Argentina
Senate, Brazil *see* Congress, Brazil
Senate, Mexico *see* Congress, Mexico
Sidus 75*n*
South Korea 35*t*, 92
Spain 35*t*, 124*n*, 174
Special 301 15–17, 53*n*,
113*n*, 239
Argentina 66–9, 72, 77, 83
Brazil 113*n*, 125, 130, 134, 212, 212*n*
Mexico 93–4
Special Commission on Industrial Property
(Brazil) 114n, 115–19, 121, 122n, 129,
130n, 138
see also Lopes, Ney
Suro-Bredie, Carmen 130
"swine flu" pandemic *see* H1N1 pandemic
Switzerland 35*t*, 113

technical assistance and
capacity-building 14–15, 20
Technological Innovation Law (Brazil) 211
Teixeira, Francisco 121*n*
Temis Lostaló 75*n*
Thailand 199*n*, 240
Todman, Terence 84*n*
Toma, Miguel Angel 70
Toscano, Miguel Ángel 189

trade agreements
  drivers of compliance and
    over-compliance 13–15, 20, 175
  preferential market access 18–19
  stabilization of trade preferences 93–4, 102,
    178, 235
  see also North American Free Trade
    Agreement (NAFTA)
trademarks 4, 23, 32*n*, 107
trade sanctions
  Argentina 65, 67, 69, 71, 73, 82–5, 135,
    150, 152
  Brazil 110–14, 130–5, 232
  general and comparative 15–18, 48, 53,
    102, 232, 235, 237, 239
  Mexico 91, 93, 102
  see also Section 301; Special 301
TRIPS 4, 171, 228
  civil society mobilization triggered by 54
  drivers of compliance and
    over-compliance 12–13, 16
  policy options compatible with
    12–13, 52–3, 71, 117, 120; *see also*
    compulsory licenses; data protection
    (and data exclusivity); mailbox; pipeline
    patents
  transition periods 36–8, 39–40, 69–70, 72,
    78–80, 110–11, 149, 201
  see also Doha Declaration on TRIPS and
    Public Health; Uruguay Round; World
    Trade Organization (WTO)
Turkey 92, 123*n*

United Kingdom 33–4, 35*t*, 174
United Nations (UN)
  Convention on Biodiversity 126

Earth Summit (Rio de Janeiro, 1992)
    126, 234
  Industrial Development Organization 46
  guidelines for examining secondary
    patents 160, 166, 190
United States Patent and Trademark
    Office 14
United States Trade Representative (USTR)
    see Section 301; Special 301
Uruguay Round 12, 37, 39, 64, 68, 92, 95, 110,
    113, 117
Uruguay Round Agreements Act (USA) 16

Venezuela 57*n*

Workers Party (Brazil, PT) 125, 194
World Bank 243
World Health Organization (WHO) 47, 52, 174
World Intellectual Property Organization
    (WIPO) 4, 14
World Trade Organization (WTO)
  Argentina 69, 71, 85, 150–2, 154
  Brazil 119*n*, 201, 212
  driver of compliance and
    over-compliance 12–14, 228
  founding 4
  Government Procurement Agreement 12*n*
  IP provisions compared with those of
    NAFTA and other trade
    agreements 13–14, 228
  most-favored nation (MFN) access 17–19
  Mexico 168
  trade sanctions 17–19, 53
  transition periods 36, 201
  see also TRIPS; Uruguay Round
Wyeth 177